German-Language Literature Today:
International and Popular?

German-Language Literature Today:
International and Popular?

edited by
Arthur Williams
Stuart Parkes
Julian Preece

PETER LANG

Oxford · Bern · Berlin · Bruxelles · Frankfurt am Main · New York · Wien

Die Deutsche Bibliothek – CIP-Einheitsaufnahme

German language literature today : international and popular? ed. by Arthur
Williams... – Oxford ; Bern ; Berlin ; Bruxelles ; Frankfurt
am Main ; New York ; Wien : Lang, 2000
ISBN 3-906764-88-5

British Library and Library of Congress Cataloguing-in-Publication Data:
A catalogue record for this book is available from *The British Library,* Great
Britain, and from *The Library of Congress,* USA

Published with the assistance of
the University of Bradford

ISBN 3-906764-88-5
US-ISBN 0-8204-5053-7

© Peter Lang AG, European Academic Publishers, Bern 2000
Jupiterstr. 15, Postfach, 3000 Bern 15, Switzerland; info@peterlang.com

Printed in Germany

CONTENTS

PREFACE

The majority of the essays in this volume were presented in their original form at the Seventh Bradford International Colloquium on Contemporary German-Language Literature held at Hinsley Hall, Leeds, in April 2000. We are deeply grateful for the continuing support of the Goethe-Institut Manchester, the Austrian Institute, London, and the University of Bradford's Department of Modern Languages, which again made the Bradford Colloquium possible.

Our thanks are due also to the University of Bradford's 'Promoting Research' Committee, which has subsidized the publication of this volume.

Many of the papers read at the colloquium have undergone various degrees of editing and revision for publication. The editors want to thank the contributors and translators for their cooperative and constructive responses to our requests and requirements. This friendly spirit of shared commitment to the study of contemporary German-language literature has always made the work on the colloquia and the resulting volumes a delight and lent them a significance beyond the finished product. On this occasion, given the current pressures on the British university system, particularly many departments of German, and the speed with which this volume has been produced, the level of cooperation and enthusiasm invested in the production of it has been exemplary; the editors have drawn great strength and lasting satisfaction from the up-front support and commitment of all of their colleagues.

I want to pay tribute here to Stuart Parkes and Julian Preece, who have been more long-suffering than anyone has a right to expect and whose sharp insights and ready humour have again been more valuable than they know.

My gratitude is due also to Anne Croasdell, Departmental Administrator in Modern Languages at Bradford, who has provided help and assistance with the production of this volume and in a multitude of other small ways which have greatly eased and expedited the completion of the project.

Arthur Williams
Bradford
31 July 2000

Editors' Note

The editors wish to point out that the opinions expressed in these essays are those of the contributors and are not necessarily shared by either the editors or the institutions which supported the original colloquium and the publication of this volume.

CONTEMPORARY GERMAN-LANGUAGE LITERATURE:
THE CHANGING AGENDA

STUART PARKES

I The German search for recognition

Many developments in Germany since 1945 can be linked with issues of recognition. In the case of the former German Democratic Republic recognition was a, if not the, key goal in a variety of areas. At the diplomatic level the GDR sought acknowledgement of its existence as a separate sovereign state by the other German state and recognition on the widest possible international footing beyond its allies in the Soviet bloc. By the mid-1970s, this target had been achieved, even if the Federal Republic still refused to consider it a foreign country. In the longer term, such acts of diplomatic recognition, since they failed to ensure its survival, clearly represented only Pyrrhic victories for the GDR. The same could now be claimed also for the country's other 'successes', such as those achieved in the area of sport, bought by the misuse of athletes' bodies, and those claimed in technological areas. It will be recalled that on the fortieth anniversary of the GDR, when the country was already in terminal crisis, Erich Honecker, apparently impervious to what was happening on the streets and at various European border crossings, lauded to a sceptical Mikhail Gorbachev the achievement of the GDR in producing a one-megabyte chip.

What the GDR sought, in its own terminology, was 'Weltklasse', not least in the cultural sphere as well. In its early days it had maintained Brecht's prestigious Berliner Ensemble, whilst the political leadership's continuing concern with cultural matters, besides having the goal of making sure that the population was not exposed to subversive ideas, was underlined in such official terms as 'die sozialistische Nationalkultur der DDR'. As the 1986 edition of the official publication *Die DDR stellt sich vor* makes particularly clear, this term implied a national achievement worthy of the widest possible recognition. The section on culture concludes with a reference to an art exhibition 'Tradition und Erneuerung' which toured Britain in 1984–1985, where its success provided '[e]in außerordentlich stark beachtetes Beispiel für die Ausstrahlung der DDR-Kunst im Ausland' (DDR 1986, 214). In other words, GDR art was, it was being claimed, nothing short of 'Weltklasse'.

It would be wrong to conclude that this question of recognition only involved the GDR, even if the insistent self-congratulatory tone of GDR pronouncements was not to be found to the same extent in quasi-official statements in the other German state. Nevertheless, there was a link between achievements in, for example, the cultural sphere and the reputation of the Federal Republic. Heinrich Böll had reason to claim that the Federal Republic was in debt to its authors in that their achievements contributed to the status of the state following its inauspicious starting point in the aftermath of political and moral humiliation (Böll 1985, 65). Willy Brandt spoke of foreign cultural policy being an integral part of foreign policy. It is, of course, true that many writers were allergic to any expression of national pride of the kind encapsulated in the cry 'Wir sind wieder wer'.[1] However, they could not avoid being linked to other parallel developments. Just as there was, in the public perception, an 'economic miracle' following the creation of the Federal Republic in 1949, the late 1950s and early 1960s were seen as the time of a 'literary miracle', with 1959 especially being picked out on the basis of the appearance of Grass's *Die Blechtrommel*, Böll's *Billard um halbzehn* and Johnson's *Mutmassungen über Jakob* in that year.

Since unification the status of all things German has again become a matter of debate. Some social critics perceive a new wave of nationalistic feeling, sometimes disparagingly referred to as 'Standortnationalismus'. This term is used particularly to refer to excessive emphasis in some quarters on the need for the Federal Republic to maintain and enhance its economic status if it is to survive in a globalized world.[2] There are also instances of similar terminology being used in relation to literature, however ironically.[3] What cannot be denied is that there has been an intense debate on the achievements of German literature over the last decade, a debate this Introduction will seek to review, as it provides the backcloth for many of the essays contained in this volume and for the question posed in its title about the extent of the international and popular qualities of contemporary German-language literature.

Before this is attempted, reference should be made to those German-language authors who do not fit neatly into the overall heading of German literature. During the division of Germany there was much debate about whether there was a second German literature in the GDR. Even after unification it is still possible to ask whether a distinctive eastern German literature is visible in some of the works discussed in this volume, particularly by Peter Graves, Tanja Nause and Astrid Köhler. Equally pertinent are questions about the existence of separate Swiss and Austrian literatures as well as about the status of works by those authors who write in German but are of non-German origin. Both Austria and Switzerland pursue active cultural policies which to some extent celebrate a distinct cultural identity. Austrian displeasure about its culture being subsumed into a single German entity was typically expressed by Alfred Missong, their former ambassador to France, in *Le Monde* in 1993. He even went so far as to speak of an 'anschluss culturel' (cit. Griotteray/Larsan 1999, 162). Since the present volume contains numerous contributions about authors and works that cannot be classified simply as 'German', the term German-language literature is preferred in its title. Nevertheless the question posed about its international and popular status applies to all the writing considered.

II 'International' and 'popular'

Any consideration of whether German-language literature at the turn of the century is 'international' and/or 'popular' cannot evade the question of what these somewhat elusive terms might actually mean in the context of literature. One starting point would be to consider what the opposite of 'international' could be. One word that arguably fits the bill is 'provincial', a term that has frequently been used in a particularly pejorative sense in public discourse in the Federal Republic. One of the uncomplimentary names for its first capital, Bonn, that became current in the 1950s when it lacked most qualities associated with a metropolis and was thought to be characterized best by its wet climate and closed level-crossing gates was 'Bundeshauptdorf'; it was a provincial backwater. When the playwright Jochen Zien put together twenty separate scenes to show the awful plainness of life in the Federal Republic, he called his work *Nachrichten aus der Provinz* (1967). How far some German intellectuals will go in their scorn of the 'provincial' was illustrated more recently by the theatre director Claude-Oliver Rudolph who was reported as saying (somewhat immodestly), when asked about producing plays in the town of Brandenburg, a place not widely seen as a centre of urbane sophistication: 'Peymann in Berlin ist Provinz, Haußmann in Bochum ist Provinz. Da, wo ich bin, kann niemals Provinz sein' (Broder 2000a, 247). Ironically this disparagement of all things provincial has taken place in a state which has undoubtedly owed some of its political and economic success to its decentralized structures. Moreover, not all have been prepared to join in. Martin Walser, who, since becoming a full-time author in 1957, has lived near the shores of Lake Constance, the area of his birth, has frequently been happy to stress his attachment to his provincial home,[4] where many of his novels are set. It can equally be pointed out that other leading authors, not least the two Nobel laureates Heinrich Böll and Günter Grass have used their provincial affiliations, Cologne and Danzig/Gdańsk respectively, for the settings of much of their work.

One change that has occurred in recent years in German literature is the increasing frequency of non-German settings. The novelist Bodo Kirchhoff, whose novels *Infanta* (1989) and *Der Sandmann* (1992) are set in the Philippines and North Africa respectively, has spoken of his inability to use purely German themes and settings. The motivation for his literary emigration, he claimed, was not that such locations were exotic, but because he needed a sense of distance from 'einer durchleuchteten Heimat mit ihrer gelüfteten Sprache. Es gab und gibt keinen anderen Weg, auf dem ich das Klügersein als mein Roman vermeiden kann' (Kirchhoff 1994, 217). It can be countered that many post-war German novels were set outside Germany, for example Wolfgang Koeppen's *Der Tod in Rom* (1954). However, the death in question is that of a former SS man, which underlines that, whatever the setting, the novel's theme is unshakably German. The same is true of Alfred Andersch's *Die Kirschen der Freiheit* (1952), where the setting is also Italian but where the theme is desertion — in this case the first-person narrator's desertion from the *Wehrmacht*. Nevertheless, German-language literature does seem to have entered new territory with a work such as Urs Jenny's 1995 *Liebesbrief für Mary*, the letter part of which is written in English but which, according to the blurb on the back of the paperback edition is still a part of German literature as the non-German part is written in a 'herrlich schauderhaften Englisch, das man nur verstehen kann, wenn man Deutsch spricht'. The letter itself is written by a friend of the narrator Helmut to a previous lover who is now living in Australia. The narrator provides the German-language commentary.

In this volume Silke Hassler discusses the work of Michael Scharang, in which American settings play a catalytic role in his innovative trajectory of liberation from the limiting aesthetic and societal horizons of contemporary Austria, whilst Ingo Schulze's *Simple Storys. Ein Roman aus der ostdeutschen Provinz*, as Graves shows, includes a first visit to Italy for previously restricted GDR citizens. Here, though, as in the earlier novels referred to above, there is an immediate link with German themes, in this case the GDR past. Given the limits placed on individual mobility by the GDR authorities, it is no wonder that travel is a recurrent theme in recent east German writing. It is the motif that is specifically examined by Köhler, who is concerned to show how the theme of travel is linked with the question of identity, itself, as Schulze knows, deeply embedded in an inescapable provincialism.

The move away from limited German themes and settings might be seen as the much desired move away from 'provincialism' to 'internationalism'. At the same time, and in this the egregious Rudolph with his separation of geography from provinciality is correct, it is more than a question of setting. Many great novels of world literature are set in provincial backwaters; a raft of novels in Balzac's *La Comédie Humaine* are subsumed under the heading *Scènes de la Vie de Province*, whilst the horrors of life in the small town of Ionville form the backcloth to Flaubert's *Madame Bovary*. In the German context, one of the few recent international successes of German literature has been Bernhard Schlink's *Der Vorleser* (1995), which deals with a quintessentially German theme and is largely set in the non-metropolitan Heidelberg area. Schlink's success also gives the lie to the idea that the inclusion of the National Socialist past in a work of art is likely to affect its chances of success, even in Germany where a weariness with such themes is often professed.[5] In fact, as far as the English-speaking world is concerned, the opposite seems more likely, as long as the public in certain countries remains obsessed with Nazism and, according to opinion surveys, the German name that most readily springs to mind even among young people is Hitler.

The example of Schlink shows that it is not the choice of theme as such that matters in either the national or the international context. The treatment of the theme and the skill of the author are obviously much more important. Whether in the case of Schlink success equals literary quality is a moot point. In this volume, Joanathan Long is most critical of this best-selling work, which he sees as a partial exculpation of those Germans involved with National Social-ism, an exculpation that is underlined by the form of the novel. If these critic-isms are at all valid, then Schlink is not an 'international' writer in the sense of Balzac and Flaubert whose literary quality and wider fame are beyond dispute.

However, it is not immediately clear how that quality can be measured. In Long's terms, it cannot be judged by our second term 'popular', if that is taken to mean solely the number of copies of a particular volume that are sold. The question that then arises is that of literary forms. Recent years have undoub-tedly brought new definitions of what constitutes culture, with traditional barriers between 'high' and 'low' culture being increasingly broken down. The message in the title of Leslie A. Fiedler's famous Freiburg lecture of 1968, which invoked a new era of post-modernity: 'Überquert die Grenze, schließt den Graben' appears to have been widely taken to heart (Fiedler 1994). Carsten Rohde points out in his essay that Rolf Dieter Brinkmann has been hailed as a writer who overcame the gap between Pop culture and literature, as demanded by Fiedler, although he then takes issue with such a simplistic view. Neverthe-less, several essays in this volume deal with works that would once have been regarded as not particularly suitable subjects for academic analysis, but are now more or less universally accepted as part of a country's literature. Christopher Jones analyses Swiss detective stories to show how they comment on such themes as the relationship between economic success in Swiss society, the use of drugs, and the suppression of a less palatable past. Colin Riordan compares Urs Richle's strongly filmic novel *Hand im Spiel* (1998) with the film *Rossini oder die mörderische Frage, wer mit wem schlief* (title of the 1997 book of the film), which is part scripted by Patrick Süskind. The title of Riordan's piece with its reference to Hollywood suggests that in this case the word popular is to be taken fairly literally.

Other areas of literary endeavour that have attracted greater interest in recent years are *Jugendliteratur* and works written in German by authors born outside Germany and who have learned German as a second language. Susan Tebbutt surveys the changing treatment of intercultural themes in Jugendliteratur, whilst Uta Aifan and James Jordan are concerned with, in the first case, Rafik Schami and Salim Alafenisch and, in the second, Akif Pirinçci. All these writers come originally from the Middle East, Pirinçci from Turkey, Schami from Syria, and Alafenisch is the son of a Bedouin tribal leader. Moreover, they are all concerned with inter-cultural understanding and have achieved popularity not only in Germany but abroad as well, as the example of Pirinçci shows.

Any international success achieved by German-language literature will inevitably depend on the translation of the works concerned. That this is a fraught business is shown in this volume by Wiebke Sievers. Translation is invariably bound up with marketing which in turn is geared to the countries in which the translated work will appear. Sievers shows the effects of this in the case of the work of Herta Müller. Her work has been marketed as a product of Ceauşescu's Romania rather than as writing primarily concerned with the position of the German-speaking minority in that country. In the same kind of area Helmut Peitsch looks at the reception of Uwe Timm in the United States. One small example from *Der Vorleser* can serve to illustrate the point about the vagaries of translation. In the German version Hanna, the former SS guard, once she has become literate, is said to be reading Holocaust literature, including the autobiography of Rudolf Höss, who was the Commandant at Auschwitz executed in Poland after the war (Schlink 1997, 193). In the English version the autobiography is that of Rudolf Hess, Hitler's deputy who flew to Britain in 1941 and spent the rest of his life imprisoned, after the war largely in Spandau in the suburbs of Berlin (Schlink 1998, 203). This change is no doubt based on a belief that English-speaking readers are more likely to have heard of Hess.

That he left Germany before the Holocaust had entered its final murderous stage and that he never wrote an autobiography is set aside.

However, just how problematical the terms 'popular' and 'international' can be is made clear by David Barnett's essay. Barnett suggests that it is inappropriate to label Werner Schwab, despite his successes, a 'popular dramatist'. Schwab's unwavering preoccupations are the essential, universal ingredients of theatre. He takes these and subjects them to a series of tensile tests, the result of which must be their destruction. His plays reveal a movement away from the popular to something which is ultimately extremely individual and esoteric. Rohde's closing identification of quality in the work of Rainald Goetz at the quiet, personal end of his lyric production also suggests an impoverishment of the popular, here Pop and Techno. And Riordan is unable ultimately to endorse the validity of the claims of international status made for Dietl/Süskind; their playful exploitation of national cultural knowledge is not without at least a hint of traditional German literary elitism.

Nevertheless, it is necessary to return to basic quantitative questions which cannot be entirely ignored in any discussion of how 'popular' and 'international' German-language literature is. In fact, the perceived lack of popularity, as reflected at home in sales figures of contemporary German literature (a look at the best-seller lists published weekly in *Der Spiegel* rarely reveals more than a couple of German titles)[6] and abroad by a dearth of translations has often been at the centre of a debate that has raged for more than a decade and will now be reviewed.[7]

III 'Die Unfähigkeit zu erzählen'

Much of the debate that took place mainly in the 1990s is encapsulated in the volume *Maulhelden und Königskinder* (Köhler/Moritz 1998). The quotation at the head of this section is from one of the earlier pieces in this collection written by Frank Schirrmacher and dates, in fact, from the autumn of 1989, shortly before Schirrmacher was to become one of the most prominent figures in the *Literaturstreit* that was to accompany the process of German unification. Whereas Schirrmacher's contribution to the Literaturstreit had much to do with writers' politics, in this essay he regrets the distance of much contemporary literature from the real world. The blame is laid at the door of literary theory which leads young authors into the trap of excessive metanarrative: 'während man eine Geschichte erzählt, davon zu reden, daß man gerade eine Geschichte erzählt' (Schirrmacher 1989, 22).

Schirrmacher's plea for a move away from theory becomes a cry for full-blooded realism in the first major contribution by the person who has undoubtedly made the most outspoken comments in the recent debate about German literature: the writer Maxim Biller. In 1991 he published an essay the title of which more or less makes clear his thoughts on what he sees as the predicament of German literature: 'Soviel Sinnlichkeit wie der Stadtplan von Kiel. Warum die neue deutsche Literatur nichts so nötig hat wie den Realismus. Ein Grundsatzprogramm' (Biller 1991). The first part of the title, it goes without saying, refers to the current products of German literature, whilst the second sentence suggests the solution. The final reference to a 'Programm' implies a rallying cry. Among those who rallied to the flag was the author Matthias Altenburg, whose 1992 essay also has a title which makes his views more than clear: 'Kampf den Flaneuren. Über Deutschlands junge lahme Dichter'. Whereas here the first part of the title may well evoke the, admittedly, no longer young Peter Handke and such works as *Nachmittag eines Schriftstellers* (1987), the text itself is redolent with direct criticisms of, for example, Thomas Hettche and his 'Suaden' and 'des großmäuligen Thorsten Becker'. What Altenburg asks for are sentences with 'Tempo' and stories with 'Drive' (Altenburg 1992, 73); at present, he claims, most books read as if they had been written on the back of a mule, whilst their authors use the Intercity Express to get from one poetics seminar to the next.

Another name that has to be mentioned in this context is that of Uwe Wittstock, who has three volumes to his name that seek to advance the cause of writing that has a wider appeal than that of most contemporary German literature.[8] His argument too is that literature should make a direct appeal to its readers, who cannot be expected to plough their way through labyrinthine textual difficulties. He underlines this point by suggesting that interest in literature is 'keine Bringschuld der Leser' (Wittstock 1995, 17) and that literature now has to compete with many other attractions, not least those offered by the media. Interestingly, he also praises American literature which is read 'in aller Welt' (Wittstock 1995, 33). This particular argument does not seem too far away from the kind of thinking, based on the concept of globalization, referred to at the beginning of this Introduction. German literature too, it would appear, must be seen as a kind of product to compete in the world market for literature.

It goes without saying that this side of the argument has not had it all its own way. Siegfried Unseld, the head of the Suhrkamp Verlag, in his 1993 essay 'Literatur im Abseits?' disputes the contention that German literature is in decline in comparison with the past. Replying to the claim that young German authors are now only published in small editions, he is able to quote examples of earlier writers, such as Hesse, Celan and Walser, whose careers made a very slow start. He goes on to attack those who merely seek 'Unterhaltung und Vergnügen im trivialen Sinn' from literature (Unseld 1993, 109). The academic Manfred Schneider, in an original contribution to the *Maulhelden und Königskinder* volume, takes the argument a step further in his satirical piece 'Einen Neckermann für unsere Dichter?'. It is not suggested that such a generous sponsor should teach writers how to ride (Josef Neckermann was an accomplished showjumper) or use them as models for mail order catalogues, Neckermann's main business interest, but that he should solve their financial problems. Then there would be the chance of such missing masterpieces as 'Fußballgedichte von Rilke, (e)ine deftige Auschwitz-Komödie von Celan' (Schneider 1998, 257).

Schneider's satire shows the vulnerability of the argument that equates or appears to equate success and entertainment value with quality. The other, largely aesthetic counter-argument is put by Heinrich Vormweg in 'Literaturzerstörung', an essay that appeared originally in 1994. He sees those who attack recent German literature, for example Schirrmacher, as wanting to turn the clock back and ignore modernism. Specifically he attacks Wittstock's 1993 essay; 'Ab in die Nische', which is also contained in *Maulhelden und Königskinder*: 'Vermengt mit erstaunlichen Gemeinplätzen und Verallgemeinerungen kommt dabei alles zum Vorschein, was auch sonst schon gegen Moderne und Avantgarde hervorgebracht worden ist' (Vormweg 1994, 123).

It is difficult to mediate between the two positions in the debate, especially in their most extreme form. It would be wrong to denigrate modernism and all its works and demand a return to traditional realistic narrative, just as it still seems to have been a blind alley, despite the possible merits of individual works, that in the nineteenth century, in the world of painting, the Pre-Raphaelites tried to go back to techniques that predated the eponymous Italian master. On the other hand, Wittstock is not decrying the whole of modernism. He is keen to point out that Kafka used the techniques of popular literature or, as he provocatively puts it, 'Kafka hatte [...] einen gut entwickelten Sinn für *special effects*' (Wittstock 1995, 23; original emphasis).

In this volume four contributions seem particularly relevant to the debate about the narrative skills of contemporary German authors. Beatrice Petz examines the problem of the narrator in Grass's *Unkenrufe* (1992), drawing attention to a narrative strategy that has been overlooked in most previous criticism of the work and may mark a change in Grass's approach to history.

Rejecting the frequently used label 'picaresque', Nause uses the term 'naive gaze' to define the narrative stance adopted in some east German post-unification novels, at least one of which, Thomas Brussig's *Helden wie wir* (1996), can be described as a popular and international success. Brussig's novel also features, alongside Timm's *Johannisnacht* (1996) and Ulrich Woelk's *Rückspiel* (1993), in Stefan Neuhaus's discussion of the 'populist' proposition that 'Erzählen ist total erotisch' (Timm 1998, 102). And Dieter Stolz, in his essay on what has been arguably the greatest international success of all, Patrick Süskind's *Das Parfum* (1985), examines specifically the role of the narrator and the technical skill of the author in a work which contains many levels. He suggests that all kinds of readers, from the casual seeker after entertainment to the specialist literary scholar, can find pleasure and satisfaction in this text. Stolz's analysis of *Das Parfum*, along with the three other essays discussed in this paragraph, suggest that any blanket claim that German authors are incapable of story-telling is far from the truth.

IV All we are saying is give us a chance

It can be no surprise that the kind of criticism of German literature outlined above has not remained unanswered. Martin Hielscher, for example, has suggested that critics' negative attitudes have an overall detrimental effect on the world of letters.[9] Writers too have sought to defend themselves by pointing out the difficulties of their position in the world of literature. Sten Nadolny, for instance, has spoken of German writing not being able to be better irrespective of the talents of individual writers. In his essay 'Roman oder Leben —?' he paints a utopian picture of a writer being able to prepare his next work over a prolonged period: 'Er wartet [...], übt andere Tätigkeiten aus und denkt nebenher gemächlich genug über sein Projekt nach. Dann schreibt er drei Jahre daran, was ihm finanziell möglich sein oder möglich gemacht sein muß' (Nadolny 1994, 235). The reality, however, is that the market will not allow this so that the situation of German literature could hardly improve 'selbst wenn die ersehnten Genies vollzählig wären' (Nadolny 1994, 236).

Nadolny's views find some support in Schirrmacher's critical essay 'Idyllen in der Wüste' referred to above. He too sees writers in a constant battle against time, with the result that much of their work remains superficial: 'Zwei Wochen New York müssen genügen, um New York zu verstehen. Einige Minuten Fernsehnachrichten reichen aus, um ein Bild vom Zustand der Welt zu bekommen' (Schirrmacher 1998, 19). That this might sometimes literally be the case is suggested by Henryk M. Broder in a highly critical review of a play about Kosovo entitled *Peace* by Falk Richter. In typically scathing manner, Broder maintains that Richter spent 'eine ganze Woche' in Kosovo (Broder 2000b). Where Schirrmacher's diagnosis appears to diverge from that of Nadolny is in the area of financial support for writers. Whereas Nadolny is demanding a degree of financial security for writers, in effect a suspension of the rules of the market economy, Schirrmacher detects negative effects in the system of subsidies that exists to help especially young writers. He sees the result of such support in endless new works that appear every year and are only distinguished by their superfluity. As for the authors, they are placed in a position of dependence on patrons who cannot be differentiated from 'den klassischen Vorbildern der Auftragskunst' (Schirrmacher 1998, 16).

One phenomenon Schirrmacher refers to is the début novel that is praised to the sky, the kind of phenomenon referred to in this volume by Stolz, who rightly condemns the sensationalist treatment of literature in parts of the media. He singles out *Der Spiegel*, which in 1999 used the kind of economics-based terminology ('Fräuleinwunder') referred to in the first part of this Introduction to celebrate the work of new women writers. The pattern of reception being criticized can be seen in relation to the Austrian writer Robert Schneider. Whereas his first novel, *Schlafes Bruder* (1992), earned unstinted and arguably excessive praise, his second work, *Die Luftgängerin* (1998), met with an almost universal negative reaction.[10] One fears that the same fate may well await some of those that were lauded by *Der Spiegel* in 1999.

Many of the relevant issues in this context were discussed in the Introduction to the previous volume in this series: *Literature, Markets and Media in Germany and Austria Today* (Williams/Parkes/Preece, 2000). That the overall situation for writers is unlikely to get better was illustrated by a recent article by Rainer Traub in *Der Spiegel* about the fate of one of the most famous names in the publishing of German literature, the S. Fischer Verlag (Traub 2000). Now part of the Holtzbrinck group, it apparently lost between 12 and 15 million Marks in 1999, losses the parent company is no longer willing to sustain. The company's plan is said to be to make around a third of the staff redundant and to produce fewer books. Even if Schirrmacher's diagnosis that too many books are produced is correct, it does not follow that the right ones in terms of quality will be axed, in particular as Fischer already publishes such a trivial author as Hertha Lind, whose portrayals of 'modern women' in such works as *Das Superweib* remain unbelievably banal.

Andreas Nentwich, writing in *Die Zeit*, whilst more discriminating than Traub (1998), comes to some broadly similar conclusions. Whilst he also believes that too many books are being produced, he is equally worried about the fate of minority authors whose work may help a publisher's prestige 'unter Kennern und Liebhabern' (Nentwich 2000, 51) but is not seen as generating enough profit. The result, according to Nentwich, is that many writers will have to turn to literary agents, a profession whose numbers have increased rapidly over recent years. This brings with it the danger of what he calls, with a reference to the fashion house of that name, 'H & M-Literatur', that is to say literature that can easily be labelled (Nentwich 2000, 51). With the end of retail price maintenance in the book trade also under discussion, the future of German-language literature, which is unlikely to appeal to a mass audience, remains less than clearcut.

V Too much politics / not enough politics

Everybody who studies post-1945 German literature quickly becomes aware that political questions have always been very much to the fore both in considerable numbers of works produced and in debates about the social role of the writer. Most famously, in the Federal Republic Günter Grass, motivated by the belief that the lukewarm or negative attitudes of writers during the Weimar Republic had contributed to the failure of the first attempt to create a democracy on German soil, has, at least since the mid-1960s, sought to involve himself in the political developments of the day, not least by frequently taking part in election campaigns on behalf of the Social Democratic Party. As for writers in the GDR, regardless of their concerns or aesthetic preferences, it was hard for them to escape the political role assigned to them by the state. Any piece of writing emanating from the GDR was invariably examined for the kind of political statement it might or might not contain.

That this kind of involvement in politics had a negative effect on literature was one of the main arguments advanced during the Literaturstreit with the use of the term *Gesinnungsästhetik* by the critic Ulrich Greiner encapsulating the argument that much post-war literature had been ruined by the propagation in it of a political viewpoint. How far the criticism was really directed at specific political stances, in particular the perceived leftist consensus that had allegedly shown too much sympathy towards communism and was now failing to welcome the achievement of German unity, remains a moot point that cannot be discussed in any detail here.[11] What is beyond doubt is that the belief that there was a dichotomy between true literature and the expression of political opinion was widespread during the 1990s. In 'Roman oder Leben —?' Nadolny states: 'der Roman [...] ist kein geeignetes Instrument zur Verbreitung lobenswerter Meinungen' and goes on to talk about 'den Meinungs-Stammtisch der Gerechten' (Nadolny 1994, 234–235). If Nadolny is being gently ironic in his dismissal of 'Meinung' in literature, Walser pulled no punches in his extremely controversial speech when awarded the Friedenspreis des deutschen Buchhandels in 1998, coining the term 'Meinungsdienst' (Walser 1998, 25), with its echoes of 'Staatssicherheitsdienst' to describe those who constantly seek to confront the German people with the Nazi past. In Walser's case one might again wonder if the major concern is a specific opinion rather than the propagation of opinions as such; what matters here though is the use of the term in such a derogatory way.

In Nadolny's latest novel *Er oder Ich* (1999), the ageing hero Ole Reuter on his train journey through the extended Federal Republic reads the work of the east German writer Daniela Dahn, who is most famous for her criticisms of German unity in such works as *Westwärts und nicht vergessen*, the volume referred to in this context. He comments: 'versuche mich politisch zu empören, egal ob im Sinn ihrer Darstellung oder dagegen' (Nadolny 1999, 231–232) and later he reflects: 'Daniela, ein schöner Name' (251). Whilst it would be far too simplistic to conclude that the character's stance reflects that of his creator, the kind of attitude displayed by Ole Reuter, that is to say indifference towards politics, became the central theme of the most recent dispute over literature (I am writing in July 2000) to come to the fore in the Federal Republic.

Referred to briefly by Nause in her essay, this latest Literaturstreit again centres around the figure of Maxim Biller. In a speech given in the early spring of 2000, Biller launched into a vituperative attack on both the society and the literature of the Federal Republic. According to him, since the 1980s there has been a lack of thinking in true political categories, only an anxious desire to maintain a comfortable existence. It was this kind of mood that Helmut Kohl pandered to and profited from: 'Er hat wie kein anderer davon profitiert, dass die Deutschen sich in ein Volk von selbstsüchtigen, neurotischen Feiglingen verwandelt hatten, die nun einzig von ihrer Angst um ihr Wohlgefühl angetrieben wurden'. Even discussions of the Nazi past fail to deal with the major issues and are 'reine Schattenkämpfe [...], wenn man bedenkt, dass hier lebende Ausländer sich in der früheren DDR genauso sicher fühlen wie ein deutscher Tourist in der Southbronx' (Biller 2000, 47). Biller sees this social malaise reflected in the unhappy state of German literature, which, because of its lack of moral concern, is characterized only by 'lauwarme Geschichten' (Biller 2000, 48). He claims: 'Moralische Vorstelling ist die handwerkliche Grundvoraussetzung eines jeden großen Schriftstellers, sie ist seine Fähigkeit zur Poesie'. His final conclusion is: 'Kunst ist Politik und Politik ist Kunst' (49).

At the political level there is much to question in Biller's arguments. However challenging at first sight, on closer examination his views appear to be very close to much of the kind of thinking that has emerged since unification. The criticism of the Germans for not being willing to face big issues is reminiscent of Cora Stephan's attack on what she saw as the 'Betroffenheitskult' in the book of that name (1993) and of Karl Heinz Bohrer's earlier attacks at the time of the Falklands War on German 'Mainzelmännchen', who, unlike the British, were unwilling to contemplate major political actions such as going to war.[12] In fact, Biller comes close to a sub-Nietzschean cult of heroism, moreover casting himself into the role of hero as he recalls his political isolation as a Hamburg schoolboy at the time of the 1977 Mogadishu hi-jacking when he agreed with the decision of the federal government to storm the aeroplane. Another dubious assertion is Biller's claim that it is necessary to have political enemies, a claim he substantiates in a reference to Brecht. Having spoken at the beginning of the essay of his previous dislike of Brecht, he later on maintains that Brecht was a great writer because he had 'ganz echte, reale Feinde' (Biller 2000, 48). This is reminiscent of the kind of rightist thinking using a concept of politics based on the question 'who is my friend? who is my enemy?' usually associated with Carl Schmitt which, if not directly akin to National Socialism, undoubtedly helped to undermine the Weimar Republic.

At the literary level, Biller was answered by Matthias Altenburg, who this time took a different side. Whereas he accepted Biller's view of German society, he rejected the claims about literature, maintaining that there was no link between the two spheres of the kind proposed by Biller. His argument is simply: 'In der Literatur haben die großen Ideen nichts zu suchen'. This is because literature is primarily concerned with detail which alone is seen as capable of moving the reader. Altenburg also defends modernism against Biller's pleas for a return to realism, asking: 'Warum sollte man zurückbleiben hinter den Fehlern und Errungenschaften der Vorgänger?' (Altenburg 2000).

In the light of the continuing arguments about morality and politics in German literature, it only seems possible to repeat the obvious: that literature has always been and will inevitably continue to be concerned with moral questions. It is only necessary to recall a classic of world literature like Dostoyevsky's *Crime and Punishment*. It is equally inevitable that socio-political issues will be raised in the literary context. What matters is how such topics and even the author's opinions are integrated into the aesthetic structure of the particular work. Interestingly, Aifan, in her essay in this volume, quotes Rafik Schami's idea of 'smuggling' his opinion into his literary work.

In the wider world of German literature, socio-political issues continue to play a significant role. In this volume, Long, Peitsch and Arthur Williams especially deal with works that might in some way be described as having political themes. Another relevant text in this context is Joachim Lottmann's recent novel *Deutsche Einheit* (1999), the title of which suggests the theme that many, in Germany at least, hope will lead to a great novel in the way that some Americans once yearned for 'The Great American Novel'. In Lottmann's case the narrative is principally about an attempt to write such a work, a sign perhaps that such an undertaking is far from easy; it also contains so many somewhat esoteric references to German cultural life (we encounter, for example, a weeping Marcel Reich-Ranicki) that it is hardly likely to be an immediate international success. Lottmann also prefaces his work with a dedication 'Für das seit Menschengedanken erste Volk des Erdballs, das, wenn auch erst seit wenigen Jahren, dafür quer durch alle sozialen Schichten, seine Vergangenheit aufarbeitet und seine Taten bereut', a claim which, whatever its veracity, again suggests that the worlds of literature and politics, not to mention 'Meinung', cannot be easily separated.

VI Conclusion

The 12 June 2000 edition of *Der Spiegel* quoted Federal Chancellor Schröder as regretting 'einen erschreckenden Mangel an Internationalität' (25) and demanding 'Wir müssen internationaler werden' (22). If German literature has become more international, it might then even be seen as setting a positive example for other areas of society. Such an impression was confirmed in the digest of press reactions to the annual conference of the German PEN contained in the June edition of the *Fachdienst Germanistik*. Referring to the previous failure of the eastern and western branches to unite until long after unification, Joachim Günter in the *Neue Zürcher Zeitung* noted: 'Die innerdeutsche Nabelschau des PEN gehört endgültig der Vergangenheit an' (Fachdienst 2000, 1). Equally praised was the choice of the writer known as SAID, who was born in Teheran, as the new president, as well as the efforts of the organization to help persecuted authors. This kind of development, along with the new mood of optimism about German literature referred to at the beginning of Nause's contribution to this volume, would seem to confirm that it is well on the way to becoming 'international' and 'popular'.

It is, however, advisable to be cautious. It is not just a case of the problems associated with the two concepts discussed above. In the media-driven age of instant sensations it is all too easy to make claims and classifications on the basis of short-term developments. This point is taken up by Katharina Döbler in a short piece 'Schnupfen' with the more revealing sub-title 'Literaturbetrieb und Tendenzwahn'. She begins her essay with the following sardonic comments: 'Wie schön ist es, wenn der Literaturkritiker etwas mehrfach Vorhandenes und zugleich Neues findet. Da ist der Jubel groß: eine Tendenz!' (Döbler 2000). She also mocks the term 'Fräuleinwunder' as coined by *Der Spiegel*, and points out that many of the women in question are not in the first flush of youth and are in some cases mothers. The point is well made. It is only necessary to recall the case of Binjamin Wilkomirski as analysed here by Long to become aware of the dangers of instant responses and classifications. What this collection of essays can be said to show is the variety of German-language literature; this is something that can be seen as positive without resort to too many labels or laboured attempts to see far-reaching developments without the necessary help of sufficient temporal distance.

Within this variety there are inevitably differences of quality, the criterion that ultimately counts more than popularity for those who study literature seriously. Given the danger that this might be forgotten in today's market and media driven world, it is small wonder that the assembled writers at the PEN meeting referred to above complained that the book market was increasingly only interested in the best seller rather than literature. Which of the works discussed in this volume possess the greatest literary merit cannot be determined here, even if such judgements were ultimately possible about a field of human endeavour which eludes exact classification. Stolz makes a stong case for *Das Parfum* which can be claimed to be both 'international' and 'popular'. Williams writes about W.G. Sebald whose vision crosses national boundaries and other barriers as well so that he can be called 'international' in a true sense of the term. One can only hope that the scholarship displayed by Williams helps to make Sebald more 'popular' or at least better understood; comparable aims can be claimed for many of the other scholarly contributions to this volume, which, like its predecessors, aims to provide its readers with new insights into the increasingly multi-faceted world of German-language literature.

Notes
1. A typical rejection by a writer of the mentality behind this kind of claim can be found in Wolf Wondratschek's text 'Hier': '"Wir sind wieder wer!" sagen sie von sich. Zurecht. Aber wer sind sie? Wieder die alten' (Wondratschek 1969, 18).
2. Christoph Butterwege's *Wohlfahrtsstaat im Wandel* (2nd edn 1999; Opladen: Leske + Budrich) provides a massive critique of the misuse of the globalization argument to demand a more competitive Germany. It uses, besides 'Standortnationalismus', the following terms in its chapter/section headings 'Standortsicherung', 'Wohlstandschauvinismus' 'nationaler Wettbewerbsstaat' to describe this kind of mood.
3. The *Berliner Zeitung* (2 April 1997) headed an article by Jürgen Busche 'Erzählstandort Deutschland in Gefahr?' (cit. Köhler/Moritz 1998, 10).
4. See, for example his essays 'Heimatkunde' and 'Bemerkungen über unseren Dialekt' in the volume *Heimatkunde* (1968).
5. In an interview with *Der Spiegel* (19 June 2000, 203) Chancellor Schröder's minister of state for culture Michael Naumann complains about films with a 'kleinen deutschen Touch', by which he means references to the German past ('Immer wirkt die SS mit'). This, he maintains, detracts from their popularity. In fact, many of the wider intellectual debates since unification have had to do with the National Socialist past, for example the reception of Daniel Goldhagen's *Hitler's Willing Executioners* and the arguments over the planned Holocaust Memorial in Berlin.
6. If the edition of 19 June 2000 is taken as an example, then the bestseller list contains only two originally German-language texts: Bernhard Schlink's collection of stories *Liebesfluchten* and Doris Dörrie's *Was machen wir jetzt?*
7. It is interesting to compare Germany and France in this area. According to Pierre Marion (1999, 149), admittedly an industrialist and former head of the secret service, France produces 'romanciers dont les traductions ne s'exportent plus et [...] films déprimistes et intimistes qui ne se vendent pas hors de nos frontières'. However, he claims there is a lack of awareness of this in France, whereas it might be argued that in Germany even minor problems are invariably turned into major crises.
8. These are an edition of *Neue Rundschau* (104/3, 1993), the edited volume *Roman oder Leben* (1994) and the authored work *Leselust* (1995).
9. See Hielscher 2000.
10. The volume *Deutsche Literatur 1998* (eds Volker Hage, Rainer Moritz, Hubert Winkels [Stuttgart: Reclam 1999]) refers in its chronicle of events to the reactions to *Die Luftgängerin* being 'einhellig negativ' (47), whilst no review of the novel is included in the new books section.
11. Books on the topic of writers and German unity are too numerous for an an exhaustive list to be given here. They include Williams/Parkes/Smith 1991 and Langguth 1997.
12. For a critique of Bohrer's attitude see Peitsch 1991, esp. 182.

Bibliography
Altenburg, Matthias 1992: 'Kampf den Flaneuren. Über Deutschlands junge lahme Dichter. (Mit Nachsatz "Aus dem Souterrain")' in Köhler/Moritz 1998, 72–78.
—— 2000: 'Alles Kohl', *Die Zeit*, 19 April 2000, 48.
Biller, Maxim 1991: 'Soviel Sinnlichkeit wie der Stadtplan von Kiel. Warum die neue deutsche Literatur nichts so nötig hat wie den Realismus. Ein Grundsatzprogramm' in Köhler/Moritz 1998, 62–71.
—— 2000: 'Feige das Land, schlapp die Literatur', *Die Zeit*, 13 April 2000, 47–49.
Böll, Heinrich 1985: 'Ende der Bescheidenheit' in Böll: *Ende der Bescheidenheit. Schriften und Reden 1969–1972*. Munich: dtv, 54–67.
Broder, Henryk M. 2000a: 'Harakari im Kleinen Haus', *Der Spiegel*, 29 May 2000, 244–247.
—— 2000b: 'Weltschmerz der Warmduscher', *Der Spiegel*, 19 June 2000, 267.
DDR 1986: *Die DDR stellt sich vor*. Dresden: Zeit im Bild.
Döbler, Katharina 2000: 'Schnupfen', *Die Zeit*, 18 May 2000, 55.
Fachdienst 2000: 'Sprache/Literatur und Öffentlichkeit', *Fachdienst Germanistik* 18/6, 1–2.

Fiedler, Leslie A. 1994: 'Überquert die Grenze, schließt den Graben' in Wittstock 1994, 14–39.
Griotteray, Alain and Jean de Larsan 1999: *Voyage au bout de l'Allemagne*. Monaco: Éditions du Rocher.
Hielscher, Martin 2000: 'The Return to Narrative and to History: Some Thoughts on Contemporary German-Language Literature' in Williams/Parkes/Preece 2000, 295–309.
Jenny, Urs 1995: *Liebesbrief für Mary*. Zurich: Diogenes.
Kirchhoff, Bodo 1994: 'Das Schreiben: ein Sturz' in Wittstock 1994, 211–219.
Köhler, Andrea and Rainer Moritz (eds) 1998: *Maulhelden und Königskinder. Zur Debatte über die deutschsprachige Gegenwartsliteratur*. Leipzig: Reclam.
Langguth, Gerd (ed.) 1997: *Die Intellektuellen und die nationale Frage*. Frankfurt am Main: Campus.
Lottmann, Joachim 1999: *Deutsche Einheit*. Zurich: Haffmans.
Marion, Pierre 1999: *Mémoires de l'ombre. Un homme dans les secrets de l'état*. [Paris:] Flammarion.
Nadolny, Sten 1994: 'Roman oder Leben — ?' in Wittstock 1994, 219–237.
—— 1999: *Er oder Ich*. Munich/Zurich: Piper.
Nentwich, Andreas 2000: 'Klein und Groß', *Die Zeit*, 21 June 2000, 51–52.
Peitsch, Helmut 1991: 'West German Reflections on the Role of the Writer in the Light of Reactions to 9 November 1989' in Williams/Parkes/Smith 1991, 155–186.
Schirrmacher, Frank 1989: 'Idyllen in der Wüste oder das Versagen vor der Metropole' in Köhler/Moritz 1998, 15–27.
Schlink, Bernhard 1997: *Der Vorleser*. Zurich: Diogenes.
—— 1998: *The Reader*. London: Phoenix.
Schneider, Manfred 1998: 'Einen Neckermann für unsere Dichter' in Köhler/Moritz 1998, 255–262.
Timm, Uwe 1998: *Johannisnacht. Roman*. Munich: dtv. (1st publ. 1996)
Traub, Rainer 2000: 'Bedrohter Kafka', *Der Spiegel*, 29 May 2000, 86.
Unseld, Siegfried 1993: 'Literatur im Abseits? Polemische Anmerkungen eines Verlegers' in Köhler/Moritz 1998, 105–109.
Vormweg, Heinrich 1994: 'Literaturzerstörung. Zur Fortsetzung des sogenannten Deutschen Literaturstreits' in Köhler/Moritz 1998, 110–125.
Walser, Martin 1968: *Heimatkunde*. Frankfurt am Main: Suhrkamp.
—— 1998: *Erfahrungen beim Verfassen einer Sonntagsrede*. Frankfurt am Main: Suhrkamp.
Williams, Arthur, Stuart Parkes and Roland Smith (eds) 1991: *German Literature at a Time of Change 1989–1990*. Bern: Peter Lang.
Williams, Arthur, Stuart Parkes and Julian Preece (eds) 2000: *Literature, Markets and Media in Germany and Austria Today*. Bern: Peter Lang.
Wittstock, Uwe 1993: 'Ab in die Nische? Über neueste deutsche Literatur und was sie vom Publikum trennt' in Köhler/Moritz 1998, 86–104.
—— 1994: *Roman oder Leben. Postmoderne in der deutschen Literatur*. Leipzig: Reclam.
—— 1995: *Leselust*. Munich: Luchterhand.
Wondratschek, Wolf 1969: 'Hier' in Wondratschek: *Morgens begann der Tag mit einer Schußwunde*. Munich: Hanser, 18–19.

PATRICK SÜSKIND'S *PARFUM*:
'NO ONE KNOWS HOW *WELL MADE* IT IS'

DIETER STOLZ

Mein Genie ist in meinen Nüstern...
(Nietzsche: Ecce Homo)

I

Also das gibt es immer noch oder schon wieder: einen deutschen Schriftsteller, der des Deutschen mächtig ist; einen zeitgenössischen Erzähler, der dennoch erzählen kann; einen Romancier, der uns nicht mit dem Spiegelbild seines Bauchnabels belästigt; einen jungen Autor, der trotzdem kein Langweiler ist. (Marcel Reich-Ranicki)

Not to him, R.-R., the preening media star of latter days, but to him, the publicity-shy creator of the *Perfume* that lingers unforgettably on, be thanks! Without his piece of artistic magic an international colloquium on contemporary German literature which examines the topic under the aspects of the popular and the international is scarcely conceivable. *Das Parfum. Die Geschichte eines Mörders* was published in 1985 by the Diogenes Verlag after several publishing houses in Germany had turned down the manuscript that ran so quintessentially counter to the *Zeitgeist* of the day.[1] The responsible editors will presumably still be kicking themselves, at least when nobody is watching them, over this glaring miscalculation, because, with his first novel, Patrick Süskind became the first author of the post-war generation to achieve success at home and abroad that has remained unparalleled until today. With more that ten million copies sold so far *Das Parfum* has even put the sales figures for *Die Blechtrommel* into the shade. Moreover, it is most warmly recommended as Europe's captivating answer to the magic realism of Latin American origin, exceptionally even in the USA, where publishers could be said to have fought each other for the lucrative rights.

It is small wonder that other writers, inspired by the desire for popular texts and extremely promising market surveys, followed the example of our successful author, with, it goes without saying, greater or lesser aversion towards the literary market place and the culture industry — and, of course, with the most varied of talents. Subsequently the supposedly entirely 'new' narrative art from European lands has undeniably achieved increasing popularity and has been enjoying an international boom for several years. This welcome development, which at times admittedly brings forth strange fruits — as is well known, the *Spiegel*-terms for it are 'Das Fräuleinwunder' (cf. Hage 1999a, 245) or, to bring the other sex into play as well, 'Grass's grandsons are coming' (cf. Hage 1999b)[2] — will have to be considered in critical discourses on the media-friendly change of paradigm. I, however, will quickly return to *Das Parfum*, the work which paved the way for the continuing current development and which remains a fascinating long seller for masses of readers. It starts with the birth of an altogether single-faceted genius ('das Denken war nicht seine Stärke' (317)) and ends with the very significant extinguishing of this insult to nature: 'Mancher der vortrefflichsten Romane ist ein Kompendium, eine Enzyklopädie des ganzen geistigen Lebens eines genialischen Individuums [...] Auch enthält jeder Mensch, der gebildet ist, und sich bildet, in seinem Innern einen Roman. Daß er ihn aber äußre und schreibe, ist nicht nötig' (Schlegel 1956, 15). This is because this task can also sometimes, as the history of literature shows, be taken over by congenial authors: 'Wieviele Autoren gibts wohl unter den Schriftstellern? Autor heißt Urheber' (Schlegel 1956, 14).

Although Süskind's success surprised aesthetic puritans, its secret is obvious to the less narrow-minded. This novel, which only at first sight (which, for similarly obvious reasons, for countless reviewers and readers may also be the last sight) trips along so lightly but is in fact highly complex, offers something for every taste. It is, as it were, superficial down to its deepest refinements of style, an example of the most subtle popular elite art. Insatiable bookworms, spurred on by the 'horrific' sub-title and the (un)ambiguous cover, enjoy looking forward to a repast spiced with eros and thanatos, amor and psyche, suppressed lust and murderous violence. This is what the despicable carnival of life brings and in this criminal case things go beyond what the police allow. Incorrigible Germanists, on the other hand, are enthused by the prospect of such 'exciting' working titles as '*Das Parfum* as a detective story', '*Das Parfum* as a Bildungsroman', '*Das Parfum* as a picaresque novel' or even 'Post-modern narrative discourse as a deconstruction of traditional structural models with regard to current religious, philosophical, psychological and macro-societal questions'. You know what I am talking about: dialogue with outstanding canonical books that in the best cases is well thought out and, perhaps, at times, even conducted systematically using such terms as style mimicry, multiple coding, intertextuality. Of course all that and much more besides is already available in the secondary literature on Süskind[3] and in the internet seminar: www.fbls.uni-hannover.de/angli/Perfume/perfume1.htm, an abstract research laboratory on the sensuous laboratory novel. Enjoy your surfing through the extensive systems of links:

Kritik und Wissenschaft haben unter anderem auf folgende Bezüge verwiesen: Claudius, Goethe, Kleist, Novalis, Chamisso, Hauff, E.T.A. Hoffmann, Eichendorff, Balzac, Flaubert, Baudelaire, Rimbaud, Huysmans, Fontane, Rilke, Thomas Mann, Nietzsche, Grass, Roald Dahl; außerdem das Märchen vom Froschkönig, Kasper Hauser und den Prometheusmythos. (Förster 1999, 178 n.18)[4]

In brief, it is clear that readers who approach the text with the most varied expectations and bring to it the most varied knowledge and competence are not disappointed in the enjoyment they experience with the biography of the French eighteenth-century murderer of maidens. Even the Federal Republic's critics enthused in rare unanimity about this anachronistic stroke of luck for German literature. Here at last was a book that once again gave aesthetic pleasure in the best sense of the term: a realistic fairy tale full of wit, esprit and imagination, endowed with a sparkling narrative and combining a wealth of imagery with gentle irony. Here was a literary work of art written in the most refined and artful prose, distilled from selected historical experiences, an ordered game in demythologized times situated beyond good and evil: 'Initiiert wird ein Spiel mit Formen und Inhalten, ein Spiel mit Realität und Fiktion, ein Spiel mit dem Leser' (Förster 1999, 148).

II

Then let us too, whilst fully aware of the multifarious complexities of this universal poetic project, deploy the tools of the 'gay literary science trade' and play along with the little game for a little while. For this is the way for us to understand a little more closely what it is in this seemingly extremely simple story of an unscrupulous serial killer that grips even proven connoisseurs of world literature. How is it that even diehard lovers of the aesthetic heights are enchanted by a quite conventionally laid out labyrinth of signs? Why do even the most demanding philologists swoon before this gruesome story with its use of trivial patterns of representation, at a horror scenario which appears more to address physical desire than to evoke illuminating intellectual debates. This game of interpretation is facilitated because I can assume that everyone knows the plot. Thus I am going to leave aside any banal reference to the content and start by problematizing a hitherto overlooked sequence from the final part of this subtle textual mise en scène.

Niemand weiß, wie gut dies Parfum wirklich ist, dachte er. Niemand weiß, wie gut es *gemacht* ist. Die andern sind nur seiner Wirkung untertan, ja, sie wissen nicht einmal, daß es ein Parfum ist, das auf sie wirkt und sie bezaubert. Der einzige, der es jemals in seiner wirklichen Schönheit erkannt hat, bin ich, weil ich es selbst geschaffen habe. Und zugleich bin ich der einzige, den es nicht bezaubern kann. Ich bin der einzige, für den es sinnlos ist. (316–317; original emphasis)

Who is speaking? If we 'moderne Menschen'(5) are not entirely deceived, Jean-Baptiste Grenouille, the main figure, is expressing his thoughts in this interior monologue. The olfactory artist who pursues his gargantuan ambitions along a path littered with corpses even seems to be reflecting, which is amazing enough, because it was already hinted that his intelligence was anything but awesome (31). What is more, his subject is himself and his greatest work, which will be discussed later. Grenouille himself, 'der solitäre Zeck [...] der Unmensch' (242) is introduced as a being without smell and godless, who actually should not exist. From his very first breath 'das geduckte Häuflein Nichts' (106) fits the cliché of the divinely gifted monster with a marked desire for self-assertion: 'Er entschied sich für das Leben aus reinem Trotz und reiner Boshaftigkeit' (28). Once cast into the world this best nose of France has clearly no other choice but to renounce love in all its forms, because wherever he sniffs, everything stinks. Instead he concentrates all his powers on the goal which promises him salvation from the infernal stench around him, namely the creation of the absolute perfume: 'Ein Parfum würde er machen nach allen Regeln der Kunst' (246).

This fundamental decision finds concentrated expression in Grenouille's linguistic development: 'Mit Wörtern, die keinen riechenden Gegenstand bezeichneten, mit abstrakten Begriffen also, vor allem ethischer oder moralischer Natur, hatte er die größten Schwierigkeiten [...] Recht, Gewissen, Gott, Freude, Verantwortung, Demut, Dankbarkeit usw. — was damit ausgedrückt sein sollte, war und blieb ihm schleierhaft' (33). Accordingly his vocabulary hardly justifies the term; what is more, he doubts the sense of language altogether. His paranormal experience of the world is based on exponentially growing fascination with combinations from the internalized 'Alphabet der Gerüchte' (35). Even when the deformed child, still without a recognizable creative principle, initially begins his imaginative yet destructive life's work by creating syntheses in the olfactory laboratory of his imagination, 'eher grob und plump, mehr zusammengepanscht als komponiert' (48), it is clear that the solipsistic revolutionary will ultimately achieve messianic greatness in the area of aromatic aesthetics: 'Hunderttausend Düfte schienen nichts mehr wert vor diesem einen Duft. Dieser eine war das höhere Prinzip, nach dessen Vorbild sich alle andern ordnen mußten. Er war die reine Schönheit' (55). Terrifying and irresistible.

There can be no doubt that what we are dealing with is a totally synthetic fictional character, a happily invented 'Wunderkind' (35), who becomes the 'größte Parfumeur aller Zeiten' (58) after a most speedily absolved apprenticeship and disappears apparently without leaving any detectable trace in history. In analogy to the aforementioned system of the 'apotheotische Parfum' (55), the unsuccessfully baptized 'Ding' (8) was distilled from countless fantastic and realistic predecessors within the universe of poetic projections and only gains his own unique features in the course of the narrative process. This distillation, which reveals a deep understanding of art, derives its convincing unity from the way that all the quoted models tell of the progressive discrediting of the idea of genius. This applies to both European intellectual history and to world politics: firstly from the Prometheus myth by way of dubious artist figures à la Cardillac or Klein Zaches and Wagner's *Rheingold*-'Kröte' up to Oskar Matzerath, who puts infantile adults under his spell with his art as a drummer-up of the past and for hard cash acts out for them, for a short time, the role of the post-war-Messiah; secondly, from the pathos of *Sturm und Drang* by way of Nietzsche's unmasking psychology up to the deluded chief ideologists of the Third Reich; thirdly, from the popes and emperors with their powers over life and death by way of Napoleon Bonaparte and Bismarck up to hypocritical princes of darkness such as Hitler and Stalin, who very quickly showed themselves to be the greatest criminals of their century. The divine right of kings, the genius cliché, the leadership principle and the Messiah imitator merge in this multi-layered context. The fateful consequences of the superstitions of fanatical camp-followers, which they continue to hold regardless of any catastrophe and which clearly can never be banished from the world, are well-known — and not only from the German past:

> Wenn es die Männer sind, die Geschichte machen, wenn große historische Entwicklungen von Einzelpersönlichkeiten eingeleitet und geformt werden, dann ist das Rätsel auch unserer Zeit nur aus der Begnadung des genialen Menschen zu erklären [...] Wir erleben das größte Wunder, das es in der Geschichte gibt. Ein Genie baut eine neue Welt![5]

Indeed, Jean-Baptiste Grenouille, this artistic creation equipped with all the attributes of the depraved original genius has, by pursuing his artifices to the point of perfection, in the end made possible the dreamed of miracle weapon. He has successfully created the super sexy, ultra-wicked, mega-strong perfume of all perfumes, a divine substance, which is to make the whole urge-driven species of homo sapiens totally compliant in a great showdown: 'Es gibt eine Überzeugungskraft des Duftes, die stärker ist, als Worte, Augenschein, Gefühl und Wille' (107). And so it turns out: Whether they want it or not, the devilishly good elixir made by the megalomanic misanthropist intoxicates all his contemporaries. Anybody who comes into context with this magical extract inevitably loses rational control. The anointed immoralist throws his followers into an ecstatic delusion in which all inhibitions are lost, the spectacle of superstition takes its course. The salvation seekers pray to the perfumed void, because this kind of love makes them blind. There are no limits to the glorification of the anointed 'Nichts' (138) by the mass of uncouth stinkers, who are touched at their erotic nerve centre. The children of God, abandoned by all their guardian angels, no longer know what they are doing. However, Grenouille, at least within the framework of the fiction, seems to be fully aware of what is happening. There comes to pass therefore what, according to his final will, was to be. The gifted monster wants the greatest finale possible. This is because he was forced to realize that his attempt to create his own authentic smell other than by means of artificial aroma surrogates was doomed to failure from the beginning: 'Nur eines konnte diese Macht nicht: sie konnte ihn nicht vor sich selber riechen lassen. Und mochte er auch vor der Welt durch sein Parfum erscheinen als ein Gott — wenn er sich selbst nicht riechen konnte und deshalb niemals wüßte, wer er sei, so pfiff er drauf, auf die Welt, auf sich selbst, auf sein Parfum' (316).

With the best good will in the world, Grenouille's power is limited to the realm of dazzlingly beautiful simulation; there is no hope anywhere of a human personality. The identity-less genius cocks a snook at the world, the omnipotent God of aromas longs for the end of all smells. In the final part of the novel things then really do reach this conclusion in scenes that are skilfully prepared in motivational terms and executed in wonderful detail. Animal-like 'Geschrei, Gegrunze, Gestöhn' (304), rituals of coupling and sacrifice, Dionysos cult, Holy Night, communion and last supper intermingle in a bacchanalian orgy of sex and crime with regressive features and metafictional dimensions. The despicable solitary genius whom nobody could stand at the beginning is now so loved that everybody could eat him up — in the most literal sense of the word. The idolized dwarf disappears completely, his will is done: redemption-hungry human animals 'hatten etwas zum ersten Mal aus Liebe getan' (320). So much for cannibalistic love within the framework of this absolutely artificial dystopia — or of the Cimetière des Innocents in Paris. The narrative circle, which also began there, 'am allerstinkendsten Ort des gesamten Königreiches' (7), has closed, and this piece of prose, which has to be read not least at the level of political allegory, ends with the sentence just quoted (320) — which leads me as if by chance back to my original question. Who is speaking?

III

Of course everything that we know about the vertically challenged grand perfumier comes from an omniscient, yet unreliable narrator, a not entirely penetrable figure who enjoys the distance created by stylization. At the same time, the narrator figure assures aesthetic unity, leaving hardly anything to chance. As a man of letters, this exceedingly well-read citizen of the twentieth century, in contrast to Grenouille, who throughout his life was no friend of language, relies on the magic of grammar. In terms of both form and content he appears to have everything firmly in control. He determines the narrative frame. He comments on and evaluates events. In spite of all the narrative experiments of modernism he manages to narrate largely chronologically and in the past tense throughout, thus guaranteeing coherence, creating connections and constructing links — or rather faking all this exactly as he likes it. Let us imagine, against this background, what would have happened if, with a wink of the eye, the long-nosed narrator had put into the mouth of the witless genius the passage about himself and his diligently created perfume of the angels quoted at the head of this essay. The sub-text of this consummately calculated fable would take on a totally different meaning. For the sake of memory:

> Niemand, weiß, wie gut dies Parfum wirklich ist, dachte er. Niemand weiß, wie gut es *gemacht* ist. Die andern sind nur seiner Wirkung untertan, ja, sie wissen nicht einmal, daß es ein Parfum ist, das auf sie wirkt und sie bezaubert. Der einzige, der es jemals in seiner wirklichen Schönheit erkannt hat, bin ich, weil ich es selbst geschaffen habe. Und zugleich bin ich der einzige, den es nicht bezaubern kann. Ich bin der einzige, für den es sinnlos ist. (316–317)

From this perspective (the internal poetological self-reflection of writing), suddenly nothing has anything to do any longer with Grenouille and his evanescent 'fabrications', everything has to do with the epic construct by the name of *Das Parfum* which is being discussed here. The reflection of the reflection cannot be overlooked, and not just in this context. On the one hand, the congenial confidence trickster is put under the spotlight and himself shown to be a necessarily dissatisfied creator of an intoxicating verbal work of art — the corpses of secondary figures litter his path as well. On the other hand, the arbitrary, omnipotent figure of the narrator appears to have dropped a subtly enlightening, yet heavy hint to his vulnerable (or rather long since seduced) readers. This is because the apparent omniscience of the narrator only exists on the surface; in reality he has led by the nose all those who admire his story without reflection or just consume it naively. One further piece of proof of many: Grenouille's first master, Guiseppi Baldini, according to the suspect narrator, was not an original inventor:

> Er war ein sorgfältiger Verfertiger von bewährten Gerüchen, wie ein Koch war er, der mit Routine und guten Rezepten eine große Küche macht und doch nie ein eigenes Gericht erfunden hat. Den ganzen Hokuspokus mit Labor und Experimentieren und Inspiration und Geheimnistuerei führte er nur auf, weil das zum ständischen Berufs

> bild eines Maître Parfumeur et Gantier gehörte. Ein Parfumeur, das war ein halber Alchemist, der Wunder schuf, so wollten es die Leute — gut so! Daß seine Kunst ein Handwerk war wie jedes andere auch, das wußte nur er selbst, und das war sein Stolz. (66–67)

Who is speaking? Even if the signals can hardly be missed by professional textual analysts, it will not be clear to all potential gullible consumers that the seasoned playmaker is concerned, within the framework of his seductive scheme, with his comfortably obvious array of narrative tricks and subtle irony, to push them back to the hard facts of reality. The practised liar, however, makes every effort to claim 'analytische Arbeit' (82): the creation of legends and transparent false scents abound; there are endless hints of cleverly blended counterfeits and plagiarized magic formulae in profusion:

> Wir werden's riechen. So wie ein scharfes Beil den Holzklotz in die kleinsten Scheite teilt, wird unsre Nase sein Parfum in jede Einzelheit zerspalten. Dann wird sich zeigen, daß dieser angebliche Zauberduft auf sehr normalem, wohlbekanntem Weg entstanden ist. Wir, Baldini, Parfumeur, werden dem Essigmischer Pélissier auf die Schliche kommen. Wir werden ihm die Maske von der Fratze reißen und dem Neuerer beweisen, wozu das alte Handwerk in der Lage ist. Haargenau wird es ihm nachgemischt, sein modisches Parfum [...] An die Arbeit jetzt, Baldini! Die Nase geschärft und gerochen ohne Sentimentalität! Den Duft zerlegt nach den Regeln der Kunst! (81)

By pulling the threads with this kind of indirect address the illusionist narrator repeatedly invites the reader to maintain a safe distance from opulently staged charades, the insubstantial ephemera of fashion, and idealistic exegeses of every kind. This includes revoltingly good propaganda speeches, sensationalistic scientific mumbo-jumbo and virtuoso literary works of art like *Das Parfum*. For this purpose he uses a poetic process of unmasking, which recalls to the reader's mind the proven devastating effects of 'scapegoat theories', of skilfully provoked mass hysteria and of pseudo-systems as promoted by various media. The aim is to put a spoke in the wheels of demagogues in their various guises and with all their false trappings of genius whenever the situation arises. Consequently claims of authenticity and truth are consistently taken ad absurdum.

By now all interested participants will know a little more about how well made it is, this experiment between Pop Art and avant-garde out of the writer's laboratory, this most seductive of honey traps for readers in the age of global inveiglement through aestheticized design: 'In der Tradition der Künstlererzählung und des dekadenten Romans angesiedelt, demaskiert er die Genieideologie und gestaltet eine Allegorie auf die Hohlheit des modernen Kulturgebarens und die Verführbarkeit des apokalyptisch disponierten Menschen' (Frizen 1994, 757).

IV

It is perhaps even possible to extend an interpretative approach which has been pursued under changing headings by adding to the question 'Who is speaking?' another about the executive director: who is pulling the strings behind the stage or rather between the lines? It may then be that the roles in this never concealed display of artifice are not so clearly allocated. It is worth imagining, as an experiment, that it is not *Das Parfum*'s teller of tall stories, prone as he is now and again to crude moralizing, but rather the one who invented him in his professional capacity who calls the shots as a second creator. This wily old devil would thus have much greater freedom of manoeuvre. He would, for instance, have the chance of capping the occasional ironical moments of his loosely controlled narrative medium through the illuminating arrangement of quotations or the seminal technique of the Romantics: ironizing irony. He would be in a position to rise on the wings of poetic reflection above both the clod-hopping ideas of his main figure and also above the limited horizons of his 'modern' narrator. Perhaps this all-powerful puppet master within the universal realm of fiction, in contrast to the anonymous narrator of the genre-transcending story, could take his perfection so far as to re-create in the light of his meticulously researched novel the efficacy graph of a progressive universal aroma capable of enticing all people equally: 'Das Parfum lebt in der Zeit; es hat seine Jugend, seine Reife und sein Alter. Und nur wenn es in allen drei verschiedenen Lebens-altern auf gleich angenehme Weise Duft verströmt, ist es als gelungen zu bezeichnen' (80). Accordingly it could be imagined that, in relation to the powerful effects of this *Perfume*, that there might be a pyramid-like line of reception, which is repeated with slight variations in every act of reading, a kind of pre-programmed arc of experience as a constant that gives rise to worry, or at least provides food for thought. This could hardly be fought against, because they, both Grenouille's unenlightened contemporaries and today's enlightened readers, were 'stinkend dumm [...]; weil sie sich von ihm belügen und betrügen ließen'(197).

Consequently things would look as follows. Exposition: at Grenouille's place of birth it stinks to high heaven. Through the conscious use of language a revoltingly indiscriminate array of odours is evoked before our eyes. The anti-image, which is necessary to establish the counter-position to the world of per-fume, is constructed. In addition, in keeping with a clearly planned strategy, far too much of a nauseating stench is presented in the exaggeratedly manneristic prologue. There is a pungent smell in the nose, an external sign that it is still impossible to speak of any symbiosis with readers' experiences. However, slowly but surely, there follows the olfactory effect and later the development of the unmistakable bouquet of a virtuoso aromatic work of art, which inspires enthusiasm through synaesthesia. Once applied, every perfume, even the best, needs its time. Finally, in the middle of the book, we briefly face the true all-enveloping climax or rather the magic mountain of the story: 'Heil Grenouille!' As we read, we experience the staging of an 'internal *Reichsparteitag*' by the great, glorious and unique Narcissus as a Wagnerian *Gesamtkunstwerk* without metaphysical roots: 'Mit beginnendem Schlaf versenkte er sich tiefer und tiefer in sich hinein und hielt triumphalen Einzug in seiner inneren Festung, auf der er sich ein geruchliches Siegesfest erträumte, eine gigantische Orgie mit Weih-rauchqualm und Myrrendampf, zu Ehren seiner selbst' (114).

The almighty Grenouille creates his own realm, and he 'sah, daß es gut war, sehr, sehr gut' (162). But then (how could it be otherwise?) the intensity of the perfectly timed, scintillating aromatic firework display accompanied by religious jingles diminishes. The intoxication of the literary ball recedes. We are approaching, with a slight hangover, the inevitable catastrophe. Nobody speaks, if it can be put that way, a redeeming word. From now on things go downhill in the truest sense of the word. There is a proliferation of repetition, the composition loses its tautness, devices from the detective story trade delay the resolution of the long-solved case and finally, logically, on this operatic world stage, as its splendour dims, all is dissipated into thin air in a final resounding pop. The symphonic aroma has melted away, because in this exactly calculated presentation of absolute artificiality, right from the beginning everything has centred around the evanescent realm of smells. The conclusion is: it is all to do with the effectiveness graph of an absolutely artificial perfume as a poetological model at the height of this 'maroden, verlotterten Zeit' (106). Accordingly the choice of book title could be seen as an act of pure genius.

It can be admitted that the interpretative approach presented here has its limits. Counter arguments relating to the rules governing the whole composition, as they have been developed here, are certainly within the realm of the imagination. Perhaps the 'Zauberlehrling' (117) or 'Hexenmeister' (118) was himself surprised by his successful recipe, perhaps the loss of suggestive force and power to convince is not at all a conscious calculation, but an aesthetic weakness.[6] Nevertheless (and this is a point which, as I approach my conclusion, is to be stressed despite possible counter claims), the heuristic structural model leads to the poetological core of the text. It is a text which reveals itself to be a seductive literary work of art with the intention of enlightenment, as a novel about the timeless art of manipulation which invites the reader to cast off his self-inflicted state of disenfranchisement: 'Er hatte sein Bestes gegeben. Er hatte all seine Kunstfertigkeit aufgebracht. Kein Fehler war ihm unterlaufen. Das Werk war einzigartig. Es würde von Erfolg gekrönt sein...' (277)

V

Thus spake the man of interpretations who was seduced to make preposterous associations by the narrative strategies mentioned above: 'Eine Formel ist das A und O jeden Parfums' (98). Or could it be that this text, which initially seems so unambitious, was really thought out or *made* in such an intricate way? Who knows? There is possibly only one person who knows more about the 'Duft-diagramm' (273) of this artificial work of art, but the 'sweet child' sagely veils himself in silence far from any media-led marketing of his person, a silence which may further intensify the aura of exclusivity. What remains is a sufficiently difficult and yet, despite that, amusing narrative experiment, a novel of enlightenment about the evanescent which is entertaining and strongly self-reflective at the same time. Moreover, this tragicomic masterpiece (unfortunately a solitary jewel in the literary oeuvre of the inventive eclectic) fortunately speaks for itself, without of course being able to turn 'die Welt in einen duften-den Garten Eden' (127).

In other words Patrick Süskind's *Parfum*, which has already made literary history, shows once again that the path from early Romanticism to post-modern late modernity is not as long as fashionable masters in the art of creating concepts constantly claim. However, before you tear me limb from limb because you think my hypotheses stink, I should like to begin my de-scent, quite discreetly, from the heights of this system of signs and do so with a ground-breaking quotation from the somewhat different history of creation contained in this anti-Bible for the fetishists of the olfactory, which itself, as my last quotation shows, should in no way be taken for an unbroken apotheosis of poetry:

> Der Große Grenouille aber war etwas müde geworden und gähnte und sprach: 'Siehe, ich habe ein großes Werk getan, und es gefällt mir sehr gut. Aber wie alles Vollendete beginnt es mich zu langweilen. Ich will mich zurückziehen und mir zum Abschluß dieses arbeitsreichen Tages in den Kammern meines Herzens noch eine kleine Beglückung gönnen.' (162)

Who is speaking?
Je ne sais pas!

P.S. Thanks be to the author!

Notes
Translation by Stuart Parkes.
1. All page references to quotations without further attribution are taken from this edition of *Das Parfum*.
2. cf. also the cover title of the same edition of *Der Spiegel* (41/1999): 'Die Enkel von Grass & Co. Die neuen deutschen Dichter'.
3. The present analysis is based principally on the research of Werner Frizen, firstly on his 1994 essay and secondly on the introduction to the text with notes for teachers (Frizen/Spanken 1996). The latter contains a useful list of secondary literature.
4. cf. also in this context the list of the novel's precursors in Frizen/Spanken 1996, 125–127. Förster significantly calls the first chapter (devoted exclusively to *Das Parfum*) of his stimulating dissertation 'Vom Plündern toter Dichter. Roman der Künstlichkeit'. His subtitles 'Geschichte als Gedankenspiel', 'Inszenierung des Erzählens', 'Masken des Authentischen' and 'Abstraktion und Entfremdung' already imply the path taken by my interpretation, albeit with different emphases.
5. Joseph Goebbels: radio speech of 19 April 1941 to mark Hitler's birthday (cit. Frizen 1994, 784).
6. cf. Reich-Ranicki 1985: 'Daß man viel Energie benötigt, um einen Roman zu schreiben, daß irgendwo in der zweiten Hälfte der Autor der Sache satt ist und schon etwas ganz anders machen möchte — Thomas Mann hat mehrfach darüber geklagt. Auch dem Anfänger Süskind blieb diese Erfahrung offensichtlich nicht erspart: Immer neue und häufig an den Haaren herbeigezogene Motive sollten ihm aus der Not helfen.'

Primary text
Süskind, Patrick 1985: *Das Parfum. Die Geschichte eines Mörders*. Zurich: Diogenes.
—— 1986: *Perfume. The Story of a Murderer*. Trans. John E. Woods. London: Hamish Hamilton (also Harmondsworth: Penguin, 1987).

Secondary literature
Förster, Nikolaus 1999: *Die Wiederkehr des Erzählens. Deutschsprachige Prosa der 80er und 90er Jahre*. Darmstadt: Wissenschaftliche Buchgesellschaft.
Frizen, Werner 1994: 'Das gute Buch für jedermann oder Verus Prometheus. Patrick Süskind's *Das Parfum*', *Deutsche Vierteljahrsschrift für Literaturwissenschaft und Geistesgeschichte*, 68/4, 757–786.
—— and Marilies Spanken (eds) 1996: *Einführung: Patrick Süskind, Das Parfum*. Munich: Oldenbourg.
Hage, Volker 1999a: 'Ganz schön abgedreht', *Der Spiegel*, 22 March 1999, 244–246.
—— 1999b: 'Die Enkel kommen', *Der Spiegel*, 11 October 1999, 244–254.
Reich-Ranicki, Marcel 1985: 'Des Mörders besonderer Duft', *Frankfurter Allgemeine Zeitung*, 2 March 1985, Literaturbeilage, n.p.
Schlegel, Friedrich 1956: *Kritische Schriften*. Ed. Wolfdietrich Rasch. Munich: Hanser.

GERMAN IDENTITIES IN TRANSITION?
THE TRANSLATION OF CONTEMPORARY GERMAN FICTION
IN BRITAIN AND FRANCE

WIEBKE SIEVERS

I Translation and inter/nationality

The translation of a book into several foreign languages tends to be equated with its international status, linked either to its popularity or to its literary merit and, in rare cases, to both. The label international best seller, for example, is not only awarded on the grounds of the copies sold worldwide; internationality also demands presence in a certain number of countries. When Akif Pirinçci's novel *Felidae*, one of the few German novels included in a British best-seller list in the last decade (cf. Blake 1994, 30), reached Britain in 1993, the literary critic Steve Crawshaw highlighted its international success: 'His (Akif Pirinçci's) novel *Felidae: A novel of Cats and Murder* has sold more than a million copies and been translated into 12 languages' (Crawshaw 1993, 29).

In general, it seems to be more difficult for a German author to find a publisher in Britain than in France. Pirinçci's text provides one of the many examples which prove that the translation of a foreign book into English often follows its translation into other languages. *Felidae* was published in Germany in 1989 and translated into French in 1992 before reaching Britain and the USA in 1993. Yet, translation into English has a significant impact on the author's worldwide reception and thus his or her international popularity. The English text might not only reach and be received by an English-speaking readership in several countries, it also facilitates the reception of the text in other countries where English might function as a lingua franca. Thus while Akif Pirinçci's *Felidae* had been translated into twelve languages in the four years after 1989, following the publication of the English version, this number increased to eighteen within a year (cf. Anon 1994, 30).

Yet despite the apparent internationalization of the translation industry, translation still seems to be affected by the nations involved in the transfer. In the context of the constructions of and debates on national identities, an apparently arbitrary choice of a particular author and text for translation acquires a wider significance in representations of the source culture within the target culture (cf. Venuti 1992, 1–17, esp. 13; Soenen 1985, 27–31). British editors and publishers might find out about a selection of German books which could be of interest to the British market from sources such as the Frankfurt Book Fair, literary agents, publishers from Germany and other countries or, since 1997, the twice yearly publication *New Books in German* (cf. Smith and note 1). While it is very difficult to establish on which grounds any one publisher decides for the publication of any particular text, the general discourses underlying these decisions can be revealed by comparing the choice of texts which manage to cross the rather wide gap of the channel with the choice of texts available in other countries. It is similarly helpful to compare the strategies employed in the different cultural contexts once these texts have been published.

Taking these premises into account, this essay will try to establish trends apparent in the particular choice of new German prose translated and published in Britain in the wake of the changes in the Eastern Bloc and after German unification, a time when German national identities were under debate in Germany as well as abroad (cf. Süssmuth 1993; Heydemann 1994; Kettenacker 1997, 213–235; Fulbrook 1999, 3–4; Paterson 1999, 263–265).[1] In the first part of my essay, however, I will concentrate on various explanations for the lack of interest in German prose in Britain and consider the influence of globalization within the publishing industry on the translation of German fiction. While the main focus will be on developments in Britain, the information will be compared and contrasted with similar data from France in order to identify trends and developments which are specific to Britain.

II Translation in the market place

British publisher Peter Owen's statement: 'What am I supposed to do with such boring stuff? Nobody here wants to read this self-satisfied rubbish' was quoted by Desmond Christy in *The Guardian* in 1992 to explain the lack of interest in German literature in Britain. Owen blames what he perceives to be the German writers' particular style for the worldwide indifference towards German literature, and he is not the only one to come to this conclusion. Several German publishers as well as critics and readers would agree with him. In fact, Christy's article is based on an account in *Der Spiegel* bemoaning the state of German literature (cf. Anon 1992, 258). The author of the *Spiegel* article quotes British as well as German publishers' attitudes towards German writers and their Anglo-American counterparts: 'Deutsche Autoren liegen wie Blei' (Geoffrey Stachan, Methuen in Anon 1992, 258), '"Deutsche Autoren", glaubt Droemer-Chef Karl H. Blessing, "können einfach nicht das bieten, was das amerikanische, britische und französische Erzählpublikum interessiert"' (Anon 1992,

260–261) and "'Die Angelsachsen", urteilt Fischer-Chef Conradi, "können einfach besser erzählen"' (Anon 1992, 263). The critical stance towards German literature within Germany, also mirrored in best-seller lists which mainly contain British and American titles in translation, has led German writers to believe that publishers and their lack of imagination in selling their German authors are to blame for the indifference towards German literature at home as well as abroad (cf. Anon 1992, 261).

While the latter argument seems to be more convincing than Owen's sweeping statement, the disdain for German literature among British publishers has to be traced back to the general lack of interest in any foreign literature — after all, it is not only German fiction that is largely ignored (cf. Hulse 1995, 139). From the 1950s to the 1990s translations published in Britain have amounted to a relatively stable 2–4% of the publications in total (with minor surges to up to 7% in the 1960s), whereas the percentage of translations published in France has increased constantly over the same period (cf. Venuti 1995, 12–13; Kreuter 1985, 103; Ganne/Minon 1992, 79). Numbers and percentages vary depending on the statistical source: thus Venuti states that in France translations constituted between 8 and 12% of the total publishing output and lay at 9.9% in 1985, whereas Ganne and Minon observe an increase from 13 to 18% between 1982 and 1991.[2] However, both accounts agree that there is considerably less demand for translation in Britain than in France. Even the total number of translations in French exceeds the number of translations published in Britain despite the considerably lower publishing output in France. The number of translations printed in France in 1991 (4,406) was three times higher than the number of translations published in Britain in 1990 (1,625) even though the grand total of publications in France in the same year (24,909) amounted to only one third of the British output (63,867) (cf. Ganne/Minon 1992, 64).[3]

These general statistics tally with my own findings. From 1980 to 1999 only 98 translations of German texts in Britain fulfilled the criteria of my database (cf. note 1), roughly a third of the titles translated in France. Despite cyclical ups and downs, the publication of contemporary German fiction in translation in France showed a general upward trend, with 60% of the 298 titles being published in the 1990s, whereas the number of translations published in the 1990s in Britain was about the same as in the 1980s.

The obviously lower demand for translations in the United Kingdom is generally attributed to the large numbers of books written in English worldwide which leads to a high degree of self-sufficiency in publishing (cf. Kreuter 1985, 106; Ganne/Minon 1992, 64; Hale 1998, 191). Like the large quantity of translations from the English language published worldwide, the lack of interest in translations in Britain confirms the Anglo-American political, economic and cultural hegemony in the global publishing industry:

> By routinely translating large numbers of the most varied English-language books, foreign publishers have exploited the global drift toward American political and economic hegemony in the post-war period, actively supporting the international expansion of Anglo-American culture. [...] British and American publishing, in turn, has reaped the financial benefits of successfully imposing Anglo-American cultural values on a vast foreign readership, while producing cultures in the United Kingdom and the United States that are aggressively monolingual, unreceptive to the foreign, accustomed to fluent translations that invisibly inscribe foreign texts with English-language values and provide readers with the narcissistic experience of recognizing their own culture in a cultural other. (Venuti 1995, 15)

The influence of Anglo-American literature and culture not only explains why German literature does not attract very much attention in Britain, it also accounts for the fact that German best-seller lists mainly contain English titles in translation. Hence, while the critical stance towards German literature within Germany might have contributed to the lack of interest in it abroad, the root cause may lie in the growing Anglo-Americanization, often referred to as globalization. Yet it also seems possible that the advance of Anglo-American cultural values in France, apparent in the growing quantity of translations from the English language, to some extent explains the level of French interest in the translation of German literature. The success of English-language literature in France has established translation as a growing and profitable business.

In Britain, by contrast, the marginalization of non-English-language literature has entailed the self-perpetuating perception of translation as a loss-making labour of love (cf. Hulse 1995, 137; Kreuter 1985, 95). These perceptions seem to be confirmed by lower sales figures. However, poor turnover does not necessarily reflect the quality of the texts and their translations; it can rather be traced back to the infrastructures of the 'translation business', the marketing and distribution processes, and the way that publishers respond to, rather than challenge, such perceptions.

In the late 1990s the British publishing industry, which consisted of about 2,000 publishers, was dominated by four major publishing groups with strong interests in general trade publishing. The new structures of these publishing conglomerates as well as their solely commercial aims have considerably changed the publishing processes. The translation of texts by relatively unknown authors, which was perceived as more experimental and risky, fell victim to these changes (cf. Kreuter 1985, 106; Feather 1993, 167–174; Hale 1998, 191). As shown above, the increasing conglomeration and globalization within the publishing industry did not particularly affect the numbers of translations from German in the 1980s and 1990s, but it has entailed changes in the names of publishers involved in the translation of German fiction. The editors of several established publishing houses in Britain, now integrated into conglomerates and reduced to imprints (e.g. Weidenfeld & Nicolson, Chatto & Windus), gave in to commercial pressures and left the 1990s niche market for German fiction in translation to smaller presses, founded in a counter-movement in the 1970s and 1980s, such as Serpent's Tail, Quartet, and Oldcastle Books. Even Secker & Warburg, who, with sixteen publications of contemporary German fiction in translation between 1980 and 1999, by far exceeded any of the other publishers' output, saw a decrease in market share from ten translations in the 1980s to six in the 1990s. Furthermore, they only issued one newcomer per decade: Erich Loest's *The Monument* (1987) and Marcel Beyer's *The Karnau Tapes* (1997). All of their other translations were of authors who had already been published in Britain at least once; some of these, such as Heinrich Böll and Günter Grass, available in Britain since the 1950s and 1960s, have a long history of translation and an established reputation. Yet the era of big-name publishing is passing: Böll's last text, *Frauen vor Flußlandschaft* (1985), was translated in 1988, and although Grass, whose books in Britain had exclusively been launched by Secker & Warburg, is still alive and writing, the licence for the hardcover of *My Century* (1999), his most recent work, was sold to Faber.[4]

The growing conglomeration had similar effects on the publishing industry in France. However, established traditions and the constantly growing position of translation within publishing has led to a relative stability in the numbers and names of publishers involved in the translation of German fiction in the last two decades. The French publishing industry has been dominated by only two groups since the late 1990s, Havas and Hachette, but their increase in power in the 1980s and 1990s was resisted and counterbalanced by the expansion of six other publishers, some of them still family businesses, into intermediate groups (cf. Piault 1998, 630–634). Among these Gallimard, Flammarion, Albin Michel, and Le Seuil have consistently been of considerable importance in the translation of contemporary German fiction and in the last two decades not only issued new books by authors already published in France but also launched new authors. That is why smaller publishers, except for the independent publishing house Actes Sud, founded in 1978 in Arles, are not as important for the translation and mediation of German literature in France as they are in Britain.

The differences in the general status of translation and the publishers involved in the publication of German literature in Britain and in France are reflected in the choice of books available. The most prolific German writer in French translation, for example, is Heinz G. Konsalik. Since his breakthrough in 1956 with *Der Arzt von Stalingrad* most of Konsalik's more than 100 novels have been translated into several languages and become best sellers (Brauneck 1995, 456–457). When Konsalik died in October 1999, *Le Monde* remembered him as the most widely read German author in the whole world whose works were still ignored by literary critics (cf. Anon 1999, 14).

In France, thirty-seven of Konsalik's contemporary novels were launched in the 1980s and 1990s, whereas none of Konsalik's many books written in the last two decades found a publisher in Britain. This is a fate he shares with other best-selling German authors. Neither the family sagas by Marie-Louise Fischer and Utta Danella nor, to cite three German authors who have recently been discovered by the French, the historical novels by Tanja Kinkel, Peter Berling, and Ashley Carrington (a pseudonym turning the German Rainer M. Schröder into a make-believe American) ever crossed the channel — which again might be attributed to the Anglo-American hegemony in these genres. While twenty-four of Konsalik's older novels were published in Britain between 1975 and 1983 (most of them by Aidan Ellis Publishing, founded in 1971) and, in the 1980s, bigger British publishers still made ventures into best-selling German fiction by authors such as Hans Hellmuth Kirst (Collins) and Wolfgang Jeschke (Century), the discovery of German crime fiction in the 1990s was largely left to smaller publishing houses. Akif Pirinçci's novels, for example, were published by Fourth Estate (founded 1984) and Jakob Arjouni's works by Oldcastle Books' No Exit imprint. It is characteristic of the new publishing mechanisms that this trend was then picked up by one of the bigger publishers, the Harper Collins imprint CollinsCrime, who published Ingrid Noll's crime novels.

Both Arjouni and Noll feature in the *Waterstone's Guide to Crime Fiction*. However, the positive reception of these two authors has not as yet contributed to a new understanding of German literature: 'In Germany, [Noll's] crime novels are massive best-sellers and, inevitably but unimaginatively, newspapers in this country have dubbed her "Germany's Queen of Crime". Potential readers should not be deterred by this less than enticing soubriquet' (Rennison/Shephard 1997, 119). The thrust of Owen's statement, cited at the beginning of this section, is also present here as a subtext; it is the fixed idea that German fiction is boring and unreadable. As the following section will show, this stereotyping of German literature runs through the discourses central to its reception in Britain.

III Contemporary German fiction in Britain

The end of the Cold War has not been reflected in an increased British interest in texts on the GDR and German unification. On the contrary, apart from two publications by established authors (Christa Wolf's *What Remains* and Monika Maron's *Silent close No. 6*; both 1993), the only German author new to the British market in the early 1990s and who fits into this category is Christoph Hein with *Der fremde Freund* (1982; *The Distant Lover*, 1991). Hein's text had already been published in France in 1985, and Christa Wolf's *Was bleibt* (1990) and *Sommerstück* (1989) were immediately translated into French, which seems to reveal more attention to the changes taking place in the German Democratic Republic than was apparent in Britain.

Most of the new German-language authors published in Britain in the wake of the changes in the Eastern Bloc, such as Herta Müller, Richard Wagner and Libuše Moníková, seem to bear witness to a curiosity to find out about the recent developments in countries such as Romania and Czechoslovakia. This new interest first became apparent with the 1989 publication of Herta Müller's *The Passport* (*Der Mensch ist ein großer Fasan auf der Welt*, 1986), a short novel portraying corruption, isolation and emotional detachment within a village community in Romania shortly before the end of the Ceauşescu regime. This work offers an interesting insight into publishing practice, for both the change in title and the whole presentation of the English and the original German editions reveal the different discourses the publishers have employed.

On the cover of the German Rotbuch edition a quotation from the book focuses on the problems of the German minorities in Romania:

> Die Traktoristen haben kleine nasse Hüte auf. Auf dem Tisch liegen ihre schwarzen Hände. 'Zeig mir', sagt einer. 'Ich geb dir zehn Lei.' Er legt zehn Lei auf den Tisch. Die Traktoristen lachen. Ihre Augen glitzern, ihre Gesichter sind rot. Ihre Blicke fingern über den langen blumigen Rock. Die Zigeunerin hebt den Rock [...]
> 'Den ganzen Sommer haben sie die Pelzleibchen an', sagt der Tischler. An seinem Daumen hängt Bierschaum. Er taucht den Zeigefinger ins Glas. 'Die Drecksau daneben bläst mir Asche ins Bier', sagt er. Er schaut den Rumänen an, der hinter ihm steht. Der Rumäne hält die Zigarette im Mundwinkel. Sie ist naß von seinem Speichel. Er lacht. 'Nix mehr deutsch', sagt er. Dann auf rumänisch: 'Hier ist Rumänien.'
> Der Tischler hat einen gierigen Blick. Er hebt das Glas und trinkt es aus. 'Bald habt ihr uns los', schreit er. (Fasan, 63–64)

This passage not only highlights the thematic relevance of this novel for a German reader: a new view of the German minority in Romania, it also conveys Müller's outstanding and highly-praised style (cf. Roberg 1997, 27). In her paratactic descriptions she excludes logical links created by subclauses of time, cause, purpose or effect and supplants these with a web of rhetorical figures such as metaphor, repetition, alliteration and anaphora (cf. Roberg 1997, 32–33).

In contrast to the Rotbuch strategy of combining thematic and linguistic features in one single quotation from the text, the Serpent's Tail edition uses short excerpts from German critical acclaim, which of course would not have been available at the time of the first publication, to describe the novel's content and its linguistic features separately; at the same time they underline its positive reception in German-speaking countries. In addition these excerpts provide the reader with a first hint to the focus of this edition. The quotation from the *Neue Zürcher Zeitung* describes the novel as revealing the 'dirty realities of a totalitarian state', and the quotation from Müller's text used inside the cover of the English edition, the words of a teacher in a lesson on Romania for small school children, further engages with this facet of the novel:

> Just as the father in the house in which we live is our father, so comrade Nicolae Ceauşescu is the father of our country. And just as the mother in the house in which we live is our mother, so Comrade Elena Ceauşescu is the mother of our country. Comrade Nicolae Ceauşescu is the father of all the children. All the children love comrade Nicolae and comrade Elena, because they are their parents. (Passport, 51)[5]

Hence, while the German edition mainly foregrounds the treatment of the German minorities in Romania, the English edition homes in on the political background and, accordingly, the blurbs concentrate on the events in the novel, the struggle to obtain passports which will enable the German citizens of this small village to escape. That the flight to West Germany ultimately does not entail happiness goes unmentioned (Fasan, 109–111; Roberg 1997, 36). The different focus of the English edition also explains the translation of the book's title. With her title: *Der Mensch ist ein großer Fasan auf der Welt*, Herta Müller uses a motif which runs through the book and which, in David Midgley's words, acquires 'cumulative resonance as the story progresses' (Midgley 1998, 27). As Müller explained in an interview, the image of the pheasant combines the contrasting connotations of the word in the German and Romanian languages: 'Der deutsche Fasan ist der Prahler, der selbstsichere, arrogante Mensch; der rumänische Fasan ist der Verlierer, der seinem Leben nicht gewachsen ist, der Vogel, der nicht fliegen kann, und der, weil er nicht fliegen kann und ziemlich groß und schwer ist, von der Kugel des Jägers getroffen wird' (Müller in Haines/Littler 1998, 16).

The German title can thus be seen to reflect Müller's very specific use of language, in this case highlighting her polyvalent imagery originating in the two languages she grew up with in Romania. The English title, *The Passport*, exemplifies the English edition's general focus on the story. These paratexts are supported by emblematic cover illustrations. On the cover of the English translation two men are trying to fell an apple tree which is devouring its own fruit; an owl circles above this scene. In the novel the recurring symbol of the owl functions as an avatar of death, while the apple tree, in one particular parabolic tale about the village's past, refers to the biblical tree of knowledge. Observed devouring its own fruit, the tree was not felled but, on the bishop's advice, burned like a witch at the stake in a 'moment of collective compulsion' (Midgley 1998, 32; Fasan, 32–36). On the one hand, this cover illustration embodies the narrative structuring of the text by images. On the other hand, the particular choice of images seems to foreground the regime's constant threat of torture and death as well as the involvement of the Church and the way people tolerated human rights abuses. The image on the German cover, by contrast, shows two people who are in the process of vanishing under long veils; it stresses the individuals' growing isolation and emotional detachment in daily life under this regime, from which even escape to West Germany cannot save them.

The visual message in the cover illustration of the Serpent's Tail edition is reinforced by a supplementary subtitle: '*a surreal tale* of life in Romania today' (Passport; my italics, WS). Yet, what Serpent's Tail describes as surreal — a word which will come up again in George Steiner's review of *The Land of Green Plums*, the second of Müller's novels published in Britain (Steiner 1998, 14) — is defined in the *bulletin critique du livre français*, a French publication mainly aiming to inform libraries and booksellers in France on new publications in French language, as 'un style particulier fait de courtes phrases, de description intégrant souvent les apports du *réalisme le plus sordide*' (Anon 1989, 202; my italics, WS).[6] While Serpent's Tail attempted to locate the text within widely known discourses on totalitarianism and Romania, which then provided the allegedly realist background for the surreal tale, the *bulletin critique...* seems to be reacting to the French publisher's decision to stress the fictional character of the book by maintaining the original imagery in the title.

The Anglo-American focus on the political situation in Romania is even more striking in the strategies unsed by Verso for their publication (1990) of Richard Wagner's *Exit* (*Ausreiseantrag* 1988). The blurb on the cover, which again focuses mainly on the plot, includes the following information:

> The monstrously repressive world of Ceauşescu's Romania provides the setting and the subject of Richard Wagner's extraordinary narrative, written shortly before the Christmas revolution.
> Stirner, the main protagonist, is an ethnic German, and lives in Timisoara, the town which was to be the revolution's birthplace.

In a preface, commissioned for this edition, Wagner 'reflects on how far life has changed since the revolution' (cover). In order to write this text Wagner returned to Temesvar, the chief town of the Banat, which, as a footnote explains, 'has a mixed population of Hungarians, Romanians, Germans, Serbs, etc. Traditionally known abroad by this, its Hungarian name, it has figured prominently in the world's press recently under its Romanian name, Timisoara' (Exit v). This footnote expressly reveals the editor's strategy of latching on to the worldwide media coverage of the Romanian revolution in order to grab the attention of the intended readership. *Exit*, the title of the book (which is described further as 'a Romanian story'), is printed in blue, yellow and red, the colours of the Romanian flag. Instead of an image the cover carries a photograph of an anti-Ceauşescu montage originally found on the side of a tank in Romania in December 1989. Both Ceauşescu's face and the colours of the Romanian flag were presumed to be familiar to people following the news at the time, whereas only a year earlier in the *The Passport* the colours of the German flag were not assumed to be immediately recognizable to the intended British readership. As the translation reveals, an explanation was deemed necessary:

> Jedes Kind hat von zu Hause ein Abziehbild in den Kindergarten gebracht. Amalie klebte die Bildchen unter die Haken.
> Jedes Kind sucht jeden Morgen sein Auto, seinen Hund, seine Puppe, seine Blume, seinen Ball.
> Udo kommt zur Tür herein. Er sucht seine Fahne. Sie ist schwarzrotgold. Udo hängt seinen Mantel an den Haken, über seine Fahne. (Fasan, 59–60)

> [Udo comes through the door. He's looking for his flag. It is black, red and gold. *A German flag.* (Passport, 50; my italics, WS)]

In contrast to the Serpent's Tail edition of *The Passport*, where at least the image on the cover and the subtitle stressed the literary elements of the fictional text, Wagner's style is described on the cover to *Exit* as 'fine, stark prose', written 'with the scrupulous detail of the best documentarists', again stressing the alleged realism with no allusion to the fragmented presentation of the so-called story, which is reminiscent of Brecht's *Geschichten vom Herrn Keuner*.

The discourses which the English publishers thus invoke in order to sell complex fictional texts as exciting stories documenting the unbearability of life under the totalitarian regime in Romania link in with a general trend in English-language writing to valorize 'the purely instrumental use of language and other means of representation' and thus to emphasize 'immediate intelligibility and the appearance of factuality' which has made 'realism the most prevalent form of narrative' (Venuti 1995, 5–6). The demand for this prevalent style is implicit in Carole Angier's review of *The Land of Green Plums*, the English translation of *Herztier*, first launched in the United States by Metropolitan Books in 1996 and published in Britain only after it had been awarded the world's biggest literary prize for fiction, the Impac Dublin Award (cf. Moss 1998, 6).[7]

Angier claims that the judges made their decision on the basis of the book's content rather than on its literary merit and concludes her review: 'Herta Müller can write, and hers is a very terrible story. If she had only told it, instead of making fine phrases – now that would have been worth a prize' (Angier 1998, 5). Despite the apparent resistance of Müller's texts to Anglo-American demands for realism, Granta's edition of her *The Land of Green Plums* relies largely on the same discourses as Serpent's Tail's *The Passport* and Verso's *Exit*. The alleged realism of Müller's text is underlined by a quotation from Ian Thomson's review in *The Guardian* which terms *The Land of Green Plums* an 'autobiographical account', while references to the narrative structuring of the text, which 'tells the story of a group of young students', describe Müller's style somewhat elusively as eloquent, exerting 'an almost hypnotic power over the reader' (Thomson 1998). The blurb as well as the darkish layout and the cover images (a woman's face behind bars) foreground the novel's 'profound illustra- tion' of 'Ceauşescu's reign of terror' (cover blurb), again ignoring the fact that 'Müller's is ultimately not a tragic world but one in which the individual survives against all the odds' (Haines 1998b, 109–110). The one-dimensional and purely negative interpretation is also reflected in the choice of the English title. *The Land of Green Plums* does keep to the principle of using a key metaphor from the text and thus anticipates the book's narrative structuring. Yet, the specific image chosen stresses an exclusively negative interpretation of life under a totalitarian regime. While the metaphor of the German title, *Herztier*, evokes a source of energy on which both human rights abuses and the struggle against the totalitarian regime can be seen to feed (cf. Schmidt 1998, 71; Haines 1998b, 117–118), the metaphor of the green plum is less ambiguous: 'Grüne Pflaumen werden so mit unbeherrschbaren, destruktiven und selbstdestruktiven Tendenzen assoziiert, die ein diktatorisches Regime im Individuum produziert' (Schmidt 1998, 69).

While Norbert Otto Eke (1991) reveals the prevalence of the debate on German minorities in Romania in the critical reception of Müller's works within the German-speaking context and argues that this reductionist approach precluded any other possibilities of interpretation (cf. Eke 1991, 107–130), many British reviews identify her and her novel as Romanian (cf. Angier 1998; Thomson 1998; Moss 1998) and, like the publishers, mainly stress the autobio- graphical and literary Romanian background of her work. Ian Thomson, for example, ascribes the image of the 'famished slaughterhouse hands who drink fresh cow's blood' to Müller's literary receptiveness 'to the Dracula legends', a rather old-fashioned and very stereotypical image of Romania, and presents the image of the cancerous dictator drinking his subjects' blood as factual rather than metaphorical: 'In the maternity clinics of Romania, children's blood is pumped out of the head of newborns (sic) with Japanese vacuum syringes. It was well known that Ceauşescu suffered from leukemia (sic) and wanted fresh red cells' (Thomson 1998, 10). It is only when Thomson refers to the protagonists' and the author's pasts that Müller's German origin suddenly takes on significance:

> The author, Herta Müller, was born in Rumania's German-speaking region of Banat. Burdened by their German heredity, the students in the novel reject their parents' Nazi past as well as Ceauşescu's cruel misrule. Müller, aged 45, is the daughter of an SS veteran and she provides a memorably vicious portrait of her Führer-doting father. An alcoholic, he laments a lost idyll of plum brandy, strudel pastry and beer-swilling Herrenvolk. (Thomson 1998, 10)

The Banat is, of course, not German-speaking but is populated by a mixture of peoples originating from various backgrounds. The review also foregrounds stereotypical images of the Germans which still prevail in Britain, while making only passing reference to the fact that the novel engages with a completely different view of German identity, namely German students trying to resist a totalitarian regime.

The fixed idea of German identities in Britain focusing on the National Socialist past and ignoring other possibilities of German identity constructions is, however, not limited to reviews. The National Socialist past has also dominated the general choice of German fiction available on the British niche market for translation over the last two decades. One quarter of all translations published in Britain, a far higher percentage than in France, deal with this topic and there are only four years in the last two decades, which did not see a publication in this area. This particular focus was already apparent before the 1980s, and the translation of several of Konsalik's novels seems to confirm that trend. These novels revolve mainly around World War II, and this topic is also particularly stressed in the translation of their titles. *Der Arzt von Stalingrad* (1956), which was first published in Britain as *The Naked Earth* in 1961 and saw three editions under this title, was republished in 1975 as *Doctor of Stalingrad*. *Die glückliche Ehe* (1969) was translated as *The War Bride* (1979) and *Sie waren zehn* (1979) as *Strike Force 10* (1981) (cf. Keenoy et al. 1997, 221–223).

In the early 1980s, new translations dealing with the National Socialist past available in Britain tended to favour popular war and espionage novels by Hans Hellmut Kirst, Will Berthold and Hans Herlin. Kirst's soldiers' novel *Heroes for Sale* (1982), the last of his novels published in Britain (*Ausverkauf der Helden*, 1980), reveals the decadent and grotesque excesses taking place in a special armed forces instruction centre in Germany shortly before the final collapse of the Third Reich. In his novels *Inferno I* and *Inferno II*, Will Berthold presents the events in World War II between September 1939 and October 1942 from the German soldiers' point of view, and the protagonist in *Siegfried's Sword* (*Ein Kerl wie Samt und Seide*, 1986) is a 'German Luftwaffe hero' who 'seeks vengeance on his arch-enemy, Günther Machoff of the SS, the man who raped his woman, tortured his friends, shipped off his cohorts to Dachau and Ravensbrück' (Sword, cover). And finally Hans Herlin's spy novel *Last Spring in Paris*, published in Britain in 1985 (*Der letzte Frühling in Paris*, 1983), mainly focuses on a German officer, based in Paris, who supplies the British Secret Service with the information they need to prepare for the landing of the British troops in France. Except for the last one, *Dernier printemps à Paris* (1984), none of these books exist in French translation, although a large number of novels by Kirst and by Berthold travelled to France before 1980 (cf. Zangl-Lorriaux 1983). Rather than the typically belated British reception of novels translated and published worldwide discussed above, the publication of Kirst's and Berthold's novels in the 1980s seems to signify a belated farewell to trends abandoned some time before by publishers in France.

Only in the late 1980s, when German popular fiction generally attracted little attention in Britain, did British publishers finally abandon the publication of German 'war and espionage' novels. This change went hand in hand with the translation of literary fiction, which presented more varied approaches to the German past. The publication, in 1987, of three novels dealing with this topic epitomized this change: Christoph Meckel's father novel *Image for Investigation about my Father* (*Suchbild: über meinen Vater*, 1980), which only reached France in 1989, Gert Hofmann's *Our Conquest* (*Unsere Eroberung*, 1984), relating the events in the immediate wake of German surrender in 1945 from a naive children's perspective, and Erich Loest's *The Monument* (*Völkerschlacht-denkmal*, 1984), a personal account of Saxon history including the Nazi period, which has yet to be translated into French. More recently still, several of texts on the National Socialist past crossed the channel before they were published in France. The more immediate response of British publishers to new developments in this area is therefore not only down to the increasing globalization in the publishing industry, it also confirms the current revival of interest in this particular topic. Edgar Hilsenrath's novel *Das Märchen vom letzten Gedanken* (1989), for example, was published in Britain within a year of the original version and preceded the edition of the French translation by two years. That the English text has as yet not been published in the United States is a further sign of a very strong British interest in this novel (cf. Möller 1996, 114–115; Kraft 1996, 241). If the early publication of W. G. Sebald's *Die Ausgewanderten* in Britain can be traced back to the fact that the author lives in England, Georges-Arthur Goldschmidt's *Die Absonderung* (1991) presents another particularly revealing example of the high level of interest among British publishers in the National Socialist past. Although Goldschmidt lives in France, his text was published in Britain (1993) before it was translated into French (1994).[8]

IV Conclusion

The complexities of cultural processes and intercultural exchanges are often prone to extreme simplification for political purposes: 'Literatur gilt als Königsweg, um Vielfalt und Denkweisen anderer Kulturen kennenzulernen. Deshalb stellt die Förderung deutscher Literatur in der Welt ein besonderes Anliegen im Rahmen der auswärtigen Kulturpolitik Deutschlands dar' (Institut für Auslandsbeziehungen 2000). And, of course the closer intercultural co-operation between Germany and France might have contributed to the comparatively large quantity of German fiction in French translation. In 1989, for example, the French Salon du Livre, an international book fair held in Paris, focused on German writing and several French publishers, in preparation for the event, commissioned new translations from German (cf. Syndicat National de l'Édition 1989). Yet, as this paper has shown, French publishers generally tend to be more receptive to literature in translation than their British counterparts, and it is rather questionable whether German foreign cultural policy is equipped to change the deep-rooted perceptions of translations within British culture. Furthermore, while the promotion of German literature by the German government might achieve an increase in translations from German, these publications do not necessarily counter the prevalent ideas about German literature and culture abroad. On the contrary, the choice of texts for translation as well as the publishing strategies seem to build on and reinforce dominant discourses, and the reception of these texts feeds on similar ideas, even though the originals might invite rather diverging interpretations. Whether the translations themselves tap into these discourses and thus aid and abet fixed ideas of German identity or whether they open up similarly heterogeneous interpretations remains to be seen.

Notes

1. The overview is based on a corpus of translations of contemporary German fiction which I collected in a database. In order to counter the notion of Germanness as a unitary category and to include as many ideas of Germanness as possible, I defined a German author as an author who writes in German and lives in Germany or is of German descent. Contemporary fiction is limited to works written and translated between 1980 and 1999. The database mainly draws upon the *Index Translationum*, a bibliography of translations published by UNESCO, as well as upon the respective National Bibliographies and, for translations distributed in Britain, upon *The Babel Guide to German Fiction* (cf. Keenoy et al. 1997) and the publication *New Books in German* (cf. Smith). *Babel Guides* are a series on contemporary world fiction available in English translation, and they include a database as well as reviews of, in their own words, 'a representative choice of books' (Keenoy et al. 1997, 1). *New Books in German* is a twice yearly journal supported by German, Austrian and Swiss governmental institutions and publishing organizations. The short descriptions of texts available for English translations as well as their authors and publishers are chiefly aimed 'at busy British and American editors who would like to publish more translations but would also appreciate help in finding the right titles from among the thousands published each year in the German language' (Smith). The 1999 and 1998 autumn journals also included a database of English translations published in recent years, which I have used to supplement the data drawn from the other sources. For the French data I additionally consulted *Französisch–deutsch–französische Übersetzungen. Les traductions de livres en langues française et allemande 1986–1989* (cf. Syndicat National de l'Édition) and *Littérature contemporaine de langue allemande: Traductions françaises des œuvres parues entre 1945 et 1982* (cf. Zangl-Lorriaux). Of course, I do not lay any claim for the information contained in my database to be complete. Several authors and works recorded in the above-mentioned sources could not be identified and have thus not been included in my database (yet) although they might be possible candidates. In addition, the sources, which are mainly based on information provided by publishers, have, in the course of my research, also proved to have gaps and to contain errors.

2. Lawrence Venuti draws on D. and M. Frémy (eds) 1992: *Quid 1992*. Paris: Laffont. Valérie Ganne and Marc Minon, by contrast, base their conclusions on a study conducted in collaboration with BIPE conseil on behalf of the Centre national des lettres.

3. For these particular numbers BIPE conseil draws upon the *UK publishing statistics* (Whitakers) and the French publication *Un an de nouveauté*.

4. This may have been at the author's request because Secker & Warburg have become part of Random House and Grass prefers independent publishers to conglomerates.

5. 'So wie unser Vater im Haus, in dem wir wohnen, der Vater ist, ist Genosse Nicolae Ceauşescu der Vater unseres Landes. Und so wie unsere Mutter im Haus, in dem wir wohnen, unsere Mutter ist, ist Genossin Elena Ceauşescu die Mutter unseres Landes. Genosse Nicolae Ceauşescu ist der Vater aller Kinder. Und Genossin Elena Ceauşescu ist die Mutter aller Kinder. Alle Kinder lieben den Genossen und die Genossin, weil sie ihre Eltern sind' (Fasan, 61–62).

6. 'a particular style consisting of short sentences and of descriptive moments of sordid realism' (my translation; WS).

7. *Herztier* was the first of Herta Müller's texts to be published in the United States. Since then *Reisende auf einem Bein* (*Traveling on one leg*. Trans. Valentina Glajar and André Lefevere. Evanston, Ill.: Northwestern University Press, 1998) and *Niederungen* (*Nadirs*. Trans. and afterword Sieglinde Lug. Lincoln: University of Nebraska Press, 1999) were published in the United States but not in Britain whereas *Der Mensch ist ein großer Fasan auf der Welt* has as yet not been published in the United States although Serpent's Tail have a branch in New York. In France only two of Herta Müller's novels have been published so far, *Der Mensch ist ein großer Fasan auf der Welt* and *Der Fuchs war damals schon der Jäger* (*Le renard était déjà le chasseur*. Trans. Claire de Oliveira. Paris: Éditions du Seuil, 1997).

8. In both countries the publication of German texts with a focus on the processes of coming to terms with National Socialism has prevailed up to the present and has provided British and French readers with a diversity of accounts which reconsider categories such as guilt and tend to blur the boundaries between victims and perpetrators. An analysis of the discourses underlying the translation, promotion and reception of these texts in Britain and France might reveal differences in German identity constructions in the two countries. Jonathan Long's essay in this volume raises a number of relevant issues (49–66 below; esp. 50–58).

Primary texts

Berthold, Will 1982a: *Inferno: Die ersten Blitzsiege*. Munich: Goldmann.
—— 1982b: *Inferno: Siege und Niederlagen*. Munich: Goldmann.
—— 1984: *Inferno I: Blitzkrieg*. Trans. Fred Taylor. London: Sphere.
—— 1986a: *Ein Kerl wie Samt und Seide*. Munich: Goldmann.
—— 1986b: *Inferno II: Bloody Turning Point*. Trans. Fred Taylor. London: Sphere.
—— 1986c: *Siegfried's Sword*. Trans. Fred Taylor. London: Sphere. (=Sword)
Beyer, Marcel 1995: *Flughunde*. Frankfurt am Main: Suhrkamp.
—— 1997: *The Karnau Tapes*. Trans. John Brownjohn. London: Secker&Warburg.
Böll, Heinrich 1985: *Frauen vor Flußlandschaft. Cologne*: Kiepenheuer & Witsch.
—— 1988: *Women in a River Landscape*. Trans. David McLintock. London: Secker & Warburg.
Goldschmidt, Georges-Arthur 1991: *Die Absonderung*. Zurich: Ammann.
—— 1993: *Worlds of Difference*. Trans. James Kirkup. London: Quartet.
—— 1994: *La ligne de fuite*. Trans. Jean-Luc Tiesset. Paris: Flammarion.
Grass, Günter 1999a: *Mein Jahrhundert*. Göttingen: Steidl.
—— 1999b: *My Century*. Trans. Michael Henry Heim. London: Faber.
Hein, Christoph 1982: *Der fremde Freund*. Berlin/Weimar: Aufbau.
—— 1985: *L'ami étranger*. Trans. François and Régine Mathieu. Aix-en-Provence: Alinéa.
—— 1991: *The Distant Lover*. Trans. Krishna Winston. London: Picador.
Herlin, Hans 1983: *Der letzte Frühling in Paris*. Düsseldorf: Marion von Schröder.
—— 1984: *Dernier printemps à Paris*. Trans. (from the English) Marianne Sinclair and Sylvette Gleize. Paris: Le grand livre du mois.
—— 1985: *The last spring in Paris*. Trans. J. Maxwell Brownjohn. London: Deutsch.
Hilsenrath, Edgar 1989: *Das Märchen vom letzten Gedanken*. Munich: Piper.
—— 1990: *The Story of the Last Thought*. Trans. Hugh Young. London: Scribner.
—— 1992: *Le conte de la pensée dernière*. Trans. Bernard Kreiss. Paris: Albin Michel.
Hofmann, Gert 1984: *Unsere Eroberung*. Darmstadt: Luchterhand.
—— 1986: *Notre conquête*. Trans Martine Keyser. Paris: Laffont.
—— 1987: *Our Conquest*. Trans. Christopher Middleton. Manchester: Carcanet.
Kirst, Hans Hellmut 1980: *Ausverkauf der Helden*. Munich: Bertelsmann.
—— 1982: *Heroes for Sale*. Trans. J. Maxwell Brownjohn. London: Collins.
Loest, Erich 1984: *Völkerschlachtdenkmal*. Hamburg: Hoffmann und Campe.
—— 1987: *The Monument*. Trans. Ian Mitchell. London: Secker & Warburg.
Maron, Monika 1991: *Stille Zeile 6*. Frankfurt am Main: Fischer.
—— 1993a: *Silent Close No. 6*. Trans. David Newton Marinelli. London: Readers International.
—— 1993b: *Rue de silence, no. 6*. Trans. Michel-François Demet. Paris: Fayard.
Meckel, Christoph 1980: *Suchbild: Über meinen Vater*. Düsseldorf: Claasen.
—— 1987: *Image for investigation: about my father*. Trans. M.S. Jones. Tayport: Hutton Press.
—— 1989: *Portrait-robot: mon père*. Trans. Michel Baillet. Paris: Flammarion.
Müller, Herta 1986: *Der Mensch ist ein großer Fasan auf der Welt*. Berlin: Rotbuch. (=Fasan)
—— 1988: *L'homme est un grand faisan sur terre*. Trans. Nicole Bary. Paris: Maren Sell. (=Faisan)
—— 1989: *The Passport*. Trans. Martin Chalmers. London: Serpent's Tail. (=Passport)
—— 1994: *Herztier*. Reinbek bei Hamburg: Rowohlt.

—— 1998: *The Land of Green Plums.* Trans. Michael Hofmann. London: Granta. (=Plums)
Pirinçci, Akif 1989: *Felidae.* Munich: Goldmann.
—— 1992: *Félidés.* Trans. Jean-Marie Argelès. Paris: Métailié.
—— 1993: *Felidae: A Novel of Cats and Murder.* Trans. Ralph Noble. London: Fourth Estate.
Sebald, W.G. 1992: *Die Ausgewanderten.* Frankfurt am Main: Eichborn.
—— 1997: *The Emigrants.* Trans. Michael Hulse. London: Harvill.
—— 1999: *Les émigrants.* Trans. Patrick Charbonneau. Arles: Actes Sud.
Wagner, Richard 1988: *Ausreiseantrag.* Darmstadt: Luchterhand.
—— 1990: *Exit: A Romanian Story.* Trans. Quintin Hoare. London, New York: Verso. (=Exit)
Wolf, Christa 1989: *Sommerstück.* Berlin/Weimar: Aufbau.
—— 1990a: *Was bleibt.* Berlin/Weimar: Aufbau.
—— 1990b: *Ce qui reste.* Trans. Ghislain Riccardi. Aix-en-Provence: Alinéa.
—— 1990c: *Scènes d'été.* Trans. Lucien Haag and Marie-Ange Roy. Aix-en-Provence: Alinéa.
—— 1993: *What remains and Other Stories.* Trans. Heike Schwarzbauer and Rick Takvorian. London: Virago.

Secondary literature
Angier, Carole 1998: 'Book: Names in search of a character', *The Independent*, 28 July 1998, 5.
Anon 1989: 'Müller, Herta: L'homme est un grand faisan sur terre', *bulletin critique du livre français* 518, February 1989.
Anon 1992: 'Gedankenschwere Nabelschau', *Der Spiegel* 12/1992, 258–263.
Anon 1994: 'Books: In the Lists', *The Independent on Sunday*, 25 September 1994, 30.
Anon 1999: 'Carnet: Disparition: Heinz Konsalik', *Le Monde*, 7 October 1999, 14.
Arnold, Heinz Ludwig (ed.) 1995: *Ansichten und Auskünfte zur deutschen Literatur nach 1945.* Munich: edition text + kritik.
Barret-Ducrocq, Françoise (ed.) 1992: *Traduire l'Europe.* Paris: Éditions Payot.
Baker, Mona (ed.) 1998: *Routledge Encyclopaedia of Translation Studies.* London/New York: Routledge.
Blake, Robin 1994: 'The Independent on Sunday Bestseller List', *The Independent on Sunday*, 25 April 1994, 30.
Brauneck, Manfred (ed.) 1995: *Autorenlexikon deutschsprachiger Literatur des 20. Jahrhunderts.* Reinbek bei Hamburg: Rowohlt.
Christy, Desmond 1992: 'Kulturmag: High Prized heels, Gazetta', *The Guardian*, 20 March 1992, 29.
Crawshaw, Steve 1993: 'Letter from Bonn: Feline Fantasies: Steve Crawshaw meets a Turkish writer who has made a home in Germany', *The Independent*, 18 September 1993, 24.
Eke, Norbert Otto (ed.) 1991: *Die erfundene Wahrnehmung: Annäherung an Herta Müller.* Paderborn: IGEL.
Feather, John 1993: 'Book publishing in Britain: an overview', *Media, Culture and Society* 15, 167–181.
Fouché, Pascal (ed.) 1998: *L'édition française depuis 1945.* Paris: Electre-Éditions du Cercle de la Librairie.
Fulbrook, Mary 1999: *German National Identity after the Holocaust.* Cambridge: Polity Press.
Ganne, Valérie and Marc Minon 1992: 'Géographies de la traduction' in Barrett-Ducrocq 1992, 55–95.
Haines, Brigid (ed.) 1998a: *Herta Müller.* Cardiff: University of Wales Press.
—— 1998b: '"Leben wir im Detail": Herta Müller's Micro-Politics of Resistance' in Haines 1998a, 109–125.
—— and Margaret Littler 1998: 'Gespräch mit Herta Müller' in Haines 1998a, 14–24.
Hale, Terry 1998: 'Publishing Strategies' in Baker 1998, 190–194.
Heydemann, Günther 1994: 'Partner or rival? The British perception of Germany during the process of unification 1989–1991' in Husemann 1994, 123–147.

Hulse, Michael 1995: 'Ach so! Deutschsprachige Literatur in Großbritannien' in Arnold 1995, 136–143.

Husemann, Harald (ed.) 1994: *As Others See Us. Anglo-German Perceptions.* Frankfurt am Main: Peter Lang.

Institut für Auslandsbeziehungen (ed.) 2000: 'Deutsche Kultur International: Deutsche Literatur im Ausland', http://www.deutsche-kultur-international.de/k/l/dldeut.htm, 1.

Keenoy, Ray, Mike Mitchell and Maren Meinhardt (eds) 1997: *The Babel Guide to German Fiction in English Translation: Austria, Germany, Switzerland.* London: Boulevard Books.

Kettenacker, Lothar 1997: *Germany since 1945.* Oxford/New York: Oxford University Press.

Köhnen, Ralph (ed.) 1997: *Der Druck der Erfahrung treibt die Sprache in die Dichtung: Bildlichkeit in Texten Herta Müllers.* Frankfurt am Main: Peter Lang.

Kraft, Thomas (ed.) 1996: *Edgar Hilsenrath: Das Unerzählbare erzählen.* Munich: Piper.

Kreuter, Uta 1985: *Übersetzung und Literaturkritik: Aspekte der Rezeption zeitgenössischer deutschsprachiger Literatur in Großbritannien 1960–1981.* Frankfurt am Main: Peter Lang.

Midgley, David 1998: 'Remembered Things: The Representation of Memory and Separation in *Der Mensch ist ein großer Fasan auf der Welt*' in Haines 1998a, 25–35.

Möller, Susann 1996: 'Zur Rezeption: Philosemiten und andere – die Verlagsstationen Edgar Hilsenraths' in Kraft 1996, 103–116.

Mommsen, Wolfgang J. (ed.) 1999: *Die ungleichen Partner. Deutsch–britische Beziehungen im 19. und 20. Jahrhundert.* Stuttgart: Deutsche Verlags-Anstalt.

Moss, Stephen 1998: 'News in brief: Romanian's plum book prize', *The Guardian,* 19 May 1998, 6.

Paterson, William 1999: 'Großbritannien, Europa und das deutsch–britische Verhältnis' in Mommsen 1999, 257–274.

Piault, Fabrice 1998: 'De la "rationalisation" à l'hyperconcentration' in Fouché 1998, 629–639.

Rennison, Nick and Richard Shepard (eds) 1997: *Waterstone's Guide to Crime Fiction.* Middlesex: Waterstone's Booksellers Ltd.

Roberg, Thomas 1997: 'Bildlichkeit und verschwiegener Sinn in Herta Müller's Erzählung *Der Mensch ist ein großer Fasan in* (sic) *der Welt*' in Köhnen 1997, 27–42.

Schmidt, Ricarda 1998: 'Metapher, Metonymie und Moral. Herta Müllers *Herztier*' in Haines 1998a, 57–74.

Smith, Rosemary (ed.): *New Books in German.* London: Society of Authors. (http://www.new-books-in-german.com/)

Soenen, Johan 1985: 'Das "Image des anderen Landes" spielt beim Übersetzen fremder literarischer Werke eine wichtige Rolle', *Babel: International Journal of Translation* 31/1, 27–40.

Steiner, George 1998: 'You're ruled by hooligans. Your friends spy on you. Hellish, isn't it?', *The Observer,* 30 August 1998, 14.

Süssmuth, Hans (ed.) 1993: *Deutschlandbilder in Dänemark und England, in Frankreich und den Niederlanden.* Baden Baden: Nomos.

Syndicat National de l'Édition (ed.) 1989: *Französisch–deutsch–französische Über-setzungen. Les traductions de livres en langues française et allemande 1986–1989.* Paris: Syndicat National de l'Édition.

Thomson, Ian 1998: 'Books: Government by ghouls', *The Guardian,* 25 July 1998, 10.

Turner, Barry (ed.) 1998: *The Writer's Handbook 1999.* London: Macmillan.

Venuti, Lawrence (ed.) 1992: *Rethinking Translation: Discourse, Subjectivity, Ideology.* London/New York: Routledge.

—— 1995: *The Translator's Invisibility: A History of Translation.* London/New York: Routledge.

Zangl-Lorriaux, M. (ed.) 1983: *Littérature contemporaine de langue allemande: Traductions françaises des œuvres parues entre 1945 et 1982. Essai de Bibliographie.* Brussels: Commission Belge de Bibliographie (Bibliographia Belgica 138).

BERNHARD SCHLINK'S *DER VORLESER*
AND
BINJAMIN WILKOMIRSKI'S *BRUCHSTÜCKE*:
BEST-SELLING RESPONSES
TO THE HOLOCAUST

J. J. LONG

I Introduction

1995 was an unsual year for German letters in that it saw the publication of two slim volumes that were to become international best sellers. Bernhard Schlink's novel *Der Vorleser* is both a love story and a Holocaust novel. Sales have surpassed the half-million mark in Germany and had reached 1.8 million in the United States by January 2000, making *Der Vorleser* Germany's greatest literary export since Patrick Süskind's *Das Parfum* (1985). Schlink has recently been awarded the Heinrich-Heine-Preis der Stadt Düsseldorf and the *Welt*-Literaturpreis, and the success of *Der Vorleser* has brought him international renown. As Tilman Krause points out, *Der Vorleser* appeals to a widely diverse readership, 'die literarischen Feinschmecker wie der kulturhungrige Friseur' (Krause 1), and Schlink's media interviews have ranged correspondingly from the cultural seriousness of *Der Spiegel* to the populism of the *Oprah Winfrey Show*.

In the same year, a publication about the Holocaust brought instant fame to Binjamin Wilkomirski, author of *Bruchstücke: Aus einer Kindheit 1939–1948*. Since 1998, it has become increasingly apparent that *Bruchstücke* is a 'fraudulent' memoir. It has transpired that Wilkomirski is the assumed name of Bruno Grosjean, a Swiss gentile whose only experiences of the concentration camps have been as a tourist. *Bruchstücke*'s exposure as a fabrication has profound implications not only for our reading of the text, but also for questions of cultural value. These issues will be discussed in Section III below. The point to note initially is that *Bruchstücke* was published as a genuine memoir and, as such, was lauded as an outstanding contribution to the literature of the Shoah. The book was first published by the highly prestigious Jüdischer Verlag, an imprint of Suhrkamp, and was brought out by similarly high-profile publishing houses in other countries: Knopf in the US, Picador in Britain. It has been translated into twelve languages and has won numerous awards, including the *Jewish Quarterly* prize for non-fiction in the UK, the American National Jewish Book

Award in the autobiography/memoir category, and the *Prix Mémoire de la Shoah* in France (Lappin 1999, 10). As a result of his book's success, Wilkomirski began to undertake regular publicity engagements, embarked on lecture tours to speak about the Holocaust, and appeared in several documentary films.

These facts alone show that *Der Vorleser* and *Bruchstücke* are both popular and international to a degree that is unusual for German-language writing. The confluence of historical catastrophe and commercial success seems at one level paradoxical — even grotesque. And yet it is also symptomatic of the 1990s, a decade that saw an exponential increase in Holocaust Studies across a broad spectrum of academic disciplines (literary criticism, theory, history, psychoanalysis), and a continued public debate about the ways in which contemporary Western culture attempts to represent, memorialize, and come to terms with Nazi genocide. The reasons for the popularity of *Der Vorleser* and *Bruchstücke* are manifold; an exhaustive study would necessitate an investigation into the cultural context of their production and reception that would exceed by far the scope of a single article. The more modest task of this essay is to analyse those formal features of the texts in question that might account for the books' popularity. I then conclude by briefly situating the texts within the wider context of Holocaust representation.

II Bernhard Schlink's *Der Vorleser*

Like Bernhard Schlink himself, the narrator of *Der Vorleser* was born in 1944; the thematic centre of the novel is the relationship of the so-called 'second generation' to the Nazi past in which many of their parents' generation had, more or less actively, participated. This had already formed the subject of the 'Vaterromane' of the 1970s and 1980s. In Schlink's text, however, the generational problem is embodied not in a family relationship, but in an erotic one. The story concerns the relationship between the narrator, Michael Berg, and a woman named Hanna Schmitz. They embark upon an affair when he is fifteen and she thirty-six, and their meetings are characterized by a repeated ritual of bathing, vigorous sex, and his reading aloud to her. The relationship comes to an abrupt end when Hanna inexplicably disappears, leaving no clue as to her whereabouts. The next time they meet, Berg is a law student following a war crimes trial in which Hanna is one of the accused. During the trial the narrator realizes that Hanna is illiterate, and her desire to conceal her illiteracy accounts for the otherwise inexplicable aspects of her behaviour during the war, in her relationship with Berg, and throughout the trial. The remainder of the novel deals with the Berg's life in the years following Hanna's imprisonment, including the re-establishment of his relationship with her whilst she is still behind bars. A day before her release, Hanna commits suicide, and charges Berg with the posthumous task of visiting the sole surviving victim of her crime, a woman now resident in America. This visit forms the last real event of the novel, whilst the last chapter is a kind of epilogue in which Berg reflects on the process of writing the text we have just read.

In this final chapter of the novel, Berg wonders 'ob ich und wie ich mich von [Hanna] hätte lossagen, loslösen müssen' (VL, 205). This represents a belated awareness of the text's central problem, for the plot of *Der Vorleser* dramatizes the inability to mourn, 'die Unfähigkeit zu trauern'.[1] Mourning is the psychological process whereby human subjects cope with the loss of a person or 'eine an ihre Stelle gerückte Abstraktheit wie Vaterland, Freiheit, ein Ideal, usw.' (Freud 1989, 197). It consists of the gradual withdrawal of 'bound' or 'cathected' libidinal energies from an object whose demise has been confirmed by the reality principle:

> Die Realitätsprüfung hat gezeigt, daß das geliebte Objekt nicht mehr besteht, und erläßt nun die Aufforderung, alle Libido aus ihren Verknüpfungen mit diesem Objekt abzuziehen [...] Jede einzelne der Erinnerungen und Erwartungen, in denen die Libido an das Objekt geknüpft war, wird eingestellt, übersetzt und an ihr die Lösung der Libido vollzogen; [...] das Ich [wird] nach der Trauerarbeit wieder frei und ungehemmt. (Freud 1989, 199)

As the bound energies are gradually loosened from the lost object, they become freed and available for new cathexis.

In Berg's case, however, the 'Lösung der Libido' never takes place. He loses Hanna twice: the first time when she inexplicably disappears, and the second time, symbolically, when his 'first love' is revealed to have been a concentration camp guard and war criminal. Yet in neither case does he go through a process of *Trauerarbeit*. In the aftermath of Hanna's first departure, he writes: 'ich [weiß], daß ich die Erinnerung an Hanna zwar verabschiedet, aber nicht bewältigt hatte. Mich nach Hanna nie mehr demütigen lassen und demütigen, nie mehr schuldig machen und schuldig fühlen, niemanden mehr so lieben, daß ihn verlieren weh tut' (VL, 84). Instead of mourning her loss, Berg merely attempts to ignore his affection for Hanna, with the result that she continues to 'bind' his libidinal energies. This accounts for the failure of all his subsequent relationships. His marriage breaks down partly because he does not tell his wife about her (164), and all his later faceless, nameless partners represent merely a chain of Hanna substitutes, betokening a kind of compulsive repetition. Berg admits to himself 'daß eine Frau sich ein bißchen wie Hanna anfassen und anfühlen, ein bißchen wie sie riechen und schmecken muß, damit unser Zusammensein stimmt' (165–166), but his failure to abandon his continued erotic attachment to her condemns him to repeat it symbolically in all his future liaisons.

This failure to mourn becomes doubly problematic during Hanna's trial. Despite the revelation of her Nazi past, Berg's attachment to her does not change. His latent libidinal investment persists, and repetition is once again the means by which it is made manifest. On seeing Hanna for the first time in the dock, he writes: 'Ich erkannte sie aber ich fühlte nichts. Ich fühlte nichts' (91). The reiteration of 'ich fühlte nichts' represents a moment of linguistic excess whose function is to imply the opposite of what it says. He then elaborates a metaphor of numbness or anaesthesia to describe the effect of the trial not only on himself but on all participants and onlookers (96–99). And yet he is plagued by repeated dreams 'in denen mich die harte, herrische, grausame Hanna sexuell erregte und von denen ich in Sehnsucht, Angst und Empörung aufwachte' (141–142). The narrator's relationship to Hanna is still governed by the sado-masochistic eroticism that had dominated their love affair, and the possibility of Trauerarbeit is blocked by the persistent invasion of the pleasure principle.[2]

In the light of this, a feature of the novel that has attracted considerable praise begins to look extremely dubious. Newspaper critics on both sides of the Atlantic interpreted Berg's avowal of his own responsibility and his refusal to pass moral judgement on Hanna as a positive feature of the text. Berg claims, for example, that the fact that he and Hanna enjoyed a sexual relationship implicates him to a greater extent than his coevals in the Nazi past, for his love for Hanna was determined not by an accident of birth, but by his own volition. As a result, he feels unable to condemn her without condemning himself:

> Ich mußte eigentlich auf Hanna zeigen. Aber der Fingerzeig auf Hanna wies auf mich zurück. Ich hatte sie nicht nur geliebt, ich hatte sie gewählt. Ich habe versucht, mir zu sagen, daß ich, als ich Hanna wählte, nichts von dem wußte, was sie getan hatte. Ich habe versucht, mich damit in den Zustand der Unschuld zu reden, in dem Kinder ihre Eltern lieben. Aber die Liebe zu den Eltern ist die einzige Liebe, für die man nicht verantwortlich ist. (162)

The problem is that Berg's repeated professions of guilt in relation to the Nazi past remain nebulous and unspecific, and critics addressing this problem have either fled into vague formulations about a 'Moment der Verantwortlichkeit' (Köster 1999, 71) or turned their back on the issue altogether (Schlant 1999, 211). This is because the text is permeated by a much more unsettling notion of guilt: Berg is unequivocal when it comes to his 'culpable' treatment of Hanna. He sees his failure to mention her to his schoolfriends in terms of betrayal (VL, 72), and sees himself implicated in her trial when he fails to divulge her secret, even though he realizes that her sentence would be commuted if the presiding judge knew of her illiteracy (VL, 132; cf. Parkes 1998, 117). In the final chapter, the entire question of his own relationship to National Socialism is swamped by a concern with his role in Hanna's life and death: 'In den ersten Jahren nach Hannas Tod haben mich die alten Fragen gequält, ob ich sie verleugnet und verraten habe, ob ich ihr schuldig geblieben bin, ob ich schuldig geworden bin, indem ich sie geliebt habe, ob ich und wie ich mich von ihr hätte lossagen, loslösen müssen' (VL, 205).

The repeated assertion that Berg is guilty of 'betraying' Hanna produces a strange inversion of values and casts her in the role of victim rather than perpetrator. In the light of Berg's inability to mourn, the question of guilt ceases to represent an exemplary sense of ethical complexity, and comes to function as a form of *apologia* for Hanna. Indeed, Juliane Köster's experience of teaching *Der Vorleser* has highlighted a strong tendency for readers to sympathize with Hanna at the expense of empathizing with her victims (Köster 1999, 75).[3] Literary texts are under no obligation to encourage identification with the victims, just as they do not have to pass moral judgement on the characters whose fates they narrate. The uncomfortable fact that the text encourages identification with Hanna, however, has been largely ignored in discussions of the book. Instead, Berg's claim that his involvement with Hanna implicates him in the Nazi past and blocks his right to pass moral judgement has met with approbation for its avoidance of the facile, self-righteous indignation that Berg himself perceives in the 1968 movement (VL, 88).

The trouble is that Berg sees no alternative to this indignation other than a retreat into a moral relativism according to which *tout comprendre, c'est tout pardonner*. This is manifested in his inability to find a middle way between condemnation and comprehension: 'Ich wollte Hannas Verbrechen zugleich verstehen und verurteilen. Aber es war dafür zu furchtbar. Wenn ich versuchte, es zu verstehen, hatte ich das Gefühl, es nicht mehr so zu verurteilen, wie es eigentlich verurteilt gehörte. Wenn ich es so verurteilte, wie es verurteilt gehörte, blieb kein Raum fürs Verstehen' (151). The false antithesis between 'verstehen' and 'verurteilen' (terms whose parallelism is orthographically reinforced by the 'ver-' prefix but which are not mutually exclusive) means that the rejection of the one legitimizes the acceptance of the other. By elsewhere rejecting condemnation (162, and the above discussion), the logic of Berg's own rhetoric means that he has to adopt a stance of moral relativism, and as a result he strives throughout the text to extenuate Hanna's crime. This in turn leads to his propagating a highly contentious view of recent German history.

The entire problem of the second generation's need to come to terms with the Holocaust, for example, is reduced to a mere generational conflict: 'Manchmal denke ich, daß die Auseinandersetzung mit der nationalsozialistischen Vergangenheit nicht der Grund, sondern nur der Ausdruck des Generationskonflikts war, der als treibende Kraft der Studentenbewegung zu spüren war' (161). On this reading, the Holocaust is just a convenient vehicle for a basically Oedipal conflict between fathers and sons, which is problematic on two counts. Firstly, it totally ignores the fact that the social phenomena against which the '68ers protested were partly attributable to the failure to work through the Nazi past, as becomes apparent in *Die Unfähigkeit zu trauern* (Mitscherlich 1990, 25). Secondly, it ignores the historical specificity of the Holocaust by turning any attempt to deal with it into an epiphenomenon of a 'timeless' generation conflict.

This intersects with a further rhetorical move on the part of the narrator, which is to conflate the perpetrators, the victims, and the post-war witnesses of the Nazi atrocities through reference to a 'Gemeinsamkeit des Betäubtseins' (VL, 99). Berg goes on to address the dubiousness of such an assertion:

> als ich dabei Täter, Opfer, Tote, Lebende, Überlebende und Nachlebende miteinander verglich, war mir nicht wohl, und wohl ist mir auch jetzt nicht. Darf man derart vergleichen? Wenn ich in einem Gespräch Ansätze eines solchen Vergleichs machte, betonte ich zwar stets, daß der Vergleich den Unterschied, ob man in die Welt des KZ gezwungen wurde oder sich in sie begeben hatte, ob man gelitten oder Leiden zugefügt hatte, nicht relativiere, daß der Unterschied vielmehr von der allergrößten, alles entscheidenden Wichtigkeit sei. Aber ich stieß selbst dann auf Befremden oder Empörung, wenn ich dies nicht erst in Reaktion auf die Einwände der anderen ausführte, sondern noch ehe die anderen etwas einwenden konnten. (99)

If, however, the differences are 'von der größten, alles entscheidenden Wichtigkeit', why assert the similarities at all? The disquieting thing about this passage is the explicit desire to assert comparability *in spite of* the differences. Tense usage and temporal adverbials stress the element of repetition: Berg tries out his comparability thesis with a series of interlocutors, and attempts to disarm them by pre-empting their objections before making his own point. Commenting on this passage, Ernestine Schlant has accused Schlink of being aware of current debates and wanting them in his novel, but of not having worked out clear positions of his own (Schlant 1999, 214). This kind of accusation, however, relies on a naive conflation of author and narrator, concentrating purely on propositional content and ignoring the question of narrative form. Rather than seeing the novel as a vehicle for Schlink's own views, it makes more sense to read this passage as a symptom of Berg's continued attachment to Hanna and a desire to exculpate her.[4]

The tendency within *Der Vorleser* to mitigate Hanna's atrocities by encouraging sympathy with her and dehistoricizing the Holocaust is one reason why the text has proven so popular. Schlink himself has said that one of his intentions was to 'humanize' the perpetrators of the Holocaust: 'Erst die menschliche Nähe zu ihnen macht das, was sie getan haben, so furchtbar. Wir hätten doch mit den Tätern schon lange abgeschlossen, wenn es wirklich alles Monster wären, ganz anders, ganz fremd, mit denen wir nichts gemein haben' (Schlink 2000, 183). Schlink is right to point out that one of the most profound moral problems facing any analyst of Nazism is, precisely, the fact that ordinary people proved capable of committing appalling atrocities. At the same time, however, overemphasizing our 'menschliche Nähe zu ihnen' runs the risk of encouraging a heightened sense of sympathy for the 'Täter' in a way that precludes critical judgement of their misdeeds. By accepting the proffered identification with Hanna, the reader can abdicate responsibility for engaging with the vexed moral questions that any serious discussion of the Holocaust necessarily raises.

The form of the novel contributes to the same end. *Der Vorleser* is a developmental narrative which Juliane Köster has characterized as a kind of *Entwicklungsroman* manqué, but which is better described by the blurb on the back of the novel, according to which it is 'Die fast kriminalistische Erforschung einer sonderbaren Liebe und bedrängenden Vergangenheit'. The similarity to the detective novel is motivated within the text by Berg's chosen profession as an academic lawyer researching jurisprudence in the Third Reich. Furthermore, Schlink is himself a practising judge, a law professor at the Humboldt University in Berlin and the author of three detective novels. So both internal and external reasons for the choice of genre seem to lie immediately to hand. This does not, however, exhaust the significance of the detective form.

As in other so-called popular genres, the conventions that govern the construction and reading of narrative in general are particularly transparent in detective novels, especially those of the classic variety. They rely on received notions of human psychology and motive, and presuppose the ultimate explicability of even the weirdest crime. They are also dependent to a high degree on the dialectic of the hermeneutic circle, according to which a preemptive conception of the whole both guides our reading of the individual narrative episodes, whilst simultaneously being corrected and modified by them. There is a general assumption that all details will somehow become meaningful from the vantage point of the end, and this expectation also subtends structures of suspense and resolution in narrative: enigmas are typically created at the beginning of the text, and our desire to keep reading is predicated on the assumption that the 'truth' will finally be revealed, no matter how many decoys and red herrings there may be along the way.[5]

This 'hermeneutic' structuring is in full evidence in Schlink's text. Wherever enigmas or gaps appear in the narrative, they are eventually explained. In fact, most enigmatic episodes are explained by one of two facts. One of these is Hanna's past life as a concentration camp guard, which accounts for her panic when Berg asks her name (VL, 34), her obsessive cleanliness (33), and her refusal to answer the narrator's questions concerning her wartime past (40). The other is Hanna's inability to read. The most significant enigma is created by the rupture in the text at the point where Hanna disappears, but her illiteracy 'explains' or 'resolves' numerous minor mysteries as well. Her relationship with Berg, for example, is characterized by highly unusual or unpredictable behaviour: her inexplicable rage when Berg tells her that he does not take school seriously (36), her anger at being temporarily 'deserted' by the narrator despite his leaving a note to explain that he had gone to fetch breakfast (54), the fact that Hanna never fills in the hotel booking forms (54), and her strange request that the narrator read to her (42). During the trial we learn that she had failed to respond to repeated communiqués from the courts (94), appears not to have read the book by a survivor on which her prosecution was based (104), and refuses to undergo a handwriting test which would have proved that she had not written an incriminating report and would have led to a lighter sentence (124).

The novel thus evinces considerable faith in the capacity of enigma, suspense and resolution to structure a linear narrative that ineluctably renders the events it represents meaningful and provides a sense of closure. In such narratives, the ending is privileged as the guarantor of meaning and the vantage point from which the significance of the foregoing can be gauged. The ending itself, however, is far from unproblematic. Hanna's suicide means that she does not have to confront the society that condemned her. Whilst Berg visits her once in prison, this remains an isolated incident; he is not forced to confront the 'real' Hanna (rather than the eroticized Hanna of his imagination) whose obesity and lack of personal hygiene would now seem to rule her out as an object of libidinal investment. In both cases, a genuine 'Auseinandersetzung' with the past is foreclosed by formal means.

In the testament she leaves behind, Hanna instructs Berg to donate her meagre savings to the sole surviving victim of her wartime crimes, a gesture which, as Ann Parry writes, 'reveals that [...] Hanna thought that a gift could be a trade-off that would somehow mitigate that "zero-moment" that occurred when she and those with her refused to release the Jewish women from the burning church' (Parry 1999, 261). The narrator conspicuously fails to provide a critical perspective on this gesture. On the contrary, he reassures the victim, now a resident of New York, that '"[Hanna wußte], was sie anderen im Lager und auf dem Marsch angetan hat. Sie hat mir das nicht nur gesagt, sie hat sich in den letzten Jahren im Gefängnis auch intensiv damit beschäftigt,"' and he goes on to explain that Hanna taught herself to read in prison, and accumulated an extensive library of Holocaust history books and survivor memoirs (VL, 202). Whilst the woman refuses to provide absolution and rejects the gift of Hanna's savings, she asks Berg to suggest a beneficiary and is perfectly happy when he proposes to give the money to a Jewish society which teaches the illiterate to read and write. By yoking together illiteracy and Jewishness, Hanna as well as her victim become the indirect recipients of the former's inheritance in a kind of belated reconciliation. Furthermore, the survivor does accept the tea caddy in which the money was kept. The concentration camp guards had confiscated a similar tin from her (202–203), and so to accept Hanna's tin amounts to a symbolic acceptance of restitution. The result of all this is that the text appears to endorse Hanna's gesture of so-called atonement, and by implication also the reader's identification with her.

In the closing chapter, Berg affirms the 'rightness' of the tale he has just told: 'es [gibt] neben der Version, die ich geschrieben habe, viele andere. Die Gewähr dafür, daß die geschriebene die richtige ist, liegt darin, daß ich sie geschrieben und die anderen Versionen nicht geschrieben habe. Die geschriebene Version wollte geschrieben werden, die vielen anderen wollten nicht' (205–206). This is, of course, highly disingenuous, the syntax of the passage suppresses the narrator's agency and obfuscates the fact that Berg is motivated by personal agendas. The reading I have proposed above, however, suggests that this particular version of the story is 'right' because it ultimately implies a world of order, rationality, and the explicability of human behaviour. The narrative form of the text contains the potential for conflict and comes to function as a compensation for traumatic experience and the inability to mourn.

It is this closure at the level of form that is so reassuring. In 1985, the German historian Martin Broszat lamented the fact that in Holocaust historiography the 'Lust am geschichtlichen Erzählen' appeared to be blocked (Broszat 1985, 375).[6] This was a plea, as Eric Santner puts it, 'for a certain primacy of the pleasure principle in historical narration even, paradoxically, when it comes to narrating events the traumatic impact of which would seem to call the normal functioning of that principle into question' (Santner 1992, 149).

Schlink's text, however, does precisely what Broszat demanded of Holocaust narration. On the penultimate page Berg writes:

> [die Geschichte] ist zurückgekommen, Detail um Detail und in einer Weise rund, geschlossen und gerichtet, daß sie mich nicht mehr traurig macht. Was für eine traurige Geschichte, dachte ich lange. Nicht, daß ich jetzt dächte, sie sei glücklich. Aber ich denke, daß sie stimmt und daß daneben die Frage, ob sie traurig oder glücklich sei, keinerlei Bedeutung hat. (VL, 206)

This stresses the capacity of the narrative form — 'rund, geschlossen, und gerichtet' — to redeem the events of the past by means of an exaggeratedly 'hermeneutic' structure and the concomitant yield of narrative pleasure.[7]

III Binjamin Wilkomirski's *Bruchstücke*

Binjamin Wilkomirski's *Bruchstücke* is situated at the opposite pole of narrative representation. It is a highly fragmentary account of the author's alleged Holocaust experiences. Despite its fragmentary structure, it is possible to reconstruct a skeletal narrative of 'what happened' to the young Wilkomirski. He was separated from his parents in Riga during the massacre of the Jews, escaped by boat to Poland, but was then taken to the Majdanek concentration camp near Lublin. From there he was moved to another camp, possibly Auschwitz. At the end of the war he was placed in a Jewish orphanage in Cracow, and then, finally, taken to an orphanage in Switzerland at the age of about seven. Here he was fostered and eventually adopted by Kurt and Martha Dössekker, but in the repressive climate of post-war Switzerland he found that society failed to acknowledge his memories or make allowances for his problems in adapting to 'normal' civilian life.

Wilkomirski came to write his memoirs after meeting a psychologist, Elitsur Bernstein, in the mid-1980s. He confided to Bernstein that he suffered from nightmares about concentration camps, and Bernstein suggested therapy. Wilkomirski rejected the idea, but his condition worsened until he could neither sleep and nor bear to be touched, especially on the back. After one particularly disturbing nightmare and subsequent hallucination in 1990, Bernstein strongly urged therapy on the grounds that what Wilkomirski was dreaming about was a part of himself. Whilst there is a certain amount of controversy over the precise nature of the therapy (some accounts talking of 'recovered memory', others of hypnosis, both of which Wilkomirski denies), the effect was that Wilkomirski began to write down what he 'remembered'.[8]

This account of the genesis of *Bruchstücke* corresponds exactly to the structure of what has been called 'traumatic memory'. In psychoanalytic approaches to the problem of trauma, theorists have distinguished two types of memory which we may respectively call 'narrative' and 'traumatic'. Narrative memory is what we would normally understand by the word: it is retrievable at will, is adaptable in the way that it links past experiences to present circumstances, and is, in part, a social act, being transmissible in the form of a story.[9] In the aftermath of trauma, however, a different form of memory emerges:

> The trauma is the confrontation with an event that, in its unexpectedness or horror, cannot be placed within the schemes of prior knowledge [...] and thus continually returns, in its exactness, at a later time. Not having been fully integrated as it occurred, the event cannot become [...] a 'narrative memory' that is integrated into a completed story of the past. (Caruth 1995c, 153)

In traumatic memory the event 'is not assimilated or experienced fully at the time, but only belatedly, in its repeated *possession* of the one who experiences it' (Caruth 1995b, 4; original emphasis). Psychoanalytic theory, from Freud's work with Viennese neurotics to Laub's work with Holocaust survivors,[10] has shown that escape from the compulsive repetition and re-living of the trauma can be achieved only by externalizing and transmitting the event in the form of narrative. The analyst's task is to facilitate the act of remembrance by simultaneously bringing the memory fragments together and, at the same time, preventing a premature foreclosure through what Dori Laub terms a cognitive suppression, an emotional catharsis, or a surrender to the ubiquity of silence (Laub 1992b, 72).

The 'Entstehungsgeschichte' of *Bruchstücke* suggests that Wilkomirski was clearly somehow 'possessed' by an experience that he had not fully grasped, not fully assimilated as part of his own life-story. In other words, his memories were 'traumatic' rather than 'narrative'. If, however, traumatic memories become available to consciousness only in the act of narrating them, then the memory-fragments contained in *Bruchstücke* cannot be seen as a direct representation of traumatic experience. They are rather a *constructed formal analogue* of traumatic recall. This becomes apparent in the preface:

> Meine frühesten Erinnerungen gleichen einem Trümmerfeld einzelner Bilder und Abläufe. Brocken des Erinnerns mit harten, messerscharfen Konturen, die noch heute kaum ohne Verletzung zu berühren sind. Oft chaotisch Verstreutes, chronologisch nur selten zu gliedern; Brocken, die sich immer wieder beharrlich dem Ordnungswillen des erwachsen Gewordenen widersetzen und den Gesetzen der Logik entgleiten.
> *Will ich darüber schreiben, muß ich auf die ordnende Logik, die Perspektive des Erwachsenen verzichten. Sie würde das Geschehen nur verfälschen.*
> (BS, 7–8; my italics, JJL)

In the italicized section, Wilkomirski's narrative techniques are announced as *self-consciously* eschewing what we would normally regard as indispensable elements of narrative representation *in order not to* falsify the experience. The formal peculiarities of the text, then, embody the desire to narrativize the experiences *somehow*, whilst avoiding the so-called falsifications that would be inherent in a closed, linear 'plot'. *Bruchstücke* can be seen as an attempt to negotiate a path, on the printed page, between the twin dangers of a resigned collapse into silence and the gratifying closure of conventional narrative, and this deliberate narrative strategy forms the plinth on which he constructs his counterfeit.

One method that Wilkomirski adopts is the disruption of chronology. In structuralist terminology, the 'story' of a text is the chronological sequence of events, whilst the 'discourse' is the verbal text responsible for their narration.[11] In *Bruchstücke*, the time structure is complex, mixing periods before, during and after the War often in the same chapter, which means that it is difficult to abstract anything akin to a story from the discourse of the text. However, it is possible, as my 'plot summary' shows, but there still are ambiguities as to when and where certain events happened. The 'memories' remain, to a certain extent, in their fractured and fragmented state, and the satisfactions of narrative form are only partially operative.

Furthermore, the text is focalized almost exclusively through the eyes and conciousness of a child. There is no specification of geographical place beyond what the child himself learns, and no attempt to explain memories in terms of 'external' history. This becomes particularly prominent in the section headed 'Der Transport' (BS, 84–91). Wilkomirski remembers the end of a journey tightly wedged in between adults in a train truck, and when smoke begins to pervade the air he is puzzled why nobody tries to move. A door is opened, and the little Wilkomirski manages to escape by being mysteriously thrown into a hole in the earth that is full of what he presumes are corpses. He then scrambles up the sides of the ditch, stepping on the distended belly of a corpse as he does so, and is dragged forcibly away by adults. There follows a short paragraph about a march, but the chapter ends with the narrator regaining consciousness 'erst viel später, als es schon kalt wurde und der erste Schnee fiel' (90). He is back in a concentration camp. The restricted focalization through the eyes and conceptual understanding of a child means that events are described at a level below the threshold of functional relevance. This is not a new device, but its effect in Wilkomirski is that readers are left to reconstruct the events themselves and situate the recounted experiences within the framework of war, race, and the Nazi genocide.

The formal features of the text that I have enumerated seem to make *Bruchstücke* an instance of a particularly sensitive, responsible Holocaust memoir that both strives to remain as true as possible to the immediate experience within the limits imposed by the exigencies of narrative transmission, and reflects on the narrative means by which this is accomplished. The reviews of *Bruchstücke*, however, suggest that the reception of the text was largely determined by quite different criteria. The verbal artifice of the text was widely ignored, and readers surrendered to the raw emotional impact of the individual fragments.[12] The techniques that seemed to invite discussion about the problems of representation, namely restricted focalization throught the eyes of a child and structural fragmentation, clearly also facilitate a mode of reading which encourages an uncritical empathic identification of the reader with the victim.

One reason for the success of *Bruchstücke*, then, is its mobilization of the existential shock-value of the Holocaust survivor-memoir. In her book *Der Betroffenheitskult*, Cora Stefan bemoans the fact that political life in Germany has become dominated by a culture of being personally affected, upset, overwhelmed, which, Stefan argues, curtails the scope for genuine political action and paralyses the decision-making process. Similarly, the institutionalization of Betroffenheit as a form of aesthetic response precludes engagement with the real historical and interpretative problems raised by a given text. By reading literature in the mode of Betroffenheit, however, what we, as readers, are doing is enlisting one of the defence mechanisms that psychoanalysts working with Holocaust survivors unwittingly employ in order to protect themselves from the atrocities being recounted.[13] One of the 'listening defenses' that Dori Laub cites is a reaction of 'awe and fear; we endow the survivor with a kind of sanctity, both to pay our tribute to him and to keep him at a distance, to avoid the intimacy entailed in knowing' (Laub 1992b, 72). The reason I dwelt on the ecstatic reception of Wilkomirski in the introduction is that the way he was feted seems to me to bear striking resemblance to this process of pseudocanonization: Wilkomirski as secular saint.

Such a reading of *Bruchstücke* might explain the furore which has surrounded Wilkomirski's exposure as a hoaxster. As has been widely reported in the media, a series of investigations by journalists and historians have proven beyond reasonable doubt that Wilkomirski was born Bruno Grosjean, illegitimate child of one Yvonne Grosjean in Biel, Switerland, in 1941 (Lappin 1999, 14). He was not born in Riga, did not experience the concentration camps of Majdanek or Auschwitz, is not even Jewish. *Bruchstücke* is 7a 'fraud'.

As soon as this suspicion had entered the public domain, journalists were virtually falling over themselves in the race to condemn the German readership of *Bruchstücke*:

> Mehrere Journalisten äußerten den Vorwurf, viele Leser, zumal in Deutschland, seien rasch zu einer völligen Identifikation mit dem Opfer bereit, schwelgten in Mitleidbekundungen, seien aber unfähig oder unwillig zu einem differenzierten, kritischen historischen Urteil. Es sei allemal bequemer, eine persönliche Leidensgeschichte zu lesen, als sich mit abstrakten Statistiken und dem umfangreichen Quellenmaterial der Historiker auseinanderzusetzen. (Bauer 1999, 10, fn. 6)

This separation of 'Quellenmaterial' and 'persönliche Leidensgeschichte' ironically reproduces the reading strategy adopted by those 'naive' readers whom journalists were so quick to criticize, for it relies on an assumption that memoirs facilitate direct and unmediated access to the author's memory, and ignores the moment of construction or fabrication inherent in any verbal representation. In the reception of Wilkomirski's text, it is not the fact that large numbers of readers failed to subject the text to a 'differentiated critical historical evaluation' that is troubling. It is rather the failure to take account of the structuring procedures that are announced by the text itself: the desire to overlook rhetoric, and its concomitant, aesthetic distance, in the desire to experience Betroffenheit.

Why Wilkomirski identifies so strongly with the Jewish victims of Nazism is a vexed question, the answers to which must necessarily be speculative. At the end of a long and meticulously researched article on the affair, Elena Lappin plausibly suggests that Wilkomirski/Grosjean projects himself into the Holocaust in order to externalize and work through his own traumatic childhood. This excessive and uncontrolled empathy with Holocaust victims is then reduplicated in the generally ecstatic reception of Wilkomirski's text itself. Once the author has been unveiled as neither a Jew nor a victim, however, he ceases to be a legitimate object of identification. Wilkomirski's 'exposure' is so shocking because the readers themselves are forced into a position of having to withdraw their libidinal investment from an object that has been lost.

Far from being dead, as Roland Barthes and others have been proclaiming for three decades or more, the author in the case of Holocaust memoirs is alive and well. More than this, he determines the forms of libidinal investment open to the reader of a given text and becomes thereby the guarantor of cultural value. Once 'the author' has been exposed as a fraudster, his text demands a radical re-interpretation as fiction if it is to retain any cultural value whatsoever. The only way in which Wilkomirski-Grosjean's text can be 'rescued' for literary history is to refuse the proffered identification with the narrator and turn attention to those formal techniques that proved so effective in creating the illusion of authenticity.

IV Conclusion

The question that ultimately presents itself is: why should two texts dealing with arguably the most 'traumatic' period in European history have become international best sellers? The success of both books is partly due to the fact that they fall into easily marketable and easily digestible genres, which itself has wider cultural significance. At the end of his book *Representing the Holocaust*, Dominick LaCapra talks of 'two complementary ways of responding to trauma' (LaCapra 1994, 192). Whilst LaCapra is talking about history and theory, his comments apply, *mutatis mutandis*, to literature as well.

His first response 'involves denial or repression, for example, in a redemptive, fetishistic narrative that excludes or marginalises trauma through a teleological story that projectively presents values and wishes as viably realised in the facts, typically through a progressive developmental process' (LaCapra 1994, 192). This clearly corresponds to Schlink's narrative, in which erotic attachment and the trauma of loss are contained by a plot structure whose resolution avoids genuine conflict and endorses the possibility of atonement. Furthermore, we have seen how the narrator of *Der Vorleser* turns the narrative into an autonomous entity that functions as a guarantor of its own rightness, thereby concealing the libidinal investments that motivate the writing process. This is what LaCapra means by 'fetishistic' narrative, a concept he borrows from Eric Santner, who defines it as follows: 'the construction and deployment of a narrative consciously or unconsciously designed to expunge the traces of the trauma or loss that called that narrative into being in the first place' (Santner 1992, 144).

LaCapra's other category of response 'tends intentionally or unintentionally to aggravate trauma in a largely symptomatic fashion'. A repeated 'acting out' of the trauma affirms 'posttraumatic fragmentation, disjunction and instability wherein the impossibility of any final unity or "suture" may become tantamount to the unavailability or elusiveness of any durable bonds or "suturing" at all' (LaCapra 1994, 193). Both the structure and the reception of Wilkomirski's text correspond to this notion of Holocaust response. The book's own fragmentariness rehearses a set of experiences but refuses to 'make sense' of them, thereby legitimizing an uncritical identification with the victim position, and implicating the reader in a process of acting out or reliving the trauma.

In both cases, a genuinely critical engagment with the problems of the Holocaust and its representation is obviated. Both the page-turning novel of suspense and the harrowing account of a traumatic childhood are commodified genres that lend themselves to easy, uncritical consumption, and this accounts ultimately for the truly international popularity of the texts under discussion here. It is precisely the task of literary studies not merely to 'consume' cultural products, however, and in the above analyses I have suggested that the ecstatic early reception of *Der Vorleser* and *Bruchstücke* could be achieved only by ignoring certain highly significant aspects of the texts: the inability to mourn in the case of Schlink, and the constructedness of memory in the case of Wilkomirski. This kind of critical practice is necessary in order to both explain and problematize the thematic and, more importantly, formal features that made Schlink's *Der Vorleser* and Wilkomirski's *Bruchstücke* best-selling responses to the Holocaust

Notes

1. Alexander and Margarete Mitscherlich's 1967 study of post-war West German society, *Die Unfähigkeit zu trauern*, pleads for the primacy of psychoanalysis as a tool of 'Menschenkenntnis' (1990, 94). More than three decades later, psychoanalysis remains a dominant discourse in the field of 'Vergangenheitsbewältigung', both in the treatment of individual victims and as a metalanguage in the study of Holocaust representation. See e.g. LaCapra 1994 and 1998, Felman and Laub 1992, Santner 1992.

2. An analogous diversion (or perversion) of mourning into pleasure can be witnessed at a collective level as well: the members of the 1966 KZ-Seminar see themselves as the 'Avantgarde der Aufarbeitung' (VL, 87) and wallow in the details of the offences they condemned: 'Je furchtbarer die Ereignisse waren, über die wir lasen und hörten, desto gewisser wurden wir unseres aufklärerischen und anklagerischen Auftrags. Auch wenn die Ereignisse uns den Atem stocken ließen — wir hielten sie triumphierend hoch. Seht her!' (VL, 88). Günter Grass had highlighted the danger of mourning turning into pleasure in his *Danziger Trilogie*, be it overtly erotic, as in the 'Zwiebelkeller' and 'Madonna 49' chapters of *Die Blechtrommel*, or aesthetic, as in the following quotation from *Hundejahre*: 'Wer mag alte Wunden aufreißen, wenn das Wundeaufreißen Lust bereitet?' (Grass 1987, 675).

3. Whilst Köster sees this problem as a side effect of the 'Dilemma der zweiten Generation', it actually plays a much more central role in Schlink's text, and her failure to address it adequately in her 'Interpretation für die Schule' is serious.

4. Berg's capacity to conflate the incommensurable emerges once more when he states, 'Hochschule und Hochschulreform waren mir letztlich ebenso gleichgültig wie Vietkong und Amerikaner' (VL, 160). His utterly apolitical stance prevents him from making important ethical distinctions.

5. Significantly, Berg (VL, 176) explicitly rejects experimental novels which might upset his faith in narrative. Schlink's own literary preferences betray a similar conservatism: he lists the nineteenth-century authors Fontane, Heine and Keller, and contemporary writers who largely eschew formal experiment: Sten Nadolny, Dagmar Leupold, Richard Ford (Schlink 2000, 181).

6. Broszat's article ultimately argues for a historiographic 'normalization' of the Nazi period, according to which it would be merely one era among many whose positive achievements could be better appreciated. The revisionist approach implied by Broszat's article makes it a kind of 'Vorbote' of the *Historikerstreit* that was to erupt in the following year.

7. Tilman Krause again echoes many German reviews of *Der Vorleser* when he stresses the book's enjoyability and its abolition of the 'Trennung zwischen E- und U-Kultur' (1999, 2).
8. See Elena Lappin's account of her interview with Bernstein (Lappin 1999, 42–43).
9. The terminology here is that of pioneering French psychologist Pierre Janet. See Kolk/Hart 1995, 163.
10. In addition to the works cited above, see Freud 1989c and Laub 1992b.
11. Beatrice Petz in this volume discusses 'story' and 'discourse' in Günter Grass's changing strategy in respect of (German) history (67–84 below; esp. 70–77).
12. See e.g. the extracts quoted on the back of the English translation (Wilkomirski 1996) and the account of readers' experiences in Bauer and Strickhausen 1999, 2.
13. A similar point was made by Lau 1999, 66.

Primary texts
Schlink, Bernhard 1992: *Selbs Betrug*. Diogenes: Zürich.
—— 1995: *Der Vorleser*. Diogenes: Zürich. (=VL)
—— 2000: '"Ich lebe in Geschichten". Spiegel-Gespräch mit Bernhard Schlink', *Der Spiegel*, 24 January 2000, 180–184.
Schlink, Bernhard and Walter Propp 1987: *Selbs Justiz*. Zürich: Diogenes.
Wilkomirski, Binjamin 1995: *Bruchstücke: Aus einer Kindheit 1939–1948*. Frankfurt am Main: Suhrkamp. (=BS)
—— 1996: *Fragments: Memories of a Childhood 1939–1948*. Trans. Carol Brown Janeway. London: Picador.

Secondary literature
Bauer, Barbara with Waltraud Strickhausen 1999: 'Reaktionen deutscher Leser auf den Fall "Binjamin Wilkomirski"', *literaturkritik.de*. (http://www.literaturkritik.de/txt/1999-02-12.html).
Broszat, Martin 1985: 'Plädoyer für eine Historisierung des Nationalsozialismus', *Merkur*, 373–385.
Caruth, Cathy (ed.) 1995a: *Trauma: Explorations in Memory*. Baltimore: Johns Hopkins University Press.
—— 1995b: 'Introduction [to Part One]' in Caruth 1995a, 3–12.
—— 1995c: 'Introduction [to Part Two]' in Caruth 1995a, 151–157.
Felman, Shoshana and Dori Laub 1992: *Testimony: Crises of Witnessing in Literature, Psychoanalysis, and History*. London: Routledge.
Freud, Sigmund 1989a: 'Trauer und Melancholie' in Freud: *Studienausgabe* III (*Psychologie des Unbewußten*). Frankfurt am Main: Fischer, 193–212.
—— 1989b: *Jenseits des Lustprinzips* in Freud: *Studienausgabe* III (*Psychologie des Unbewußten*). Frankfurt am Main: Fischer, 213–272.
—— 1989c: 'Erinnern, Wiederholen, Durcharbeiten' in Freud: *Studienausgabe* Ergänzungsband (*Schriften zur Behandlungstechnik*). Frankfurt am Main: Fischer, 205–215.
Friedlander, Saul (ed.) 1992: *Probing the Limits of Representation: Nazism and the 'Final Solution'*. Cambridge, Mass.: Harvard University Press.
Grass, Günter 1987: *Hundejahre* in Grass: *Werkausgabe* III. Ed. Volker Neuhaus. Darmstadt/ Neuwied: Luchterhand.
Köster, Juliane 1999: 'Bernhard Schlink: *Der Vorleser* (1995) — Eine Interpretation für die Schule', *Der Deutschunterricht* 4/99, 70–82.
Kolk, Bessel van der and Onno van der Hart 1995: 'The Instrusive Past: The Flexibility of Memory and the Engraving of Trauma' in Caruth 1995a, 158–182.
Krause, Tilman 1999: '*Welt*-Literaturpreis für Schlink. Liebe zu guten Geschichten: Ein Porträt des Berliner Schriftstellers', *Die Welt*, 16 Oktober 1999 (http://www.welt.de/daten/1999/10/16/10141w133616.htx).
LaCapra, Dominick 1994: *Representing the Holocaust: History, Theory, Trauma*. Ithaca: Cornell University Press.

—— 1998: *History and Memory after Auschwitz*. Ithaca: Cornell University Press.

Lappin, Elena 1999: 'The Man with Two Heads', *Granta* 66, 7–65.

Lau, Jörg 1998: 'Ein fast perfekter Schmerz: Die Affäre um Binjamin Wilkomirski zieht weitere Kreise', *Die Zeit*, 17 September 1998.

Laub, Dori 1992a: 'Bearing Witness; or, The Vicissitudes of Listening' in Felman/Laub 1992, 57–74.

—— 1992b: 'An Event Without a Witness: Truth, Testimony and Survival' in Felman/Laub 1992, 75–92.

Mitscherlich, Alexander and Margarete 1990: *Die Unfähigkeit zu trauern: Grundlagen kollektiven Verhaltens*. Leipzig: Reclam.

Parkes, Stuart 1998: 'The Language of the Past: Recent Prose Works by Bernhard Schlink, Marcel Beyer, and Friedrich Christian Delius' in Williams/Parkes/Preece 1998, 115–131.

Parry, Ann 1999: 'The caesura of the Holocaust in Martin Amis's *Time's Arrow* and Bernhard Schlink's *The Reader*', *Journal of European Studies* 24, 249–267.

Santner, Eric 1992: 'History Beyond the Pleasure Principle: Some Thoughts on the Representation of Trauma' in Friedlander 1992, 143–154.

Schlant, Ernestine 1999: *The Language of Silence: West German Writers and the Holocaust*. London: Routledge.

Stefan, Cora 1993: *Der Betroffenheitskult. Eine politische Sittengeschichte*. Berlin: Rowohlt.

Williams, Arthur, Stuart Parkes and Julian Preece (eds) 1998: *Whose Story?: Continuities in contemporary German-language Literature*. Bern: Peter Lang.

GÜNTER GRASS SINCE THE *WENDE*:
GERMAN AND INTERNATIONAL

BEATRICE PETZ

I Introduction

The decision of the Swedish jury to award the last Nobel Prize for Literature of the twentieth century to Günter Grass would seem to imply that the works of the veteran of German post-war literature are both popular (although not in the sense of *Trivialliteratur*) and international. Persistently high sales figures and translations into many languages also attest to the popularity of his works both in Germany and abroad. However, the popularity is by no means universal, except perhaps in the sense that Grass is the German writer whom some critics and other public figures most love to hate — notwithstanding some apparent coat-turning when prominent people were interviewed for television after the announcement of the Nobel Prize. Grass's work has always ruffled feathers; since the *Wende* it would appear that the criticism has become sharper and more personal in tone, and not only in the German media. At the 1999 Sydney German Studies Symposium, for example, the side-swipes taken at 'the most original and versatile writer alive today' (John Irving cit. Mews 1983, x)[1] by both Australian and international scholars were so numerous that one wondered whether the word-field around the term 'granny-bashing' might not be extended to include 'Grass-bashing'. For the most part, however, criticism of Grass centres on what is perceived as his refusal to move with the times and stop harping on about the National Socialist legacy, especially now that the Wende has supposedly brought the post-war period to an end. In this essay it is contended that Grass does indeed move with the times and that his novels, *Unkenrufe* (1992) and *Ein weites Feld* (1995) may read as evidence of this.[2]

The unification of Germany was welcomed by many, including critics like Frank Schirrmacher (1990) and Ulrich Greiner (1990), as an historical watershed which entailed release from the pressures of *Gesinnungsästhetik*. David Roberts has shown how Gesinnungsästhetik is a category that applies to a period when writers felt obliged to take a position in relation 'zum öffentlichen Verbrauch der Historie, zur kritischen Funktion der Literatur und zum morali-schen Engagement in der demokratischen Erneuerung der Gesellschaft: d.h. die Verpflichtung eben zu einer Gesinnungsästhetik, die von der Erfahrung und dem Bewußtsein der Folgen eines verbrecherischen Nationalismus nicht zu

trennen ist' (Roberts 1994, 236). For Greiner and Schirrmacher Gesinnungsästhetik was merely a 'Vernunftehe' (Greiner 1991, 211) of literature and morality. Their calls for a new German literature, which had begun even before the
Wende, seemed to find legitimation in the political events of 1989–1990. In
their view the literature of engagement, which had arisen out of the reaction
against a literature tarnished by complicity or silence in the face of immense
immorality, had run its course, and was due to be replaced by a 'depoliticized'
literature (Bullivant 1994, 182). Just as the changes in German literature in the
early post-war period were slow to emerge, and just as that new literature
required a new generation to bring it into being, there are signs that now, too, a
radically new literature is a concomitant of a generational changing of the guard
(Bullivant 1994, 13–32; 161–162). Yet as we scan the literary landscape in
search of new developments in the train of the political and social upheaval
surrounding the Wende there are some changes discernible in the work of the
'old guard' — although not of the kind advocated by the critics just mentioned,
who, using Gesinnungsästhetik as a 'Knüppelwort' (Grass 16, 366), would
condemn engaged literature, with its commitment to extra-literary values, to the
historical scrap heap as both a sham and no longer relevant.

   Given such sentiments, and the obituaries for the respective literatures of
East and West Germany, one might well have expected to observe a move away
from 'German' themes. It is, of course, not surprising that Grass has experienced no release from his perceived obligation to keep Germany's history in the
public domain, or that he has refused to present the reading public with 'eine
pflegeleichte Literatur, die Pfötchen gibt' (Grass 16, 336). What Habermas
(1986) calls the 'public use of history' remains a persistent feature of Grass's
literary output in which the processes and consequences of Germany's past continue to find expression. This essay will attempt to show that Grass's concern
with history since unification goes beyond specifically German problems, and
beyond history itself, to embrace an issue that has been the subject of international debate for the last three decades or so, namely the problematical nature
of the representation of historical events and processes. It will be seen that
Grass's work is at once German and international, for it places German history
and its telling within the context of this international discussion. From this point
of view it is possible, moreover, to speak of the new and the old in Grass's
narrative fiction because of the different ways in which the theme of historical
representation is developed. This is an aspect of Grass's post-unification fiction
that does not seem to have been accorded much attention to date. A possible
explanation for what appears to be a lack of interest or awareness of this

particular supra-national dimension might be found in the Gesinnungsästhetik of the critics, whose expectations determine their reading of Grass's work as representations of domestic political issues, and thus deprive other features of the works of the recognition they deserve.

From our vantage point at the turn of the century it can be observed that a distinguishing characteristic of Grass's prose fiction of the last decade has been the appearance of a new type of narrator figure. The narrators in the works written during the 1970s and 1980s are constructed using a stylistic device that invites the reader to identify the narrator figures with their creator. This is an affect of style that gives the reader the feeling that s/he has been given access not only to the world of the fictional characters, but also personal access to the author's own 'real' world — a technique that undoubtedly exacerbated a practice about which Grass complained in his Sonning Prize speech, only a few years later, when he likened his 'I' to a collector's specimen which could not evade 'jene berufsnotorischen Spürnasen, die in jedem zweiten Nebensatz den Autor zu hören meinen und die dessen Ich schon längst aufgespießt und zwischen anderen Schmetterlingen in Kästchen gesperrt haben' (Grass 16, 448). One could extend Grass's butterfly metaphor and say that if the narrators of the works of the 1970s and 1980s had distinctive markings to make them resemble their creator, the narrators that Grass has created in the 1990s appear decidedly unmarked in terms of personal identity. They are not created in the image of their maker, nor do they assert their personal identity within their fictional worlds as the narrators of Grass's works of the 1950s and 1960s do. The first-person narrator of *Unkenrufe* (1992), Grass's first post-Wende work, is a singularly colourless fellow. He does not give his name, and it is hard for the reader to determine the 'true' relationship between him and the story he tells, and between him and the main protagonist.[3] In fact, he is so sketchily defined that he barely rated a mention in reviews of the work.[4] The anonymity of the narrators is even more extreme in Grass's following work, *Ein weites Feld* (1995). Here there are a number of narrators who usually refer to themselves in the first person plural, but sometimes the first person singular is used. Although changing to the singular would necessitate a transition from one narrating voice to another, the transitions are not marked, so that the narrators maintain their individual anonymity. None of them has been given a name, and we do not even know how many there are. The presentation of the stories in *Mein Jahrhundert* by means of a 'choir' (Grass in Geisler 1999) of narrating voices also precludes the development of individual narrators of the kind found in Grass's earlier work.[5] The colourless, in some aspects even marginal, nature of the narrator figures in the works of the 1990s contributes to a certain tension between the narrators and the stories they tell, as their position on the margins, or outside of the action, conflicts with their central significance to the narratives as first-person narrators. The tension can be resolved, however, if the narrative process itself is taken to be a central concern of the works under consideration.

In order to view the narrative process it is necessary to separate it temporarily from the subject matter of the narratives and to concentrate on the texts as discourse. To do so is to be concerned, like Seymour Chatman in his theoretical work on the nature of narrative, 'with form, rather than content, or with content when it is expressible as form' (1978, 10). Chatman explains how narratives have two major constitutive elements: story and discourse. The story is the content of the narrative, or *what* the narrative depicts. The discourse is the means by which, or *how* the story is communicated (19). The narrator, regardless of the degree of her/his involvement *in* the narrative, is the vehicle for its discourse aspect, and therefore provides the key to the interesting aspect of Grass's new prose fiction being addressed here. Viewed from the perspective of their discourse both *Unkenrufe* and *Ein weites Feld* can be read as dramatizations of the process of history writing. The narrator of *Unkenrufe* is commissioned by Alexander Reschke to write up the history of the Reconciliation Cemeteries Association on the basis of a bundle of primary material which Reschke posts to the narrator shortly before his death in a single-vehicle motor accident. The narrators of *Ein weites Feld* are a group of archivists who bring an historical figure back to life and engage in various decidedly unorthodox kinds of behaviour for their profession as they tell their story.

As Grass's use of first-person narrators is critical in both works, it will be helpful to review some of the aspects of first-person narration that contribute to its aptness for the kinds of concerns that these works address. According to Franz K. Stanzel's narrator typology, first-person narrators present the fictional world from their own vantage point within that fictional world, so their representation of it is marked by uncorrected subjectivity and fallibility (1985, 24). Their representation is also determined by the existential link between their own subjective experience and the process of telling the story. Nilli Diengott has shown that Stanzel's model is mimetic, as it supposes 'person-like' narrators and is couched in terminology that is steeped in psychological and existential bias: subjectivity, credibility, embodiment, deixis, motivation and so on (1987, 523–534). Therefore, we can say that the dramatization of the subjectivity of perception performed by first-person narration, as described by Stanzel, is an imitation of reality. This is what makes Stanzel's model of first-person narration so useful for my focus on the narrative process in Grass's work. The substantial contribution of the storytelling process itself to the meaning of the literary work can easily be overlooked by the reader who is eager to find out 'what happened, and what happened next'. So, while it is certainly true that the story of Alexandra and Alexander's project and their wheeling and dealing with death and Deutschmarks forms a substantial component of *Unkenrufe*, and that *Ein weites Feld* is about the revival or continuing presence of 'the Immortal', Theodor Fontane, and some hallmarks of his age that can be found in the Berlin of 1990, it is also true that the manner in which these are conveyed to the reader by the first-person narrators has meaning as well.

Although the basic structure of *Unkenrufe* is easy to categorize as a 'Rahmenerzählung' because it is structured on the principle of the narrator telling a story on the basis of material he receives, a too hasty dismissal of the 'frame' as such, would be to disregard the importance of the narrator's difficulties in his task as historiographer. The frame in this work is a means by which the constructed nature of historical accounts is foregrounded, as can be shown if we approach *Unkenrufe* focusing on the *process* by which the reader is informed, that is, on *how* the story of Alexander and Alexandra and their Reconciliation Cemeteries Association is conveyed, rather than on *what* is conveyed. This approach does not imply a blurring of the ontological categories of reality and fiction as far as the book *Unkenrufe* itself is concerned. Rather, the narrator's implicit presentation of himself as an historiographer within the fictional world of the text is understood as mimetic, that is, as 'die Interpretation des Wirklichen durch literarische Darstellung oder "Nachahmung"' (Auerbach 1946, 494). It is a representation in fiction of the real process of writing history and what it entails. The narrator's utterances are understood, to use Käte Hamburger's term, as 'fingierte Wirklichkeitsaussage' (1957, 271–277).

II *Unkenrufe*

Unkenrufe begins with this short paragraph:

> Der Zufall stellte den Witwer neben die Witwe. Oder spielte kein Zufall mit, weil ihre Geschichte auf Allerseelen begann? Jedenfalls war die Witwe schon zur Stelle, als der Witwer anstieß, stolperte, doch nicht zu Fall kam (12, 7).

The position of these three sentences in a paragraph of their own at the beginning of the text imbues them with thematic importance.[6] Yet there is little tangible information to be found in them. In fact, they present the reader with a lack of information, with gaps. Who is speaking? Who is the widow, who the widower? Why did he stumble, and where? There are gaps for the narrator too, but they are of an entirely different kind. The fact that a widower stumbled and a widow was there seems to be of less importance to him than the question as to how to interpret this event. Moreover, the choices for interpretation that he sees open to him do not lie in the category of immediate physical causes, like an uneven pavement, or a shove from a passer-by, but in terms of universal causes: *Zufall*, or, as the mention of the date as being All Soul's Day suggests, *Fügung*. The narrator has a conundrum that causes him to stumble into the narrative in the same way as his protagonist stumbles into the story.

The brief opening paragraph is, in fact, a very concise presentation of an event and its cause — those elements which E. M. Forster described as the two aspects of plot (1927, 16). Here, however, there is a significant variation: the narrator presents the reader with an event and a *search* for a cause. The narrator is certain as far as the event is concerned; he is uncertain as to how to explain it. The presentation of the choice between two possible interpretations opens out, as the work progresses, to embrace the problematic distinction between 'historical' and 'fictional' discourse, as well as some of the fundamental issues associated with understanding and writing about history. This occurs in the story as well as in the discourse aspects of the work. On the story level the liberal use of actual events, real people, significant dates in German history and clearly described real locations encourages the reader to read the work as an historical novel. The fantastic excesses of the plot, like Reschke's 'Zeitsprünge', the international success of Chatterjee's enterprise, or the erection of cool storage facilities to house the disinterred remains of displaced people, work against such a reading.

On the discourse level, Grass strengthens the 'historical' feeling of the novel by making many of the narrator's statements conform to the epistemological constraints that would apply to a biographer or historian who writes within the discourse of history. The narrator often admits, for example, that he does not know certain facts because he can find no record of them in the documents. These unknown 'facts' range from the make of Reschke's car to information about Reschke's feelings and intentions. In such cases, the narrator's recourse is to conjectural and inferential statements like, 'Ich frage mich, ob er seine Währung kopfrechnend in Vergleich zu den vielstelligen Zahlen der Zloty-Scheine gebracht […] hat' (12, 12), and, 'Das Spielen mit dem Computer muß Reschke Spaß bereitet haben' (12, 94). Not only do such expressions serve as reminders that the narrator is, as he calls himself, only the

'Berichtender' (12, 87), an 'Außenstehender' (12, 92), they also imbue the rest of the narrator's account with an air of historical authenticity.

In her 'Fictional *versus* Historical Lives: Borderlines and Borderline Cases', Dorrit Cohn observes that 'the reason why a biographer tends to favor the must-have construction is that it allows him to look inside his subject's mind without transforming him into an imaginary being'. She points out that 'the *form* of an inferential statement puts a stamp of historicity on the text that contains it' (1989, 10), and that 'in a novel, it is the reversion to quasi-factual discourse [...] that draws attention to itself' (1989, 9). Thus it is that our attention is drawn, (or could be drawn) to the discourse aspect of *Unkenrufe*. However, the *Unkenrufe* narrator's mimicking of the language of historical discourse is undermined at times by his apparent inability to approach his task dispassionately, by the freedom with which he handles his 'props', like Reschke's beret for example (12, 14; 16; 60), and by the instances where he suspends the passage of time — 'So bleiben sie stehen. Oder: so stehen die beiden mir, damit ich mich gewöhne, ein Weilchen und noch ein Weilchen Modell' (11–12).

Unkenrufe is far from being merely the story, or history of the Reconciliation Cemeteries, as it has been *re*-presented by most critics. Rather, the text is the narrator's presentation of himself in his activity as historian. His historical method conforms in part to that of the narrative historian as described by Hayden White, namely in 'the investigation of the documents in order to determine what is the true or most plausible story that can be told about the events of which they are evidence' (1987, 27). But as both White and the fiction of *Unkenrufe* show, the task is much more complex.

The narrator's investigation of the evidence leads to a kind of dialogue between himself and his image or projection of Reschke. The two most significant aspects of the dialogue revolve around the clash between Reschke's and the narrator's world views, and the influence of the conflicting motivations of the commissioner of the history, on the one hand, and the writer of the history, on the other. These are some of the issues which impinge repeatedly on the narrator as he tries to write the history of the Reconciliation Cemeteries. Grass has long been concerned with the problems of historiography, commenting in 1977, 'wie sehr unsere Geschichtsschreibung, die sich als authentisch ausgibt, weil sie auf Dokumentation fußt, Fiktion ist: nicht zugegebene Fiktion' (Arnold 1978, 31). At that time his concern was with the tendentious nature of historical documents, and the fact that they had only survived by chance. He saw it as the fiction writer's task to fill the gaps left by conventional historiography, and 'genauere Fakten zu erfinden, als die, die uns angeblich authentisch überliefert wurden' (Arnold 1978, 31).[7] Since the Wende, and the *Historikerstreit* of the 1980s, that 'seismographische Antizipation des Kommenden' (Roberts 1994, 237), issues of much wider historiographical relevance are to be found in Grass's prose fiction.

As we become privy to the narrator's concerns about his task in *Unkenrufe*, the relevance of some of White's other observations about history writing becomes clear: 'Narrative is not merely a neutral discursive form that may or may not be used to represent real events in their aspect as developmental processes but entails ontological and epistemic choices with distinct ideological and even specifically political implications' (1987, ix). As we have seen, in the opening paragraph of *Unkenrufe* it is with just such choices that the narrator is confronted. He cannot begin to tell the story with authority until he has decided which world view his history is to be based upon. Because he cannot decide between the world views that are subsumed under the terms Fügung on the one hand, and Zufall on the other, the narrator is condemned to presenting two accounts of events — one in keeping with each world view. The narrator presents the first of these world views, that which Reschke espouses, in the form of his selection of excerpts from Reschke's diaries, and also in his reconstruction of events from Reschke's point of view. Some of the incidents thus presented are then described again from the narrator's point of view. A good example of this can be seen in the two descriptions of Alexander and Alexandra's first meeting. The narrator describes the lovers' first meeting as follows: 'Er stellte sich neben sie. Schuhgröße dreiundvierzig neben Schuhgröße siebenunddreißig' (12, 7). The antagonism between the two world views is clear from the narrator's remark that it was Reschke's diary that had 'given away' the sizes of the couple's shoes (12, 7). In other words, by including commonplace details in his diary Reschke had furnished the narrator with the means of presenting events in a banal manner completely devoid of the instrumentality which we will see is characteristic of Reschke's presentation of events. In contrast to the narrator's presentation of the meeting as, 'bigger feet beside smaller feet' (an image that calls to mind television footage of the commonplace, chaotic movement of feet, filmed at pavement level) Reschke's description of the event in his diary reads: 'Es mag an diesem Tag, zu dieser Stunde — schlag zehn Uhr — Fügung gewesen sein, die uns zusammen führte' (12, 7). The narrator's satirical remarks reveal his leaning towards a world view that understands events as being determined by chance. He casts scorn on Reschke's world view by referring to Fügung, or providence, as 'die dritte, stumm vermittelnde Person' (12, 7). When Alexander discovers that his new acquaintance has a name which matches his own, his belief in Fügung is further reinforced. For the narrator, on the other hand, Alexandra and Alexander remain 'dieses vom Zufall verkuppelte Paar (12, 21). The reader cannot be certain which account of events, each relying on a different world view, is legitimate, especially as the narrator's indecision causes his manner of narration to become a constant *sous rature*, that is, he crosses out Reschke's account, while ensuring that it remains visible.[8] This also has the effect of preventing the reader from privileging one world view over the other. On a more prosaic level, the reader is uncertain whether the narrator is simply rude and lacking in respect for Reschke's noble enterprise; or whether Reschke is just a pompous old fool with a uncanny gift for making money. Only by making moral decisions of their own can readers find their way in the two contradictory worlds which exist simultaneously in Grass's *Erzählung* — the narrator's chaotic world of chance occurrences and Reschke's world whose processes are determined by Fügung.

Readers who concentrate on the story aspect of the text seem to pass over these incongruities, constructing their own version of what must have happened. For readers who concentrate on the discourse aspect of the text, the play of possibilities enriches the text with its metahistorical implications. Another contributing factor is the way Grass uses first-person narration in the work, for unlike most first-person narrators, the narrator of *Unkenrufe* is not a direct eye-witness to the events he must describe. The main protagonists of his story are presumably dead at the time he begins his work, so his knowledge of events is second-hand, derived from Reschke's documents and statements made by other parties. He therefore lacks the authority that the first-person narrator-as-eye-witness can enjoy. The uncertainty is further complicated by issues of guilt and indebtedness between the two men. The sources of these obligations are hinted at in fragments of information from which readers must draw their own conclusions. The only authority that the narrator does have lies in the documents in front of him, but as Grass's observations cited above show, this is a dubious authority. Furthermore, White's observations indicate that real historiography requires much more than this raw material. Epistemological and ontological choices must be made concerning the significance and meaning of the 'data' before the historian can construct the story which will become the historical record.

The information that what Reschke is asking of the narrator is a *chronicle* of the Reconciliation Cemeteries is reserved until close to the end of the work, where its importance is stressed by the repetition of the word (five times in a page and a half of text; 12, 293–294). This is the piece of information from which the conflict of world views presented in the opening sentences, and which runs as an undercurrent throughout the story, receives its poignancy, for the traditional chronicle would not require the narrator to choose between Zufall and Fügung to fulfil his task, as it merely lists events in the temporal order of their occurrence. The traditional chronicle was informed by an underlying belief in a master-plan, the *göttlicher Heilsplan*, to which all events conform. It was this world view which gave the events their *plot*, their causal link. Although the narrator does not engage in theoretical discussions of the problems of historiography, his sardonic references to plot as he works through Reschke's documents tie his deliberations in with the international debates of the last decades about the nature of historical discourse.[9]

The narrator of *Unkenrufe* seems to take for granted that a plot must be imposed upon the events in order to make them into a story for his history of the Reconciliation Cemeteries Association. According to White, plot, that aspect of narrative which 'imposes a meaning on the events that make up its story level by revealing at the end a structure that was immanent in events all along', is a means by which historical stories can be given narrative closure, but only at the expense of portraying a world whose completeness and fullness we can only imagine, but never experience. Plot is therefore an embarrassment to historical narrative, giving to reality 'the odor of the ideal' (White 1987, 20–21).

> The embarrassment of plot to the historical narrative is reflected in the all but universal disdain with which modern historians regard the 'philosophy of history' of which Hegel is the modern paradigmatic example. This [...] form of historical representation is condemned because it consists of nothing but plot; its story elements exist only as manifestations, epiphenomena of the plot structure, in the service of which its discourse is disposed. Here reality wears a face of such regularity, order and coherence that it leaves no room for human agency. (White 1987, 21)

This seems to be the sort of approach that Reschke would have liked the narrator to take in his account of the Reconciliation Cemetery Association. Reschke's view of the world is 'verhegelt', to use Grass's term from *Aus dem Tagebuch einer Schnecke* (7, 50). Grass rejects Hegel's world view: 'Dessen Hineininterpretieren von Sinn in die Geschichte liegt mir genausowenig wie die Vorstellung von der ewigen Wiederkehr, mit der man die völlige Hoffnungslosigkeit des Geschichtsprozesses versinnbildlicht. Ich glaube, daß die Geschichte ein absurder Prozeß ist, aus dem zu lernen schwer fällt' (Köhler/ Sandmeyer 1995, 59). The narrator's approach to the historiographical exercise with which he has been entrusted in *Unkenrufe* illustrates White's description of 'emplotment' in the historical narrative. The historian is faced with a chaotic mass of events that are '*already constituted*', and from these he must choose elements for his story. This entails the selection and rejection of events, as well as processes of subordination and stress. These processes are carried out 'in the interest of creating *a story of a particular kind.*' (White 1973, 6; original emphasis). Emplotment is the way in which a sequence of events fashioned into a story is gradually revealed to be a story of a particular kind — Romance, Tragedy, Comedy, or Satire (1973, 7). All of these employ some form of closure. The lack of closure, the open-endedness, of much of Grass's prose fiction is explained in part by Grass's statements in an interview with Manfred Durzak, in which he spoke of his belief in the necessity of expanding our understanding of history to include the absurd, the disparate, and the contradictory. He also expressed the view that such an approach would not have appeared strange to historians like Burckhardt and Mommsen (Durzak 1985, 16). White's description of Burckhardt's approach to historiography explains why Grass would find it attractive, for White associates Burckhardt's approach with a move from processionary history to structural history, in which 'the element of theme tends to override the element of plot, at least insofar as plot may be conceived to be the strategy by which an *unfolding* story is articulated' (1973, 230; original emphasis). Paradoxically, *Unkenrufe* can be seen as a work in which there is closure in the form of the deaths of the main protagonists. This apparent closure, however, makes the discourse aspect of *Unkenrufe*, that is, the way the narrator tells the story, resemble White's description of one mode of 'explanation by emplotment' namely that of tragedy.

Despite his early references to 'plot' the narrator of *Unkenrufe* seems to feel towards the end of the work that he has succeeded in resisting the lure of 'novelistic' or 'romanhafte' representation. However, the events with which the narrator chooses to end his account show that he has not succeeded in freeing himself from the explanatory patterns of the archetypes listed above. Although he expresses the desire, 'meinem Bericht hier den Schlußpunkt zu setzen', asking: 'Ist den nicht alles gesagt?' (12, 294) he finds that he cannot end his report at that stage. If his account were really a chronicle, he could end it at any stage, because the chronicle does not require closure. But the narrator's aim is to write a story, to provide explanations, not merely a record of events. He says: 'Ich habe versucht, mich nicht einzumischen. Allzu romanhafte Ausflüge konnte ich mir verkneifen. Aber mußtet ihr unbedingt diese Hochzeitsreise machen, verdammt!' (12, 298). It is as if the narrator is blaming the protagonists for the form his account takes, namely, that of the tragedy. Indeed, it is now easy to see, as White described in his explanation of plot, that the structure of tragedy was 'immanent in events all along' (1987, 20). It is not only Alexander and Alexandra's deaths in fulfilment of the saying 'See Naples and die', and Alexandra's prophetic, 'Na, wenn ich schon gesehn hab' Neapel, kann ich ja sterben gleich' (12, 181), that indicate a tragic mode of emplotment. It now becomes clear that the narrator's manner of portraying the fictitious world within the text simultaneously from two points of view serves a second purpose beyond that of dramatizing the fact that ontological and epistemological choices underlie representations of history even in such a minor form as his history of the Reconciliation Cemeteries Association. The narrator's ambiguous presentation of Alexander and Alexandra which has been shown to proceed from his inability to make these choices, simultaneously facilitates the presentation of the two main protagonists, his hero and heroine, as being neither thoroughly good, nor thoroughly bad, but a mixture of both, in the manner of tragic heroes. Reschke's *hubris*, and the couple's decision not to retain the right of veto at Association meetings now assume significance as *hamartia*. The fourth and central chapter of *Unkenrufe* provides a virtual plethora of statements that can be interpreted as the ignored divine warning in the tradition of the classical tragedy. The most significant of these is, of course, the excursus on the role of the *Unke* as a prophetess of doom, which is indebted for its detail to one of Grass's favourite sources, *Grimms Wörterbuch*. But they also include Reschke's observations, '[...] wir bekommen die Quittung für unser Tun und Nichtstun, wenn nicht morgen, dann übermorgen' (124); and 'Glaub mir, Alexandra, wie der Raps zu früh blüht, rufen Rotbauchunken und Gelbbauchunken zu früh. Sie wollen uns etwas sagen' (12, 127); not to mention the narrator's insightful 'Doch nicht nur der zu früh blühende Raps gab seine Vorahnung' (125). Moreover, Reschke's political intransigence is prefigured in the way he refuses to react appropriately to Alexandra's complaint, 'Mich fressen mücken auf!' (12, 127). In Chapter 5 there is an ironic evocation of pity for the tragic hero when the narrator exclaims: 'Reschke, der arme Reschke' (12, 202).

Tragedy is a mode of emplotment which is consonant with the interests of those historians who conceive of events as belonging to 'an ongoing structure of relationships or an eternal return of the Same in the Different' (White 1973, 11). It is therefore not surprising that tragedy is the archetype that informs the narrator's approach to the task of constructing a story from Reschke's documents. His view of history as cyclic and absurd, as expressed by such off-hand remarks as 'Die wenigen Touristen und einige betende Polen verloren sich in der Hallenkirche, deren neugespanntes Gewölbe von sechsundzwanzig achteckigen Freipfeilern bis zur nächsten Zerstörung getragen wird' (12, 60) — is a view not unlike that expressed by Grass himself: 'Mein Geschichtverständnis ist nicht resignativ, es ist skeptisch. Es ist ein den absurden Prozeß mithineinbeziehendes Verständnis, das aber nicht mit Fatalismus abgetan werden darf' (Hofer 1995, 443).

As the narrator is forced by his work on the history of the Cemeteries Project to engage more and more with the events of the past that led to the desire for cemeteries for exilees in the first place, he finds himself unable to maintain the divided stance that has demanded his continual presentation of two world views. In a rare outburst of emotion he breaks off his account of Alexandra and Alexander's activities, as he recalls events towards the end of the war, how he and Reschke were thrown into the *Endkampf* in 1944 (12, 263–264): 'Und zufällig — Reschke, hörst du! — rein zufällig, nicht dank höherer Fügung, kamen wir davon, überlebten wir, blieben wir bis auf ein paar Schrammen heil und retteten uns in den Westen' (12, 264). The narrator's insistence that he and Reschke survived by chance coincides closely with Grass's conviction that he only survived the war, and indeed was only able to remain innocent, by chance — a view that he has repeated many times over the years (e.g. Arnold 1978, 3; Grass X, 166; Grass 16, 447).

The novel ends on an ambivalent note, so typical of Grass's prose fiction, with a satirical twist which seems to cast doubt on the adequacy of the tragic mode of emplotment as an explanation of the events. The narrator's story, which, in mapping out Reschke's childhood, youth, manhood and death, is as much a biography as an account of the Reconciliation Cemeteries Association, conforms so well to White's explanation of the tragic mode as 'a revelation of the nature of the forces opposing man' (1973, 10), and the view that 'the reconciliations that occur at the end of Tragedy [...] are more in the nature of resignations of men to the conditions under which they must labor in the world', and that these conditions 'set the limits on what may be aspired to and what may be legitimately aimed at in the quest for security and sanity in the world' (1973, 9). Yet the narrator relativizes these conditions of tragedy with an ironical question slipped into the middle of a crucial sentence about Alexander and Alexandra's deaths: 'Auf einer kurvenreicher Strecke muß es sie — doch wer ist Es? — aus der Kurve getragen haben' (12, 299). Given that in his outburst about having survived the war by chance the narrator has committed himself to a world view which rejects Reschke's belief in Fügung, there is only one answer to this question within the framework suggested by the text as a whole, and that is Zufall.

III Conclusion

The narrator's impassioned commitment in *Unkenrufe* to Zufall in connection with his war experience is followed immediately by a cryptic hint about the narrator's identity (cf. Petz 1999) that directs the informed reader towards the works of the Danzig Trilogy and their central concern with *Vergangenheits-bewältigung*. However, to understand this as simply a reversion to old themes, or to call it 'more of the same' would be to ignore significant developments in Grass's fiction writing, for there are two important differences that distinguish Grass's post-Wende writing from that which went before. The first difference concerns the international discourses which have a bearing on his writing. The earlier works can be placed under the heading of 'metafiction'. They conform to Patricia Waugh's description of such works as being 'constructed on the principle of a fundamental and sustained opposition: the construction of a fictional illusion (as in traditional realism) and the laying bare of that illusion' (1995, 43). Two frequently cited examples of this in Grass's early prose fiction are Oskar's references in *Die Blechtrommel* to such technical concerns as where to begin his novel, and to the importance of the hero in the novel despite assertions that heroes in novels are no longer possible (3, 12); and in *Katz und Maus*, Pilenz's reference to the fact that someone invented him 'von berufswegen' (4, 6). In this way these works, and their narrators in particular, draw attention to their ontological status as fiction. This is not the case with the two post-Wende novels. In *Unkenrufe* and *Ein weites Feld* it is not the texts' own fictionality to which attention is drawn, but rather the fictive nature of historical recon-structions, and the uncertain ontological status of historical discourse in general to which the texts draw attention. They dramatize some of the concerns of the international discourse of 'metahistory', and are informed by an underlying interest in how historical events and the documents which provide the raw data come into being, and how these raw data are incorporated during the process of historiography. They are illustrations of Louis Mink's statement: 'It is salutary to be reminded that historiography is a matter of fallible inference and inter-pretation, but the reminder does not touch the point of the common-sense distinction between history and fiction' (1978, 131).

While *Unkenrufe* is clearly a work of fiction, the piece of writing that its narrator has been asked to produce within the fictional world that Grass creates in *Unkenrufe* is to be 'history'. But the insight that the text gives us into how that piece of history comes into being casts a degree of doubt on the ontological status of the narrator's history of the Reconciliation Cemeteries Association, despite the fact that we, as readers, are not privileged with a view of the narrator's finished work of historiography. The narrator's commentary points up the inadequacy of 'the common-sense distinction between history and fiction' that Mink describes, and demonstrates White's concern that 'where the aim in view is the telling of a story, the problem of narrativity turns on the issue of whether historical events can truthfully be represented as manifesting the structures and processes of events met with more commonly in certain kinds of "imaginative" discourses, that is, such fictions as the epic, the folk tale, myth, romance, tragedy, comedy, farce, and the like' (White 1987, 27).

The narrator is obliged by Reschke to produce an account which is supposed to be an historical record of true events (true within the fictional world), namely, the founding and subsequent development of the German–Polish– Lithuanian Reconciliation Cemeteries Association. His enterprise is threatened on two fronts, one particular and one general. Firstly, there is the fact that the history has been commissioned to achieve a particular aim. The reason why first Wrobel and then the other founders of the Association want the history of the Reconciliation Cemeteries to be written in the first place, is because they believe that it will vindicate them — 'Solche Chronik möge alles zurecht-rücken' (12, 293). This is a condition that has the potential to preclude the report from being objective, especially in the light of the narrator's indebtedness to Reschke. Secondly, doubt is raised concerning the possibility of 'true' representations in general in the light of the wider ontological and epistemological considerations described above. With the narrator of *Unkenrufe* Grass has created an historian whose approach to his task illustrates what White describes as 'the fictive character of historical reconstructions', which has been stressed by 'continental European thinkers from Valéry and Heidegger to Sartre, Lévi-Strauss, and Michel Foucault' (White, 1973, 1–2).

The second important difference between Grass's post-unification works and his earlier ones concerns stylistic choices with regard to the narrator types. The narrators of his earliest works, with their very distinctive personalities, their names, family trees and so on, drew attention to themselves both as highly idiosyncratic characters central to the texts which they narrated, as well as fictional entities. The narrators of the 1970s and 1980s with their resemblance to Grass himself continue this in some ways, but may also be interpreted as a resistance to the (international) critical tendencies associated with Roland Barthes's 'La mort de l'auteur' (Barthes 1977, 142–148), with their presentation of a representation of the author within the texts themselves. David Roberts notes, for example, in *Aus dem Tagebuch einer Schnecke* 'hat sich Grass in der ersten Person seiner Gegenwart, seiner Präsenz schreibend versichert (Roberts 1994,

242). What we see in *Unkenrufe* and *Ein weites Feld*, however, is the appearance of a new type of narrator; and with this new narrator type a substantial shift in emphasis. The absence of names and other information about the narrators in the newer works is a device that directs attention away from the narrators as individuals towards the narrators as performers of a specific, socially and politically relevant task — namely the collation of historical documents and the interpretation of these documents. In short: historiography. As individuals the narrators of *Unkenrufe* and *Ein weites Feld* are forgettable. Something one could never say of Oskar, Pilenz, or the fictional Grass in his space capsule in *Die Rättin*. In the post-Wende novels there is a shift in emphasis away from the 'selves', from the individual identities of the narrators towards an emphasis on a specific social and historical 'role' as the new, unnamed, relatively undefined narrators attempt to grasp and shape the chaotic events of which 'history' is made up. Thus, while both of the new works cited are 'about' German issues, and I am certainly not suggesting that these issues are of secondary importance to the matters I have discussed here, the works are simultaneously representations of a concern which is international, and that is the challenge of historiography, the possible modes of the presentation and understanding of history, and the ends which it serves. The narrator of *Unkenrufe* shows the reader historiography 'from below', employing some of the conventions of factual discourse while flaunting others. His simulated naiveté as an historiographer, and his satire (not only of the protagonist Reschke, but also of his own narrative) unmask the dependence of narrative historiography on ontological, epistemological, moral and aesthetic choices.

Notes
I am indebted to Jonathan Long whose approach to the problems associated with the intersection of fictional and historical discourses (Long 1996) provided a stepping-off point for one section of this article. Any misconceptions, however, are my own.
1. cf. 'John Irving gegen Reich-Ranicki', an interview with Sven Bürgel in: *Prinz*, October 1995, reprinted in Negt, 1996 445–449.
2. These two works have been discussed previously in this series by Paver (2000) and Stolz (1998) respectively. The approaches are quite different from mine here.
3. I am aware of Volker Neuhaus's view that the narrator of *Unkenrufe* is a fictionalized version of Günter Grass, like the narrators of the works since *Aus dem Tagebuch einer Schnecke* (Neuhaus 1993, 187), but, for reasons which I have elaborated briefly elsewhere (see Petz 1999), I do not share that view. cf. also Mayer 1993.
4. Most reviewers and critics described *Unkenrufe* simply as a story told in the first-person by an old school friend about a geriatric love affair between Alexandra and Alexander and their remarkable Reconciliation Cemeteries scheme.
5. I am grateful to Dieter Stolz for the observation that *Mein Jahrhundert* conforms to the periodization of Grass's work suggested here.
6. Grass has frequently referred to the importance of the opening sentence. See, for example, Köhler/ Sandmeyer, 1995, 58.

7. See Bond/Preece, 1992 for an excellent description of how Grass employs history and its documentation in his earlier work.
8. The term 'sous rature' (under erasure) is used by Derrida in *Of Grammatology* (1967). He places a large X over some words so that they are crossed out but remain legible. Such words must still be read as part of the text. The English translator explains in his 87-page 'Translator's Preface' that Derrida uses this strategy when words or concepts are still valuable as tools, although their truth value is rejected (xiii–xix). 'It is a process of using the only available language while not subscribing to its premises, or operating according to the vocabulary of the very thing that one delimits' (xviii). He also refers to 'the schizophrenia of the "sous rature"' (lxxviii). McHale 1987 draws on Derrida's practice and writes of 'Worlds Under Erasure' (99–111), by which he means a narrative technique in which 'mutually-exclusive states of affairs are projected by the same text' (101).
9. cf. White 1973, 1–2 and 1987, esp. 30–38; also Canary/Kozicki 1978.

Primary texts

Grass, Günter 1997: *Werkausgabe*. Ed. Volker Neuhaus and Daniela Hermes. Göttingen: Steidl.
References in the text by volume and page number are to this edition, unless the volume number is in Roman numerals, in which case the reference is to Günter Grass 1987: *Werkausgabe in zehn Bänden*. Ed. Volker Neuhaus. Darmstadt: Luchterhand.
The volumes referred to in the text are:
Volume 7:   *Aus dem Tagebuch einer Schnecke* (1972)
Volume 12:   *Unkenrufe* (1992)
Volume 13:   *Ein weites Feld* (1995)
Volume 16:   *Essays und Reden* (1980–1997)
Volume X: *Gespräche mit Günter Grass* (1958–1986)

Secondary literature

Anz, Thomas (ed.) 1991: *Es geht nicht nur um Christa Wolf*. Munich: Spangenberg.
Arnold, Heinz Ludwig 1978: 'Gespräche mit Günter Grass' in Arnold (ed.): *Text und Kritik. Zeitschrift für Literatur*, 1/1a, June 1978, 1–39.
Auerbach, Erich 1946: *Mimesis*. Bern: Francke.
Barthes, Roland 1977: 'The Death of the Author' in Barthes: *Image — Music — Text*. Trans. Stephen Heath. New York: Hill and Wang, 142–148. Orig. Roland Barthes: 'La mort de l'auteur' in *Mantéia* V, 1968.
Bond, D. G. and Julian Preece 1992: '"Cap Arcona" 3 May 1945: History and Allegory in Novels by Uwe Johnson and Günter Grass', *Oxford German Studies* 20/21, 1991–1992, 147–163.
Bullivant, Keith 1994: *The Future of German Literature*. Oxford/Providence: Berg.
Canary, Robert H. and Henry Kozicki (eds) 1978: *The Writing of History. Literary Form and Historical Understanding*. Madison: University of Wisconsin Press.
Chatman, Seymour 1978: *Story and Discourse. Narrative Structure in Fiction and Film*. Ithaca: Cornell University Press.
Currie, Mark (ed.) 1995: *Metafiction*. London: Longman.
Derrida, Jacques 1967: *Of Grammatology*. Trans. Gayatri Chakrovorty Spivak. Baltimore/London: John Hopkins University Press.
Diengott, Nilli 1987: 'The Mimetic Language Game and Two Typologies of Narrators', *Modern Fiction Studies* 33/3, Autumn, 523–534.
Durzak, Manfred 1985: 'Geschichte ist absurd. Eine Antwort auf Hegel'. Ein Gespräch mit Günter Grass' in Durzak (ed.): *Zu Günter Grass. Geschichte auf dem poetischen Prüfstand*. Stuttgart: Klett, 9–19.
Forster, E. M. 1927: *Aspects of the Novel*, London: Edward Arnold.

Geissler, Cornelia 1999: 'Hundert Jahre in hundert Geschichten' [Interview with Günter Grass], *Berliner Zeitung*, 7 July 1999.
Greiner, Ulrich 1990: 'Die deutsche Gesinnungsästhetik. Noch einmal: Christa Wolf und der deutsche Literaturstreit. Eine Zwischenbilanz', *Die Zeit*, 2 November 1990.
—— 1991: 'Die deutsche Gesinnungsästhetik' in Anz 1991, 208–216.
Grimms Lexicon 1984. Munich: dtv. (Orig. Leipzig: Hirtel, 1854).
Habermas, Jürgen 1986: 'Vom öffentlichen Gebrauch der Historie', *Die Zeit*, 7 November 1986.
Hamburger, Käte 1957: *Die Logik der Dichtung*. Stuttgart: Klett-Cotta.
Hofer, Hermann 1995: 'Ich sitze nicht auf der Bank der Sieger', *Lübecker Zeitung*, 24. October (Negt 1996, 444–449).
Köhler, Joachim and Peter Sandmeyer 1995: 'Der Leser verlangt nach Zumutungen!', *Stern* 34/1995, 57–61.
Long, Jonathan 1996: 'History as Biography as Fiction: Wolfgang Hildesheimer's *Marbot. Eine Biographie*' in Williams/Parkes/Preece 1996, 31–50.
Lützeler, Paul (ed.) 1994: *Poetik der Autoren. Beiträge zur deutschsprachigen Gegenwartsliteratur*. Frankfurt am Main: Fischer.
Mayer, Sigrid 1993: 'Politische Aktualität nach 1989: Die Polnisch–Deutsch–Litauische Friedhofsgesellschaft oder *Unkenrufe* von Günter Grass', *Amsterdamer Beiträge zur neueren Germanistik* 36, 213–223.
McHale, Brian 1987: *Postmodernist Fiction*. London/New York: Routledge.
Mews, Siegfried 1983: *"The Fisherman and his Wife": Günter Grass's* The Flounder *in Critical Perspective*. New York: AMS.
Negt, Oskar (ed.) 1996: *Der Fall Fonty*. Göttingen: Steidl.
Neuhaus, Volker 1993: *Günter Grass*. 2nd edn. Stuttgart: Metzler.
—— and Daniela Hermes (eds) 1991: *Die 'Danziger Trilogie' von Günter Grass: Texte, Daten, Bilder*. Frankfurt am Main: Luchterhand.
Paver, Chloe E.M. 2000: 'Jesus in the market place: Ethical capitalism in Günter Grass's *Unkenrufe*' in Williams/Parkes/Preece 2000, 71–83.
Petz, Beatrice 1999: 'The Toad and the Toady — Günter Grass's *The Call of the Toad*' in Squires 1999, 79–87.
Roberts, David 1994: '"Gesinnungsästhetik"? Günter Grass, *Schreiben nach Auschwitz* (1990)' in Lützeler 1994, 235–261.
Schirrmacher, Frank 1990: 'Abschied von der Literatur der Bundesrepublik. Neue Pässe, Neue Identitäten, neue Lebensläufe: Über die Kündigung der Mythen des westdeutschen Bewußtseines', *Frankfurter Allgemeine Zeitung*, 2 October 1990.
Squires, G. (ed.) 1999: *Language Literature, Culture. A Selection of Papers Presented at Intercultural Studies '98*. Newcastle (Australia): Dept. of Modern Languages, University of Newcastle.
Stallbaum, Klaus 1991: '"Der vitale und vulgäre Wunsch Künstler zu werden" — ein Gespräch' in Neuhaus/Hermes 1991, 11–33.
Stanzel, Franz K. 1985: *Theorie des Erzählens*. 3rd rev. edn. Göttingen: Vandenhoek & Ruprecht.
Stolz, Dieter 1998: 'Nomen est omen: *Ein weites Feld* by Günter Grass' in Williams/Parkes/Preece 1998, 149–166.
Waugh, Patricia 1995: 'What is Metafiction and Why are They Saying Such Awful Things About it?' in Currie 1995, 39–54.
White, Hayden 1973: *The Historical Imagination in Nineteenth Century Europe*. Baltimore/London: Johns Hopkins University Press.
—— 1987: *The Content of the Form*. Baltimore/London: Johns Hopkins University Press.
Williams, Arthur, Stuart Parkes and Julian Preece (eds) 1996: *Contemporary German Writers, Their Aesthetics and Their Language*. Bern: Peter Lang.
—— (eds) 1998: *'Whose Story?' — Continuities in contemporary German-language Literature*. Bern: Peter Lang.
—— (eds) 2000: *Literature, Markets and Media in Germany and Austria Today*. Bern: Peter Lang.

IMAGES OF SWITZERLAND

IN

SWISS CRIME FICTION

CHRISTOPHER JONES

I Preamble

This essay looks at some recent Swiss crime fiction texts and examines the images of Switzerland presented there, making some suggestions for their interpretation. Popular fiction in Switzerland has been forced to overcome many hurdles as Michael Böhler (1992) shows in his study 'Triviale Lesestoffe in der Schweiz'. At one extreme it has been the target of book burning; at the other even those who read it have felt unable to admit to such a habit. This situation has changed recently and Swiss crime authors have been gaining much recognition outside their homeland over the last decade, thus Peter Zeindler was awarded the Deutscher Krimipreis in 1992 for *Feuerprobe* and Alexander Heimann received the same award in 1997 for *Dezemberföhn*. Wolfgang Bortlik (1999) hints at one of the reasons for this recent resurgence in Swiss crime writing when he associates it with the publication of the works of Friedrich Glauser in a paperback edition (by Arche, in the 1980s).

Glauser is arguably Switzerland's most famous crime writer thanks mainly to his creation of *Wachtmeister* Studer, who combines fatherly warmth with an unswerving determination to get at truth and justice. Some commentators are keen to put Glauser forward as the only key influence on the Swiss tradition. Thus, in the introduction to his *Banken, Blut und Berge* anthology, Zeindler is happy to make the following generalization: 'Schweizer Autoren, in Studers Nachfolge, sind Seelenforscher' (Zeindler 1995, 11). In the course of this essay it will become clear that this oversimplifies the picture considerably and overlooks other strands of at least equal significance and influence.

The only other author with a claim as Switzerland's best known writer of crime fiction is Friedrich Dürrenmatt, on the basis of his 1950s novels: *Der Richter und sein Henker*, *Der Verdacht* and *Das Versprechen*. Dürrenmatt used the genre to consider notions of good and evil, guilt, personal responsibility, and the role of chance in human affairs. Given these higher goals and his more significant work in other genres it is perhaps not entirely appropriate to consider him as a crime writer at all, yet he and Glauser are often regaded as the backbone of a Swiss tradition. For those Swiss writers who have chosen to use the *Kriminalroman* as a vehicle for the purposes of moral enquiry and argument Dürrenmatt remains a key figure; however, it is important not to overestimate the influence of Glauser and Dürrenmatt. Roger Graf, for example, when faced with the interview question: 'Als Schweizer Autor liegt es natürlich nahe, Sie nach Glauser und Dürrenmatt zu fragen' gave the following reply:

> Das ist in der Tat eine Standardfrage. Meist ist sie mit der Frage gekoppelt, wo ich mich selber ansiedle in der Schweizer Krimitradition. Eine lächerliche Frage. Ständig lese ich etwas über eine Schweizer Krimitradition und überall stehen dann die Namen Glauser und Dürrenmatt. Das ist eine lausige Tradition, die sich auf gerade zwei Namen berufen kann, wovon der eine, Dürrenmatt, nebenbei manchmal einen Krimi geschrieben hat. Glauser war toll, Dürrenmatt ebenfalls, wobei ich die Krimis nicht für seine besten Werke halte, aber es gibt keine Krimitradition in der Schweiz. (Graf no date)

While Graf has the utmost regard for both Glauser and Dürrenmatt, it is the attempt to force them into the role of founding fathers to which he objects. The extent to which his own work belongs to a different strand will be considered below in a discussion of it and that of Willy Bär.

Irrespective of tradition, much crime fiction is linked by the use it makes of the past, in many cases resulting in a form of double narrative in which real events are obscured by a narrative deliberately constructed to hinder the investigation of a crime. It is only when the fictitious nature of this second narrative has been revealed that the real course of past events can be discerned. In the four texts under consideration here, it is the treatment of *history* which is a major linking element. In a recent conference paper, Aaron Kelly (1999) put forward the view that the thriller can be regarded as the dominant mode of fictional representation of Northern Ireland. By analysing our four texts it may become possible to suggest a similar role for Swiss crime fiction and to answer the question whether it is the ideal medium of the moment to represent some intrinsic quality of Switzerland.

II Alexander Heimann: *Dezemberföhn*
The story in *Dezemberföhn* (1996) centres on the village of Hinterzünen somewhere in the vicinity of Bern. The setting for the book is the 1950s. The narrative rests on the supporting pillars of two characters: Gottfried Jost ('Josi') and Josua Kniehorn. Josi is a young good-for-nothing with a bad reputation, although so far this reputation has been unwarranted. Indeed one of the major facets of the book is Josi's struggle to overcome his reputation. Kniehorn is an artist and writer who arrives in the village just before a series of disturbing

events. It soon becomes clear what the villagers think of such outsiders: 'der Schriftsteller musste sich sagen lassen, was für ein grosser Löl er sei und dass ein fremder Fötzel besser den Rand halte, besonders wenn er kein berndeutsch rede' (Df, 40). This tension between an outsider and the villagers allows Heimann to present stereotypical characters and situations in a way which demands a stereotypical reaction of his reader. When he then proceeds to take the story down unexpected twists and turns, he not only explodes the clichés, he also pulls a metaphorical rug from under the reader who is then forced to analyse this new direction and to re-assess earlier reactions to characters and incidents.

Of these earlier incidents it is probably the mystery of the dead cat and Helena Wüthrich's experiences in the fog which set the tone and draw the reader down a well-trodden path of predetermined reaction. A cat is killed in a particularly gruesome way. Helena is followed in an unusually thick fog. Much of the tension in the story then comes from the fact that these mysterious events are not resolved until nearly the end, inviting the reader to reach a premature conclusion about Josi's involvement. Heimann places the reader in the role of Josi's fellows, who judge him on the strength of hearsay and gossip. In the story, Ernst Gantenbein most embodies local prejudice: the secret dislike he harbours for Josi fits very badly with his role as teacher. It may, of course, be Heimann's intention to create in the educated Gantenbein a character with whom the reader is likely to identify. The journey which Gantenbein takes from prejudice to understanding may therefore be one which Heimann hopes the reader will also undertake. Reactions to Josi are thus partly a barometer of prejudice or tolerance towards others. However, any sense of satisfaction which may be derived from monitoring the liberalness of one's attitudes is rudely shattered when it is revealed that it was after all Josi who both killed the cat and stalked the girl. If Josi's subsequent decision to reject evil is to have any dramatic impact, it must be taken by someone who has at least some capacity to do wrong.

Heimann plays in a similar fashion with expectations of Kniehorn, who is established early on as the outsider. Kniehorn functions not merely as the focal point for the villagers' prejudices and suspicions, he also provides Heimann with a viewpoint slightly outside the village: 'Hinter der Schwärze des Vorplatzes erblickte er vereinzelte, rötlich erleuchtete Fenster, die ihm jetzt nicht heimelig erschienen wie sonst, sondern heimtückisch und geierig' (Df, 63). The reader is drawn into Kniehorn's point of view and builds up sympathy with this victim of the villagers' xenophobia. Heimann's decision to give no indication of the guilty party before the end means that both of his central characters can serve a purpose over and above their roles as suspects in a mystery: Josi reveals the reactions of the villagers to one of their own whom they do not much care for; Kniehorn is the lightning conductor for their fear and distrust of strangers.

Dezemberföhn becomes a genuine Kriminalroman when a young girl is raped and murdered — not in the village of Hinterzünen, but in the same canton. The reader must take sides with Josi or Kniehorn. Towards the end of the book Heimann brings these two main characters together for a showdown by the river when Josi finds Kniehorn attacking Verena, a young woman from the near-by village of Krälligen. On one level the mystery is resolved: Kniehorn is the killer. However Heimann creates a confrontation that is stylized in the extreme. He weaves a tapestry of theatrical allusion around the action which gives it an air of staged artifice:

> Als Gantenbein einmal aufblickte, sah er die Krähen, die zurückgekommen waren und die nun ringsum im Halbdunkel der Bäume hockten, als befänden sie sich auf den *Logenplätzen* eines *Theaters* [...] die nachmittägliche Sonne [fand] im Gewirr der Äste und Sträucher erneut eine Lücke und richtete eines ihrer Strahlenbündel auf Gantenbein und Verena, so dass sie *angeleuchtet* wurden wie *Schauspieler* auf der *Bühne*. (Df, 144–145; my italics, CJ)

This provides a suitably unreal setting in which the protagonists face each other as mirror images separated by the stream. Both Kniehorn and Josi are armed with knives and both have violence on their minds, indeed the reader may well remember Josi's own thoughts about Verena: 'aber diese verfluchten Weiber, die schon immer über ihn die Nase gerümpft hatten, sollten sich bloss vorsehen, besonders dieses Flittchen Verena Andrist' (46). On the level of the Kriminalroman this is an essential element in creating suspense about the identity of the villain. On the psychological level, which Heimann introduces here at the climax of the story, it underlines the mirror-image relationship between Josi and Kniehorn and makes their meeting a shock to both of them: 'Totenbleich starrten sie einander über den Bach hinweg an, und keiner von beiden konnte sich bewegen' (133). For Josi the descent into the tree-covered darkness has been a symbolic descent into the depths of his being in which a possible future self is revealed to him in the form of his older Doppelgänger: it is only Kniehorn who has now taken the final irreversible step, as he has in the past, of actually carrying out his impulses by attacking Verena. Josi's fear is therefore partly a fear of himself brought on by the realization of where such violent impulses can lead: 'Er *musste* stehenbleiben und sich diese schrecklichen Schreie anhören, und er *musste* hinüberschauen [...] aber er *musste* hinüberschauen, ob er wollte oder nicht' (132; my italics, CJ). The fight between the two men then becomes a symbolic struggle between Josi and his evil side. Thanks to the arrival of Gantenbein and to the sound of *Landjäger* Röthlisberger's approaching motorcycle

Josi is able to gain an advantage and strike Kniehorn from behind, hold him down in the river and finally kill him. Verena is saved and although Josi is arrested his fellow villagers seem to be warming to him.

This tale of redemption certainly has much in common with Dürrenmatt's crime fiction. The 1950s village setting of Hinterzünen seems highly reminiscent of *Das Versprechen* and the dramatic overtones at the end show the influence of *Der Verdacht*. However, closer reading reveals a divergence in aim in the social element which Heimann has included. If Dürrenmatt was concerned primarily with notions of good and evil as moral absolutes which transcend geographical and political borders, Heimann attempts to use his Swiss setting in a rather different way. This is seen most clearly in his two protagonists. There is definite evil in Josi which manifests itself in his attack on the cat and his desire to frighten Helena. However Josi and his misdeeds seem to embody a different form of evil to Kniehorn's. Josi represents a different social class to Kniehorn, and his turn to evil is based partly on his inability to break out of his suffocating environment. The reader is able to witness Josi's attempts to change, seen most poignantly in the waterwheel which he builds and which is then symbolically smashed. Evil in Kniehorn does not come from without, it is rooted in himself, and in Heimann's simplistic view of the past is associated with the growth of the urban, materialistic society which Switzerland so often represents. The choice of setting in the past makes Heimann's aims even clearer as it becomes an attempt to show where things started to go wrong:

> Dass die Lebensbedingungen sich praktisch für jedermann verbesserten, Konjunktur und Wohlstand zunahmen, war sicher erfreulich. Leider gingen mit dem wirtschaftlichen Fortschritt auch gravierende Verschlechterungen einher. Sittenlosigkeit und Verbrechen nahmen, wie Figura zeigte, zusehends überhand, und die Verderbtheit, die ehemals bloss in den Städten grassiert hatte, griff langsam, aber sicher auf ländliche Gegenden über. (Df, 98)

But it is *not* Kniehorn as an interloper from the city who is the focus of *Dezemberföhn*, it is Josi, who, although driven to rage and violence by his situation, is saved from himself by a moment of heightened insight and revelation. In spite of all the bloodshed Heimann seems concerned to end on a note of hope with Josi's (re-)integration into the village community, emphasizing once more the rejection of urban civilization and its corrupting influence.

III Ulrich Knellwolf: *Klassentreffen*

A group of Swiss men now in their 80s, who were in the same class at school, meet regularly for their reunion (the *Klassentreffen* of the title) with fewer and fewer of them attending as death takes its toll. Shortly after this particular reunion, Philipp Lützelschwab, who has been living in Argentina calling himself Felipe, travels back to Europe. The arrest of Rolf Floßmann, an old Nazi also in hiding in Argentina, is the catalyst for Lützelschwab's decision to leave and return to Europe. Lützelschwab had deserted Switzerland during the war and gone to Germany to work for the Nazis: 'Ich war von den technischen Leistungen der Deutschen begeistert' (Kt, 133). Although he worked as an overseer of *Zwangsarbeiter*, he states that he always did his best to look after them. Once back in Europe, he travels to Leipzig where he learns that he has a daughter and where he meets up with Esther, a niece of one of his school comrades, Gerold Meyer. Esther is a journalist and is keeping tabs on Lützelschwab on behalf of her uncle. Whilst all this is happening, the old schoolfriends are dying one by one; but none of them is murdered. Indeed, by the time Lützelschwab returns only one other member of the old class is still alive; their heated confrontation leads to both their deaths by natural causes.

The past plays a defining role in this novel. This is achieved partly through Esther's questioning; she must discover for herself what happened to Lützelschwab. '"Und dieser Lützelschwab war Schweizer?" fragte Esther. "Ein Schweizer, der zu den Nazis übergelaufen ist. Begreifen Sie, daß wir nichts mit solchen Leuten zu tun haben wollen?"' (Kt, 50). Lützelschwab's return is the trigger for old secrets to be dragged back into the light, whether these are broad issues such as Switzerland's neutral status during the war, or more personal matters which individuals would rather remained forgotten. Lützelschwab, although no saint himself, becomes the embodiment of the past; his journey from South America is also a journey out of that past into the Swiss present. But if Knellwolf's book is explicitly a Kriminalroman, where are the crimes? There are certainly vague plans to bring Lützelschwab to some sort of lynch-mob justice, by hanging or shooting him; but as these plans come to nothing, it is clear that the crimes with which Knellwolf is concerned in *Klassentreffen* lie elsewhere, with Lützelschwab's school comrades during the war years.

Lützelschwab's journey back to his old home dredges up the past in such a way that the reader is at first reminded of Claire's homecoming in Dürrenmatt's *Der Besuch der alten Dame*, given that both of them are old, both are returning after many years of absence, and both are the instigators of lethal consequences. However, the resemblance is only superficial. The key difference lies in Lützelschwab's lack of intent to cause harm. He is not seeking revenge or any form of justice. Floßmann's arrest was a shock which spurred him to return to see the places of his youth once more before his death. The other men from his class all carry the seeds of their own doom within themselves.

The first to die is *Pfarrer* Theophil Kellerhals. Kellerhals witnessed first-hand the turning away of Jews at the Swiss border during the Third Reich and now finds it is too painful a memory. He dies 'an einem akuten Anfall seiner chronischen Herzschwäche' (Kt, 83). In the case of Lukas Rothpletz, we hear him imagining what Lützelschwab will say to him when he arrives back home, forcing him to remember the National Socialist era when he took advantage of a Jewish rival for a post at the Kunstmuseum: 'Du, Rothpletz, kamst aus begütertem Haus. Dir hätte es nichts ausgemacht zu warten. Du wußtest, daß Weisensee der begabtere von euch beiden war, und auch, daß er auf die Stelle angewiesen war und daß er nun als Stellenloser damit rechnen mußte ausgewiesen zu werden' (120). Weisensee had hanged himself rather than be forced to return to Germany. Now Rothpletz must face his doubts: 'Bin ich *schuld* an Weisensees Tod? [...] Kann man uns das als *Schuld* anrechnen?' (122; my italics, CJ). Shortly after these reflections he is found dead in a fountain in Basle full of sleeping tablets and whisky, a very determined suicide. Gerold Meyer seems to have no direct reason to have a guilty conscience, but his family is certainly not without its dubious past: it was his uncle, Friedrich Lauer, who had made Lützelschwab's desertion possible. When Meyer and his wife are killed in a road accident, it may therefore be viewed as divine retribution. And there is Otto Frischknecht, who survives until the final encounter with Lützelschwab. Frischknecht is not without an ambiguous past; he sold armaments to Germany on behalf of his company. As Lützelschwab says of him: 'Ich ging zu den Nazis und habe ihnen meine Haut verkauft. Mehr nicht. Er ging zu ihnen und hat ihnen Geschütze verkauft. Ich habe meine Russen gut behandelt. Seine Geschütze haben vielen Russen das Leben gekostet' (183). Lützelschwab's role is not that of an avenging angel: his hands are too bloodied for that. But he is also too aware of events to be dismissed as a scapegoat, taking pains to distance himself from those he considers to be the real collaborators: 'Die wirklichen Nazifreunde saßen im Schweizer Generalstab und in den leitenden Posten der Industrie' (137). He functions as a manifestation of a collective guilty conscience, powerful enough to destroy frail old men.

As Dürrenmatt before him in *Der Verdacht*, Knellwolf uses the Kriminalroman genre to evaluate the role of Switzerland and the Swiss during the Nazi past. Whereas Dürrenmatt had been primarily concerned with the notion of evil in absolute terms, Knellwolf looks at evil in its shades of grey, whether it be Rothpletz's ambitious opportunism or Frischknecht's materialism. It should, of course, not be overlooked that these characters have enjoyed success as pillars of the community: their personal guilt seems to indict the complicity of Swiss society as a whole. Viewed in this light, *Klassentreffen* becomes an effective misappropriation of the genre, setting up expectations of murder and its investigation where none are to be found. Disconcerted by this absence, the reader is forced to look elsewhere in the story for other crimes and other types of criminal, becoming in the process an investigator who participates in the allocation of blame and guilt. Knellwolf guides the reader in this task by directing him or her to the unusual deaths of the school comrades. It is through an analysis of the causes of these deaths that the reader will glimpse Knellwolf's vision of the world in which a relentless Nemesis refuses to forget the crimes of the past, even if contemporary Swiss society is prepared to do so.

IV Willy Bär: *Tobler*

Published in 1990, Bär's *Tobler* set the scene for much Swiss crime fiction in the following decade. Avoiding the tradition handed down by Glauser and Dürrenmatt, Bär draws on a very different background, tapping into the hardboiled school developed in the 1920s and 1930s by Dashiell Hammet and Raymond Chandler. Bär gives us a private detective for the Zurich of the late twentieth century: the eponymous hero Serge Tobler, freelance journalist and occasional private investigator. Asked to look into the suspicious death by drug overdose of Peter Bigler ('Bigi'), an apparently clean former heroin addict, Tobler takes the reader deep into the Zurich drug culture of the 1980s. The depiction of this milieu is Bär's primary interest; he is less concerned with the resolution of the mystery element of the novel. After a number of blind alleys and red herrings, he takes the reader to a denouement which reveals that the death was the result of a misunderstanding rather than a premeditated murder. Sonja, a young drug user, gave Bigi a shot of heroin in the mistaken belief that that was what he wanted; but as Bigi had been off the drug for some time, the dose was too high and proved fatal. As Gämperle, the crooked policeman, explains: "'Sie hatte keine Ahnung, dass Bigi clean war. Glaub' mir, sie wollte ihm nur helfen, aber ihre Dosis war viel zu stark für ihn [...] Auch ein Arzt hätte nichts mehr ausrichten können"' (Tob, 178–179). Stock Kriminalroman elements are introduced to provide narrative structure and to trick the unsuspecting reader into not noticing that Bär has hijacked the genre as a vehicle for his views on drug use. Gämperle is responsible for fooling Tobler in almost exactly the same way that Bär fools the reader. Thus Gämperle constructs a mystery where there is none: by moving Bigi's corpse, by supplying Tobler with documents incriminating Jacky Bucher, and by having Tobler beaten up. Gämperle creates a fiction and thereby becomes Bär's counterpart in the novel, leaving the bemused reader to identify with Tobler, who has had the wool well and truly pulled over his eyes. The double narrative of the Kriminalroman with a misleading narrative obscuring the real events is mirrored partially in the experience of reading *Tobler*; the dialogue Bär is hoping to establish on the subject of drug use is disguised by the structures and clichés of a well known genre. However, it is not merely on a narrative level that Bär's prudent choice of genre becomes clear. From a thematic point of view as well it aids Bär's cause to use a Kriminalroman to focus on criminal activity. By revealing that the supposed murder of Bigi was in fact not a crime, Bär is tempting the reader to consider the possibility that other crimes which may appear clear-cut should also be re-evaluated. The laws relating to drugs are made susceptible to debate.

Bär not only breaks with tradition as far as the story is concerned, he also subverts the usual expectations of a Kriminalroman set within an urban drug culture. 'Das läuft anders hier in Zürich' (Tob, 8), is how Tobler establishes this facet in the first few pages of the novel; indeed, Bär is constantly at pains to point out that he is not working with a model of Swiss society in order to illustrate how organized crime and drug dealing are inevitable concomitants of the modern world. Here, crime is simply not the best option for making money fast:

> Für einen Schweizer, der ums Verrecken eine Haufen Kohle machen will, ist doch beispielsweise der Immobilienhandel nicht nur naheliegender und ohne Risiko, sondern wahrscheinlich auch lukrativer. Im Heroinhandel gibt es in der Schweiz jährlich ein paar hundert Millionen zu verdienen, im Boden- und Immobilienhandel sind es Milliarden. (Tob, 79)

Bär is able to site his story in one of the few locations in the world where it is possible to deal with the concept of a drug culture relatively free of notions of drug-related crime. Bär's reason for doing this seems to be that he is less concerned with the supply of drugs, which is the criminal aspect, than with the use of drugs. The latter affords an insight into the nature of modern Swiss society: 'Es ist doch nicht dieses weisse Pülverchen, das die Süchtigen schafft, sondern es gibt in dieser Stadt eben Tausende und Abertausende von Leuten, deren soziale und psychische Lage sie für ein Betäubungsmittel wie Heroin empfänglich macht' (Tob, 78). In order to examine this situation, Bär creates a *dramatis personae* of various drug users and strange characters and makes effective use of cynical humour to breathe life into them.

However, it is vital to realize that *Tobler* is not an indictment of a repressively rigid society which forces individuals to extreme measures as they seek to cope with it. Nor is it a society in which the individual is stifled and turns to drug use as a means of self-expression and fulfilment. Nor is there any sense of Zurich being a less forgiving environment of non-conformity than any other major city. Indeed, many of the characters Bär introduces revel in their rejection of standard patterns of behaviour and beliefs, such as Marie-Theres and her various associates with their alternative therapy sessions, or Frau Meili-Stähelin's recordings from beyond the grave. Zurich does not break free will and individuality; the issue here is pressure of work in a country which values success above all else. The character of Röfe makes Bär's aims clear when he recounts his own experiences. Röfe makes explicit references to the implicit values of the good Swiss citizens: 'Auch später im Heim, nachdem sie mich mit sechzehn aufgegriffen hatten, realisierte ich sehr schnell, auf was es ankam: Pünktliches Aufstehen, diszipliniertes Arbeiten, Reinlichkeit und Ordnungs-liebe' (Tob, 65). Equipped with this insight, Röfe is able to fit in very quickly. However this apparent adherence to these core values is humorously under-mined when Röfe continues: 'Dabei [...] wusste jeder, dass ich die ganze Zeit über gefixt habe. Sonst hätte ich es ja gar nicht ausgehalten' (65). The implic-ation that heroin use is a prerequisite for coping with Swiss values of law and order is an amusing paradox that forces the reader to attempt its resolution. Another example is to be found in the character of Schimmerle whom Bär intro-duces in the penultimate chapter: 'Ich war auch clean. Dann habe ich diesen Scheissjob angenommen [...] Irgendwann wurde der Stress so gross, dass ich mir wieder einen Schuss gesetzt habe' (167–168). The link between pressures of work and increased drug use is explicit.

There are, of course, some characters to whom success comes naturally, such as Jacky Bucher, who, in spite of, or possibly thanks to, a criminal past, is now a wealthy businessman. His function in the novel is to provide a blind alley for Tobler in his investigations, but the significant aspect of this is that it oper-ates on two distinct levels. On one level, it is a structural feature of the genre which allows Bär to create suspense about the identity of Bigi's killer. On a higher level, it serves as an indicator of how Swiss society reacts to successful businessmen with a shady past: the very idea of blackmail is the blind alley — if being successful is the only thing that matters, then a criminal past becomes irrelevant and the foundation for blackmail disappears.

V Roger Graf: *Zürich bei Nacht*

It has become something of a commonplace to associate Graf with Raymond Chandler on the basis of those of Graf's works that feature Philip Maloney, a parody of Chandler's hardboiled detective Philip Marlowe. More recently Graf's works have taken a darker path with his Marco Biondi stories and if there is still a useful connection here it is that Chandler showed both sides to life on the American West Coast, the glamorous and the dark underbelly, and, in Marlowe, he created a character who could move easily between the two. Graf operates with a similar polarization of society in Zurich, 'eine Stadt der Extreme auf kleinem Raum' (ZbN, 178), in which there seem to be only success stories and losers. His Biondi is also able to move freely between the two worlds; indeed Biondi refers to himself self-reflectively as a 'Pendel' (ZbN, 237). What sets Graf's work apart from Chandler's is, amongst other things, Graf's desire to analyse the roots of this polarization.

Zürich bei Nacht (1996) is the first of Graf's novels to feature Marco Biondi, who is a television scriptwriter as well as a private investigator. In Zürich bei Nacht, Biondi is asked by Katharina Boxler to find her brother Martin. The latter turns up as a corpse dumped in a lake; the mystery can begin. Biondi soon discovers that Martin's girlfriend, Anna Reber, is also dead. She has been run over by a car (it is later revealed that there is nothing suspicious about her death). Going through Martin's things, Biondi is surprised to find an old photograph of himself taken with his two friends, Linus Fischer and Christoph Fröhlich. His investigations then reveal that Christoph has committed suicide, and that Martin and Anna had been planning to blackmail someone. The key to the mystery is, quite literally, Martin's safety deposit key. Biondi finds this and it gives him access to some documents which Martin had found whilst living in Christoph's old place. These documents include the latter's diary and his confession to the rape and murder 15 years ago of a young heroin addict, Tanja Sonderegger. The confession also reveals that Linus had taken part in the rape. Linus had murdered Martin.

As indicated at the start of this essay, the persistence of the past plays a large part in the Kriminalroman genre because it is typically in the recent past that a crime has been committed. The solution of the mystery in Zürich bei Nacht will also necessitate a re-examination of the past; in fact, the investigation of the murder becomes an investigation of Biondi's own past as well. He is forced to retrace the route which brought him and his contemporaries to the present and to the people that they are now. This strategy gives Graf an opportunity to chronicle the lives of several contemporaries and allows him to illuminate a process of social assimilation. It is this that gives Zürich bei Nacht much of its impact. As Biondi tells one addict: 'Vor zwanzig Jahren sind meine Kumpels genauso rumgehockt wie ihr, haben gekifft und gestunken, und was ist aus Ihnen (sic) geworden? Die hocken jetzt in der Regierung und in den Direktionsetagen, (ZbN, 39). This process of assimilation from rebellious youth to model citizen has already been discussed with reference to Bär's work. It does not seem to matter how people behave in their youth as long as they are willing to become part of society as adults. Phil, the dealer who helps and hinders Biondi with his investigations, has a similar tale to tell when he recollects his youth: 'Mensch, waren das verrückte Typen, taten so, als würden sie sich irgendeiner Terrororganisation anschließen... Doch irgendwann war das vorbei. Der blöde Phil sumpfte noch immer herum, wähend die Herren Studenten sich ihrer Karriere widmeten und Häuschen im Tessin erbten' (116). And there is the story of Jerry, the successful head of a concert agency, who can look back on a past in which he beat up a policeman and spent time in gaol. Graf dots his narrative with these anecdotes and character portraits to reinforce the view that the past is unimportant in society's judgement. This is not to suggest that Swiss society is all-forgiving; it is rather to shift the focus firmly onto present achievements and status.

The past resurfaces for Biondi initially with the photograph and then on a grander scale with the film project *Zürich bei Nacht*. Biondi, Linus and Christoph had intended to make the film together. It is through Biondi's musings about the film project that the notion of assimilation becomes most clear. He ponders: 'Was ist nur aus *uns* geworden... Vielleicht wurde Christoph damit nicht fertig. Zuzusehen, wie man sich verändert, wie man langsam zu dem wird, was man einst bekämpft hat. Auf Linus traf das nicht zu, er wollte immer das Arschloch werden, das er jetzt war' (198). Linus and Christoph represent two extremes and illustrate what could have become of Biondi himself. They are like distorting mirrors of him: his depressions could lead him to suicide like Christoph, yet his greatest fear seems to be of becoming like Linus. This would explain his outrage when Linus states: 'Dabei haben wir beide auf ganz ähniche Weise Karriere gemacht' (191). Biondi keeps himself in check, but he admits: 'Ich wollte aufstehen, ihn anschreien, ihn deutlich machen, daß sich alles in mir weigerte mit ihm verglichen zu werden' (191). It is only someone like Biondi, who can move, like Marlowe before him on a different continent, between the two domains, who is able to resist the process of assimilation and retain his own values and sense of self.

In Graf's novel Zurich becomes a testing ground, sorting the winners from the losers. It assimilates the winners, while the losers find themselves marginalized and stripped of power. Graf's vision of Swiss society is therefore one of extremes, where people succeed and are assimilated or where they fail and are even made to feel guilty for it. As Christoph's diary entry sums up: 'Eigentlich habe ich mich immer schuldig gefühlt in meinem Leben, schuldig an meinem Scheitern' (271). Yet Biondi himself also seems to embody Graf's message about the divisive effect of Zurich. Biondi's insight into the two halves of a split Swiss society prevents him fitting into either properly. On the one hand he is successful as a scriptwriter and so removed from the world of losers, yet on the other hand he is enough of an outsider to know that he does not want to fit into the mould of a typical Swiss success story. His encounter with Linus has made him aware of the real nature of this aspect of Swiss society: 'ich spürte einen tiefen Groll gegen Linus, gegen alle, die waren wie Linus, gegen die erfolgreichen, die dafür sorgten, daß ich mich schäbig vorkam in meiner Unentschlossenheit dem Leben gegenüber' (256). Biondi thus typifies the clasic figure of the detective as an outsider; he is not just unable to join society, he is unwilling to join it and through this unwillingness, he defines both himself and, significantly, also that society.

VI Conclusions

As indicated at the start of this essay, it is possible to discern three key strands in the Swiss tradition. These are represented, firstly, by those contemporary authors, such as Heimann, who follow in Glauser's footsteps and concentrate on the psychological aspects of crime and punishment; secondly, by those, such as Knellwolf, who have continued in Dürrenmatt's legacy of moral philosophical investigation; and, thirdly, by writers such as Bär and Graf who have been influenced by the hardboiled school in their depiction of urban crime. Given these different aims it is no surprise that these authors have approached the task of dealing with the past in their own ways. Nevertheless common ground is established through the use of Switzerland as an essential protagonist in the criminal activities which are portrayed. As the discussion above has made clear Switzerland as a milieu clearly has much to offer the writer of crime fiction. It provides a broad resource stretching from a claustrophobic backwater village, such as Hinterzünen in *Dezemberföhn,* to a modern city such as Zurich in the works of Bär and Graf. The latter sums up the appeal of Zurich to a writer thus: 'Ich glaube ein Grossteil der Faszination dieser Stadt macht der Umstand aus, dass diese übersichtliche Weltstadt auf einer relative kleinen Fläche alles beherbergt, was man auch in London, Paris, Berlin oder einer anderen Metropolen findet' (Graf no date).

Returning to the question posed at the start of the essay it is now possible to suggest that Swiss crime fiction has the potential to be a defining genre of Swiss literature not merely from a psychological point of view as Zeindler proposes but rather from the interrogation of social norms which it facilitates. As I have shown, crime in these novels becomes a vehicle to throw an unsettling light on the nature of the relationship between a social structure and its inhabitants. The four authors whose works I have analysed have chosen to portray Switzerland as a closed environment with a high expectation of its population and a tendency to overlook or forgive a dark and unpleasant past. Josi in *Dezemberföhn* is a telling example of what can happen to an individual who is excluded from a community when he is unable to meet their expectations; the crimes of the war years in *Klassentreffen* can remain in a forgotten past as long as the perpetrators fulfil their social function in today's Switzerland; *Tobler* demonstrates that the same issue of keeping up with the expectations of current Swiss society is not easy, and shows how increased drug use is one way of coping; and a violent past in *Zürich bei Nacht* is easily overlooked in the case of financially successful members of society. It seems that success in the present is all that matters. The modern Kriminalroman with its typically cynical tone and outlook is perfectly suited to this task of exposure, and here Switzerland has much to offer as a setting with a relevance far beyond its own borders.

Note

I would like to thank Dr William Adamson and Dr Christian Timm at the *Raymond-Chandler-Gesellschaft* for the loan of some of the texts used for this paper.

Primary texts

Bär, Willy 1990: *Tobler*. Zurich: Limmat. (=Tob)
Graf, Roger 1996: *Zürich bei Nacht*. Zurich: Haffmans. (=ZbN)
Heimann, Alexander 1996: *Dezemberföhn*. Muri bei Bern: Cosmos (cited here from the 1998 btb [Munich] edn). (=Df)
Knellwolf, Ulrich 1995: *Klassentreffen*. Zurich/Hamburg: Arche (cited here from the 1997 Fischer, Frankfurt am Main, edn). (=Kt)

Secondary literature

Böhler, Michael 1992: 'Triviale Lesestoffe in der Schweiz' in Hugger 1992, 1331–1341.
Bortlik, Wolfgang 1997: 'Löcher in der Schweizer Leiche' in Schindler 1997, 180–187.
Graf, Roger no date: 'Interviews' at <www.access.ch/rgraf/inti.html>, accessed 12 April 2000.
Hugger, Paul (ed.) 1992: *Handbuch der schweizerischen Volkskultur*. Zurich: Offizin.
Kelly, Aaron 1999: '"The Green Unpleasant Land": The Political Unconscious of the British "Troubles" Thriller'; conference paper given at "No end to Thrills? Genre, death and pleasure in the thriller", University of Lincolnshire & Humberside, 25–27 June 1999.
Schindler, Nina (ed.) 1997: *Das Mordsbuch*. Hildesheim: Claassen.
Zeindler, Peter 1995: 'Vorwort' in Zeindler (ed.) 1995: *Banken, Blut und Berge*. Reinbek bei Hamburg: Rowohlt, 9–14.

W. G. SEBALD:

A HOLISTIC APPROACH

TO

BORDERS, TEXTS AND PERSPECTIVES

ARTHUR WILLIAMS

I Preamble

W.G. Sebald has been proclaimed the saviour of German literature in English translation (Howald 1998); indeed, the international aspects of his life and work are so numerous and so fundamentally important that he becomes an automatic subject for study in any consideration of the international dimensions of contemporary German-language literature. This essay will explore the way in which Sebald profits, in particular, from his knowledge of Austrian literature and of both literary and cultural theory characteristic of post-modern thinking to arrive at a presentation of German issues in a framework which is anything but German and may even be felt to display some anti-German features. His work can be read as a journey through academic fields into a literary universe which, by dint of its creative openness and powers of association, allows him to revisit a history which is German but which is revealed increasingly as more broadly European. As it progresses, his oeuvre becomes as much an ethical as an aesthetic statement about our common heritage, increasingly about the growing threat to the natural world that sustains us; a threat we may fail to see if we allow our thinking to remain entrenched in received readings of the past. Sebald's work seeks neither to conquer nor to relativize the German past; it is rather an engagement with and an acceptance of a past whose imprint we need to throw off if we are to invest in a new approach to the future of our planet.

There are two principal keys to Sebald's aesthetics and ethics which enable him to arrive at this position. One is his interest in and exploitation of the techniques and theories of the visual arts. He is, to adapt the subtitle of a review of *The Rings of Saturn* (Angier 1998), 'Europe's great painterly writer'. At the same time, he remains at heart a committed teacher. For him learning and literature are part of the same continuum. His view of the world is holistic so that his work can also be read as representing a case for anti-modular man.

II Sebald's movement outward from his German roots

Sebald was born in 1944 in Wertach in the Allgäu and received his schooling in Sonthofen and Oberstdorf. He has a Swiss LèsL (Fribourg), an English MA (Manchester) and PhD (East Anglia), and a German Dr phil habil (Hamburg). He taught briefly in Sankt Gallen and, apart from a short break when he returned to Switzerland, not Germany, he has lived and worked for over three decades in England, first in Manchester (from 1966) and then (since 1970) in East Anglia. He holds the Chair of German at the University of East Anglia and has received many awards for his literary works, most recently the most prestigious Düsseldorf Heine Prize (December 2000).

Sebald's academic writing as evidenced mainly in his two collected volumes of literary essays concentrates mainly on Austrian literary figures. There is a strong interest in Jewish themes, which links by extension to migrant figures and exiles, to the qualities of uprootedness, outsider or disenfranchised status, and to the attendant loss, duality, or ambivalence of identity. Writers known by their pseudonyms are prominent, as are figures with schizophrenic tendencies. The subjects of Sebald's essays are often victims of the aberrations of European history in the twentieth century. There is a marked emphasis on the socio-political context of their writing, particularly during the transition from bourgeois capitalism to the period of high capitalism, while the major historical events themselves tend to remain in the background.

On the basis of the same evidence, it also seems possible to argue that Sebald the academic was aware at a very early point (i.e. by the mid 1970s at the latest) of the emergent theoretical debates in literary and cultural theory — at a time when the work of German writers and scholars, including British Germanists, focused almost exclusively on internal German issues and responses to them. The main exception to this was probably women writers, specifically where they had a pronounced feminist profile. Sebald himself indicates something of the then prevalent climate in German Studies in his 1986 essay on Hermann Broch. Perhaps anticipating reactions to his own essay, he refers to the way negative criticism of established figures can be dismissed:

> Das ist insofern nicht erstaunlich, als kritische Eingriffe in das Werk eines einmal kanonisierten 'großen Autors' in der Germanistik nach wie vor nicht gern gesehen sind. Das Berufsethos einer in weiten Bereichen immer noch arg retardierten Wissenschaft verlangt von ihren professionellen Vertretern, daß sie [...] das Werk weniger verstehen als durch die Eruierung seiner Quellen und Bezüge legitimieren sollen. (Heimat, 127)

In the light of this, it seems hardly surprising that Sebald should gravitate towards non-German thinkers and theorists, or to German figures who stand somewhat apart from mainstream literary traditions. Perhaps the figure who most fascinates him is Kafka, to whom he dedicates two important analyses in the collected essays on Austrian literature (Unglück, 78–92; Heimat, 87–103) and who can be identified as the main model for *Schwindel. Gefühle.* (Isenschmid 1990: 'Diese Kafka-Erzählung ['Der Jäger Gracchus'] ist der heimliche Motor von Sebalds Buch [...] Er hat seine Biographie gleichsam kafkaisiert'; cf. Williams 2000, 66–67). An omnipresent éminence grise in many aspects of his work is Walter Benjamin, whom he cites in many of his essays at a time when the seminal nature of Benjamin's work was perhaps still being digested. Susan Sontag's splendid introductory essay to the English edition of Benjamin's *One-Way Street and Other Writings* (1978) could almost be the template for Sebald's aesthetics (Sontag 1983). Wittgenstein is much more present than Nietzsche. Lévy-Strauss and Barthes are directly addressed as are Bakhtin, Berger, Sontag and Bataille, whilst Schiller and Goethe enter his discussions only obliquely. I have yet to identify a reference to Hegel. Sebald, on this evidence, can be located in traditions which are not particularly German — an appraisal which can be further supported by reference to his apparent knowledge in the 1970s and 1980s of issues in 'cultural studies' (e.g. in addition to the above, Foucault), a field which is only now beginning to take hold in Germany.[1]

When Sebald's creative writing is examined for similarly 'non-German' features, two further pieces of evidence can be adduced. There is, firstly, an extension of his subject matter to include writers in French and in English; again they are writers marked by exile. In the case of English writers, the most prominent are of non-English origin: Nabokov in *Die Ausgewanderten* and Conrad in *Die Ringe des Saturn*, for example. His main 'German' figures are also long-term English residents who were driven out of Germany by the Nazi persecution of the Jews: Michael Hamburger (*Die Ringe des Saturn*) and the painter Frank Auerbach (*Die Ausgewanderten*). Secondly, the geographical range of his literary horizons marked out by the travels of these figures, whether historically accurate or a product of Sebald's literary musings, extends increasingly beyond Europe (criss-crossed by his 'twin' first-person narrator in *Schwindel. Gefühle.*) to embrace much of the world: the Americas, Africa, China and the Indian subcontinent all feature in *Die Ringe des Saturn*. In his first literary work, *Nach der Natur*, we are taken to imperial Russia, the Baltic states and the Arctic Circle, while *Die Ausgewanderten* (anchored, like *Die Ringe des Saturn*, in England) spans Europe and America. Sebald's native Germany only appears as a place visited, usually in search of answers to gaps in his knowledge about the past (e.g. 'Il ritorno in patria' — the fourth part of *Schwindel. Gefühle.*, and the stories of 'Paul Bereyter' and 'Max Aurach' in *Die Ausgewanderten*); or it is the setting for a dilemma he needs to confront, as in *Luftkrieg und Literatur*.

The point of origin of Sebald's oeuvre and the fixed centre around which it circles is his awareness of the gaps in his knowledge and his need to find an appropriate form for the literary processing of them. In his introduction to *Luftkrieg und Literatur*, he reveals that his motivation for writing these, now much edited, lectures on poetics (first delivered in 1997 in Zurich), was his need to come to terms with the circumstances prevailing at the time of his birth:

> Im Mai 1944 in einem Dorf in den Allgäuer Alpen geboren, gehöre ich zu denen, die so gut wie unberührt geblieben sind von der damals im Deutschen Reich sich vollziehenden Katastrophe. Daß diese Katastrophe dennoch Spuren in meinem Gedächtnis hinterlassen hat, das versuchte ich [in Zürich] anhand längerer Passagen aus meinen eigenen literarischen Arbeiten zu zeigen. (Luftkrieg, 5)

This self-quotation has been edited out of the published volume, but the letters he had received since Zurich had re-confirmed that 'die in den letzten Kriegsjahren von Millionen gemachte Erfahrung einer nationalen Erniedrigung sondergleichen nie wirklich in Worte gefaßt und von den unmittelbar Betroffenen weder untereinander geteilt noch an die später Geborenen weitergegeben worden ist'. This leads him to observe that it is 'als seien wir Deutsche heute ein auffallend geschichtsblindes und traditionsloses Volk' and he reinforces this by comparing Germany with Britain. He identifies a source for this in post-war German writing: 'Die Hervorbringungen der deutschen Autoren nach dem Krieg sind [...] vielfach bestimmt von einem halben oder falschen Bewußtsein, das ausgebildet wurde zur Festigung der äußerst prekären Position der Schreibenden in einer moralisch so gut wie restlos diskreditierten Gesellschaft'. He cites Alfred Andersch, the subject of the essay appended to the volume, as a prime example of the process of image construction: 'In solcher Präokkupation mit der Nachbesserung des Bildes, das man von sich überliefern wollte, lag, meines Erachtens, einer der wichtigsten Gründe für die Unfähigkeit einer ganzen Generation deutscher Autoren, das, was, sie gesehen hatten, aufzuzeichnen und einzubringen in unser Gedächtnis' (Luftkrieg, 6–8).[2]

This situation may, in turn, relate to two further aspects of Sebald's essentially alienated relationship to the land of his birth. Firstly, its apparent absence from his work — a sleight of hand which elicited the comment from one reviewer that *Schwindel. Gefühle.* 'hat mit unserer deutschen Gegenwart auf herrliche Weise nichts zu tun' (Isenschmidt 1990). This is wrong, unless by the German present (in autumn 1990, of course) we understand simply issues of unification, Stasi IMs and the like. If Germany is largely absent as a direct subject of Sebald's work, it is an incontrovertible subliminal presence; the

Holocaust is present almost throughout as a palimpsest. Secondly, when there is direct reference to Germany, and this is most particularly the case in *Die Aus-gewanderten*, there is an immediate association with ugliness and antisocial behaviour. We are brought face to face with 'die häßlichen Deutschen'. There is a certain anti-German element about Sebald's work.[3]

Sebald's work, then, is characterized by a self-imposed exile from a Germany he seems not particularly to like, but which, perhaps for this reason, is a constant nagging presence in his self-reflection. His international search for answers to this conundrum takes him, perhaps inevitably, into new realms of aesthetics and thus permits him new perspectives on old problems. As part of the same search for perspective and orientation, the geographical peregrinations in Sebald's creative work are also associated with travel through time and with fluent transitions across genres and media. In particular, he devotes a lot of thought to the visual arts, contrasting painting advantageously with photography. His readings of paintings, and again German works are underrepresented, are quite remarkable, but of greatest significance is his constant exploration of perspective, of viewpoint, of technical aids to vision, and of the attainment of depth within two-dimensionality. He visits and re-visits the 'vanishing points' in the local studies and vistas of history he is contemplating in order to break through to the other side of the visible picture.[4]

Sebald's journeys are dual. The boundaries he crosses, his re-locations, the new perspectives he gains and the re-interpretations he attempts occur in the realms of aesthetics, literature, the visual arts and history, but they are part and parcel of a similar, less overt process in his relationship to his German inheritance. Beyond this, because he adopts a vantage point which is uniquely his, our shared European past and the world which is the product of our culture and history are brought increasingly into the frame; his greatest commitment is revealed as that to the natural world we inhabit, our real homeland, which we seem determined to destroy. I shall return to this point below.

The stations of Sebald's literary itinerary are significant. They lead us, after the volumes of essays, from the *Elementargedicht, Nach der Natur* (really three long poems) through the three volumes of prose which have now been translated into English to the 1997 Zurich lectures on poetics (published last year in the volume *Luftkrieg und Literatur*) and his hitherto latest work, the 1998 volume of essays on figures associated with his native, Alemanic, corner of the world: *Logis in einem Landhaus*. The latter ends with an essay on the painter Jan Peter Tripp, one of Sebald's schoolfriends and one of the people he writes about who have required psychiatric treatment.[5] The essay thus rounds off a literary journey which had started when the first lines of *Nach der Natur* had set in motion Grünewald's Lindenhardt Altarpiece. Sebald moves its wings in towards the centre (Natur, 7–9) and then proceeds to deconstruct and reconstruct the person, life and times of its creator, Matthaeus Grünewald, and his generally acknowledged alter ego, Mathis Nithart — or is it a case of two men and a 'Männerfreundschaft' overlayered by history (16–19)? The poem highlights the distortion of Grünewald's life, much of which was spent in exile, in a volume presented to Hitler on his birthday in 1938 (13).

Sebald's itinerary thus commences with a German masterpiece from the great period of German painting and sculpture associated also with Riemenschneider, Holbein the Younger, Dürer and Altdorfer (Natur, 8, 10, 74, 97–99) in a time of terrible devastation by both war and disease, when prejudice against religious and other minorities was structural and callously executed. It reaches its interim conclusion in the Germany of his own time, in the region of his birth, with Tripp, another German painter born at a time of great upheaval who suffers from a split personality. On the way, he has visited a curiously encrypted literary and cultural past (*Schwindel. Gefühle.*), the phenomenon of European anti-Semitism and, as part of that, the vicitims of the Holocaust (*Die Ausgewanderten*), and then the history of European colonialism and conquests, exploitation and extermination of peoples, individuals and nature (the silken thread that runs through *Die Ringe des Saturn*). German atrocities are always present, but they are beginning to take their place in a pattern of behaviour which is characteristic of our so-called civilization, particularly in the age of great industrial expansion, the age of high capitalism. Only when he has completed this pilgrimage, ostensibly into the heart of the Suffolk countryside but which entails reaching back into the 'heart of darkness' (Ringe, 141–149; esp. 143, 145), does he address the real absence in his own life identified in the introduction to *Luftkrieg und Literatur*: the absence of an adequate representation of the sufferings of the German civilian population in the Second World War.

Tracing his steps in this way, we can perhaps begin to see in Sebald a writer whose work ultimately places the German problem in the context of a wider history and, consequently, opens up perspectives for the future. He achieves this as a result of a combination of his physical distance from Germany, his journey through time and also, crucially, his engagement with aesthetic theories of the post-modern, which are essentially theories about perception and identity, both of which have implications for our reading of history and historiography. It is a normal process of history that each generation must revisit the past and re-read it in the light of the advantages gained from new analytical tools and perspectives. In the case of readings of German history in the twentieth century, because of the inhumanity and degradation that marked its course, any hint of a new perspective risks the immediate accusation of minimizing, relativizing or even revising the evil perpetrated. Some aspects of the interpretation of Sebald's work offered in this essay may seem to suggest that his contribution takes him in the direction of a relativization of the Nazi past. There is no suggestion of this in his work, and none in any of the secondary literature. There are at least four reasons why such a view would not be tenable. Firstly, at no point does he deny or minimize the facts of German history. Secondly, his somewhat negative view of his compatriots and their social behaviour is of a piece with his constant identification with the victims of history. Thirdly, he applies exactly the same method of reading to all of his subject matter and it is a method which relies on the retrieval of information and personal commitment in its interpretation. Fourthly, he never forces his view on his reader; his aesthetics places his reader in a position to empathize and to think for herself or himself about the new associations and significations he has placed on offer.

Sebald belongs to the generation for whom the impact of the Nazi years was indirect and secondhand, yet for whom the sense of having received only a much-filtered and carefully edited text is precariously balanced by the knowledge of having been alive at the time, and thus of having been at risk and potentially part of it.[6] The 'Gnade der späten Geburt' carries with it neither closure nor absolution; it implies rather the acknowledgement of a responsibility which, of course, cannot be directed at something one did or one can change. It is a sense of responsibility which is almost destined to remain frustrated — unless, as in the case of Sebald, it finds expression in a commitment to fundamental humanity and, by extension, in a moral approach to our environment.

Essentially, Sebald's saturnine melancholia (e.g. Natur, 76, 85; Ringe, 11) is triggered by our inability as human beings to overcome our natural bent to destroy everything we touch. Already at the end of *Nach der Natur*, in the third, overtly autobiographical poem, he scans the horizon where the freighters

> [hinüberziehen] in eine andere Zeit,
> gemessen am Ticken
> der Geiger im Kraftwerk
> von Sizewell, wo sie langsam
> den Kern des Metalls
> zerstören. Raunender
> Wahnsinn auf der Heide
> von Suffolk.
> (Natur, 94–95)

This poem contains the whole problematic and ethos of Sebald's oeuvre in just a few brief pages. Andreas Isenschmidt (1990), who got it wrong about the German connections of *Schwindel. Gefühle.*, got it right when he identified the coherence and integrity of Sebald's work: 'ein Zusammenhang [ist] auf jeder Seite aufs Nachhaltigste und Unheimlichste zu spüren'.

III The unity of Sebald's intellectual world

There are some hints in the recent secondary literature on Sebald that increasing note is being taken of his academic persona. One reviewer, perhaps reflecting Sebald's own interest in figures with dual or split personalities, notes how 'sich der Dichter W. G. und der Germanist Max Sebald auf geglückte Weise vereinigen' (Pfohlmann 1999), describing the academic essays as 'Stoff- und Motivsammlungen für Sebalds eigene literarische Produktion'. It is a valid point, even if the relationship between the two is more complex than this. What the critics are beginning to identify is the deep integrity of Sebald's work to date, without which his calculated destabilizing of genre would probably prove aesthetically disastrous. It is the unity of content and form realized through his mobile and flexibile use of genre that has earned Sebald the praise of critics in Germany and in England. Kurt Flasch (1998), for example, speaking of *Logis in einem Landhaus*, says: '[Der analytische Ertrag ist] erheblich, besonders in dem Essay über [Robert] Walser. Ich sagte: Essay, aber dies Wort muss ich wieder zurücknehmen; es klingt zu glatt und distanziert für Sebalds Notate seiner Wanderungen zu verstörten Brüdern'. And the review of *The Rings of Saturn* in *The Guardian* is prefaced by the questions: 'Fiction? Travel? History? Or all of these? His own publishers cannot quite classify W G Sebald's latest book'; Sebald is 'a master of the strange and sublime' (Wood 1998).

Introducing his first collection of essays in early 1985, Sebald himself observes that his analytical method changes according to the difficulties of the subject 'ohne viel Skrupel'. This accords with 'der vorbedachten Rücksichtslosigkeit, mit der in der österreichischen Literatur traditionelle Grenzlinien etwa zwischen ihrem eigenen Bereich und dem der Wissenschaft übergangen werden' (Unglück, 9). This illustrative example is deliberately chosen; it establishes an indissoluble link between his own twin fields of activity. This is not to suggest, however, that the two have remained equally important to him. Creative writing may be seen to have gradually assumed the ascendancy over the academic. Again the introduction to the first set of essays provides the essential clue. Sebald notes that Austrian literature is more than just a 'Vorschule der Psychologie', it is 'den Einsichten der Psychoanalyse in vielem gleichwertig und in manchem voraus' (Unglück, 9), thus echoing Heinrich Mann's observation: 'Was eine Gesellschaft oder ein Jahrhundert werden, weiß die Literatur im voraus — oder niemand weiß es' (Mann 1935, 285). And, writing of the messianic tradition in an essay on Kafka's *Schloß* first published in 1975, he explores the ambivalence of messianic figures, shifting between 'Repräsentanz und Außenseitertum' (the deliberate choice of example here is mine; AW) and emphasizing that 'Invariabel und bestimmend ist hier einzig die Hoffnung als Prinzip der Theorie und der Praxis' (Heimat, 91–93), a point he repeats later in the essay (99), making reference (which today may seem obvious) to Ernst Bloch. There is an underlying and unifying belief here in the power of literature to open up horizons and keep hope alive; but it is also a principle of fundamental importance to every teacher. I shall return to this point.

All of Sebald's texts, including some of the essays, have a strong first-person-singular presence. It is this that sustains his virtuosic juggling with the author-text-reader relationship. It is a truism that all art must start within its creator. There may, however, be something very special and relevant to our time in Sebald's conscious exploitation of the presence of a first-person narrating persona in his texts. Where Rimbaud gave us his famous 'Je est un autre' (1960, 344) and Barthes proclaimed 'The Death of the Author' (1968) as part of his liberation of the reader–text relationship, Sebald turns to the visual arts and takes the exploration of perception and responsibility a step further. He quotes Maurice Merleau-Ponty (1964) and his concept of the 'regard préhumain': '[...] umgekehrt sind [...] die Rollen des Betrachters und des betrachteten Gegenstands. Schauend gibt der Maler unser allzu leichtfertiges Wissen auf; unverwandt blicken die Dinge zu uns herüber. "[...] on ne sait plus qui voit et qui est vu, qui peint et quit est peint"' (Logis, 174). The quotation is from the important essay on Jan Peter Tripp referred to above, but Sebald had already used the idea in his 1986 essay on Gerhard Roth's *Landläufiger Tod*, where he describes a moment of complete self-oblivion as the 'Tante des Sohns des Bienenzüchters' gazes down from the mountain top into the valley. 'Der metaphysische Augen- und Überblick entspringt einer profunden Faszination, in welcher sich eine Zeitlang unser Verhältnis zur Welt verkehrt. Im Schauen spüren wir, wie die Dinge uns ansehn, verstehen, daß wir nicht da sind, um das Universum zu durchdringen, sondern um von ihm durchdrungen zu sein' (Heimat, 158). It is the essential and necessary response to the alienation of nature by its incorporation into the categories of our civilization to which so many of his essays refer.[7]

The inversion of subject and object experienced when the contemplation of nature or a work of art inspires us to leave behind all barriers and inhibitions has implications for Sebald's concerns and yields direct outcomes in his writing. His most telling use of the technique is probably the closing paragraph of *Die Ausgewanderten*, which is something of a literary tour de force; significantly, he applies the same aesthetic strategy at the end of *Logis in einem Landhaus*. In both cases the narrator is scrutinized by the image and a level of reader involvement with the text is mediated which demands both further contemplation of the text and, significantly, also of the self.

In *Die Ausgewanderten*, the reader is first told of the Genewein photographs from the Łódź ghetto and then presented with a description, purportedly of one of them.[8] It contains many motifs from the book it both closes and re-opens, challenging the reader to explore both its visual and literary substance:

> Wer die jungen Frauen sind, das weiß ich nicht. Wegen des Gegenlichts, das einfällt durch das Fenster im Hintergrund, kann ich ihre Augen genau nicht erkennen, aber ich spüre, daß sie alle drei herschauen zu mir, denn ich stehe ja an der Stelle, an der Genewein, der Rechnungsführer, mit seinem Fotoapparat gestanden hat. Die mittlere der drei jungen Frauen hat hellblondes Haar und gleicht irgendwie einer Braut. Die Weberin zu ihrer Linken hält den Kopf ein wenig seitwärts geneigt, während die auf der rechten Seite so unverwandt und unerbittlich mich ansieht, daß ich es nicht lange auszuhalten vermag. (Ausgewanderten, 353–354)

The first-person narrator may be able to turn away from the photograph, but the eyes continue to follow the reader, gazing at us from beyond the divide scored in history by the Holocaust. In the later essay (Logis, 171–188; here 185–188), it is again the barrier of passed time which is removed as a new immediacy is gained together with a new awareness of the brief span of our human life.

A small painting by Tripp (which is reproduced in the text) contains in a dominant, central position an earlier, larger one by the same artist of a pair of women's shoes discarded on a tiled floor. A young woman now sits facing the older painting, lost in deep contemplation of it. Her shadow falls to her left and rises to cross into the older painting, where it merges with the short, midday shadow cast by one of the shoes. She is wearing one of the shoes. In the foreground, just left of centre, a dog looks straight out at us. Its image does not break the frame of the earlier painting, but it does obscure part of the woman's shadow, while its own shadow extends directly left and out of the boundary of its own painting. It has a shoe at its feet. This shoe is one of the pair we find in the left foreground of Jan van Eyck's 1434 painting known as 'The Arnolfini Marriage'. In that painting, a little dog occupies the centre foreground, its shadow falling to the right onto the woman's gown. In his reading of the paintings, demonstrating an uncanny skill he deploys at many points in his work to decisive effect,[9] Sebald brings out the multiple intertextualities of Jan Peter Tripp's work (as indicated here) and concludes his essay as follows:

Der Hund, der Geheimnisträger, der mit Leichtigkeit über die Abgründe der Zeit läuft,
weil es für ihn keinen Unterschied gibt zwischen dem 15. und dem 20. Jahrhundert,
weiß manches genauer als wir. Aufmerksam ist sein linkes (domestiziertes) Auge auf
uns gerichtet; das rechte (wilde) hat um eine Spur weniger Licht, wirkt abseitig und
fremd. Und doch fühlen wir uns gerade von diesem überschatteten Auge durchschaut.
(Logis, 188)

We may have imposed our patterns of life on nature, but its fundamental essence is more permanent and more constant than any of these.

Sebald's first-person narrator and the first-person essayist are both at once intermediary and interpreter; the dual burden of responsibility is awesome. If Rimbaud steps away from himself to a creative distance which is at once alienating and liberating, libertine even, and if Barthes takes away the author's responsibility for his work, but without visiting new responsibilities upon the reader, who is free to re-write the text he reads according to his own ludic lights, Sebald the author re-enters his text as both first-person narrator and as reader.[10] However, he does not remain an uninvolved reader by proxy for those who cannot or will not read, he is no mere 'Vorleser', his well-documented scruples as a creative writer[11] are complemented by his scruples as a creative reader and this in turn means scrutiny of himself as the reader. He is examined by the text he reads and is thus affected, changed by the text. It is not difficult to see how a principled and responsible reading of a text, no matter how defined, becomes a factor for change in the reading subject. This is what Sebald seems to learn from the visual arts, particularly from Merleau-Ponty's observations, and since his subject is his German problem and our European problem it seems not unreasonable to argue that he has found, and benefits from, a German application of an eminently French approach to contemporary aesthetics.

Or perhaps, bearing in mind Sebald's preferences, it is an Austrian adaptation of a French model to a German dilemma, for the above are examples of aesthetic border-crossings of a kind only great art can achieve; and border-crossing, as Sebald points out, is a particular feature of Austrian, as opposed to German, literature. At the same time he reminds us of a further quality his work embodies which has been hinted at above and which again he claims is an Austrian trait; and one related to a disastrous history:

Es ist schwer zu sagen, wo das in der österreichischen Literatur zum Ausdruck kom-
mende Interesse an Grenzüberschreitung sich herschreibt und ob es vielleicht damit
zu tun hat, daß das nach einem langwierigen historischen Debakel noch übrigge-
bliebene Österreich [...] 'das einzige Nachbarland der Welt' ist, was man wohl dahin
gehend verstehen muß, daß man in Österreich, wenn nur mit dem Denken einmal ein
Anfang gemacht ist, bald auch schon auf den Punkt stößt, wo man über das vertraute
Milieu hinaus und mit anderen Systemen sich auseinandersetzen muß. (Unglück, 10)

Austrian writers have a longer history of disaster to learn from than their German counterparts. Since the two histories coincide in their darkest moments, it is possible that German writers (and others) can learn from their openness to other systems and the continuity of learning and experience (it is an argument which perhaps carries less weight now than it did in the early 1980s).

We have returned to the integral unity of Sebald's work; it is nowhere more crucial than in the identity of academic and creative writer. And he has reminded us that the border-crossing and intellectual wanderlust he identifies as characteristic of Austrian literature is also part and parcel of an approach to learning which may differ considerably from German traditions: '[die] in der literarischen Tradition Österreichs, im Gegensatz etwa zur reichsdeutschen, so wichtig[e] Kategorie der Lehre und des Lernens' (Unglück, 13). It is a thought he had developed at some length into an important statement which, in the present context, acquires the status of a philosophy of life. I quote from his 1983 essay 'Summa Scientiae. System und Systemkritik bei Elias Canetti' (Unglück, 93–102; here 101–102):

> Wie wenige hat Canetti die verhängnisvollen Prozesse unseres Jahrhunderts, den Aufstieg des Faschismus, die hypertrophische Entwicklung der Machtapparate, die Ermordung der Juden, das Ausmaß atomarer Vernichtung überdacht, und wie wenige andere Schriftsteller ist er im Lauf seiner Entwicklung zu der Einsicht gekommen, daß es mit Repräsentationen des Endes nicht getan ist. Sein Ideal ist nicht das des Propheten, sondern jenes des Lehrers, dessen Glück es ausmacht, daß [...] das Lernen nicht endet. Bleibt der Machthaber immer an seinem Platz, so ist der Lernende stets auf der Reise. 'Das Lernen muß ein Abenteuer bleiben, sonst ist es totgeboren. Was du im Augenblick lernst, soll von zufälligen Begegnungen abhängig sein und es soll sich so, von Begegnung zu Begegnung, wieder fortsetzen, ein Lernen in Verwandlungen, ein Lernen in Lust.' Die zentrale Aktivität des Lernenden aber ist nicht das Schreiben, sondern das Lesen. 'Lesen, bis die Wimpern vor Müdigkeit leise klingen.' [...] Lernen scheint Canetti identisch mit dem Leben selbst, so wie es sein sollte. Damit steht er in einer langen jüdischen Tradition, in der der Ehrgeiz des Schriftstellers nicht auf das von ihm geschaffene Werk, sondern auf die Erhellung der Schrift geht. Die literarische Form, derer die Illuminierung sich bedient, ist die auch für Canetti bezeichnende des Exkurses, des Kommentars und des Fragments [...] Für Canetti besteht ein entscheidender Unterschied zwischen dem Vorgang des Lesens und der Aufnahme von Wissen, das hinauswill auf Macht. Freiheit scheint ihm 'die Freiheit *loszulassen*, ein Aufgeben von Macht'. Die Haltung, auf die hier angespielt wird, ist die des Weisen, der den Verlockungen des Wissens, das er in sich trägt, zu widerstehen vermag.

The link between order and power is one that Sebald explores in a number of his collected essays, it is axiomatic to his thinking.[12] Whilst his essays appeared originally as discrete entities, each fashioned according to its own analytical method, his collections of them and the incorporation of their content into more creative forms allow him to make the partitioning walls porous and demonstrate the inherent closure of vision that the single modularized item may encourage. His creative writing embraces the ideal form he ascribes to Canetti: 'des Exkurses, des Kommentars und des Fragments' — all of which suggest at once incompleteness and complementariness.

Sebald's 'Austrian' willingness to cross borders allows him to break through predictable thought patterns — and to display his obvious enjoyment in communicating knowledge. This is nowhere more apparent than in *Die Ringe des Saturn* where every step of his walk leads him into himself to contemplate the associations he perceives in the traces of the past still surviving in the Suffolk countryside. The result is a display of prodigious learning which never becomes self-advertisement. The reason why he manages to avoid this pitfall lies in his deep seriousness, his characteristic melancholy, about our human predicament and his unequivocal identification with the victims of the power-systems on which our civilization has been built.

Again the introduction to the 1985 set of essays contains a further clue to the source of Sebald's world view: 'Kafkas Einsicht, daß all unsere Erfindungen im Absturz gemacht werden, ist ja inzwischen nicht mehr so leicht von der Hand zu weisen. Das Eingehen der uns nach wie vor am Leben erhaltenden Natur ist davon das stets deutlicher werdende Korrelat'. But he goes on, as a true teacher must: 'Melancholie, das Überdenken des sich vollziehenden Unglücks, hat aber mit Todessucht nichts gemein. Sie ist eine Form des Widerstands. Und auf dem Niveau der Kunst vollends ist ihre Funktion alles andere als bloß reaktiv oder reaktionär [...] Die Beschreibung des Unglücks schließt in sich die Möglichkeit zu seiner Überwindung ein' (Unglück, 12).

To the readers of *Die Ringe des Saturn* and, indeed, to readers of the second set of essays, this positive credo may now seem less intact. I quote the final paragraph of the introduction to the latter. One message that can be read out of representative Austrian texts is

> die [...] allmählich aufdämmernde Erkenntnis der im weitesten Umraum sich vollziehenden Dissolution und Zerrüttung der natürlichen Heimat des Menschen. Lag die Restaurierung der gesellschaftlichen Heimat kraft des rechten Wortes immerhin noch im Bereich des Möglichen, so scheint es in zunehmendem Maße fraglich, ob solche Kunst hinreichen wird, das zu erretten, was wir, über alles, als unsere wahre Heimat begreifen müßten. (Heimat, 16)

There is a deep saturnine melancholy about the implied thesis that human progress is bought at the cost of destruction, be it of nature or of our fellow human beings (and Sebald often poses the question about man's over-determination and over-exploitation of nature, particularly in the age of advanced capitalism[13]). That the history of mankind is a history of combustion and consumption is one of the key themes of *Die Ringe des Saturn*; he develops it particularly at the beginning of his seventh chapter (201–203) as the first-person narrator is on his way to Middleton to call on a friend. The passage, which culminates in an apparent return to his point of departure and an overwhelming sense of vertigo and disorientation (204–208), opens in Britain with '[die] über Millennien fort-schreitende[.] Zurückdrängung und Zerstörung der dichten Wälder' and pro-gresses via the forest fires in the Amazon and Borneo to Brazil, which 'verdankt [...] seinen Namen dem französischen Wort für Holzkohle', and climaxes with:

> Die Verkohlung der höheren Pflanzenarten, die unaufhörliche Verbrennung aller brennbaren Substanz ist der Antrieb für unsere Verbreitung über die Erde. [...] alles [ist] Verbrennung, und Verbrennung ist das innerste Prinzip eines jeden von uns her-gestellten Gegenstandes [...] Die ganze Menschheitszivilisation war von Anfang an nichts als ein von Stunde zu Stunde intensiver werdendes Glosen, von dem niemand weiß, bis auf welchen Grad es zunehmen und wann es allmählich ersterben wird.

The friend who lives in Middleton is Michael Hamburger who escaped the Holocaust when his family moved to Britain in 1933. It is as if the first-person narrator lived or had lived in Michael's house, as if the items in the study were his own and not the belongings of the poet who is in so many ways his precursor (cf. Ringe, 218–224; esp. 218–219) and who can be seen to represent the central dilemma in Sebald's personal and literary world. The two figures begin to be two sides of the same German and European catastrophe. The peaceful domestic visit triggers recollections of the fate of Michael's Berlin home and members of his family (210–216), but the associations are still strong with the narrator's apocalyptic thoughts a few pages earlier. It is a coherence which is curiously strengthened by the intervening, contrasting episode in which the first-person narrator is treated like a suspicious alien by a shopgirl who, wrenched away from her television, is inarticulate and can only offer him the comfort of that symbol of our consumerist society, an ice-cold can of Cherry Coke (209). This everyday experience comes at the moment when the narrator most needs succour after the labyrinthine displacement of time and space; and it contrasts completely with the Hamburgers' hospitality. Their genuine humanity rises above, but cannot extinguish, the disconcerting undertow of the omni-present past.

The implicit, therefore incontestable unity of these associations, mediated as ever by the first-person narrator's musings, will not tolerate a modular parti-tioning and petrification of history and of learning. The apocalyptic labyrinth inescapably enfolds also the firestorms set off by the allied area bombing of Hamburg, Nuremberg and Dresden to name but three cities which were the target of Operation Armageddon. The awareness of this history has been with us since the early pages of the book, as has the subliminal presence of the 'anti-modular' theme which was introduced when the first-person narrator (is it Max or is it W.G.?) reports the deaths of two revered colleagues and pays tribute to these two 'old-fashioned', deeply humane and anything but modular, academics (14–19). In the opening lines of the book this narrator, who is separable from the author only as a result of his translation into text, has dragged himself across the floor of the hospital room where he is recovering from an operation on his spine to pull himself upright in order to gain a bird's-eye view of the city of Norwich through a window which is curiously veiled by a squared net curtain (11–14). He then sets out on his 'English pilgrimage' (the subtitle of the German, but not of the English edition) through the Suffolk countryside, his pilgrim's progress through European colonial history and man's inhumanity to man. But he makes doubly sure at the outset that his reader is aware of the backcloth for his inner journey through our common past: it is the now of Thatcher's Britain (56), where true scholarship seems unable to survive, and the here of the air bases whose bomber squadrons carried Armageddon to the German cities (52–55). He rejects the drawing of neat frameworks which compartmentalize history, events, places, and people. After all, Southwold, one of his points of orientation on his pilgrimage, had been the vantage point from which the naval battle of Sole Bay had been observed — in which so many had died, combusted in their wooden warships in 1672 (95–97). The grid of the net curtain is quickly replaced by the figure of the quincunx, the mysterious lattice which represents the recurring pattern which underlies life itself (30–32), which existed before human beings came on the scene and will continue after they have joined the extinct sea-monsters they are already beginning to resemble (88).

IV Envoi

Each of Sebald's two collections of essays contains a discussion of a work by Gerhard Roth. The 1984 essay on *Winterreise* ('Der Mann mit dem Mantel. Gerhard Roths *Winterreise*'; Unglück, 149–164) ends with an adapted quotation from James Joyce:

> Vergleicht man das Verhältnis, in dem die irische Tradition zur englischen steht, mit dem, das die österreichische Literatur auch heute noch über die gemeinsame Sprache mit dem deutschen Ausland verbindet, dann liegt die Vermutung nicht fern, daß die Krankheit, an der der Schullehrer Nagl leidet, am genauesten diagnostiziert werden könnte als 'that hated brown Austrian paralysis' — eine Spekulation, an die sich allerhand weiterführende Hypothesen anschließen ließen.

Much of the essay (153–161) is devoted to a discussion of the structural features of pornographic texts which draws on the work of John Berger, Beatrice Faust, Georges Bataille, and Susan Sontag. Roth's text is shown to be a failure because it exemplifies all the worst techniques of pornographic writing, which 'nach und nach ein nicht intendiertes System [ausbilden], das die Denk-freiheit sowohl der Erzählfigur als auch des Lesers aufhebt' (153). What has been lost is 'die Zeit zum genaueren Anschauen und Überdenken' (152); Roth allows 'weder sich noch uns, lang genug bei dem zu verweilen, was sehens- und bedenkenswert wäre' (151).

Two years later, 'In einer wildfremden Gegend — Zu Gerhard Roths Romanwerk *Landläufiger Tod*' (Heimat, 145–161) applies the same criteria and reaches the diametrically opposite conclusion. Here, Ascher, 'über sein Mikro-skop gebeugt', attempts 'hinter die Natur der Dinge zu kommen' as Roth adopts a new technique which 'besteht in der Dissolution der (erzählerischen) Vernunft durch die Intensität poetischer Imagination' (145). It is a technique which 'offensichtlich von einer Sammlertätigkeit bestimmt wird, die jedes gefundene Objekt, jedes Fragment der Natur und jedes Bruchstück zertrümmerter Ge-schichte, das dem Autor unter die Hände kommt, als Baumaterial in den Prozeß der Rekonstruktion eines in zunehmendem Maß im Verschwinden begriffenen Lebens einbringt' (149). Sebald's model, on this occasion, is Lévy-Strauss. Roth's technique of constantly changing perspectives (150), his 'exzentrisch[e] Proliferationen', mean the 'die Abweichung [wird] zur Agentur einer neuartigen Erkenntnis' (151). Underlying Roth's work and its uncanny resemblance to Sebald's own (or is it again Sebald the viewer who is placed on display to us?) is a conjecture which could also be Sebald's: '[er begreift] die Geschichte der Menschheit nur als eine besonders virulente und vielleicht die letzte Phase der Naturgeschichte' (154), and he offers a model for the tendency now endemic in our civilization towards ruin (155). 'Der spezifische Schock, den diese Ge-schichten Roths vermitteln, ist der der Einsicht in das Alter der Zeit und in ein Leben, das sich selbst überlebt hat', we have only survived beyond our natural span because of our ability to think: 'Die Denkfähigkeit ist als das Instrument des Überlebens der Zwang, unter dem wir kontinuierlich stehen' (156).

With this scenario in mind, it is not inappropriate to turn, finally, to the essay in which Sebald brings together two figures he greatly reveres, Joseph Roth and Walter Benjamin: 'Ein Kaddisch für Österreich — Über Joseph Roth' (1989; Heimat, 104–117). Roth had an uncanny sense of impending disaster. In 1927 he had used the term 'Konzentrationslager' and in the early 1930s spoken of being 'fünf Minuten vor dem Pogrom' (106–107). His world lies in the past; 'Die Zukunft hingegen ist ein Trugbild' (104–105). His writing provides an example of 'einer Kunstübung, die, ihrer scheinbaren Anspruchslosigkeit zum Trotz, nirgends mit dem Vordergründigen sich zufriedengibt' (112). 'Was unter solchen Auspizien thematisiert wird, das ist nicht die Geschichte, sondern der Lauf der Welt, der, wie gleichfalls von Benjamin angemerkt wird, außerhalb aller eigentlichen historischen Kategorien steht. Die andere Weltzeit, um die es [...] geht [...] ist die der naiven Dichtung' (113). It is a deeply moral stance: 'Es geht [...] im Bereich der Ästhetik letzten Endes immer um ethische Fragen' (115). We return to Sebald and his own position in relation to his work and history when he goes on to quote Benjamin: 'Benjamin war der Auffassung, daß der wahre Erzähler nicht der Geschichte, sondern der Naturgeschichte tribut-pflichtig sei' (115).

Notes

1. The essay 'Eine kleine Traverse. Das poetische Werk Ernst Herbecks' (1981; Unglück, 131–148) contains passages (esp. 132–133, 139–140) which show Sebald drawing on aspects of cultural studies related to discourse and power (the canon and the role of 'kleine Literatur'). See also the interesting review article by Naumann (1999) of two new books, both introductions to 'cultural studies', both drawing on English-language sources and both with English titles: *Cultural Studies. Grundlagentexte zur Einführung* (Bromley/Göttlich/Winter; Lüneburg: zu Klampen) and *The Contemporary Study of Culture* (Bundesministerium für Wissenschaft und Verkehr/Internationales Forschungszentrum Kulturwissenschaften; Vienna: Turia und Kant).
2. cf. ZDF film by Volker Hage and Matthias Ziemann: 'Tabu Vergeltung. Die Literaten und der Luftkrieg' (28 March 2000, 22.45–23.30) in which, in particular, Wolf Biermann, Monika Maron, Walter Kempowski, Klaus Harpprecht, Rolf Hochhuth, Harry Mulisch and Dieter Forte recall and discuss their experiences and the role of literature. Alongside a few short comments from Sebald, the film includes several contributions from Marcel Reich-Ranicki and also Gert Ledig's last interview before his death in 1999.
3. On these aspects see *Die Ausgewanderten*, esp. 238–240; Williams 1998b, esp. 98–99, 109–110; and Williams [2000], esp. [75–77, 81]. But note also the fourth part of *Schwindel. Gefühle.* where the first-person narrator returns on foot (202–210) across the Alps to pause at a chapel with badly painted, now decaying but no less horrendous, mid-eighteenth-century depictions of the Stations of the Cross, before passing the scene of the last local action of the war. The grave of the fallen with its iron cross can be found in the village; the thought of it triggers memories of the gypsies and his father's photographs of his 'Polenfeldzug'. In the village itself (232–238) everywhere reflections of the heyday of Nazi art survive in the murals and other works by a local artist whose fame in the 1930s spread even as far as Munich.
4. Sebald's works, particularly *Die Ausgewanderten* and *Die Ringe des Saturn*, are rich in references to perspective and such optical aids as glasses, microscopes, reversed telescopes, watchmakers' eye-glasses. His first-person narrators often overfly areas or stand on high vantage points, sometimes in dreams, affording them and the reader a bird's eye view of world, revealing its past and hinting at its future (Natur, 85: 'Flugzeuge, die grauen Brüder der Vorzeit'). On perspective and the influence of paintings, see Williams 1998b, 99–104, 106–108; and Williams [2000, 69–71, 80].
5. Sebald's introduction to the volume closes with a remarkable tribute to Tripp (7): 'Daß am Ende ein Aufsatz steht über einen Maler, das hat auch seine Ordnung, nicht nur weil Jan Peter Tripp und ich eine ziemliche Zeitlang in Oberstdorf in dieselbe Schule gegangen sind und weil Keller und [Robert] Walser uns beiden gleichviel bedeuten, sondern auch weil ich an seinen Bildern gelernt habe, daß man weit in die Tiefe hineinschauen muß, daß die Kunst ohne das Handwerk nicht auskommt und daß man mit vielen Schwierigkeiten zu rechnen hat beim Aufzählen der Dinge.'

6. The comparison and contrast with Botho Strauß, who is just a little older than Sebald, may be instructive. Many of Strauß's statements, for example about his position in time ('eine Zwischenzeit'), about his desire for a history of his own ('weder dürftig noch blutig'), about his commitment to writing ('Man schreibt einzig im Auftrag der Literatur. Man schreibt unter Aufsicht alles bisher Geschriebenen'), or about his ambivalent relationship to the German language ('Es schafft ein tiefes Zuhaus und ein tiefes Exil, da in der Sprache zu sein'), could be used as points of departure for an analysis of Sebald's work. The findings would be fundamentally different in the two cases. For a discussion of some of the issues raised here see Williams 1990, 283–284, 288–293; Williams 1991, 452–453; Williams 1998a, 9–16; Williams [2000, 71–74].

7. Of particular relevance are the essays on Stifter ('Bis an den Rand der Natur. Versuch über Stifter' and 'Helle Bilder und dunkle — Zur Dialektik der Eschatologie bei Stifter und Handke'; Unglück, 15–37, 165–186) and on Bernhard ('Wo die Dunkelheit den Strick zuzieht. Zu Thomas Bernhard'; Unglück, 103–114). Stifter is the key figure in this context (cf. Heimat, 12); one quotation from the first essay will makes the point (Unglück, 25): 'Die Poetisierung der Natur im Blick des Betrachters vermittelt einen Begriff von Landschaft, in dem sich die Zivilisation schmerzlos arrangiert mit dem, worüber sie sich erhebt [...] Problematisch bleibt [...], daß die Natur eben nur vom Standpunkt der Zivilisation aus wirklich "schön" erscheint. Die Beschreibung der Natur, auch die literarische, entwickelte sich erst mit der kommerziellen Erschließung der Welt, und es spricht einiges dafür, daß Stifter die Kunst der prosaischen Landschaftsmalerei von Autoren [...] gelernt hat [...] in deren Werk die Ästhetisierung der Topographie ideengeschichtlich bereits dem Kolonialismus beizuordnen wäre'. The passage goes on to highlight the 'Funktionszusammenhang von Natur und Wirtschaftsgeschichte' and to compare Stifter's way of looking at nature with that of a man looking at the body of a sleeping woman; the eye is the original 'Organ der Besitzergreifung und Einverleibung' (26).

8. The photograph itself is not reproduced in the text, which contains many photographs. In the BBC 'History Zone' account of the Łódź Ghetto based on the Genewein slides, one of his photographs records women making bags from straw (of which also shoes were made in the 'Strohschuh-Abteilung'). Another shows three women winding the straw; they somewhat resemble Sebald's three carpet weavers. The documentary refers to 'rugs' made in the Ghetto; I have been unable to establish the relevant German term. There is a significant em dash in the text before this 'photograph' is brought to life.

9. The most significant example of this is his reading of Rembrandt's 1632 painting 'The anatomy lesson of Professor Tulp', which he introduces, significantly, in the first chapter of Die Ringe des Saturn (22–27; cf. 102). Another key reading is of Grünewald's Isenheim Altarpiece in Die Ausgewanderten (252–254), where, of course, the techniques of the eponymous painter Max Aurach [Frank Auerbach] provide essential clues to Sebald's own techniques (237–240). Other paintings he describes include Altdorfer's 'Battle of Alexander' (Natur, 97–99) and Jakob van Ruisdael's 'View of Haarlem with Bleaching Fields' (Ringe, 102–103; cf. Unglück, 184–105: Ruisdael's 'Der große Wald'). The reading of paintings and drawings plays a significant role in Logis in einem Landhaus; the Mörike essay (77–94) is a particularly interest case.

10. See Williams 1998b, esp. 100–105; Williams [2000, 77–78.

11. See esp. Korff 1998, esp. 169–171; also note 10 above.

12. See esp. the opening pages of the essay 'Summa Scientiae. System und Systemkritik bei Elias Canetti' (Unglück, 93–95) which discuss the relationship between historiography and power ('Geschichte [wird] von Standpunkt der Stärkeren geschrieben') and link it to imperial expansionism into the realms of both space and time until only the powerful remain alive ('bis schließlich der "ideale" Machthaber allein "auf einem riesigen Leichenfeld lebend noch steht"'); the [Nazi] 'Sehnsucht nach totaler Ordnung bedarf nicht des Lebens', but is essentially 'mörderisch', striving for total power. And, by extension: 'Die planmäßige Einteilung der Welt in Felder des Todes durch den paranoischen Machthaber wird in bescheidenerem Maßstab fortlaufend praktiziert als die Organisation des normalen Lebens. "Die Strenge der Fachdisziplinen", von der Canetti wenig hält, ahndet Grenzverletzungen und zwingt die Wirklichkeit ins System ihrer Kategorien.'

13. cf. note 7 above, also the first essay in *Unheimliche Heimat*: 'Ansichten aus der Neuen Welt. Über Charles Sealsfield' (17–39; esp. 34–37). Sebald introduces a quotation from Sealsfield's *Cajütenbuch* ('Die Passage hat als Indiz für das Verhältnis von Mensch und Natur in der ersten Hälfte des 19. Jahrhunderts wohl nicht leicht ihresgleichen') with a depiction of Sealsfield's view of nature as 'das prinzipiell Fremde', showing how '[die] zerstörerische Dynamik' between man and nature 'durch die kapitalistische Waren-wirtschaft erst wirklich virulent wurde'. He closes the discussion, which also touches on male violence to women (developed further in his essay on Schnitzler; Unglück, 38–60) and Foucault's analysis of the discourses of sexuality, with the view that these depictions of nature 'entstanden auf einem entscheidenden Wendepunkt, an dem die Natur end-gültig aufhörte, die natürliche Heimat des Menschen zu sein'. The changing role of the city is highlighted in the essay on Peter Altenburg (Heimat, 65–86; esp. 68, 75).

Primary texts

Sebald, W.G. 1985: *Die Beschreibung des Unglücks. Zur österreichischen Literatur von Stifter bis Handke.* Salzburg/Vienna: Residenz. (Fischer TB 1994 = Unglück)
—— 1988: *Nach der Natur. Ein Elementargedicht.* Nördlingen: Greno (Eichborn 1989). (Fischer TB 1995 = Natur)
—— 1990: *Schwindel. Gefühle.* Frankfurt am Main: Eichborn. (Fischer TB 1994 = Schwindel)
—— 1991: *Unheimliche Heimat. Essays zur österreichischen Literatur.* Salzburg/Vienna: Residenz. (Fischer TB 1995 = Heimat)
—— 1993: *Die Ausgewanderten. Vier lange Erzählungen.* Frankfurt am Main: Eichborn. (Fischer TB 1994 = Ausgewanderten)
—— 1995: *Die Ringe des Saturn. Eine englische Wallfahrt.* Frankfurt am Main: Eichborn. (Fischer TB 1997 = Ringe)
—— 1998: *Logis im einem Landhaus. Über Gottfried Keller, Johann Peter Hebel, Robert Walser und andere.* Munich/Vienna: Hanser. (=Logis)
—— 1999: *Luftkrieg und Literatur. Mit einem Essay zu Alfred Andersch.* Munich/Vienna: Hanser. (=Luftkrieg).

English translations by Michael Hulse (all Harvill, London)
The Emigrants (1996)
The Rings of Saturn (1998)
Vertigo (2000)

Secondary literature

Angier, Carole 1998: 'In the killing fields. W G Sebald is England's — and East Anglia's — great German writer', *Independent Saturday Magazine*, 23 May 1998, 9.
Barthes, Roland 1977: 'The Death of the Author' (1968) in Barthes: *Image–Music–Text.* Trans. and ed. Stephen Heath. London: Fontana, 142–148.
Braese, Stephan (ed.) 1998: *In der Sprache der Täter. Neue Lektüren deutschsprachiger Nachkriegs- und Gegenwartsliteratur.* Opladen: Westdeutscher Verlag.
Flasch, Kurt 1998: 'Landhaus mit Wasseradern. W. G. Sebalds Wanderungen zu verstörten Brüdern', *Neue Zürcher Zeitung*, 6 October 1998 (http://www.nzz.ch/online/ 02_dossiers/buchmesse98/nzz981006flasch.htm).
Howald, Stefan 1998: 'Es hilft, dass W.G.Sebald in England lebt', *Tages-Anzeiger* (Kultur), 11 July 1998 (wysiwyg://89/http://www.tages-anzeiger.ch/archiv/98juli/980711/ 45910.HTM).
Isenschmid, Andreas 1990: 'Melencolia. Prosa zwischen Protokoll, Zitat und Traum. W. G. Sebalds "Schwindel. Gefühle."', *Die Zeit*, 21 September 1990, 75.
Korff, Sigrid 1998: 'Die Treue zum Detail — W.G. Sebalds *Die Ausgewanderten*' in Braese 1998, 167–197.
Mann, Heinrich 1935: 'Die Macht des Wortes', *Die Neue Weltbühne*, 4/10, 7 March 1935.

Merleau-Ponty, Maurice 1964: *L'Œil et l'Esprit*. Paris: Gallimard.

Naumann, Barbara: 'Wenn alles Kultur ist. Über zwei neue Einführungen in die Kulturwissen-schaft', *Die Zeit*, 40, 30 September 1999, 57.

Pfohlmann, Oliver 1999: 'Ausblicke von Schönheit und Intensität. W. G. Sebald: "Logis in einem Landhaus"', *literaturkritik.de*, 1/1999 (http://www.literaturkritik.de/txt/1999-01-27.html).

Rimbaud, Arthur 1960: 'A Georges Izambard' (letter of [13] May 1871) in Rimbaud: *Œuvres*. Paris: Garnier, 343–344.

Schmitz, Helmut (ed.) [2000]: *An End to* Vergangenheitsbewältigung? *Representations of National Socialism in post-'89 literature*. Aldershot: Ashgate [forthcoming].

Sontag, Susan 1983: 'Under the Sign of Saturn' in Sontag: *Under the Sign of Saturn*. London: Writers and Readers Publishing Cooperative Society Ltd (New York: Farrar Straus Girous, 1980. Original essay 1978, introduction to Walter Benjamin: *One-Way Street and Other Writings*. New York: Harcourt Brace Jovanovich).

Williams, Arthur 1990: 'Botho Strauß and the land of his fathers. From *Rumor* to *Der junge Mann*' in Williams/Parkes/Smith 1990, 279–307.

—— 1991: 'Botho Strauß. From identity crisis to German ennui — whither the poet?' in Williams/Parkes/Smith 1991, 449–470.

—— 1998a: 'German-language literature after the diversion' in Williams/Parkes/Preece 1998, 1–20.

—— 1998b: 'The elusive first person plural: real absences in Reiner Kunze, Bernd-Dieter Hüge, and W.G. Sebald' in Williams/Parkes/Preece 1998, 85–113.

—— [2000]: '"Das korsakowsche Syndrom": Rembrance and responsibility in W.G. Sebald' in Schmitz [2000], 65–83.

——, Stuart Parkes and Julian Preece (eds) 1998: *'Whose Story?' — Continuities in contemporary German-language Literature*. Bern: Peter Lang.

——, Stuart Parkes and Roland Smith (eds) 1990: *Literature on the Threshold. The German Novel in the 1980s*. Oxford: Berg.

——, Stuart Parkes and Roland Smith (eds) 1991: *German Literature at a Time of Change, 1989–1990. German unity and German identity in literary perspective*. Bern: Peter Lang.

Wood, Jarnes 1998: 'A death artist writes. Fiction? Travel? History? Or all of these? His own publishers cannot quite classify W G Sebald's latest book', *The Guardian*, 30 May 1998, saturday 8.

MICHAEL SCHARANG:
FROM FLORISDORF TO NEW YORK
AND BACK AGAIN

SILKE HASSLER

The Austrian Cultural Institute in Cairo is happy to extend invitations to Austrian authors, on one condition: that they do not give a reading from their work. Why? Because only two people attend these receptions: the ambassador and the ambassador's wife. In the winter of 1999, Michael Scharang spent several weeks in Cairo, where he carried out research for a new novel and did not give a reading from his work. He and the ambassador got along famously.

While Scharang has travelled a great deal since the beginning of the 1990s, especially in America, his preoccupation with setting out, taking leave, and moving on dates back much further. His whole literary career, which began with his move, as a young student, from Styria to Vienna, from Kapfenberg to Florisdorf, can be seen as an accumulation of new beginnings, as a succession of new literary methods and their subsequent rejection, as a continual process of testing words against reality and of testing methods against the intended effect. Many Austrian authors have, in the course of their career, developed a method, perfected it, and made it their own. Scharang, by contrast, has left at least six literary methods behind. The only persistent refrain in this changeable career is his rallying cry 'Auf nach America', which rings out whenever his literary homeland becomes insufferable and impossible to live in.

It is in his two most recent novels, *Auf nach Amerika* (1992) and *Das jüngste Gericht des Michelangelo Spatz* (1998), that Scharang makes the cleanest break with his literary past and travels furthest: from Florisdorf to New York and back again. His two main characters, the anonymous first-person narrator and his girlfriend Maria, meander back and forth through both novels and between the continents with no respect for the laws of logical and chronological narration. Can it be that the inveterate realist Scharang, the boy from Kapfenberg who made it to Florisdorf, the author of great realist novels such as *Charly Traktor* (1973) and of realist screenplays such as *Der Sohn eines Landarbeiters wird Bauarbeiter und baut sich ein Haus* (broadcast by ARD 1975; book 1976) has become the literary equivalent of a stunt pilot, with his clever and daring tricks? Not quite. Realism has not disappeared altogether from his latest fiction, it has simply assumed new guises, becoming cleverer and more cunning.

Scharang scorns the narrative conventions of the media, whose watchwords are 'quick, short, and easily digested'. Disdaining the breakneck pace of our modern age, he sets against it his own deliberate slowness.[1] Thus, between the protagonist's leaving the precincts of J.F.K. Airport and his arrival at the New York apartment where he is to look after his girlfriend's convalescing dog, a good deal of time elapses. Time enough to expatiate on such subjects as airport taxis and their deceitful drivers, the searing heat under the glass roof of the airport terminal and the desolate streets of New York; time enough to cause a traffic jam and to observe its effect on car drivers; and time enough to make the acquaintance of an Italian confectioner. The key to this slow-motion effect is humour, coupled with precise observation of human behaviour and a profound understanding of human psychology.

The route from this, Scharang's latest literary method to his earliest, from the 1990s back to the 1960s, from New York back to Florisdorf and from there back to his starting point, in Kapfenberg, is a long and tortuous one. Back then, in the 1960s, a whole generation of provincial writers, mostly the sons and daughters of workers, farmers and *Kleinbürger*, left Kapfenberg, Maria Saal (Peter Turrini), Griffen (Peter Handke) and Steyr (Elfriede Jelinek) for Vienna: the big city, the seat of power. Here, they thought, the traumas of the post-fascist provinces would be overcome; the silence of the older generation (the *Wiederaufbaueltern*), who had kept their counsel through the tight-lipped 1950s, would be broken so that the truth about fascism and its continued legacy in the post-war years might finally be told.[2] However, the Austrian establishment, in the form of reactionary members of the PEN Club and those artists manqués, the cultural functionaries, showed no interest in these angry young men from the country with their inflammatory language. Just as Austria made no effort to secure the return of its writers in exile, so it preferred not to discover its youngest literary talents. Scharang and his generation could only get their work published abroad, if at all (principally by West German publishers: Luchterhand, Rowohlt and Suhrkamp). As a result, a whole generation of writers emigrated, at least as far as their writing was concerned, even before they could put down roots in their own country.

The young writers despised a society which refused to acknowledge its own contradictions, which coined the watchword 'A New Beginning' and promptly set the workers to do the donkey-work while behind their backs the new state was carved up in accordance with the time-honoured principles of cronyism and patronage. Instead of a new beginning, the old order was simply dressed up in new clothes. Such was their contempt for this society that the writers did not even want to share a language with it. Literature withdrew from the official language and turned instead to experimental language. According to Scharang, looking back from the vantage point of 1985, this linguistic experimentation, with its defamiliarization of language, was necessary

> weil die von den Nazis vergewaltigte Sprache in der Nachkriegszeit, statt fürsorglich aufgepäppelt zu werden, gleich wieder mißbraucht wurde, diesmal zur Sprachlüge von der sozialpartnerschaftlichen Gesellschaft [...] Zumindest solange die Konjunktur anhielt, wurde sprachlich so getan, als wären die Herrschaften letzte Nacht besoffen mit dem Volk im Straßengraben gelegen. (BPW, 109)

The fifteen texts which make up Scharang's 1969 anthology *Verfahren eines Verfahrens* are characterized by a two-pronged critique: of language and of traditional narrative forms. At times in this collection, Scharang's language reaches such a level of abstraction that the reality behind the words is barely distinguishable. Where once there would have been a narrator, a story and characters, we find instead an excess of syntactical structures: convoluted and labyrinthine sentences with no typographical signposts to help the reader find a way through.

Scharang had found his first literary method, or rather, it had found him, for none of his departures and new beginnings, none of his literary excursions has been an end in itself: each represents a writerly response to changing realities. No sooner had Scharang postulated the necessity of defamiliarization than he recognized the dangers inherent in it. In 1970, he published a volume of prose entitled *Schluß mit dem Erzählen und andere Erzählungen*, in which he called programmatically for the end of storytelling, whilst countering ironically that he himself, no matter how radically he called into question the business of storytelling, could ultimately do no other than write stories. Looking back, Scharang writes that the logical endpoint of the attempt to avoid all conventional modes of writing and speech is a position of pure opposition, of complete abdication, from which one can no longer communicate with one's readership or audience. Poetic language, he argues, cannot be random invention, and the defamiliarization of everyday language cannot be an arbitrary act, but must be backed up by concrete thinking, by concrete political thought (BPW, 109). For Scharang, then, every linguistic critique is also a social critique.

With this realization, Scharang had arrived at his next literary method, which he practised from the 1970s onwards. He called his writing from this period 'proletarianized' ('proletarisiert') and described it as 'vulgär', in the sense of 'accessible to the masses': 'Sie [die proletarisierte Literatur] weiß, je gewählter der Ausdruck, desto abgefeimter die Lüge'. Proletarianized literature 'plant nicht den Aufstand als literarische Methode. Sie gibt sich weder heroisch noch empfindlich. Sondern sie ist mißtrauisch, listig, spöttisch [...] Wenn sie sich schwer macht, dann nicht, um in die Tiefe zu sinken, wie man es von ihr erwartet, sondern um auf dem Boden zu bleiben, von dem man sie vertreiben will' (LK, 24).

In 1973, Scharang published a novel about the labourer Charly Traktor. The simplicity of the story, narrated from the perspective of the hero, is matched by the simplicity (not to say *Vulgarität*) of the language. Charly Traktor's problem is that he cannot make sense of the experiences that he amasses in a string of firms where he works until he is either fired or leaves of his own accord. He lacks a language in which to formulate his ideas, and he lacks the kind of colleagues who could show solidarity with him. Consequently, in 'Die Geschichte vom Wähler' (published in the 1974 anthology *Bericht an das Stadt-teilkomitee*), concrete individuals are no longer depicted: all that remains are linguistic processes in which the voter of the title no longer has the power to intervene. His story, his career aspirations and his hopes for a contented lower-middle-class existence collapse under the oppressive weight of the relative clauses describing his dependencies. This torrent of relative clauses is halted only once, at the end of 'Die Geschichte vom Wähler', when the narrator calls on voters, and that includes writers, to take control of their own stories, to achieve their objectives in life (Scharang uses the Marxist term 'in der Praxis') by means of self-determination and by organizing themselves politically. *Selbstbestimmung* and *Selbstorganisation* are two concepts that run like a thread through Scharang's essayistic work, acting as leitmotifs and rallying calls (Bekes 1998).

When, in the mid 1970s, Scharang's generation of authors took stock of the relationship between their language and proletarian reality, they found that traditional storytelling no longer fitted their purpose.[3] Scharang calls those who turned this situation into a crisis foolish, because for him the word 'crisis' implies a desire to restore the state that prevailed prior to the crisis. Here, too, Scharang sought a new way forward: 'denn wie man etwas erzählen oder be-schreiben kann, hängt nicht bloß vom subjektiven Willen dessen ab, der das tun will oder tut, sondern vor allem von der objektiven Beschaffenheit der Dinge, die erzählt oder beschrieben sein wollen. Die Frage nach der Erzählbarkeit oder Beschreibbarkeit ist eine [...] gesellschaftliche Frage' (Einer, 7). 'Die Beschaf-fenheit der Dinge', or, to put it another way, social development in its increasing complexity, had pulled the rug from under traditional forms of narrative, leaving only one option: to take whatever material was available (which in Scharang's case was language) and to relate it to real social conditions. With his *O-Ton-*

Hörspielen (in which workers with no training as actors speak about themselves and their environment), Scharang added documentary literature, in particular its documentation of the world of work, to the list of staging posts on his literary odyssey. The project was based on an idea which Scharang formulated as early as 1971 in his essay 'Zur Emanzipation der Kunst': 'die Aneignung der für eine zeitgemäße Kunstproduktion notwendigen Kunstmittel durch die Kunstproduzenten' (EK, 24). Only through such an appropriation, Scharang argued, could art emancipate itself from the bourgeois-capitalist sphere of influence and reestablish its political basis.

At this time, in the early 1970s, the only group to declare their solidarity with the working classes were the young realist writers; but the working classes were unwilling to accept help from this quarter. Despite the best efforts of the writers, the relationship between the two groups remained deeply strained and most writers let it wither when their efforts at *rapprochement* fell flat. All sorts of people attended readings of 'proletarianized' literature; the proletarians themselves stayed away. Many of the most politically committed writers of the period took refuge from this dilemma in increasing aestheticization and held the working classes responsible for their own apathy. Scharang held himself responsible and applied himself to the task of finding a new literary method.

The short story 'Harry. Eine Abrechnung' (1984) presents itself as a sequel to Scharang's realist novel *Charly Traktor*: Harry is the illegitimate son of Traktor. However, the story does not chronicle Harry's life. Instead, he sits in a pub in Vienna's Tenth District, facing the writer who has written the novel about his father, and explains to this writer that he (Harry) objects to him (the writer), writing a book about him (Harry). As in reality, so in literature: a working-class man rebuffs the writer's advances, providing Scharang with a clever premise for an examination of the role of the socially engaged writer. Increasingly, the story becomes a critical examination of Scharang's 'old' realist narrative techniques and raises questions about what form realist writing might take in the mid-1980s, given the background of a continually changing society and given the disillusionment of the working classes. The fictitious Harry says to the real writer Scharang in the story: 'Es führt zu nichts, glauben Sie mir, mich mit meinem Vater zu vergleichen. Ich lebe in einer anderen Welt. Er [Charly Traktor] fordert Gerechtigkeit ein. Ich verzichte darauf. Ich werde sie mir eines Tages nehmen. Das habe ich schon gelernt: Von denen etwas einzufordern, die taub sind, das macht nur heiser' (H, 130).

Harry's sober attitude corresponds to a very real development in Austria: by the end of the 1970s, Austria had made a success of itself, in its own eyes and in the eyes of the world. Austria was a reconstructed democratic country, the world had forgotten its involvement in Hitler's fascism, Waldheim was a big noise at the UN, and Austria was a thriving holiday destination, 'das Hawaii Mitteleuropas' (Turrini 1988, 144). The price for this picture-postcard idyll was paid twice over: in the lie that was propagated about Austria's political past and in the paralysis of the working classes. Those who were lucky may have managed to raise themselves to the ranks of the house-owning lower-middle classes, but the price they paid for this minimal economic advance was to surrender completely their agency in the political process. The social democrat functionaries were in cahoots with the employers and it was the employers who were calling all the shots.

From the early 1960s onwards, the Viennese Activists (cf. Roussel 1995) protested in their own, polemical way against this picture-postcard Austria, against a homeland under whose fields the war dead lay buried: they slung mud at the shining white innocence in which Austria cloaked itself in order to expose what lay behind it: the War, the lies, the unburied dead. Scharang, who had no time for things, for 'material action', for activism, but — as ever — only for language, later formulated this situation in the following words, extending his judgement to the whole of Europe:

> Ausgerechnet in Europa, dachte ich, wo Kultur nur mehr ein weißes Leinentuch ist, strahlend weiß, weil jede Woche frisch gewaschen, gebleicht und gebügelt, ein Leinentuch, das sich leuchtend über Abermillionen Tote breitet, über die Opfer von Völkermord, Weltkriegen, Massenmord. Wenn die Europäer [...] meinen, sich in ihrer Kultur zu sonnen, genießen sie in Wirklichkeit nur den Widerschein jenes Leichentuches. (MS, 130)

Although this passage is taken from a novel, Scharang's latest, it has the force of his essayistic work. It is possible to see the whole of Scharang's *oeuvre* as essayistic, to see the changes in his literary methodology as the constant struggle of the essayist Scharang to identify society's weak point: the point at which language is misused. To this extent, Scharang is the Styrian reincarnation of Karl Kraus, and *Die letzten Tage der Menschheit* do not end on the battlefields of the First World War, but live on in a factory canteen in Kapfenberg, spreading from there via Florisdorf as far afield as America. Scharang has devoted his entire literary career to denouncing the dishonest use of language, in order to unmask the dishonest thoughts and actions which lie behind it. In the novel *Charly Traktor*, the communist *Betriebsrat* decides to hand in his notice, saying: 'Ich wäre ein Masochist, wenn ich in diesem Betrieb bleiben würde'. The foreman could not agree more: 'Für Maoisten', he declares, 'ist hier kein Platz' (CT, 33).

In his novel about the eponymous Michelangelo Spatz, Scharang alludes to one of Karl Kraus's essays on language, in which Kraus explains the distinction in meaning between the phrases 'nur noch' and 'nur mehr' (Kraus, 1987, 16–18). Where Kraus theorizes, Scharang humanizes. A former burglar, the embodiment of every social worker's hopes, confronts the deputy director of the *Deutsches Haus* in Washington Mews in New York and threatens him with a sub-machine gun. He tells the director that he wants to get to the bottom of the distinction between 'nur mehr' and 'nur noch' once and for all, even if it means resorting to armed force. The deputy director offers to call a German writer currently staying in New York, but by the time the writer arrives the armed man has already been shot dead by the police. The punchline is an ironic comment on the writer's lack of a useful social role: 'Verflucht sei dieser Tag, rief der Schrift-steller. Wenn einmal jemand etwas wissen will, das nur ich weiß, wird er, ehe ich mich mitteilen kann, erschossen' (MS, 47).

In the 1980s and 1990s, Scharang frequently organized his own readings. He adapted his literary method yet again, broadening it to encompass the location in which his method would be put into action. He read from his work himself, in a wonderfully memorable way, checking the lights and microphone beforehand. The writer as artisan, working not just with his hands, but also with his mouth, to the evident enjoyment of the audience and to the annoyance of certain feuilletonists and of the newspaper editors and political parties to whom they are accountable.

In 1986, Erhard Busek, the then Secretary General of the Austrian People's Party (ÖVP), declared in an interview with the Austrian daily news-paper *Die Presse* (27 September 1986): 'Die Intellektuellen sollen ins Ausland fahren und erklären, warum Österreich doch so gut ist, daß sie hier leben'. Scharang took Busek at his word and responded: 'wir werden dieser Aufforde-rung selbstverständlich nachkommen. Da wir im Ausland nichts anderes sagen werden als hier, ist damit zu rechnen, daß uns Herr Busek nicht mehr einreisen läßt' (both WÖ, 47). During the 1990s (Busek had, meanwhile, resigned), Scharang travelled frequently, to America. For the first time he took literally his lifelong rallying call 'Auf nach Amerika'. Arriving in New York, he discovered that the city was an enormous theatre complex:

die Hauptbühne, auf der die wichtigsten Aufführungen stattfinden, heißt Manhattan; drumherum Probe- und Nebenbühnen, Kulissenwerkstatt, Technik, Verwaltung, Kan-tine. Orginellerweise ist die Beleuchtung außerhalb des Theaters angebracht, am Himmel, und besteht nur aus einem einzigen Scheinwerfer, der Sonne. Wenn der sich bewegt, kommen die Kulissen [...] erst richtig zur Geltung [...] Ein Wolkenkratzer

> spiegelt sich in der Glasfassade des anderen, dieser im nächsten, so daß sich nicht
> sagen läßt, was Wirklichkeit ist, was Spiegelbild. Der Vorwitzige, der der Sache
> nachgeht, wird zu Recht bestraft. Bewegt er sich auf die Kulissen zu, weichen die
> Spiegelbilder vor ihm zurück. (BPW, 76)

Scharang would not be Scharang if the idea of New York as a theatrical city and
the discovery of America did not lead immediately to the discovery of a new
literary method: 'Bislang war immer ich es gewesen, der die Dinge betrachtete.
In New York geht das nicht. Da betrachteten die Dinge mich' (MS, 12).[4]

The comparison of New York to a theatre complex is not just the result of
free association. It is a genuine experience, one which every theatregoer
recognizes to some degree: you sit in the theatre, your eyes fixed on the action
unfolding on stage, and all the while you are being controlled by objects and
stories outside of yourself.

> Um diesem Drama zu entgehen, übte ich im Zimmer: setzte mich als Schriftsteller
> kostümiert ins Fenster, mit Buch, Notizblock, Bleistift in der einen, mit der Brille in
> der anderen Hand, die Augen und den Kragen des Sakkos hochgeschlagen. Im Fenster
> gegenüber erblickte ich einen Mann, der als Silberschmied verkleidet vor einer
> kleinen Flamme saß und so tat, als wäre er beschäftigt. Und ich tat, als würde ich
> dichten. (BPW, 77)

Here, Scharang's focus has shifted from defamiliarized language to the defamiliarizing gaze. The narrator, who is asked by his girlfriend Maria to come to New
York for a few days to look after her dog (the one that is convalescing), soon
decides to stay on, because the city has so much to tell him. It is not a case of his
choosing things to go and see; rather, things and events choose him. They work
to their own peculiar poetic timescale, conform to no fixed laws and impose
themselves arbitrarily. Which brings us to the very latest Scharangian literary
method. 'Der Mut des Dichters ist der Übermut', writes Scharang in a review of
the premiere of Handke's *Zurüstungen für die Unsterblichkeit* (1997). Literature
is not courageous ('mutig'); it is high-spirited ('übermütig').

These same literary high spirits inform one strand of the action in the
novel: the first-person narrator and Michelangelo Spatz come up with an idea for
keeping people glued to their television sets (the holy grail of television making)
and offer to sell it to an American TV channel. They invent a hero, 'der in einer
Fernsehserie auftritt, der aber auch in allen anderen Sendungen plötzlich und
unerwartet auftreten [...] kann. So daß man, um der Serie folgen zu können, Tag
und Nacht fernsehen muß' (MS, 411). Thus Scharang, himself the author of
several screenplays,[5] recognizes (albeit, perhaps, with a measure of irony) the
incompatibility of literature and the media. In an article for *Der Standard* in
which he is ostensibly writing about Handke, but doubtless also reflecting on his

own latest literary method, Scharang locates the source of the media's hostility towards Handke in this very incompatibility:

> Als empörend, vermute ich, wird empfunden, daß Handke die Gesetze des Erzählens, also dessen Gesetzlosigkeit, auch dort achtet, wo Politik und Medien bereits eine hierarchische Gesetzmäßigkeit durchgesetzt haben: den Vorfall des Tages, das Ereignis der Woche, die Sensation des Monats, das Problem des Jahres, mitsamt Lösungsvorschlägen, vorzugsweise militärischen. Das Wesen des Erzählens aber — und deshalb sind Erzähler bei den Autoritäten so unbeliebt — ist Gleichheit. Nichts erträgt die Erzählung, was Vorrang hat vor irgend etwas anderem; was als wichtig anerkannt wird, um anderes als unwichtig wegzudrängen, [...] kein Gedanke, der sich Nebengedanke schimpfen lassen muß; keine Erinnerung an Vergangenes, die sich bieten läßt, von der Gegenwart unaktuell gescholten zu werden. Die Erzählung [...] wird von denen, die auf Information gedrillt sind, als obszöne Ausschweifung empfunden. (EsF)

Both Scharang's latest novel, *Das jüngste Gericht des Michelangelo Spatz*, and the previous one, *Auf nach Amerika*, constitute one long 'obszöne Ausschweifung'. They exemplify perfectly the latest Scharangian literary method. Here we are in that taxi from the airport again:

> Ich schaute durch die Heckscheibe. Eine Leitschiene, in die einmal ein Auto gekracht war, lag zerbeult und verrostet am Straßenrand. Seit die neue Leitschiene geliefert worden war, dürfte schon einige Zeit verstrichen sein. Sie war noch nicht montiert und lag ebenfalls rostig am Straßenrand [...] Das schien mir keine Notiz wert zu sein. Doch jedesmal, wenn ich dachte, nun sei der richtige Moment, ein Wort zu Papier zu bringen, fuhren wir durch ein Schlagloch, und der Bleistift, der auf dem Papier zu schreiben begonnen hatte, schrieb auf meiner Wange weiter. Was dort geschrieben stand, konnte ich aber nicht lesen, weil ich keinen Taschenspiegel bei mir hatte. Wenn die Umstände, dachte ich, unter allen Umständen verhindern, daß ich erste Eindrücke festhalte, dann ist diesen ersten Eindrücken auch nicht zu trauen. Und die waren: New York wird eben erst gebaut. Aber auch: New York zerfällt bereits. (MS, 14)

At the journey's end, the taxi driver exhorts the narrator, by way of a parting shot, to give his regards to his (the narrator's) fellow Egyptians on his return to Cairo. He has, says the taxi driver, always got on well with Egyptians. The narrator reflects for a moment:

> Da er so aufrichtig gesprochen hatte, wollte ich es mir nicht zu leicht machen. Ich wollte nicht einfach sagen: Danke, ich werde die Grüße bestellen. Und so sagte ich, auch meine Sympathie gehöre den Ägyptern, ich aber sei Österreicher. Der Taxifahrer lächelte. Ich weiß alles, sagte er. Es passieren schreckliche Dinge in Ägypten, Touristen werden erschossen, zu Pyramiden aufgetürmt und brennend in den Nil geworfen. So daß ein Ägypter im Ausland lieber sagt, er sei kein Ägypter. Ich erlebe das täglich, sagte der Taxifahrer. Ich habe jeden Tag Dutzende Fahrgäste, die Ägypter sind, das aber angesichts der schrecklichen Erlebnisse in ihrem Land nicht zugeben. (MS, 19–20)

In this, his latest literary method, Scharang, a *Kapfenberger* born and bred, has metamorphosed into an Egyptian in New York. But only momentarily, for it is the people, the things, the events, which scrutinize him (not the other way around), and when — in their own time — their gaze moves on, then the first-person narrator (whose time in America is spent searching for his grandmother, finding love again, and thinking about a Styrian coal merchant) insists on his own story. No matter what gazes or people or objects light upon him, no matter how much distance he puts between himself and Florisdorf or between himself and Kapfenberg, he always ends up back in Austria:

> Ich war bei der Erforschung der Lebensläufe der Großmutter und des Kohlenhändlers so tief in die Geschichte Österreichs eingedrungen, daß ich, gegen meine Absicht und gegen mein Interesse, auf dem Weg war, Historiker zu werden. Auf diesem Irrweg hielt ich erst ein, als ich sah, daß zu Beginn der neunziger Jahre die österreichische Nachkriegsgeschichte wieder dort war, wo sie begonnen hatte, bei der Sehnsucht nach zuverlässiger Führung: nach dem Kaiser, der das Land in den Ersten Weltkrieg, nach dem kleinen Diktator, der es in den Bürgerkrieg, nach dem großen Diktator, der es in den Zweiten Weltkrieg geführt hatte. Nun, in den neunziger Jahren, wird abermals nach einem Führer verlangt, zu haben ist aber nur mehr einer, der das Land an der Nase herumführt. (MS, 207–208)

Scharang is back on home ground, in the thick of issues that have preoccupied him throughout his life. The stunt pilot has landed, on an open field near the Bisamberg and, after thirty years of flying stunts and fighting battles and cautioning against *Nasenherumführer*, a journalist with the *Standard*, Michael Cerha, has the temerity to mock him. After Haider's success at the polls, writes Cerha, artists should assemble post-haste at the 'Gewissensfront', for he has doubts, after this election result, about 'die Effizienz der geleisteten Überzeugungsarbeit. Der Stimmengewinn der FPÖ ist eine Herausforderung für Kunst und Kultur' (1999). And Scharang answers, in a letter to the *Standard*: 'Wir sind nicht nur auf verlorenem Posten, wir sind auf gar keinem Posten. Zum Glück!' (quoted in Vujica 1999). What do the media have to offer, after all? Only fanfares, headlines and insinuation. Literature, on the other hand, offers whimsical detail:

> Der kräftige Hauptsatz lockt die Schergen herbei, währenddessen sich die vielen listigen Nebensätze zu den Menschen durschschwindeln. [...] Wir stecken in der Scheiße, gewiß. Aber nicht in unserer eigenen. Wen dieser Unterschied nicht zuversichtlich stimmt, der wird auf seiner Schwermut sitzen bleiben, anstatt sich auf dem Trampolin auszuprobieren. (LK,13)

In December 1999, Michael Scharang climbed on to the trampoline and flew off to Egypt in search of his next literary method...

Notes
Translation by Chloe E M Paver.
1. cf. the essay by Uta Aifan, 237–253 below.
2. cf. Halsall1998.
3. cf. Lengauer 1990.
4. cf. the essay by Arthur Williams in this volume, esp. 107–109).

5. These include 'Der Lebemann' (1979), 'Das doppelte Leben' (1981), 'Die Kameraden des Koloman Walisch' (1984) and 'Eine Heimkehrergeschichte' (1985).

Primary texts

Scharang, Michael 1969: *Verfahren eines Verfahrens*. Neuwied/Berlin: Luchterhand.
—— 1970: *Schluß mit dem Erzählen und andere Erzählungen*. Neuwied/Berlin: Luchterhand.
—— 1971: *Zur Emanzipation der Kunst. Essays*. Neuwied/Berlin: Luchterhand. (=EK)
—— 1973a: *Charly Traktor*. Darmstadt/Neuwied: Luchterhand. (=CT)
—— 1973b: *Einer muß immer parieren. Dokumentationen von Arbeitern für Arbeiter*. Darmstadt: Luchterhand. (=Einer)
—— 1974: *Bericht an das Stadtteilkomitee*. Darmstadt/Neuwied: Luchterhand. (=BS)
—— 1976: *Der Sohn eines Landarbeiters*. Darmstadt/Neuwied: Luchterhand [book of the television film].
—— 1986: *Die List der Kunst*. Darmstadt: Luchterhand. (=LK)
—— 1991: *Das Wunder Österreich*. Frankfurt am Main: Luchterhand. (=WÖ)
—— 1992: *Auf nach Amerika*. Hamburg/Zurich: Luchterhand.
—— 1993: *Bleibt Peymann in Wien oder kommt der Kommunismus wieder*. konkret Texte 3. Hamburg: Gremliza. (=BPW)
—— 1996: 'Erfahrung schrecklicher Fremdheit', *Der Standard*, 24 January 1996. (=EsF)
—— 1997: 'Der Mut des Dichters ist der Übermut. Notiz zu Handke', *Die Presse*, 5 March 1997.
—— 1998: *Das letzte Gericht des Michelangelo Spatz*. Reinbek bei Hamburg: Rowohlt. (=MS)
—— 1999: *Harry. Eine Abrechnung*. Vienna: Libro. (=H)

Secondary literature

Bekes, Peter 1998: 'Michael Scharang', *Kritisches Lexikon der Gegenwartsliteratur*, 60th instalment, October 1998.
Cerha, Michael 1999: 'Das Gewissen muß sich melden', *Der Standard*, 9 October 1999.
Halsall, Robert 1998: 'Language and Silence: Gerhard Roth's *Die Archive des Schweigens*' in Williams/Parkes/Preece 1998, 133–147.
Kraus, Karl 1987: *Die Sprache*. Frankfurt am Main: Suhrkamp.
Lengauer, Hubert 1990: 'Beyond reality: Theory and practice of Austrian prose in the 1980s' in Williams/Parkes/Smith 1990, 169–186.
Roussel, Danièle 1995: *Der Wiener Aktionismus und die Österreicher. 50 Gespräche*. Klagenfurt: Ritter.
Turrini, Peter 1986: 'Die touristische Bananenrepublik. Essay', abridged preview, *Der Spiegel*, 46/1986. With the title 'Die Deutschen und die Österreicher. Chronik einer touristischer Begegnung' in Turrini: *Mein Österreich*. Hamburg: Luchterhand, 1988, 137–147.
Vujica, Peter 1999: 'Frontbericht', *Der Standard*, 27 May 1999.
Williams, Arthur, Stuart Parkes and Roland Smith (eds) 1990: *Literature on the Threshold. The German Novel in the 1980s*. Oxford: Berg.
Williams, Arthur, Stuart Parkes and Julian Preece (eds) 1998: *'Whose Story?' — Continuities in contemporary German-language literature*. Bern: Peter Lang.

ENLIGHTENMENT AND ENTERTAINMENT — STILL?
UWE TIMM'S NARRATIVE MODEL
AND HIS RECEPTION
IN THE USA AND IN GREAT BRITAIN

HELMUT PEITSCH

I Preamble

In 1972, Uwe Timm published the essay 'Zwischen Unterhaltung und Aufklärung' in *kürbiskern*. In it he drafted out a narrative model which sought to
combine accessibility for a large number of readers with the discovery of a new
social reality: 'Selbstverständlich wäre es falsch, [...] die vorliegende Aufklä-
rungsliteratur mit der vorliegenden systemkonformen Unterhaltungsliteratur zu
kreuzen [...] Gemeint ist vielmehr die Verbindung — eine langfristige Arbeit —
zweier literarischer Tendenzen' (Timm 1972, 88).

Timm's narrative model, which was shared in the 1970s by those associated with him in the *AutorenEdition* publishing collective, provoked a chorus of
violent polemic from left-wing and liberal critics and authors — from Heinz
Ludwig Arnold and Lothar Baier to Jörg Drews, from H.C. Buch to Hermann
Peter Piwitt, the 'naive[.] Darstellungsverfahren' of realist narrative (Laemmle
1976, 153) were rebutted and the standards of modern narrative theory re-
asserted, some citing Brecht, others Adorno as their authority. And Timm's
novels based on this model, from *Heißer Sommer* (1974) to *Der Schlangenbaum*
(1986), provided prominent critics with opportunities for model slatings: Ulrich
Greiner (1974), Volker Hage (1976), Werner Fuld (1986), Christian Schultz-
Gerstein (1974), Heinrich Vormweg (1986) and Stephan Reinhardt (1984),
whether they were writing in the *Frankfurter Allgemeine Zeitung*, *Die Zeit*, *Der
Spiegel*, *Süddeutsche Zeitung*, or *Frankfurter Rundschau*, were united on the
absence of aesthic value. However, Fuld's attack on *Der Schlangenbaum* employed a new yardstick. His points of reference were not Brecht and Adorno,
they were 'angelsächsische[.] Vorbilder, die dieses Genre mit bekannter Leichtigkeit und Routine beherrschen'; 'Uwe Timms Parabel vom Sieg der Natur ist
schief konstruiert. Dies entspricht der falschen Seriosität dieses verhinderten
Abenteuerromans, dem sein literarisches Hemd so angegossen sitzt wie eine
Zwangsjacke' (Fuld 1986). Where Timm's narrative model had previously been
termed a 'Trivialform' 'eines Bertelsmann-Romans' (Laemmle 1976, 163, 162),

now it appeared to be not 'trivial' enough, it was too serious. With *Kopfjäger* (1991), however, the tables began to turn; and they turned completely with *Die Entdeckung der Currywurst* (1993). The number of reviews doubled from an average of twenty to more than forty (cf. Basker 1999, 123–145) and the majority agreed that the 'wunderbare Geschichte', in Fuld's words, deserved fulsome praise: 'so [ist] [...] bei uns schon lange nicht mehr erzählt worden [...], ohne Sentimentalitäten und [...] stets ganz dicht an der Wirklichkeit' (Fuld 1993). Just one reviewer had a sufficiently good memory (or archive) to recall Timm's 1972 essay: 'Der Balanceakt zwischen "Unterhaltung und Aufklärung" ([...] eine Forderung der Postmoderne) ist seit 20 Jahren erklärtermaßen das Ziel Uwe Timms — er ist ihm hier gelungen' (Boedecker 1992).

In the first part of this essay, by approaching Timm's narrative model as an example of committed literature, I want to suggest an alternative to the interpretation that sees the combination of enlightenment and entertainment as 'postmodern' and seeks to highlight the continuity in Timm's oeuvre. In the second part, I shall outline the changes in the conditions affecting the reception of his work in the 1990s, in particular the critics' demand for 'angelsächsich[es] Erzählen'. In the third and fourth parts, I take the reception of *Kopfjäger* and *Die Entdeckung der Currywurst* in the USA and Great Britain as the litmus test of whether Timm's entertaining novels were perceived as examples of an international post-modernism, as products of westernized German literature, or as traditionally German.

II Committed literature?

Timm wrote his first *kürbiskern* essay as a direct response to Peter Handke's *Ich bin ein Bewohner des Elfenbeinturms*, his critique of Sartre's concept of commitment. The 'Scheinalternative': 'Entweder Politiker oder Schriftsteller' (Timm 1970, 619), was rejected by Timm as merely reproducing the division of labour and alienation. The 'engagierte Autor' (Timm 1972, 79) avoided the separation imposed by the literary market between serious and light literature, between entertaining 'beruhigende Fiktionalität' and empty 'Irritation' (82). The blind spot common to both serious and light literature was the 'soziale Wirklichkeit' (82), as he put it in 'Zwischen Unterhaltung und Aufklärung', where he first described the so-called negative *Entwicklungsroman*, the narrative model which typified the AutorenEdition. Once the concept of realism had been established in the programme of the AutorenEdition, that of commitment slipped into the background in Timm's essays. He limited it to the political sphere, e.g. in a discussion with Klaus Konjetzky, at that time like Timm a member of the

DKP, who defined literary commitment as the inadequate preliminary stage of party-political commitment in literature (Konjetzky 1977, 134). Timm distanced himself from this definition by identifying political commitment as the prerequisite for the real literary work of the author. However, Timm did not uphold this distinction between party-political commitment and literature as a linguistic schooling in social responsiveness in the year of Biermann's expatriation from the GDR; quite the opposite, his renunciation of the DKP appears to have made it easier for him to hold on to his concept of literary commitment: 'politische, aufklärerische, engagierte Literatur' (Timm 1976b, 176) are synonymous concepts for him, together with 'politisch engagierte Prosa' (Timm 1976c, 24). He places the opposite of this: '"freie, reine oder autonome Literatur"' in ironic inverted commas and doubly criticizes formalistic literature for literature's sake: because of its refusal to engage with reality and because of its corruption of the representation of what is a social privilege to make it appear endowed with intrinsic value (Timm 1976b, 175). Timm responds to Drews's attack on 'alle engagierten Autoren' (Timm 1976b, 170) who seek to break down the binary division of literature into 'anspruchsvoll' and 'anspruchslos' (169) thus: 'Hier verteidigt ein Bildungsprivilegierter seine Privilegien, die zu festigen jede seiner Kritiken beiträgt' (170).

In the year of the *Wende*, Timm contributed an article to a poetological collection by Kiepenheuer & Witsch authors, the publishers he moved to on the demise of the AutorenEdition, and included in its subtitle the concept which had replaced realism as the new buzz word of the day: 'Ästhetik des Alltags'. At the same time he reaffirmed his position as an 'engagierter Schriftsteller' and defined his texts as 'engagierte Literatur' (Timm 1989, 204).

Four years later, in his Paderborn lectures on poetics, he used the adjective again, but his supplementary qualification reveals the defensive stance that had become characteristic of any declaration of commitment in the 1990s. He depicted himself as an 'engagiert[er] Ethnograph[..]' who did not dip into the 'ideologischen Schwitzkasten' but looked instead at 'das Alltägliche mit dem Blick des Fremden' (Timm 1993b, 144). This insistence on individual, subjective experience and perception, on the one hand, and on distance and the power of language, on the other, implied a programme which placed a dual expectation on narration: 'in Distanz zur Sprache [zu bringen]' (54) and to mediate 'Identität', 'ganz normal in der Sprache [...] sein' (45–46).

For Timm, committed narration remained 'Deutung der Zeitläufte' (98), but, compared with the realism of the AutorenEdition, the accent no longer lay on the future (utopia) but on the past (106). He explained the change in a discussion with Manfred Durzak, on the one hand, in terms of the insight 'daß es kein handelndes Subjekt mehr gibt, kein revolutionäres Subjekt' (Durzak 1995, 336) and, on the other, in terms of the refusal 'sich [...] zynisch in einer Gesellschaft, die Ungleichheit [...] produziert, ein[zu]richten' (330–331). Timm defined 'engagiert' as '[d]ie Erfahrung: daß man aus seiner Isolation herauskam, [...] aus einem Subjektivismus' and thus, describing his politicization through the 1960s, preserved his concept of commitment as an 'Entdecken von Gesellschaft, von einem Gegenüber': 'Aus meiner Haltung, die damals elitär isoliert war, wurde eine, die sich gesellschaftlich verstand. Ich versuchte nun, auch in der literarischen Form Menschen und Dinge anders zu reflektieren, nämlich deren gesellschaftliche Bedingtheit mitzubedenken' (312–313).

Two details of form and one of content from *Kopfjäger* and *Die Entdeckung der Currywurst* reveal that Timm's narrative in the 1990s continued to reflect a model of commitment based on taking an involved position. The first detail indicates the narrative position of both texts, the second is indicative of the central system of imagery (which also provides the titles), the third is a secondary figure common to both texts.

The narrative present of the first-person narrator in *Kopfjäger*, Peter Walter, is riddled with limitations signalled through the uncle figure. At the narrative time of the action in his childhood and youth his uncle is presented as admired by the mother he does not love, while at the narative time of his flight he appears as the persecutor. On top of this, during the actual process of writing, he becomes a negative point of reference. In this way the text establishes a distance from the first-person narrator which is perceived by its addressee. The first-person narrator's mockery of his uncle as a committed writer 'lamentierend', 249; 'Sozialspanner', 314; 'Schnee von gestern', 249) takes on an air of cynical clarity about the way the critic belongs in the society he criticizes; correspondingly, the first-person narrator depicts the sole situation which might possibly show him adopting a position of committed involvement: 'In den sechziger Jahren wollte irgendein wahnsinniger Stadtplaner den Kanal zuschütten und darauf eine Stadtautobahn bauen. (Ich habe damals, mein bislang einziges politisches Engagement, Flugblätter verteilt, bei dem Treppauf-Treppabjagen nach Zeitschriftenabonnenten. Kam durch die Flugblätter mit den Leuten schnell ins Gespräch und auf einen guten Abonnentenschnitt.)' (316). The first-person narrator 'sees through' the way the political end becomes a means to private gain.

At the level of the novel's imagery, the same revelatory effect is achieved by equating the cannibalism on Easter Island with, on the one hand, present-day capitalism and, on the other, literature. For the first-person narrator both the uncle collecting his stories and Rob are the 'größte [...] Headhunter Deutschlands': 'Er [...] schloß sich Meinungsumschwüngen schon in einem sehr frühen Stadium an, um die vorausgeahnten Meinungen sodann mit Überzeugung und Geschick zu vertreten — und half so, ihnen Geltung zu verschaffen. In der Minderheit zu sein, war für ihn wie ausgeschlossen zu sein, in der Ecke stehen zu müssen, nicht mitspielen zu dürfen' (254).

The metaphorical equating of the 'Überzeugungs-Opportunisten' (255) and the 'committed' person, however, as with the mockery mentioned above, is undermined by the contrast which distinguishes playing the stock market from the game of literature: it sharpens the difference in approach to boredom which lies at the heart of the cannibalism metaphor. At the end of the novel, the first-person narrator, on Easter Island, formulates his theory which is to solve the mystery of the statues and the cannibals: 'Eine kolossale kollektive Langeweile brach aus, die [...] zu der Herstellung dieser kolossalen Statuen führte, was aber auch nur in Wiederholung, also Monotonie mündete, in Langeweile, und diese [...] wird am leichtesten durch Aggression aufgelöst, durch [...] rituellen und kulinarischen Kannibalismus, Mord und Totschlag' (441). The central metaphorical idea of boredom encompasses, on the one hand, a narrative which corresponds to dealing in commodity futures: it is allowed to disappear into the black hole of indifference, and, on the other, a narrative of recollection: it 'passes on' desires (313). At the end, the first-person narrator's text is transferred on diskette to become part of the uncle's work, 'der ja alles ausplündert. [...] Er gibt dafür seinen Namen, darf aber nichts, nicht ein einziges Wort ändern' (433).

The narrative situation is again linked with the metaphor in the title in *Die Entdeckung der Currywurst*: 'Frau Becker behauptete, [...] ihre [...] Currywurst, die löse die Zunge, die schärfe den Blick' (13). Where the sharpening of the eye, which is aimed at indifference and boredom, is directed can be seen by reference to a secondary figure who appears in the two texts under two different names: it is the old boat builder called Behrens in *Kopfjäger* and called Junge in *Die Entdeckung der Currywurst*. In *Kopfjäger*, the world of skilled work posesses such an attraction for the first-person narrator that (for the one and only time) he runs out of business-related lies: 'Es war der Moment, als ich still wurde, als mir keine Geschichte einfiel, der Moment, in dem ich mich so fühlte, wie der Onkel sich das vermutlich vorstellt, ich dachte an mich, und ich fand mich abstoßend, voller Ekel dachte ich an mich' (Timm 1991, 383–384). Both at the narrative time of the court hearing and also at the narrative time of the stock-market trading the look at the boatbuilder, who loses 'vierzig Jahre Arbeit' (381) in Walter's and Dembrowksi's business, places the first-person narrator in the wrong in his own eyes: 'Um ehrlich zu sein, nicht alle Leute die vor Gericht aussagten und ihr Leid klagten, waren mir gleichgültig [...] Seinem Auftreten im Zeugenstand sah ich nicht nur mit Unbehagen und Unruhe, sondern mit einer gewissen Angst entgegen' (379). The opposite of this fear is the wish the first-person narrator is unable to fulfil when he pays a business visit:

> Ich wäre gern nur zum Zuschauen in der Werkstatt gewesen, [...] ohne Absicht, ohne Zwang, etwas sagen zu müssen über Gewinnspannen, Preisverfall und Börsentrends, vor allem aber, ohne lügen zu müssen. Einfach zuschauen können, wie sich unter einem Hobel die Holzspäne herausdrehten, wie die Hand des Gesellen prüfend über die Planke fuhr, dabeistehen zu dürfen, wie man als Kind anderen bei der Arbeit zuschauen durfte. (382)

The resurfacing of the reality of the majority of working people, which had disappeared from his mind, also occurs in a scene in New York, which is recalled by a trip to negotiate with brokers: 'Danach war ich durch die Straßen gelaufen, hatte am Broadway einen Mann entdeckt, der gerade dabei war, eine Scheibe einzupassen. Ich blieb stehen, und mit mir immer mehr und mehr Leute, Leute in Anzügen oder Kostümen, mit Aktentaschen in den Händen. Wir alle schauten zu' is how the first-person narrator recalls the scene and then goes into increasingly detailed description of the individual operations, until finally he states: 'Die Neugierigen, und ich mit ihnen, gingen weiter. Wir alle waren Zeugen einer seltsamen, fremden Tätigkeit geworden' (382).

III Timm's German reception in the 1990s

In the 1990s, dominant west German literary criticism structured what was regarded as legitimate in the literary field within a system of opposites which justified the exclusion of committed literature. This is most obvious in the offensive mounted by publishers and other middlemen, who (unlike the critics) did not attack the authors directly but claimed instead to represent the interests of the readers. They set the needs for popular entertainment against elitist concepts of art. The competing sides designated the two poles in different ways, but Hubert Winkels, a commissioning editor with Kiepenheuer & Witsch, is right when he speaks of a 'Feld mit halbwegs einheitlichen Regeln und deutlichen Gegensätzen' (Winkels 1998, 5). Thus, for example, Uwe Wittstock (1993, 330) and Siegfried Unseld, representing the different sides, both invoke Enzensberger's dictum that literature should neither legitimate nor challenge legitimacy, only the one does so in support of entertainment, while the other concludes that 'man sich in der Literatur über Literatur verständigt' (Unseld 1993). Jürgen

Neven du Mont, director of Kiepenheuer & Witsch, sees the opposition as one between 'durch Moderne geläutertem Realismus' and 'Hermetik' (Geisel 1993); Maxim Biller and Matthias Altenburg, two of his authors, describe the opposition as that between 'Welthaltigkeit' and 'Rückzug auf Textualität' (Biller 1993; Altenburg 1993). Michael Krüger, who is the director of the Hanser Verlag, publishes journals and is also an author, sees the two sides as the 'book light' and a 'Spezialliteratur' marked by 'Komplexität' (Krüger 1993, 198, 203). The superficial nature of these evaluative patterns becomes clear when we take account of the polemic between Kiepenheuer & Witsch commissioning editor Martin Hielscher and Karl Heinz Bohrer. Hielscher's charge of 'Elitismus' (1995, 59, 61, 68) caused Bohrer to set himself apart from the 'Spießer' (1995, 1058) and 'Kleinbürger' (1061). Both Hielscher and Bohrer are, in fact, equally signalling an 'Abschied' (Hielscher 1995, 63) from a literature of commitment. While Bohrer locates commitment on the side of the 'Spießer', for the advocates of entertainment it is a component of elitism. Hielscher sees in commitment a variant of the elitist 'Deutungsprivileg', the 'politisch-moralische' variant, which competes with the metaphysical privilege of the 'Dichter-Seher', repre-sented by Handke and Strauß (Thomalla 1996). Bohrer aims his polemic directly at the Zeitroman, which is 'engagiert', i.e. it is 'Gesinnungsliteratur' (Bohrer 1995, 1061). Unlike Bohrer, however, most attempts to depict the situation which see 'das Zentrum der Debatte' (Rathnow 1998) as located in the contrast between light and serious literature are silent about commitment. In this way, critics and authors alike contribute to the exclusion of commitment, they con-stantly define the poles exclusively in terms of amusement and self-referen-tiality. This is true whether they see the structural conflict within the field as between entertainment and formalism (Seibt 1995), between entertainment and the specifically literary (Drews 1998), between realism and aestheticism (Mo-dick in Buselmeier 1995) or realism and anti-realism (Biller in Wieviel Literatur 1992, 125), between the naive narrative and the ivory tower (Politycki in Rath-now 1998) or naive realism and 'traumhaft heiterem Realismus' (Koneffke in Wieviel Literatur 1992, 127) or epigonism and avant-garde (Spinnen 1995, 208).

To put it bluntly, the exclusion of commitment from the field of legitimate literature constitutes a falsification of literary history. With total disregard for very basic facts, Grass and Wolf are lumped together in generalizations about a 'German' (i.e. West and East German) post-war literature defined by generation which (as committed literature) 'vierzig Jahre lang den Widerstand gegen Hitler nachholte' (Anz 1995, 83). In the context of commitment, the authors them-selves have provided the critics with two authoritative slogans, which they hardly ever fail to quote. Both support the *Sonderweg* thesis and can be integrated, thanks to literary historians, into the great metanarratives of post-modernism.

In 1987, Enzensberger povided the classic signal for the end of commitment: 'Langsam, aber sicher breitet sich unter den Intellektuellen die Einsicht aus, daß ihre alte Präzeptorenrolle ausgespielt ist. [...] es ist eine Vergesellschaftung solcher Rollen eingetreten. Wir haben Heinrich Böll verloren. Aber dafür haben wir amnesty und Greenpeace' (Enzensberger 1987). Enzensberger's claim has been quoted ever since — no less uncritically than Rolf Schneider's classification of GDR literature as 'Ersatzöffentlichkeit', which turned literary commitment into a 'Publizistikersatz' within a dictatorship (Schneider 1997). These two concepts have often appeared since 1989–1990 in combined form, as the democratization of the role of intellectuals and the release from the compulsion to be political (cf. Emmerich in Beutin 1992, 610).

The two pseudo-historical relativizations of commitment as the German Sonderweg open up two routes to normalization: one is preferred on the level of entertainment literature and is called internationalization, the other (nationalization) obtains on the level of serious literature. In both cases, as the term normalization implies, literature is instrumentalized for 'morality' and nation. Critics and commissioning editors alike make the assumption that a capitalist society with a democratic, parliamentary constitution has no need for commitment in literature. More precisely, any commitment that does happen to crop up is morally reprehensible, to the extent that it constitutes a threat to the socially guaranteed autonomy of art (of the elite) or to entertainment (of the masses). A typical *Frankfurter Rundschau* article (23 October 1997) accuses Grass and, in immediate associaton with him, Rühmkorf, Loest, Hein, Wolf and Braun, as 'politisierende Literaten', of being 'unpolitisch, antiliberal und antiwestlich'. In relation to GDR writers, Iris Radisch, for example, uses the terms 'DDR-Nostalgie' (*Die Zeit*, 4 June 1993) and 'Ostalgie' (Emmerich 1996, 502); this implies a lack of affirmation for capitalism and democracy, while both are seen to be subsumed by the term 'western'. 'Western', however, is not meant to stand just for the societal elements of modernity, but also for the aesthetic elements as well — especially when critics see themselves engaged in the struggle against 'deutsche Zivilisationskritik und das neue Antiwestlertum' (Richard Herzinger in *Die Zeit*, 4 June 1993).

And the normality of the West, at least in literature, takes on two guises: as international post-modernism and as national tradition. In the first case, the yardstick is the degree to which entertaining literature can be translated; in the second, it is the continuity of national self-awareness. The ambivalence of 'westernization' as a norm, since it means both international and national at the same time,[1] is what informed Schirrmacher's 'Abschied von der Literatur der Bundesrepublik'. On the one hand, he measured the latter against the 'Literaturen der Nachbarländer', where (he was speaking of the period 1959–1965) 'der Abschied von einem stabilen, selbstbewußten Ich längst vollzogen war', while, on the other, he criticized German literature for having '[den] Raum der [deutschen] Geschichte [...] versperrt', '[d]en Zusammenhang mit der Vergangenheit [...] objektiv suspendiert', and of limiting '[den] Umfang des produktiven Gedächtnisses' (Schirrmacher 1990). Where Bohrer and others place their faith in the national tradition to end the German Sonderweg, Wittstock turns to the 'angloamerikanischen Romancier[s]' (Wittstock 1993, 319): 'Weder in England noch in Frankreich, weder in Italien noch in Nord- oder Südamerika wird das Recht und Pflicht des Schriftstellers, Vergnügen zu bereiten, mit soviel Mißtrauen beäugt wie hierzulande' (326).

IV Timm's reception in the USA

If we move on to ask the question about the pleasure taken by American and British critics in the 1994 and 1995 translations of Uwe Timm's books, what we find in their reviews initially is distrust of a different kind, but which seems to constitute a mirror-image of Wittstock's thesis: it is a fundamental distrust of narrative texts translated from German, which appears to presuppose that, as a rule, these do not promise enjoyment.

The reviews of *Headhunter* and *The Invention of Curried Sausage* rarely miss an opportunity to convey a negative stereotype of German literature. Even when they set out to except the individual case 'under review', the positive impression of this example of German literature becomes the exception that proves the rule. The first sentence of the discussion of *Headhunter* in the *Cleveland Plain Dealer* runs: '*Headhunter* is remarkable for a trait you might not associate with German literature: humor' (Zafris 1994).

With *Headhunter* and *The Invention of Curried Sausage*, Uwe Timm succeeded, at least in the United States, in getting reviews in daily newspapers with a nationwide circulation: *Headhunter* in the *Washington Post* and the *Wall Street Journal*, *The Invention of Curried Sausage* in the *New York Times*. Reviews of this kind provide a good indication of the success of a translation because they enhance its chances of selling the 2,000 copies usually printed (Sander 1986, 487) and thus save the book from the usual fate of being sold off cheaply after only a short time (cf. Frielinghaus 1998).

The most significant difference between the reception of the two volumes in the USA and Great Britain lies in the fact that, in the USA, it successfully breached the barrier succinctly expressed by Volkmar Sander: 'außerhalb der amerikanischen Germanistik findet deutsche Literatur in Amerika nicht statt' (Sander 1986, 488; cf. Klüger 1995, 135). The academic character of the British reception contrasts starkly with the journalistic approach of American critics. The difference in the appraisals of the two 'national' dailies which reviewed *Headhunter*, *Washington Post* and *Wall Street Journal*, is plain to see, all the more so since both reviews agreed about the novel's 'Germanness': the German element was identified as non-American, but it was detected in the first case in the protagonist's focus on pleasure and his capacity for enjoyment, and in the other in the moral criticism of capitalism, which was taken as explicitly anti-American. Both notices made reference to the Nazi past: Paul Kafka (*Washington Post*) regarded its anti-asceticism as the conquest of a military past which had demanded heroic self-sacrifice, while Bruce Bawer (*Wall Street Journal*) felt that its moralism was nothing less than the continuation of a Nazi attitude of mind. Kafka reviewed Timm's novel together with an Indian one, an Israeli one, and one from 'South California', so that the emphasis on national differences which opens the review becomes especially important: 'Every good novel constitutes an authentic, living world. [...] *Headhunter* is an innocent book that no American could write, burdened as we are with Protestant anxiety around the making of money. We must read and envy, because Peter Walter is a man who enjoys everything' (Kafka 1994). Bawer, in his very different reading of the first-person narrator as a moralist, takes the metaphor of cannibalism as his starting-point, specifically the sentence about Rob's '"serious mistake of putting headhunter into German and introducing himself as *Kopfjäger*"'; this sentence allows Bawer to identify 'Mr. Timm's tendency to play down German failings and blame the U.S.'; he finds support for this tendency in the way the Nazi past appears in the novel: 'Not too far beneath Mr. Timm's preoccupation with contemporary brutality lies a vivid sense of the horror of World War II. Yet that war is remembered not for its death camps (the only Nazi is a Latvian SS man who is disarmed by Walter's grandmother), but for Allied bombing of German residential neighborhoods. Likewise Mr. Timm implicitly ascribes the aspects of German finance that he finds offensive not to individuals, but to the influence of the financial establishment of another country (America)' (Bawer 1994).

These two very different readings by Kafka and Bawer were also in agreement that the positive qualities of the novel lay in its elements of reflection, rather than its naive narrative stance: 'something fresh, quirky, unexpected and illuminating' (Bawer 1994), that, however, (altogether at odds with the description given) the distance from the first-person narrator created through the text had been ignored.

The magazines also read the novel as a 'meditation' (Bawer 1994; *The Bookseller's Network*, 6 April 1994, 10; *The New Yorker*, 2 May 1994, 109) on the capitalism of the 1980s, but the moral and political assessment of the first-person narrator tended to slip completely into the background to make way, on the one hand, for appraisals of the tension created by the structure and episodic nature: 'fast moving engrossing narrative' (*The Bookseller's Network*), 'cliff-hanger after cliffhanger' (*The New Yorker*), 'abundance of earthy anecdote' (*Kirkus Review*, 1 November 1993), 'A page turner' (*The Bookseller's Network*), and, on the other hand, for judgements based on the potency of the imagery: *The Bookseller's Network* continues 'A page turner that haunts long after it is put down'. *The New Yorker* makes a similar comment: 'an allegory with the ear-marks of a suspense thriller'. The reviewers felt that the success of the novel stemmed from the 'proper mélange of elements to guarantee the reader's interest' (Byrne 1994); 'there's so much fun along the way [in] [...] this comic, disabused fantasia on themes from *das Kapital*. Marx would have cracked a grudging smile' (*Kirkus Review*). Even *Border Patrol*, the journal of the International Association of Crime Writers, joined in the praise of the structure and imagery: 'The construction is nonlinear [...]. Nevertheless the story rips right along and the [narrator's] [...] cynical and amusing remarks spice up the prose constantly' (*Border Patrol* 1994, 10).

The anti-Americanism of the imagery, of which the *Wall Street Journal* made a central issue, served as the basis for the only slating of the novel. It is hardly a coincidence that this appeared in the *Executive Recruiters News*: 'it all comes down to portraying the language of American business as a savage proposition'. Yet the only discussion of the book which did not focus on the structure and the imagery, concentrating instead on the first-person narrator, ended with a comprehensive offer of identification to American readers: 'Peter Walter embodies impulses all of us share: to rewrite our own histories, to escape boredom and to find meaning' (Zafris 1994).

When *The Invention of Curried Sausage* appeared in 1995, the controversy about the treatment of the German past was repeated in the daily press, this time between two New York newspapers, the *New York Times* with its nationwide circulation and the more local *New York Newsday*. Francine Prose, writing in the *New York Times*, more or less picked up where the *Wall Street Journal* had left off, charging Timm with silence about the Holocaust (Prose

1995). By contrast, Richard Eder's review in the *New York Newsday* worked out what appeared to be Timm's 'vision' and 'idea' on the basis of the figures of Frau Brücker and Bremer:

> Curried sausage [...] stands for his vision of a German tradition different from both the Nazi past and the overstuffed present. It is proletarian, irreverent, skeptical and spirited: [...] a North Sea socialism. [...] Half shirker, half compulsive believer, Bremer seems to be Timm's idea of what the average wartime German was actually like. The comedic [...] figure of Lena [...] is what Timm believes the average German could be, then and now. She is his national hope, and sometimes he makes her a little too readily splendid. Seeing photographs of Buchenwald in the paper, she [...] ends the charade [...]. It is not unbelievable, but tidier than it ought to be. (Eder 1995)

Only one magazine took up the question over which the *Times* and *Newsday* disagreed about the credibility of the 'tale of Germany's transition from Nazi totalitarianism to the "sweetly pungent anarchy" of modern Germany' (*Publishers Weekly*, 27 March 1995); the majority concentrated on Lena and were thus implicitly convinced through the figure of the woman (or the structure of 'persuasive romance'; *Recommended Reading*) of the 'redemption of a people out of war and madness' (Massaro 1995): 'her lust for life and unerring sense of right and wrong' (*Kirkus Review*, 15 March 1995, 342). This character was generally identified with the metaphor of the book's title and with the text as a whole: 'full of life, heart, spirit, and laughter, all seasoned delicately with sorrow and hope' (*Kirkus Review*; cf. Betsy Levins, Internet). Only the *Publishers Weekly* cast serious doubt on the image suggested by the title: 'Still, modern German history is a lot of weight to lay on one spicy wurst'.

Just as opinion about its imagery was divided, so there was also a lack of agreement about the book's position in literary tradition. On the one hand, the Germanness of Timm's *Novelle* was emphasized by its inclusion among internationally recognized post-war German literature — in a manner which had been anticipated by just one review of *Headhunter*; the way this achievement was qualified, however, was in itself indicative of the other way in which its humanistic quality was highlighted: 'Timm does for Hamburg what Gunther Grass [sic] has done for Danzig — make it more real for you than the place you grew up' (Kafka 1994). In this sense, what predominated were associations with English-language and other non-German narrative traditions: Frau Brücker was compared with the Wife of Bath (*Kirkus Review*, 15 March 1995, 342; Pratt 1995), the Good Soldier Schwejk (Eder 1995), and Anna Magnani's roles in neo-realistic films (*Kirkus Review*); Timm's Hamburg was compared with Saul Bellow's New York 'in his vital youth': 'like Bellow, he's in love with his hometown, the patrician-proletarian port city of Hamburg, and stuffs his book with street names, legends, weather, landscapes, and history' (*Kirkus Review*, 1 November 1993).

While the first-person narrator is only rarely the subject of commentary (only the *Los Angeles Reader* praised the 'perfectly poised tension' between him and the heroine; Mastaro 1995) extremely laudatory adjectives were heaped upon the story and the characterization: 'engaging' (Bill Meyers, Internet), 'captivating', 'heart-warming' (Betsy Levins, Internet). Characteristic of the predominant tone were slogans for the author like 'a world-class story teller' (Bill Meyers) and 'the skillful Timm' (*Kirkus Review*, 15 March 1995, 342) and for the book like 'the German version of "Like Water for Chocolate"' (Prose 1995) and 'an ideal summer read' (Pratt 1995).

V Timm's reception in Great Britain

In assessing the British reception, it is important to be aware of the discrepancy between the academic regard for Timm among British Germanists and his status in the Federal Republic. Timm's first literary distinction was the invitation to him in 1981 to become writer in residence at the University of Warwick, at a time when the Volkswagen Foundation had stopped financing the programme there and the DAAD had not yet taken it over (Bullivant 1989, 9). In the years that followed, Keith Bullivant, who was in Warwick at the time and is now professor in Gainesville, Florida, became the most important champion of Timm's work. From his lecture at the 1982 DAAD conference for British and Irish Germanists (Bullivant/Althof 1986) and his monograph on the contemporary West German novel *Realism Today* (1987) to his book on the literary consequences of unification *The Future of German Literature* (1994), Timm and his latest novel have always been at the centre of Bullivant's attention. Moreover, his narrative technique has served as the yardstick for the evaluation of other writers and texts (Bullivant 1987b, 2). The net result is that the British contribution to research on Timm in terms of books and journal articles is considerably greater than in the case of Böll or Grass, where the statistics are already quite remarkable (cf. Engel 1997, 257–261). Bullivant is the co-editor of the only book to appear in the Federal Republic on Timm and also a contributor to the volume edited by David Basker in the series *Contemporary German Writers*, which resulted from Timm's period as writer in residence in Swansea. Notable for their absence from the German-language part are the 'Aufsätze [...] deutscher Germanisten', which are promised on the dust-jacket (Basker 1999). Since Bullivant is listed there, in spite of the fact that he is now based in America, as a 'britisch[er] Germanist[..]', British Germanists are, as it were, very much in their own company in this second book on Timm. Even in the volume co-edited by Bullivant and two west German professors, published by Timm's publishers, Kiepenheuer & Witsch, there is a massive preponderance of extraterritorial German scholars: the two colleagues from Paderborn and Passau are almost lost from view among the seven (often originally from the Federal Republic) based in Australia, Italy, South Africa and the United States (Durzak 1995).

The interest in Timm shown by Germanists outside Germany was supported by west German institutions to the extent that the Goethe-Institut published a brochure to coincide with Timm's acceptance of the New York scholarship of the Deutscher Literaturfonds, which canonized the author to a degree quite at odds with his recognition in the Federal Republic. Whilst Ackermann and Borries's 1988 brochure made Timm a figure of central importance for the external impact of German literature, Timm was not once (then or since) chosen for the *Bestenliste* (Lodemann 1995), not once was he discussed by the *Literarisches Quartett* (*Stiftung Lesen* 1997), nor was he ever invited to give the Frankfurt Lectures on Poetics (Lützeler 1994). Timm never had a chapter in any of the anthologies of nineties' literature (Arnold 1992; Delabar/Jung 1993; Kramer 1996; Weniger/Rossbach 1997; Knobloch/Koopmann 1997; Erb 1998), the only monograph on nineties' literature to mention him (in footnotes) is Nikolaus Förster's *Die Wiederkehr des Erzählens* (1999, 192, 217). The first time a review of Timm's work was included in one of the Reclam *Deutsche Literatur* annual volumes was in 1994 (Görtz/Hage/Wittstock 1994, 228–231). *Fachdienst Germanistik* ignored both *Kopfjäger* and *Die Entdeckung der Currywurst*, but did at last include a cross-section of the discussions of *Johannisnacht* (*Fachdienst Germanistik* 14/12, 1996, 16).

If Timm was supported in Warwick, New York and Swansea as part of an external cultural policy which had an interest in critical self-representation (Enzensberger 1996, 37), then it was not to be disappointed. Critical interest was indeed directed at the home country and its literature (cf. Görner 2000)[2] — this becomes clear in Bullivant's case from his polemical references to contemporary British literature (Bullivant 1987b, 2). In both of the Timm-anthologies (Kiepenheuer & Witsch; Swansea), Bullivant's use of the term 'engagiert' (Bullivant 1995, 233) differs markedly from, on the one hand, the objective appraisal of an 'attitude towards committed writing' (Basker 1999, VIII) and, on the other, the prevalent positioning of Timm's narrative within a triangle of self-reference, entertainment and everyday ethnology. In the volume edited by Hartmut Steinecke and Manfred Durzak, entertainment became the common denominator on which all interpreters could agree, whether they tended towards a '"chaotische" Zirkulation der Zeichen' (Horn 1999, 199) or a 'Madeleine der Alltagsästhetik' (Steinecke 1999, 217).

From Bullivant's explanation of what is to be understood by the 'ethnographic perspective' (43) which is characteristic of *Die Entdeckung der Currywurst* and, particularly, *Kopfjäger*, it becomes clear why he was still able to talk of Timm's commitment:

> In these works our modern world is [...] anthropologized as a historically peculiar value system based on exploitation and confronted with alternative values. By doing this Timm hopes to go some way towards breaking the 'momentan allgemeine[n] und zugleich lähmende[n] Konsens' as to the profit motive and to generate a 'kritische, eine radikal subjektive Wahrnehmung des Älltäglichen' [...] in the mind of his reader that might possibly lead to a quizzical attitude towards the given and seemingly self-evident. (Bullivant 1999, 45–46)

The world which Bullivant called 'ours' is obviously not just a German one; but when he collaborated with a west German scholar, his perspective changed dramatically. In the essay he wrote together with Klaus Briegleb, 'Die Krise des Erzählens — "1968" und danach', Timm's contributions to the realism debate in the 1970s were reduced to a 'helpless' encounter with Adorno and classified as proof of 'die Stärke der Verdrängung' of the fascist past: 'Wir finden keine Auseinandersetzung mit der "Negativität des Positiven" in Adornos Denken nach Auschwitz' (Bullivant/Briegleb 1992, 329–330).

VI Conclusion

Both the journalistic reception of Timm's novels in the United States and the academic reception of them in Great Britain provide evidence that the German past determines any interest shown in reviewing and appraising contemporary literature; together they undermine any simple equating of 'international' and 'popular'. But this is not the only reason why it is wise to be cautious when 'international' is used by publishers as a slogan and by critics as a yardstick. With his eye on the international market, Bernd Lunkewitz, director of the Aufbau-Verlag, turned the popular success of Viktor Klemperer's diaries (which have also been translated into English) into one of the guiding principles of his publishing programme: 'Nach der Wiedervereinigung mußte eine Literatur entstehen, die [...] emotional packt'; '[...] daß die Leser eine Katharsis erleben, also eine tiefe Erschütterung und Befreiung'; 'Die Zeit zwischen Mitte der sechziger und Ende der achtziger Jahre ist vorbei. [...] Es ging um die Bewältigung des Krieges und seiner Folgen, natürlich auch um Auschwitz'; 'die westdeutsche Literatur hat fast 30 Jahre lang nicht emotional packend geschrieben' (Lunkewitz 1998). In the same breath, Lunkewitz refers to the Berlin Verlag, which

'eigentlich ja Manhattan Verlag heißen' 'könnte', as 'die Agentur des amerikanischen Kulturimperialismus':[3] 'Die veröffentlichen rund 80 Prozent ausländische Autoren' (Lunkewitz 1998).

The way in which international popular success can serve nationalist ends
becomes clear in an article by the critic Thomas Medicus on the success of
Bernhard Schlink's *Der Vorleser* in the United States and Great Britain. Without
naming Lunkewitz, he quotes the publisher's central concepts of 'Emotion' and
'Katharsis' in order to explain Schlink's national and international success.
Schlink united popular 'transatlantische Form' and the theme of the Germans in
such a way that he became a 'kathartisch[es] Sprachrohr ihrer Gefühlslagen':
'Daß wir uns — jenseits von Geschichtsrelativismus und Moralkeule — zu uns
selbst als Deutsche bekennen müssen, lautet das belletristisch gut versteckte und
[...] aufklärerische Credo' (Medicus 2000). What kind of 'enlightenment' might
be meant here was made obvious by the award to Schlink of the newly endowed
Die Welt literature prize to mark the occasion of his appearance on an American
coast-to-coast talkshow:

> dieser Gipfelstürmer der deutschen Gegenwartsliteratur unterläuft so ziemlich alle
> Klischees, die über deutsche Schriftsteller immer noch im Umlauf sind. Das
> begnadete Gestammel [...] ist ebensowenig seine Sache wie das zornbebende
> 'Engagement' von Autoren, die in verbohrter Besserwisserei das selbstauferlegte Amt
> des Mahners und Wächters ausüben. (cit. Dotzauer 1999)

This contrasting of linguistic reflection and popular, internationally successful
narration and also the exclusion of commitment were common to *Die Welt* and
to *Der Spiegel*, although Volker Hage's international legitimation (in the latter)
of the nationalist message was not based on Schlink's appearance on the
American talkshow but on the German edition of *TLS*. Without acknowledging
the author, Hage quoted a sentence from Peter Graves's composite review article
in which he notes 'the appearance of an unusually large number of accomplished
first novels by younger German authors' (Graves 1999, 7). Hage ignored
Graves's meticulous, strongly nuanced location of texts by five young writers
within the west German literary debate of the 1990s.[4] Instead of addressing
Graves's reminder of 'the East German tradition of critically committed
literature' and 'socially engaged writing in general', he incorporated his praise
into a text which used multiple repetitions to hammer home the terms 'Selbst-
bewußtsein', 'Unbekümmertheit', 'Unbefangenheit' and 'Unverschämtheit'
(Hage 1999).

Just one unfortunate error slipped into this proclamation of national self-
confidence by means of popular, international narratives;[5] we can read it as the
resurfacing of the repressed. Hage chose to quote, of all things, Sartre's 'What is

Literature?', specifically his definition of 'speech' as 'action', in order to play off the debutants of 1999 against post-war literature: 'Übermächtige Schuldgefühle waren es [...], welche die deutschen Autoren nach 1945 immer wieder hinderten, literarisch zu handeln, mit Worten vital nach der Welt zu greifen und so einen neuen Blick auf die Dinge zu öffnen' (Hage 1999, 248). And this is no more and no less than the definition of commitment, for Sartre elucidated his 'action through revelation' precisely as an appeal to the readers to change the world (Sartre 1958, 17).[6] In his Paderborn lectures in 1993, Uwe Timm said: 'Das Erzählen ist immer auch Stellungnahme, also politisch [...] Das muß in einer Zeit, in der absichtslose Literatur gefordert wird, in der Autoren auf Einmischung verzichten und bereitwillig die Folgenlosigkeit ihres Schreibens beteuern, hervorgehoben werden' (Timm 1993b, 103).

Notes
Translation by Arthur Williams.
1. For the ideological aspects of the discussion of the neoliberal concept of globalization as well as the political and economic aspects see: Bauman 1996, Burchardt 1996, Bieling/Deppe 1996, Haug 1996, Milios 1996. In different ways they thematize the connection between the apparently internationalist solution 'globalization' and the promotion of *Standortnationalismus* and also the internal social consequences of the deregulation carried out as part of this process. Enzensberger, for example, draws a picture of globalization as conflict between cultures (not consensus) used as an excuse for a power-conscious, 'egoistical' involvement of the national culture in the conflict (Enzensberger 1996, 41). On Enzensberger's source, Samuel P. Huntington, see Senghaas 1997. The concept of westernization (or Jürgen Habermas's 'kulturelle Westorientierung', 1995) is reduced by Bernd Greiner and Heinz Bude to Americanization; it corresponds to what Susan Willis calls the 'Begriff des demokratischen Konsums' (Willis 1991, 737), for Greiner mentions the following 'neutral' synonyms for Americanization: mass culture, consumer society, democratization, modernization (Greiner 1997, 5). Bude emphasizes two aspects of the Americanization of the Federal Republic: the adaptation of the concept of the political to mean democratic processes and the establishment of a popular schema for the regulation of behaviour and feelings: clever, cool and laid-back in place of heroic (Bode 1997, 45). Thus the concept identifies that which analyses of 'popular culture' differentiate: active everyday practices and conformist, homogenized consumption (Mayer 1998, 432). In order to highlight the inherent contradictions, Perry Anderson has suggested the (Brechtian) term 'plebianization' for the post-modern equating of democracy with marketization (Anderson 1998, 113–114). Anderson's differentiation of a citra-modern and an ultra-modern within the post-modern, however, merely reproduces the polarization between serious and light literature along the line 'availability' and 'immediate intelligibility' (102). On the pre-history of the concept 'cross the border, close the gap' in Leslie Fiedler's writings (Wittstock 1994, 14–39) see Anderson 1998, 13 and, particularly, Ross 1989, 14 on Fiedler's 1953 and 1955 essays: 'Afterthoughts on the Rosenbergs' and 'The middle against both ends'. In them he condemns to death the petty bourgeois nature of stalinist socialist realism in the name of a clean distinction between avant-garde and mass culture and between fact and fiction (32).
2. 'Worauf es [...] ankommt, ist, wechselseitig auf die Entwicklung eines kritischen Selbstverständnisses in Britannien und Deutschland Einfluss zu nehmen' (Görner 2000). Without naming the essay, Görner is referring to Doris Bachmann-Medick's 'Interkulturelle Beziehungen als "dritter Raum"'. Her emphasis on the 'erstaunliche Verwandtschaft' of post-colonial cultural theory with 'ökonomische Expansion und Fusion' (1999, 527–528)

tends to weaken the critical potential by the shift into aesthetics: 'Interpretations-offenheit', 'Perspektivenreichtum an Ausdeutbarkeit und an Infragestellung' (530). On this, cf. Anderson 1998, 113: 'a vast broadening of the social basis of modern culture and a great thinning of its critical substance'.

3. There is a similarly problematical concept of cultural imperialism in Politycki 2000a, 2000b. As a purely cultural category it never throws into question a societal system of exploitation and suppression, it simply marks the difference. Politycki's 'third way' between serious and light literature is distinctive only by dint of its oppositional position vis-à-vis the United States. He defines European literature explicitly as elitist and himself as Nietzschean. His use of names is particualrly irritating: he uses 'ein gewisser' or 'heißen' to mark the ones that are supposed to sound 'Jewish'. Arend 2000 is very carefully critical of Politycki.

4. Graves discussed Karen Duve: *Regenroman*, Christoph Peters: *Stadt Land Fluß*, Judith Hermann: *Sommerhaus, später*, Kathrin Schmidt: *Die Gunnar-Lennefsen-Expedition*, and Michael Kleeberg: *Ein Garten im Norden*. His principal theme was the 'new realism'. He was particularly critical of 'the populist blood and guts' of Duve and of Schmidt's 'curiously old-fashioned' 'essentialist view of women'. He commented positively on 'the space between words' (Peters), on the 'sophisticated' Hermann as well as on Kleeberg's confrontation with German history.

5. See, however, Kraft 1999, 141, who closes his survey of the prose of the 1990s: 'Damit soll nicht verhohlen werden, daß deutsche Literatur im Ausland weniger Chancen hat als andere Qualitätsprodukte aus Wolfsburg, Stuttgart und Leverkusen. Ist das so schlimm? Es ist zu bezweifeln, daß gerade die italienische Literatur den amerikanischen oder die spanische den russischen Markt erobert. Wozu eigentlich die Aufregung? Man fühlt sich [...] an die Fußballnationalmannschaft erinnert.'

6. [Translator's note] Sartre's essay: 'Qu'est-ce que la Littérature?' was first published in 1948 in the volume *Situations II* (Paris: Gallimard) where the relevant passage can be found: 'Il n'est plus temps de *décrire* ni de *narrer*: nous ne pouvons pas non plus nous borner à *expliquer*. La description, fût-elle psychologique, est pure jouissance contemplative: l'explication est acceptation, elle excuse tout; l'une et l'autre supposent que les jeux sont faits. Mais si la perception même est action, si, pour nous, montrer le monde c'est toujours le dévoiler dans les perspectives d'un changement possible, alors, dans cette époque de fatalisme nous avons à révéler au lecteur, en chaque cas concret, sa puissance de faire et de défaire, bref, d'agir' (349–350;original emphasis).

Primary texts
Timm, Uwe 1970: 'Peter Handke oder sicher in die 70er Jahre', *kürbiskern*, 4, 611–621.
—— 1972: 'Zwischen Unterhaltung und Aufklärung', *kürbiskern*, 1, 79–90.
—— 1975: 'Realismus und Utopie', *kürbiskern*, 1, 94–101.
—— 1976a: 'Sensibilität für wen?', *kürbiskern*, 1, 118–122.
—— 1976b: 'Von den Schwierigkeiten eines Anti-Realisten' in Laemmle 1976, 164–177.
—— 1976c: 'Über den Dogmatismus in der Literatur', *kontext* 1, 22–31.
—— 1989: 'Der Blick über die Schulter oder Notizen zu einer Ästhetik des Alltags' in *Es muß sein...*, 186–208.
—— 1991: *Kopfjäger. Bericht aus dem Inneren des Landes. Roman*. Cologne: Kiepenheuer & Witsch.
—— 1993a: *Die Entdeckung der Currywurst. Novelle*. Cologne: Kiepenheuer & Witsch.
—— 1993b: *Erzählen und kein Ende. Versuche zu einer Ästhetik des Alltags*. Cologne: Kiepenheuer & Witsch.
—— 1994: 'Der politische Ästhet. Alfred Andersch lesen', *Neue deutsche Literatur* 42/4, 168–175.

Secondary literature
Ackerman, Irmgard and Mechthild Borries (eds) 1988: *Uwe Timm*. München: Goethe-Institut.
Anderson, Perry 1998: *The Origins of Postmodernity*. London/New York: Verso.

Arend, Ingo 2000: 'Zwei Sprachen. Leipziger Buchmesse. Europa und die Literatur', *Freitag*, 31 March 2000.

Arnold, Heinz Ludwig (ed.) 1992: *Vom gegenwärtigen Zustand der deutschen Literatur*. Munich: edition text + kritik.

—— (ed.) 1995: *Ansichten und Auskünfte zur deutschen Literatur nach 1945*. Munich: edition text + kritik.

Bachmann-Medick, Doris 1999: '1 + 1 = 3? Interkulturelle Beziehungen als "dritter Raum"', *Weimarer Beiträge* 45, 518–531.

Bauman, Zygmunt 1996: 'Globalisierung oder: Was für die einen Globalisierung, ist für die anderen Lokalisierung', *Das Argument* 38, 653–664.

Basker, David (ed.) 1999: *Uwe Timm*. Cardiff: University of Wales Press.

Bawer, Bruce 1994: 'It's Dog-Eat-Dog in Deutschland', *The Wall Street Journal*, 28 February 1994.

Beutin, Wolfgang et al 1992: *Deutsche Literaturgeschichte. Von den Anfängen bis zur Gegenwart*. 4th rev. edn. Stuttgart: Metzler.

Bieling, Hans-Jürgen and Frank Deppe 1996: 'Gramscianismus und Internationale Politische Ökonomie', *Das Argument* 38, 729–740.

Biller, Maxim 1993: 'Soviel Sinnlichkeit wie der Stadtplan von Kiel. Warum die neue deutsche Literatur nichts so nötig hat wie den Realismus. Ein Grundsatzprogramm' in Görtz/Hage/Wittstock 1993, 281–289.

Boedicker, Sven 1992: 'Mit Geschichten Geschäfte machen. Uwe Timms neuer Roman "Kopfjäger": Balance zwischen Unterhaltung und Aufklärung', *Der Tagesspiegel*, 13 October 1992.

Bohrer, Karl Heinz 1995: 'Erinnerung an Kriterien. Vom Warten auf den deutschen Zeitroman', *Merkur* 49, 1055–1061.

Briegleb, Klaus and Sigrid Weigel (eds) 1992: *Gegenwartsliteratur seit 1968*. Munich: dtv.

Bude, Heinz 1997: 'Unser Amerika', *Mittelweg 36* (6/5), 41–48.

Bullivant, Keith 1987a: *Realism Today. Aspects of the Contemporary West German Novel*. Leamington Spa: Berg.

—— (ed.) 1987b: *The Modern German Novel*. Leamington Spa: Berg.

—— (ed.) 1989: *Englische Lektionen. Eine andere Anthologie deutschsprachiger Gegenwartsliteratur*. Munich: iudicium.

—— 1994: *The Future of German Literature*. Oxford/Providence: Berg.

—— 1995: 'Uwe Timm und die Ästhetik des Alltags' in Durzak 1995, 231–242.

—— 1999: 'The Writer as Anthropologist: The Works of Uwe Timm' in Basker 1999, 38–46.

—— and Hans-Joachim Althof (eds) 1986: *Subjektivität — Innerlichkeit — Abkehr vom Politischen? Tendenzen der deutschsprachigen Literatur der 70er Jahre. Dokumentation der Tagungsbeiträge des Britisch–Deutschen Germanistentreffens in Berlin vom 12.4.–18.4.1982*. Bonn: DAAD.

—— and Klaus Briegleb 1992: 'Die Krise des Erzählens — "1968" und danach' in Briegleb/Weigel 1992, 302–339.

Burchardt, Hans-Jürgen 1996: 'Die Globalisierungsthese — von der kritischen Analyse zum politischen Opportunismus', *Das Argument* 38, 741–756.

Buselmeier, Michael 1995: 'VorOrt Deutschland: '89er-Literatur? Zeitschriften-Rundschau', *Frankfurter Rundschau*, 24 June 1995.

Byrne, Jack 1994: 'Uwe Timm. "Headhunter"', *Review of Contemporary Fiction*, 1994, 220.

Cassidy, Bruce 1994: 'Uwe Timm', *Border Patrol*. International Association of Crime Writers, 10–11.

Delabar, Walter and Werner Jung (eds) 1993: *Neue Generation — neues Erzählen. Deutsche Prosa-Literatur der achtziger Jahre*. Opladen: Westdeutscher Verlag.

Dotzauer, Gregor 1999: 'Scharf geschossen. Über Spatzen und Kanonen im deutschen Literaturbetrieb', *Der Tagesspiegel*, 17 October 1999.

Drews, Jörg 1998: 'Zwischen Traditionalismus und Internet. Zur Beschleunigung der Literaturkritik', *Merkur* 52, 531–537.

Durzak, Manfred et al. (eds) 1995: *Die Archäologie der Wünsche. Studien zum Werk von Uwe Timm*. Cologne: Kiepenheuer & Witsch.

Eder, Richard 1995: 'From Bad to Wurst', *New York Newsday*, 4 June 1995.

Emmerich, Wolfgang 1996: *Kleine Literaturgeschichte der DDR*. New edn. Leipzig: Gustav Kiepenheuer.

Engel, Henrik D.K. 1997: *Die Prosa von Günter Grass in Beziehung zur englischsprachigen Literatur*. Frankfurt am Main: Peter Lang.

Enzensberger, Hans Magnus 1987: 'Die Gesellschaft ist keine Hammelherde', *Der Spiegel*, 19 January 1987.

—— 1996: 'Auswärts im Rückwärtsgang' in Sartorius 1996, 36–43.

Erb, Andreas (ed.) 1998: *Baustelle Gegenwartsliteratur. Die neunziger Jahre*. Opladen/Wiesbaden: Westdeutscher Verlag.

Es muß sein. Autoren schreiben über das Schreiben. Cologne: Kiepenheuer & Witsch. 1989.

Förster, Nikolaus 1999: *Die Wiederkehr des Erzählens. Deutschsprachige Prosa der 80er und 90er Jahre*. Darmstadt: Wissenschaftliche Buchgesellschaft.

Frielinghaus, Helmut 1998: 'Deutsche Literatur interessiert die Amerikaner durchaus' *Frankfurter Rundschau*, 12 September 1998.

Fuld, Werner 1986: 'Die Sandbank im Regenwald. Uwe Timms Roman "Der Schlangenbaum"', *Frankfurter Allgeimeine Zeitung*, 29 September 1986.

—— 1993: 'Affäre fürs Leben. Uwe Timms süß-scharfe Geschichte', *Frankfurter Allgemeine Zeitung*, 2 October 1993.

Geisel, Sieglinde 1993: 'Vertrauenssache. Reinhold Neven Du Mont über den Beruf des Verlegers', *Der Tagesspiegel*, 23 October 1993.

Görner, Rüdiger 2000: 'Ein jeder hat ein Skelett im Schrank. Third Way und andere Abwege: Gedanken zur wechselseitigen Wahrnehmung deutsch–britischer Kultur', *Frankfurter Rundschau*, 8 April 2000.

Görtz, Franz Josef, Volker Hage and Uwe Wittstock (eds) 1993: *Deutsche Literatur 1992. Jahresüberblick*. Stuttgart: Reclam.

—— 1994: *Deutsche Literatur 1993. Jahresüberblick*. Stuttgart: Reclam.

Graves, Peter 1999: 'Replanting the garden of the North', *The Times Literary Supplement*, 8 October 1999, 7–8.

Greiner, Bernd 1997: '"Test the West". Über die "Amerikanisierung" der Bundesrepublik Deutschland', *Mittelweg 36* (6/5), 4–40.

Greiner, Ulrich 1974: 'Allem Anfang wohnt ein Zauber inne. Uwe Timms "Heißer Sommer": der erste Roman über die Studentenbewegung', *Frankfurter Allgemeine Zeitung*, 8 October 1974.

Habermas, Jürgen 1995: 'Aufgeklärte Ratlosigkeit. Warum die Politik ohne Perspektiven ist. Thesen zu einer Diskussion', *Frankfurter Rundschau*, 30 December 1995.

Hage, Volker 1976: 'Realismus — wo denn? welcher? von wem? für wen? "Kontext 1" und anderes zu der Frage, was realistische Literatur sein kann oder sein soll', *Frankfurter Allgemeine Zeitung*, 7 December 1976.

—— 1999: 'Die Enkel kommen. Aufbruchstimmung bei deutschen Schriftstellern und ihren Verlegern', *Der Spiegel*, 11 October 1999, 244–254.

Hage, Volker, Rainer Moritz and Hubert Winkels (eds) 1998: *Deutsche Literatur 1997. Jahresüberblick*. Stuttgart: Reclam.

Haug, Wolfgang Fritz 1996: Editorial, *Das Argument* 38, 635–639.

Hielscher, Martin 1995: 'Literatur in Deutschland — Avantgarde und pädagogischer Purismus. Abschied von einem Zwang', *Neue Rundschau* 106/4, 53–68.

Horn, Annette and Peter 1999: '"Poesie heißt nämlich nichts anderes als Schöpfung durch Verlust". Die "chaotische" Zirkulation der Zeichen in Uwe Timms Roman "Kopfjäger. Bericht aus dem Inneren des Landes"' in Durzak et al.1995, 199–215.

Kafka, Paul 1994: 'Fiction', *Washington Post*, 20 February 1994.

Klüger, Ruth 1995: 'Zur Rezeption der deutschen Literatur im 20. Jahrhundert in den USA' in Arnold 1995, 132–135.

Knobloch, Hans-Jörg and Helmut Koopmann (eds) 1997: *Deutschsprachige Gegenwartsliteratur*. Tübingen: Stauffenburg.

Konjetzky, Klaus 1977: *Was interessiert mich Goethes Geliebte? Tendenziöse Gedanken und Gespräche über Literatur und Wirklichkeit*. Munich: Bertelsmann.

Kraft, Thomas 1999: 'Franz Beckenbauer und der Realismus. Anmerkungen zur Erzählliteratur der neunziger Jahre', *Neue deutsche Literatur* 47/5, 123–141.

Kramer, Sven (ed.) 1996: *Das Politische im literarischen Diskurs. Studien zur deutschen Gegenwartsliteratur*. Opladen: Westdeutscher Verlag.

Krüger, Michael 1993: 'Bücher im Überfluß. Ein paar Anmerkungen', *Neue deutsche Literatur* 41/8, 194–199.

Laemmle, Peter (ed.) 1976: *Realismus — welcher? Sechzehn Autoren auf der Suche nach einem Begriff*. Munich: edition text + kritik.

Lodemann, Jürgen (ed.) 1995: *Die besten Bücher. 20 Jahre Empfehlungen der deutschsprachigen Literaturkritik. Die 'Bestenliste' des Südwestfunks*. Frankfurt am Main: Suhrkamp.

Lützeler, Paul Michael (ed.) 1994: *Poetik der Autoren. Beiträge zur deutschsprachigen Gegenwartsliteratur*. Frankfurt am Main: Fischer.

Lunkewitz, Bernd 1998: '"Ich wollte immer im geistigen Brennpunkt der Nation sein". Der Verleger Bernd Lunkewitz über sein Verhältnis zu Literatur und Gesellschaft', *Berliner Zeitung*, 2/3 May 1998.

Malchow, Helge and Hubert Winkels (eds) 1991: *Die Zeit danach. Neue deutsche Literatur*. Cologne: Kiepenheuer & Witsch.

Mastaro, John 1995: 'The Invention of Curried Sausage', *Los Angeles Reader*, 16 June 1995.

Mayer, Ruth 1998: 'Populärkultur' in Nünning 1998, 432–433.

Medicus, Thomas 2000: 'Populäres Sprachrohr der Katharsis. Warum der Schriftsteller Bernhard Schlink bei uns und anderswo so erfolgreich ist', *Frankfurter Rundschau*, 18 February 2000.

Milios, Jean 1996: 'Internationalisierung des Kapitals, Gesamtkapital und Nationalstaat', *Das Argument* 38, 713–724.

Nünning, Ansgar (ed.) 1996: *Metzler Lexikon Literatur- und Kulturtheorie. Ansätze — Personen — Grundbegriffe*. Stuttgart/Weimar: Metzler.

Politycki, Matthias 2000a: 'Wir wollen doch alle Ravioli. Im Gespräch über Bestseller, Spätavantgarde und das Bedürfnis nach Trivialliteratur', *Freitag*, 10 March 2000.

—— 2000b: 'Der amerikanische Holzweg. Am Anfang vom Ende einer deutschsprachigen Literatur', *Frankfurter Rundschau*, 18 March 2000.

Pratt, Sharon 1995: 'The Invention of Curried Sausage', *Nuvo*, Indiana, 7/1995.

Prose, Francine 1995: 'Spicy Business', *The New York Times*, 11 June 1995.

Rathnow, Thomas 1998: 'Das Ende des Abgesangs. Jahrelang wurde die Krise der neuen deutschen Literatur proklamiert. Inzwischen hat sich der Wind gedreht', *Der Tagesspiegel*, Berlin, 5 December 1998.

Reinhardt, Stephan 1984: 'Vom Farbenreichen. Uwe Timms neue Prosa', *Frankfurter Rundschau*, 3 October 1984.

Ross, Andrew 1989: *No Respect. Intellectuals & Popular Culture*. New York/London: Routledge.

Sander, Volkmar 1986: 'Zum deutschen Buch in Amerika: Produktion und Rezeption', *Deutsche Vierteljahrsschrift für Literaturwissenschaft und Geistesgeschichte* 60, 484–495.

Sartorius, Joachim (ed.) 1996: *In dieser Armut — welche Fülle! Reflexionen über 25 Jahre auswärtige Kulturarbeit des Goethe-Instituts*. Göttingen: Steidl.

Sartre, Jean-Paul 1948: 'Qu'est-ce que la Littérature?' in Sartre: *Situations II*. Paris: Gallimard.

—— 1958: *Was ist Literatur? Ein Essay*. Trans. Hans Georg Brenner. Reinbek bei Hamburg: Rowohlt.

Schirrmacher, Frank 1990: 'Abschied von der Literatur der Bundesrepublik. Neue Pässe, neue Identitäten, neue Lebensläufe: Über die Kündigung einiger Mythen des westdeutschen Bewußtseins', *Frankfurter Allgemeine Zeitung*, 2 October 1990.

Schneider, Rolf 1997: 'Kann die Kunst die Welt verändern? Über literarische Mythen, Hoffnungen, Selbsttäuschungen. Eine Betrachtung', *Die Welt*, 9 August 1997.

Schultz-Gerstein, Christian 1974: 'Wetterberichte von der Apo-Front. Ein Roman um die Studentenbewegung herum', *Die Zeit*, 1 November 1974.

Seibt, Gustav 1995: 'Langer Samstag. Die deutsche Literatur in diesem Herbst', *Frankfurter Allgemeine Zeitung*, 7 October 1995.

Senghaas, Dieter 1997: 'Die fixe Idee vom Kampf der Kulturen', *Blätter für deutsche und internationale Politik* 42, 215–221.

Spinnen, Burkhard 1995: 'Erzählen Geschichte auch Geschichte?', *Neue deutsche Literatur* 43/4, 203–209.

Steinecke, Hartmut 1999: 'Die Entdeckung der Currywurst oder die Madeleine der Alltagsästhetik' in Durzak 1995, 217–230.

Stiftung Lesen 1997: 'Leseempfehlungen 108', *Das Literarische Quartett 1997*. Mainz: Stiftung Lesen.

Thomalla Ariane 1996: 'Deutsche Querelen, fortgesetzt. Tagung über "Kulturkämpfe und kulturelle Deutungsmacht"', *Frankfurter Rundschau*, 12 December 1996.

Unseld, Siegfried 1993: 'Literatur im Abseits? Polemische Anmerkungen eines Verlegers', *Frankfurter Allgemeine Zeitung*, 18 August 1993.

Vormweg, Heinrich 1986: 'Auf Wasser gebaut. Vorzüglich nur im Handwerklichen: Uwe Timms neuer Roman', *Süddeutsche Zeitung*, 1 October 1986.

Weniger, Robert and Brigitte Rossbacher (eds) 1997: *Wendezeiten — Zeitenwenden*. Tübingen: Stauffenburg.

'Wieviel Literatur im Leben, wieviel Politik in der Poesie? Eine Umfrage unter deutschsprachigen Schriftstellern der Jahrgänge 1950 bis 1966', *Neue Rundschau* 103/2, 1992, 95–130.

Willis, Susan 1991: 'Die "Erdbeben-Ausrüstung". Zur Politik des Trivialen', *Das Argument* 33, 735–748.

Winkels, Hubert 1998: 'Zur deutschen Literatur 1997' in Hage/Moritz/Winkels 1998, 5–36.

Wittstock, Uwe 1993: 'Ab in die Nische? Über neueste deutsche Literatur und was sie vom Publikum trennt' in Görtz/Hage/Wittstock 1993, 313–331.

—— (ed.) 1994: *Roman oder Leben. Postmoderne in der deutschen Literatur*. Leipzig: Reclam.

Zafris, Jim 1994: 'Novel captures need to flee life's tedium', *Cleveland Plain Dealer*, 18 July 1994.

'ERZÄHLEN IST TOTAL EROTISCH':
LITERATURE, PLEASURE AND DESIRE
IN NOVELS BY
THOMAS BRUSSIG, UWE TIMM AND ULRICH WOELK

STEFAN NEUHAUS

Es scheint, daß unsere gesamte Seelen-
tätigkeit darauf gerichtet ist, Lust zu
erwerben und Unlust zu vermeiden.
(Sigmund Freud 1999, XI, 369)

Erotik, das ist auch so ein Kapitel
(Martin Walser 1997, VIII, 318)

I Introduction

Eroticism in literature has seldom been examined by literary specialists. This is surprising if one considers that most literary texts contain at least erotic undertones. Over the past ten years eroticism has featured increasingly as a central theme, or at least as an important motif, in literary texts. With few exceptions this, too, has largely been ignored. Perhaps the most likely explanation is that eroticism and sexuality are still often taboo subjects. Yet authors have a licence to undermine taboos; indeed they must, if they are to make an impact.

It is the aim of this essay to show that authors of the 1990s like to use erotic connotations in a positive way and as an integral part of their work. This was not the case in the past. Up to and into the twentieth century texts took care not to violate taboos too blatantly and the limits to which authors could venture were much tighter than today. There were, of course, portrayals of sexuality (they are as old as literature itself), but with the rise of the bourgeoisie in the late eighteenth century descriptions of sexuality became much more covert. It is even possible that authors were not always aware of the sexual connotations in their works; the obvious exceptions were such great figures as Goethe, Friedrich Schlegel and especially Theodor Fontane. However, in comparison with the sexual content of more recent texts, they are very subtle.[1]

These traditions continue today. Light fiction still uses innuendos which are open to interpretation by the reader's imagination. Moreover, the high literature of the twentieth century abounds with examples of the subtle portrayal of eroticism; one obvious example are the works of Thomas Mann.[2] At around the turn of the last century many authors started describing sexuality more openly, albeit not always as something positive. Many portrayals were written in a more or less threatening or critical manner in an attempt to undermine rigid taboos or to compensate for their effect. In the latter group it was often the author's intention to shock the reader.[3] Even the (for the time) very open and positive portrayal of sexuality in the works of Arthur Schnitzler or Frank Wedekind is a kind of protest literature, directed against bourgeois concepts of morality. That is why their protagonists cannot live out their sexuality and achieve fulfilled love. Other authors as different as Bertolt Brecht, Franz Xaver Kroetz, Martin Walser,[4] Werner Schwab and, last but not least, Elfriede Jelinek break taboos by portraying sexual desire in an exaggerated and shocking way, focusing on its negative aspects. Jelinek's highly praised novel *Lust* (1989) was published just before the period under review, but since it illustrates the way eroticism was previously portrayed, I shall discuss it briefly.

The blurb on the inside cover of *Lust* cites a review in *Der Spiegel* with the obvious intention of preempting misunderstanding: 'als böse Porno-Parodie könnte "Lust" gelesen werden, die durch den Rhythmus der Sätze, durch Wiederholungen die stets verfügbare Frau, den immer potenten Mann der Lächerlichkeit preisgibt, abrechnet mit Männerphantasie und Männerrede'. Even allowing for the use of the subjunctive, this interpretation hits the nail on the head. Jelinek describes sexual intercourse in such a repelling and obscene manner that every possible erotic feeling the reader may have turns into abhorrence — assuming s/he does not enjoy scenes in which humiliation and rape are the order of the day. Jelinek describes an apparently exemplary marriage as pure hell. An affair serves only to confirm that all men are pigs. The woman is left with no other alternative than to kill her son, who has developed a similar attitude to sexuality as his father, thus enabling the latter to be portrayed as typical of all men. The book conveys an extreme feminist streak with a degree of radicalness which is new and innovative. One example of how Jelinek creates a feeling of abhorrence in the reader must suffice in the present context: 'So steht die Frau still wie eine Klomuschel, damit der Mann sein Geschäft in sie hineinmachen kann' (Jelinek 1999, 38). The generic terms 'Frau' and 'Mann' emphasize the universal applicability of the relationship as depicted. The grotesque and exaggerated nature of some of the scenes may appear to offer a potential counterweight to feminist trends; it would then represent an attempt to attenuate the shock effect and thus increase the text's general impact. This view is open to debate; even so, it shows that the novel intentionally creates, at least as far as human sexuality is concerned, the opposite to what the title promises: *Lust*.

Opinion among literary critics soon polarized. There were those who felt the book undermined a taboo they considered an important part of society's moral fabric and displayed a distorted view of reality. The other camp hailed the book as a successful and long-overdue breaker of taboos.[5] The literary awards Jelinek received for this novel will undoubtedly help the work go down in literary history; they also underline the fact that the opinion of that particular group of professional readers has asserted itself against the disapproving voices.

The debate about *Lust* (cf. Schlich 1994) illustrates once more that to many readers arousal and abhorrence have always been two sides of the same coin. From as early as the nineteenth century, light fiction pandered to voyeuristic desires by portraying eroticism as a threat to moral values while always ensuring that the latter ultimately won through. Freud created the famous analogy between the dream or daydream and the work of fiction, showing that 'der Dichter uns in den Stand setzt, unsere eigenen Phantasien nunmehr ohne jeden Vorwurf und ohne Schämen zu genießen' (Freud 1999, VII, 223). The author achieves this by satisfying both the id and the superego, by stimulating erotic feelings and yet not allowing their unrestricted fulfilment within the plot. Popular texts such as these represent a point of departure and comparison because, on the surface, they seem to support the taboos that later authors, such as Jelinek, vehemently attack with innovative literary strategies.

My contention in this essay is that a change in direction can be adduced from texts published in the last decade. Not only is sexuality not portrayed negatively; sometimes it is portrayed very positively. It is no longer its function to break taboos. Perhaps our post-modern society has become more liberal and tolerant, paving the way for authors to integrate sexuality into their literary texts as a part of everyday life. This development must be seen within the context of a shift in the entire literary arena. At the beginning of the 1990s, there were many complaints that German writing was boring and could not compete with foreign imports. In several important instances the plaintiffs were authors or editors, i.e. people who, at the time of the accusations, were already in the process of changing what they criticized.

In 1995, Uwe Wittstock, the German literature editor of Fischer-Verlag, published a book with a title indicative of its central theme: *Leselust. Wie unterhaltsam ist die neue deutsche Literatur?* He shows that Germany boasts authors who can produce both sophisticated and entertaining literature. Two of the three novels he selects as the principal evidence for his case, Sten Nadolny's *Die Entdeckung der Langsamkeit* and Patrick Süskind's *Das Parfum*, were indeed overwhelming successes among the general public and were appreciated by the critics. However, the praise Wittstock showers on the third writer, Ulrich Woelk, is of greater importance in the context of this essay. Wittstock concludes: 'Vor dem hier skizzierten intellektuellen Hintergrund nehmen sich die meisten autobiographischen Produkte der Neuen Subjektivität in mehrfacher Hinsicht naiv aus' (Wittstock 1995, 135). 'Einfalt' and 'Schlichtheit' is the damning judgment passed on the mainstream German literature of the 1970s and 1980s. The weaknesses of 'Neue Subjektivität' are highlighted in a chapter devoted to two authors he considers to be the key representatives of this phenomenon: Christa Wolf and Peter Handke (Wittstock 1995, 91–113). However, he never questions the qualities of their texts.

Wittstock is only one of many literary specialists who, in the 1990s, voiced their opinion publicly in a debate about the state of contemporary German literature. Despite several critical comments, the call for more 'entertainment' seemed to meet with widespread approval.[6] In 1993, Uwe Timm commented: 'Wer heute die verschnarchte, blutleere deutsche Literatur beklagt, darf sich nicht wundern. Diese Anämie hat — neben vielen anderen — zwei plausible Gründe. Einmal ist sie in der Biographie der Schreibenden zu suchen, zum anderen ist der deutschen Literatur das Erzählen ausgetrieben worden' (Timm 1993, 83–84). The move away from traditional narration in a complex and entangled world, coupled with the avant-garde attempt 'to always be new', had led to this dead end. Ever the pragmatist, Timm sees literature in direct competition with cinema and television and evolved the strategy that is reflected superbly in the novel discussed below, *Johannisnacht*. Timm states:

> Ich sehe im Lesen denn auch eine Chance, sich gegen die Opulenz des Visuellen zu wehren. Und gerade die Prosa kann hier (natürlich nur in einem bescheidenen Adressatenkreis) ihre Möglichkeiten entfalten. Sie kann — unspektakulär und leise — Bilder wieder aufbrechen, die uns von der medialen Wirklichkeit simuliert wurden bzw. die wir uns von der Wirklichkeit selbst gemacht haben. (Timm 1993, 137)

He is one of several authors who have followed in the footsteps of the older generation as far as quality is concerned — without sharing their stance, described thus by Martin Hielscher: 'Die Ästhetik der Moderne hat insofern die pädagogische Tradition fortgesetzt, als sie im Choc, im Verfremden, mit Montage, Polyperspektivität, Identifikationsverbot etc. eine identifikatorisch-einfühlende Kunsterfahrung zerstören und die Leser, Hörer oder Betrachter aus der Unmittelbarkeit "heraussprengen" wollte' (Hielscher 1998, 152).

Fundamentally there is, of course, nothing wrong in the narrative strategy described here. The debate about contemporary German literature and its simultaneous transformation have, however, shown that literary quality and popular success need not rule each other out. Authors such as Jelinek belong to the

'Ästhetik der Moderne' tradition, a tradition they continue to develop, causing sensations with their texts and contributing to the reputation of German literature, whilst reaching a comparatively small section of the population. At the same time a new form has emerged which latches onto older narrative traditions, reviving and adapting them to today's expectations. Light fiction stands beside these as the only constant factor. Its forms and content may move with the times (for example, the depictions of the sexual act have become increasingly explicit), but its fundamental conceptual framework, by which the author seeks to satisfy both id and superego at the same time, has remained unchanged.

II Sexuality in light fiction
From what we know about the reception of depictions of the erotic, it seems possible to assume that the repressive forces in people's minds have to be taken into account and that descriptions of unproblematical sexuality are immediately suspected of being pornographic.[7] Perhaps with the exception of borderline cases, this is quite understandable. If they are simply an end in themselves, such descriptions seek only to stimulate the corresponding impulses in the reader. There is nothing wrong in this except that they might be deemed to be out of place in high-quality literature. Sexuality as an end in itself is inevitably trivial. Roland Barthes formulated this most eloquently and accurately: 'So-called "erotic books" [...] *represent* not so much the erotic scene as the expectation of it, the preparation for it, its ascent; that is what makes them 'exciting'; and when the scene occurs, naturally there is disappointment, deflation. In other words these are books of Desire not Pleasure' (Barthes 1990, 58; original emphasis).

As I have already indicated above, the category of the 'trivial portrayal of sexuality' can be applied not just to pornographic texts but also to light fiction in which sexuality is used to make the text more interesting for the reader.[8] The difference between pornographic and trivial texts is that the latter disguise their aim of giving people this type of pleasure. One example are the best-selling novels by Tanja Kinkel, which purport to be historical novels. The tone set at the beginning of *Die Löwin von Aquitanien* (1991), however, reveals just how 'historical' they are: 'Was ich tue und mit wem ich ins Bett gehe, entscheide alleine ich!' (9). The language and the moral ideas of the characters belong in the present; they are simply projected back into the twelfth century. When the author alludes to the first act of sexual intercourse just a few pages into the same book, explicit descriptions of sexuality that could meet with the disapproval of the general public are avoided:

> Sie spürte, wie er sie in ungewohnter Heftigkeit an sich preßte, und war zugleich erfreut und beunruhigt. Bisher war er wohl zärtlich, aber kaum leidenschaftlich ihr gegenüber gewesen. Diesmal küßte er sie mit der Verzweiflung eines Erstickenden, hob sie auf und trug sie zu ihrem Lager. Dieser Nacht der Liebe, des Zorns und Hasses, des Verlangens und der Erbitterung verdankte Alienor ihr Leben. (Kinkel 1991, 13)

It is a perfect illustration of Barthes's 'Desire'. It is noteworthy that the last sentence of this quotation contains all the ingredients of a true piece of light fiction. However, the context and the clichés make it unlikely that such ironic self-reflection ('Selbstreflexivität') was intended by the author.[9]

III Thomas Brussig: *Helden wie wir*

Few books aroused as much attention in the 1990s as Thomas Brussig's second novel.[10] His first, *Wasserfarben,* which appeared in 1991 was a respectable success among critics but was hardly noticed by the general public. *Helden wie wir* appeared at the beginning of 1996. By the autumn of the same year it was already in its eighth printing. Its success is unlikely to be rooted solely in the novel's high narrative quality. Two other factors, apparent in the reviews, no doubt played an important role. The novel drew attention, first because of the centrality of the theme of German unification and, secondly, due to the great detail of sections of the text which portray the sexual development of a young man. *Helden wie wir* was often described as 'lacking respect' — and this was intended as acclamation. The scathing criticism of the GDR's past (Brussig grew up in East Germany) was in keeping with the political mood of the time, the witty, sometimes sad, portrayal of sexual experiences complied with what I believe to be the continuing call for 'entertaining reading'. The synthesis is that Brussig describes East Germany's history, reflected in the life of a character, as a series of obscenities. This no doubt made it easier for many critics and readers to express their appreciation the book. After all, the sexual scenes are not there as an end in themselves; they serve to make a critical point.

Although Brussig seems to fall into line with the apparently traditional concept of negative sexuality, on closer inspection the text reveals a slightly different story. Brussig's way of undermining taboos can be divided into exaggerated obscenities (the great majority), on the one hand, and descriptions containing positive connotations, on the other. Indeed, it is the unspoken goal of the protagonist Klaus Uhltzscht, to develop a normal sexuality. The language chosen to describe the only act of sexual intercourse Brussig allows his pitiful and paranoid anti-hero before the collapse of the Berlin Wall is youthful and humorous, bringing a gain in credibility:

Wir zerrten ihr den Slip herunter, auf dem sie saß [...]. Sie zog die Beine an und fuhr mit ihren großen Zehen zielsicher in den Gummi meiner Unterhose und zog sie herunter, indem sie in sanften Hin- und Herbewegungen den Spann ihrer süßen Füßchen eng an meinen Lenden herunterschob. Synchron dazu fädelte sie sich meinen Schwanz ein. (Helden, 128)

Although the portrayal is detailed, it cannot be described as pornographic: the scene is fully integrated into the context of the novel; it also reflects the mixture of irony and humour which is characteristic of the entire work. *Helden wie wir* appeals because of its liberal, but not voyeuristic, treatment of sexuality. The absence of taboos could hardly be more complete. Even if Brussig is neither the first nor the only author to describe male masturbation (well-known examples are Frank Wedekind's *Frühlings Erwachen* and Günter Grass's *Katz und Maus*, and the most recent, perhaps, Martin Walser's *Ein springender Brunnen*[11]), he takes it a decisive and unique step further. He attempts to describe this act onomatopoeically — and not just for its own sake. When Klaus Uhltzscht makes 'Minister Mielke' the 'Objekt meiner Wichsphantasien', Brussig is again emphasizing the parallel between what is still often regarded as sexual perversion and the real perversion of the state (196–198).

IV Uwe Timm: *Johannisnacht*

Uwe Timm is a significant German-language author of the so-called 'middle generation'.[12] His novel *Johannisnacht* (1996) constitutes a post-modern game with literary quotations, cross references and meanings but never falls prey to the post-modern 'anything goes' phenomenon. The following words from one of the characters could be seen as the motto for the entire text: 'Gute Geschichten sind wie Labyrinthe' (Johannisnacht, 197). One can assume that Timm's text is consciously conceived in this manner, not least since Timm shed light on his approach to writing and his literary strategies in his five Paderborn poetics lectures. Using Freudian terms, he describes his relationship with language as 'libidinös' and regards the creation of a montage of quotations (in the wider sense) to form a text as 'lustvoll' (Timm 1993, 14, 28).

It is apparent from the many reviews of *Johannisnacht* by well-known critics in major national newspapers that Timm is deemed one of Germany's leading contemporary authors from whom quality texts can be expected.[13] Although criticism of the novel is voiced, it is not widespread and is primarily the result of careless reading. Some find fault with the apparent lack of coherence between the many small stories in it — a reproach which, as I shall show, is unfounded. In fact, every part of the plot is linked with the others in a complicated web of cross-references. Those who praise the book also see the openness of the text as a positive aspect.[14]

For readers with a knowledge of the calendar and of literature, the book's title indicates that the author is proffering a variation on Shakespeare's *A Midsummer Night's Dream*, a link which is immediately confirmed by the author's epigraph, which is a quotation from the play. Moreover, the novel is peppered with many other allusions to Shakespeare's text.[15] The natural phenomenon of the equinox already prompted Shakespeare to tell complicated love stories. Alongside such significant parallels as the changing of spouses, the theme is brought into the present by the way eroticism is presented and by a major recent artistic event: Christo's wrapping up of the Berlin Reichstag in 1995. The hotel doorman explains to the protagonist:

> Danach wird etwas anders sein, ich bin überzeugt, daß diese Verhüllung etwas verändert. Das Geheimnis liegt darin, daß etwas anders sein könnte. Übrigens ist keinem dieser Kunstkritiker aufgefallen, daß die Verhüllung am 23. Juni vollendet wird, also der Mittsommernacht, in der es ja kunterbunt zugeht, Verwechslungen, Verkleidungen, Vertauschungen sozusagen zur Tagesordnung gehören. Es ist die ästhetischste Nacht des Jahres. Die Dinge zeigen sich von einer anderen Seite, wie auch die Menschen. Fräulein Spinnweb und Frau Bohnenblüte lassen grüßen. Wenn Sie die treffen wollen, müssen Sie sich heute ein Reggaekonzert anhören. Einen Augenblick überlegte ich, ob ich ihm sagen sollte, daß ich Frau Spinnweb schon getroffen hätte. (Johannisnacht, 193)

'Fräulein Spinnweb' is a young woman who meets the older married narrator (69) during his stay in Berlin. The name is indicative of the web she spins around the first-person narrator, in which he remains trapped until he finally manages to tear it asunder.

The narrator has undertaken his journey to Berlin to research the topic of a history he is writing (of the potato). This, too, has erotic connotations. Accompanied by the sounds of a couple having sexual intercourse in the room next door, the narrator reads that, because of its nutritional value, the potato was once reputed to be an aphrodisiac (74). Humour and irony are undoubtedly in play here; throughout the text they help shape the book's labyrinthine character, which is probably designed to evoke an atmosphere similar to midsummer's night. If this were pornographic or trivial literature, the narrator would most likely be stimulated by what he reads and hears; in fact, his reaction is somewhere between neutral and negative.

When he talks on the phone to the 'student' who purportedly wrote an essay on the 'potato in literature', he is greeted with similar background noises, for which, initially, he has no explanation. The narrator does not pose this question, it is left to the reader whose confusion grows with the description of 'Frau

Angerbach' ('Übrigens, ich heiße Tina'; 109): 'Zwei Tische waren besetzt, an einem saß ein Mädchen, an dem anderen eine Frau, stark überschminkt, plastikrosa gefärbte Haare' (94–95). That the two women happen to be sitting at neighbouring tables is no coincidence; however only a second reading of the text makes it clear that the artificial appearance of the second woman is a signal for the fact that the first one, the girl, is not what she appears to be. 'Höchstens für zwanzig hatte ich sie auf den ersten Blick geschätzt, nein, noch jünger, eine Schülerin vielleicht, dieses kindlich glatte Gesicht, eine zarte Nase, weißblondes Haar, kurz geschnitten, eine Stoppelfrisur, die bei mir den Reflex auslöst, darüberzustreichen' (95). The Lolita syndrome made famous by Nabokov's novel enters the text: the narrator is old enough to be her father, yet experiences her appearance as erotic:

> Sie schlug die Beine übereinander, nackte braungebrannte Beine, die unter einer weiten Lederjacke verschwanden. Der Rock mußte extrem kurz sein, denn es war kein Saum zu sehen. Sie hatte meinen Blick bemerkt. Und wie zufällig, aber doch auf diesen Blick hin, zog sie den Reißverschluß der Jacke auf. Unter dem T-Shirt zeichneten sich zwei zarte Brustwarzen ab. Auf dem T-Shirt ein roter Stern, der Sowjetstern mit einem T darin. Tupamaros, fragte ich, die Stadtguerilla? Da lachte sie und sagte: Sie kommen noch aus der guten alten Zeit. Nee, das heißt: Texaco. Ihre Generation sieht überall politische Signale, selbst wenn nur ein Zapfhahn gemeint ist. (95–96)

The question of generation is thus linked with the theme of eroticism. The age difference but also the significant changes Berlin is undergoing as a result of unification are factors which make it hard for the narrator from Munich to conduct his research. In contrast to other novels (cf. my comments below on Woelk's *Rückspiel*), *Johannisnacht* is not a story about the narrator's alienation ('Ich-Dissoziation'); this again is simply a part of the author's totally 'virtuous' game. Moreover, it is no coincidence that the narrator talks to the young lady as dusk is gathering, outdoors, in a street café. Once again the theme of transformation hinted at in the title re-emerges, something with which the young woman has more to do than the reader suspects.

The signals described lead us to assume that we are at the beginning of a love story, an erotic relationship. Our expectations now focus on the course this relationship will take. Our curiosity is nourished further by the narrator's observation of the woman's body and the explanation for the background noises on the telephone. This is 'wie mein Firmenschild', says Frau Angerbach:

> Übrigens O-Ton, sagte sie und wechselte die übereinandergeschlagenen Beine [...] Ich verdiene mein Geld mit Telefonsex. [...] ich laß Geschichten entstehen, Möglichkeiten, es entsteht was im Kopf, wie beim Lesen. Insofern hat mir auch das Studium

geholfen. Erzählen ist total erotisch. Bekommen die heimlichen Wünsche etwas Luft unter die Flügel. (101–102)

This is yet another analogy between the text we are reading and the (not only written) text which the woman invents to satisfy her listeners. At this point, our text becomes self-referential, another game the author plays with his readers. With his description of this erotic relationship he too conjures up images in the readers' mind which, at least in this form, will never be fulfilled. The analogy is taken further when Frau Angerbach reports on her literary research. The sentence 'Kartoffel und Sex, das finden Sie nur bei Grass', ceased to apply as soon as Timm wrote it. The following passage carries the irony to the extreme:

> Habe in der Kundschaft Politiker und Politikerinnen, vor allem viele Geistes-wissenschaftler, zum Beispiel Germanisten, übrigens auch Frauen, Germanistinnen, die über Visualisierung von Texten gearbeitet haben, also literarische Barbiturate, gerade die sind ganz scharf am Telefon [...] Das sind diejenigen, die immer Angst haben, sich unter ihrem Niveau zu amüsieren. Die sind von einem berserkerhaften Ernst. Kommen ja meist aus kleinbürgerlichen Verhältnissen. Kenn ich von mir selbst, geistige Höhe durch Tiefe. Hat einige Zeit gedauert, bis ich das als ziemlich breiten Quark erkannt habe. Hat mir mein Beruf geholfen. Ich schneide die Gespräche mit. Will ich mal veröffentlichen, vielleicht, irgendwann: das Selbstreferentielle und die Selbstbefriedigung. Da werden einige Leute ganz schön dumm aus der Wäsche gucken. (105)

Those who understand the allusion to modern literary theory und criticism ('Niveau', 'das Selbstreferentielle') are more than likely, depending of course on their perspective, either to do precisely that ('dumm aus der Wäsche gucken') or to laugh along with Timm. But the irony and humour inherent in the novel are not completely revealed until the end when the narrator makes a shocking discovery whilst dancing: 'Nur einmal bekomme ich von hinten einen kräftigen Stoß und fliege förmlich auf sie, nein in sie hinein, spüre ihren Körper, zart und weich, habe einen Moment den Eindruck, mit einem Mann zu tanzen, als sei da etwas, was nicht zwischen die Beine einer Frau gehörte. Ihre echten-unechten Haare fliegen' (215). Once again the sexual connotations are obvious ('Stoß', 'in sie hinein'), but for the first time the tentative suggestion is made that Tina is a transvestite.

To the careful reader, this assumption becomes a certainty when Tina makes the narrator an offer and, with the visit to the swimming pool in mind, he secretly steals away (217). During a telephone conversation (188–190) she had told him in great detail about an affair in the same swimming pool to which she invites him with the ambiguous question: 'Hast du Lust?' (125). Even after the page-long description of an erotic telephone experience which is likely to have a certain effect on even the most detached reader, the characters do not have sexual intercourse: when the narrator comes to the pool, Tina does not appear to be there. The short-sighted narrator can only see enough to establish that she is not in the water: 'Es war, als hätte ein Altersheim einen Ausflug gemacht. Lediglich am Beckenrand hing an einer Schwimmangel ein blonder Junge' (126). When the narrator later flees from Tina and, in doing so, remembers the blond boy, the careful reader realizes that the two were, in fact, the same person.[16]

Tina is a transvestite; and the theme of homoerotic attraction is also dealt with in a parallel story. The narrator realizes that the dark-skinned person observed on the patio of a mansion was not a woman but a man. The 'Bedouin Prince' Moussa has followed the Buchers (a married couple) to Berlin where he has accompanied them everywhere and has thus caused their separation; both fell in love with him. Bucher's wife attempts unsuccessfully to seduce Moussa and Bucher comments: 'Ich habe nie gedacht, dass ich mich für Männer interessiere, aber als ich ihn nackt sah, diesen durchtrainierten, gleichmäßig braunen, muskulösen Körper, kam immer häufiger dieser mich zutiefst irritierende Wunsch in mir auf, die Muskeln, die den Arm hier mit der Brust verbinden, zu berühren' (155). When the narrator meets Moussa, the latter gives him a ring (160), the possible symbolic meaning of which makes him feel uncomfortable. Not without reason: when he leaves Berlin, he leaves behind both Tina and also a sleeping Moussa, who had suddenly appeared in the narrator's hotel (232).

The motif of the transvestite and the references to Shakespeare's comedy shed light on each other. This can best be illustrated by an allusion. As mentioned above, the narrator equates Tina with 'Frau Spinnweb'. This is the name of an elf. When 'Spinnweb' introduces himself, 'Zettel' answers: 'Ich wünsche näher mit Ihnen bekannt zu werden, guter Musje Spinnweb'. Spinnweb is male; and not just in Schlegel and Tieck's translation. In Shakespeare's original Bottom says to Cobweb: 'I shall desire you of more acquaintance, good Master Cobweb' (IIIi). In fact, it is logical that Spinnweb is addressed as a man: in Shakespeare's time women were not allowed to act on stage, and it must have been difficult to fill all the female roles with effeminate men or boys (cf. Schabert et al. 1992, 122–123). The fact that the doorman and the narrator mistakenly think that Frau Spinnweb is a woman can now be seen to reflect more than one aspect of Timm's narrative strategy.

Timm skillfully arouses his readers' curiosity. He turns them into voyeurs, inviting them to identify with the mostly passive protagonist, to imagine what he feels and hopes, while the author himself remains inexplicit. Although homoeroticism is not new to literature (one need only think of Thomas Mann's *Tod in Venedig*; cf. Deuse 1992), some facets do appear new, or at least newer: the detail in which the erotic scenes are described, the positive or subtly ambivalent connotations of the scenes, and the irony with which they are undermined without any loss of their erotic potential (something that occurs frequently in earlier texts by Timm). In spite of the irony the imagination is given free rein in this novel. The readers can decide for themselves whether to join the author's game or to read the text in their own way and fill it with different meaning.

V Ulrich Woelk: *Rückspiel*

In Woelk's *Rückspiel* (1993), eroticism and sexuality are not the main focus of attention; however, they remain a fundamental component of the book's structure, which is so complex that only a preliminary appraisal is possible in the present context.[17] Like *Johannisnacht*, *Rückspiel* can also be read as a postmodern work. The author makes abundant cross-references (above all, of an historical nature) and plays with the reader's expectations. Susanne Schaber has noted: 'Ulrich Woelks Buch ist ein kompliziertes, hochartifizielles Gebilde, das zudem eine Entsprechung in einer scharfen, luziden Sprache findet [...] Ein ungemein sinnlicher, ungemein spannender Roman, der leichten Fußes daherkommt' (Schaber 1993).[18]

In contrast to Timm's novel, *Rückspiel* is lacking in reconciliatory irony. It is not until the open, but sad, ending that one realizes that the complete mental disintegration of the protagonist is caused by the times in which he lives and could not be halted. *Rückspiel* is a detached critical appraisal of society over the period leading up to 1989–1990. This becomes obvious after the first few sentences: 'Klar bin ich auf der Flucht. Sind doch alle. Wer will denn heute bleiben, wo er ist?' Much the same is true of the narrative situation which the first-person narrator describes in the following manner: 'Also erzählen, die Minuten, die Stunden, die Tage, eine Geschichte, deren Ende ich nicht kenne, und ich sehe nicht, wie der Anfang einer Geschichte zu bestimmen ist, deren Ende man nicht kennt' (Rückspiel, 7).

This fictional text, as the critics agree, is a generational novel.[19] The feeling of the younger, largely unpolitical generation, represented by the first-person narrator, Johannes Stirner, that they have been just thrown into the world is blamed on the fathers (the Nazi generation) and older brothers (the generation of 1968). The latter is represented by Stirner's brother Kurt and his friends, the former by his old teacher Kampe and one of the teacher's acquaintances. The former National Socialists, or simply nationalists, lead lonely lives; their relationships have broken down as a result of historical events. Stirner experiences a passionate love affair, only to lose the object of his love to a '68er. Kurt marries at the beginning of the novel, thus betraying his principled opposition to marriage, without seeing it as a U-turn. The 'symmetry', as Stirner initially concludes from his investigations (245), appears to lie in the comparability of their lives. Kampe, Kurt and Johannes are all devastated by the unhappy ending of a relationship; in all three cases this is caused by a representative of an older generation. However, this construct suddenly collapses when it is revealed to be nothing more than an episode in Woelk's post-modern game with the meanings of terms and content.

The arrogant Kurt and his equally over-confident friend Johnny, whom Stirner visits in Berlin, are the catalysts of the plot. Kurt's marriage, coupled with the accusations he directs at the former teacher, change Stirner's life fundamentally. He shares his journey to Berlin, organized by an agency for arranging lifts, with the young and beautiful Lucca. He stays on in Berlin because of her; although he doubts whether he is doing so for the right reasons:

> Diese ganze Reise nach Berlin! Da war eine Lüge eingebaut, und ich kam nicht dahinter, wo. Daß ich Lucca getroffen hatte, machte die Sache nicht leichter. Andernfalls hätte ich mir jederzeit eingestehen können, daß ich hier in Berlin nichts verloren hatte. Es wäre möglich gewesen, mich in den Zug zu setzen, nach Hause zu fahren und alles auf sich beruhen zu lassen. (193)

The romance with Lucca comes to an end because neither of them can solve their problems, and Lucca takes up a relationship with Johnny. At the end of the novel, Stirner, whose name may be symbolic of his tendency to let his mind rule his heart, is left alone in the unfamiliar metropolis. A return home is impossible, yet there is no way forward. The situation could hardly be more hopeless.

In this analytical novel (Stirner is recording his experiences retrospectively), the breakdown of the relationship between Lucca and Stirner is hinted at even before it begins. Stirner tells Lucca about something he once witnessed in a bar. At the time, Johnny owed Kurt DM50. In lieu of payment he offered his friend a date with his girlfriend. 'An das Gesicht des blonden Mädchens meine ich mich noch zu erinnern, wegen der Tränen vielleicht' (78). Later Stirner came to believe that Kurt was in love with the girl. However, ultimately it becomes clear that this was not the case; nor was Kurt's accusation of Kampe true, which had prompted Stirner to go to Berlin. Kampe is blamed for expelling one of Kurt's friends, Klausen, from school, who is supposed to have committed suicide as a result. In fact, Klausen committed suicide because he was in love with the blonde girl, who had suffered a serious accident as she tried to fend off his overtures (208).

A further matter that only becomes clear at the end of the book is that Stirner started writing about the beginning of his relationship with Lucca after discovering that she was having an affair (153). Helmut Peitsch (1998) believes that Johannes tries to 'escape' from this discovery by writing about it. In fact, Johnny and Kurt are the cause of his plight because they use and abuse people. Stirner and Lucca both let themselves be used as they know neither what they want nor where they belong. What lies behind this complex plot and the constellation of characters is substantial criticism of the 1968 generation, people who, when *Rückspiel* was published, were beginning to occupy leading positions in the Federal Republic. A revealing quotation conveys Stirner's late realization of the essence of the situation. The 'vielleicht' it contains is characteristic of a novel in which there are no absolute truths:

> Es ist immer leicht, Widersprüche bei anderen aufzudecken, aber manche finde ich so offensichtlich, daß sie mich wütend machen. Und bei meinem Bruder machen sie mich besonders wütend, wohl weil ich ihn immer als Vorbild gesehen habe, als einen, der weiß, wo es langgeht. In den letzten Jahren hat sich das dann gedreht. Am Ende konnte er machen, was er wollte, für mich war alles nur noch eine einzige Lüge. Vielleicht lag hier der eigentliche Grund für meine Fahrt nach Berlin. (281–282)

The motif of sexuality in the novel fits in with the overall ambivalence of the structure described here. A conversation between Stirner, Lucca and one of her friends marks the beginning of this motif:

> Samstags war es in manchen Kneipen so voll wie in der U-Bahn zu Stoßzeiten. Es war zu laut, um über komplizierte Dinge zu reden, lediglich einmal, erinnere ich mich, kam es zu einer Debatte über Pornografie, weil einer eine kennengelernt hatte, die das machte. Der eigentliche Skandal, hatte er sich überlegt, sei nicht die Pornografie selbst, sondern die Art, in der die Gesellschaft mit ihr umging. — Zum Vögeln brauch ich keinen Fernseher, meinte Lucca. Luccas Bekannter produzierte Argumente, die auch ich jederzeit aus meinem Fundus hätte abrufen können: die Kommerzialisierung von erotischen Chiffren in Werbung und Alltag einerseits, bei gleichzeitiger nach wie vor prüder Sexualmoral andererseits, das Ideal der Zweierbeziehung mit der implizierten Behauptung, daß nur dort sexuelle Erfüllung zu finden sei — das müsse zu Widersprüchen und unlösbaren Konflikten im Triebleben führen, die mit der Pornografie wiederum kommerzialisiert würden. (185)

Later in the conversation, the contrast between the familiar ground of the intellectual debate and Lucca's 'Anarchie' becomes clear: 'Zum Vögeln brauch ich keinen Fernseher [...] Sex braucht man sich nicht anzuschauen, Sex macht man' (185). The narrator thinks the situation is 'ungeheuer komisch'; however, seen in the context of the novel, it is almost tragic.

Stirner's tendency to rely on his intellect and Lucca's refusal to discuss intellectual views mark a decisive difference between the two which ultimately leads, or at least contributes to, the breakdown of their relationship. The beginning of the end occurs symbolically on the night of the opening of the Berlin Wall. Stirner wants to continue his investigation into the former Nazi teachers' past (a story which has its own erotic side; 241–243). Lucca insists on living in the present; she has no interest in the past (cf.225). Stirner's brooding causes them to lose sight of each other (212–213) and, as we learn later on, Lucca meets Johnny and their relationship begins (289–290).

Immediately after the conversation about pornography, Stirner manages to smooth over the difference between Lucca and himself, perhaps because he has consumed a great deal of alcohol and is feeling less pensive. They go on to make love for the first time. The description of the sexual act is unsentimental and realistic, but never goes into great detail and never becomes pornographic (cf. 186); rather the passion of a fresh relationship is evoked. The tragedy of their relationship becomes apparent when the conversation between the two lovers is considerd within the context of the novel. On the evening after Lucca has betrayed Stirner and while he is still unaware of this, she reveals her problems to him. Full of despair, she describes the difficulties she has keeping steady relationships and the childhood trauma that is the cause of the problem. Her much loved father had left the family for another woman. This has left Lucca unable to feel deep love for any man. Relationships without the 'fear' of separation are only possible for her if she remains emotionally detached and regards them as a 'game' (233–234). Stirner fails to recognize this cry for help. Once again, he fails to react correctly by not reacting at all.[20]

The ultimate catastrophe occurs at another symbolic event — a New Year's Eve party 1989–1990, thrown by an artist known as 'van Gogh'. Stirner discovers a nude picture of Lucca and assumes she has had an affair with the painter. He tries to make love to her in an adjacent room, but she refuses (249–250). He tells her about his investigations, but they do not interest her — perhaps because of her refusal to acknowledge the analogy between the results and her life. She reproaches him and he does not know how to react: 'Ich wollte das nicht, wollte diesen Streit nicht, ich liebte sie' (270). Although the sultry atmosphere at the party, with its abundant use of alcohol and drugs, would have made it easy for him to seduce someone else (274), Stirner resists all temptation and keeps a relatively clear head. Finally, he finds Lucca again:

> Johnny lag auf dem Rücken, Lucca kniete über ihm, bewegte sich auf und ab, er hielt ihre Brüste mit seinen Händen. Sie bemerkten mich nicht, waren fünf, sechs Meter entfernt auf einer Matratze vor der hinteren Fensterfront. Sie verschränkte ihre Arme über dem Kopf, ich sah ihren Überkörper im Profil, die Linie von ihrem Hals bis hinunter zu ihrem Geschlecht, das auf und nieder ging über Johnny, der jetzt ihre Hüften umfaßte und den Rhythmus gab. (277)

The tragic climax is reached in the final discussion between Stirner and Lucca. She confesses that she has been unfaithful to him for the past two months. Her line of argument is transparent to the reader, who will still have her account of her parents' separation in mind. The extent to which Stirner thinks of it remains a matter of speculation. We must assume that he is not able to see the link because he has been hurt too much by his discovery. He is truly in love as he makes one final useless attempt: 'Ich will dich. Ich will dich immer noch' (291). He undresses her and thinks in terms of rape; but almost bursts into tears 'weil man nicht vergewaltigen *wollen* kann' (292), and, as is readily apparent, he is unable to perform the act. Lucca does not put up a fight, she remains detached and ends the scene with the comment on her affair with Johnny: 'Vielleicht hat er mich nur gereizt, seine Art, daß er einmal eine Frau herumgeschubst und benutzt hat' (293).

In spite of the closure of the plot and the interpretations offered in this essay, the novel does not contain a definite statement or an interpretable conclusion. The final words of the novel could not be more post-modern in character: 'In mir ist nur noch ein weißes Blatt, auf das ich systemlos schreibe, was ich für den Augenblick zu fassen kriege. Und alles endet in dem Moment, in dem ich die Finger von den Tasten hebe' (295).

VI Conclusion

The similiarities between the three novels chosen for this essay have already been discussed. They describe sexuality without the obvious intention of breaking or undermining taboos. The erotic scenes serve a function, they are a component of the overall structure and, as far as can be ascertained, of the intended meaning of the text. All three novels play with the meanings of terms and content, even though this is less obvious in Brussig's novel than in Timm's or Woelk's works. They are all texts which intend to entertain their readers or, in Wittstock's terms, to create 'Leselust'.

Leaving aside light fiction at this point, I believe that it is possible to offer a concluding hypothesis based on my initial distinction between two lines of contemporary literature and my discussion of the specific examples of texts by Brussig, Timm and Woelk. Texts which fall into the category of 'Ästhetik der Moderne' are directed towards readers who transform their feelings of displeasure ('Unlust') created by the text in a variety of ways (by shocking the reader, by complex language and the overall aesthetic value) into feelings of pleasure ('Lust'). This can only be done if the reader does not question the general consensus that literature must break away from traditions both in form and content. On the other hand, there are authors who do not primarily intend to arouse feelings of displeasure ('Unlust') but still create texts which compete in intensity and complexity with those of their rivals. Something these texts have in common with those of the traditional authors (e.g. Fontane or Mann) is that the effect of simplicity and lightness they create is the result of hard work. The return to more traditional narrative qualities can be termed innovative if one shares Wittstock's view: 'Mit Konventionen zu brechen gehört mittlerweile selbst zur literarischen Konvention' (Wittstock 1995, 27).

There are substantial similarities between these authors, but beyond these there are also differences which can be identified. In Brussig's novel the sexuality of his characters seems tragicomical, in Timm's amusing, and in Woelk's tragic. Brussig's novel contains page after page of detailed sexual passages. Timm limits himself, despite the central role of sexual attraction in the structure of the novel, largely to suggestion. The sexuality of Woelk's protagonists is probably similar in significance to what one would expect in reality. His descriptions of sexuality are relatively reserved. None of the texts is in any way pornographic. And yet, when compared with earlier texts in literary history, all are characterized by a greater openness and freedom from prejudice. Sexuality is treated as what it really is: a part of everyday life. The days of taboos and of taboo-breaking appear, at least for these authors,[21] to have passed.

Notes

Translation by Isabelle Esser.

1. For an introduction to the complicated relationship of literature to pleasure or desire see Anz 1998. With reference to strategies and forms of presentation up until the nineteenth century cf. Schlaffer 1971. With reference to Fontane cf. Grawe 1998.
2. cf. the balanced and enlightening analysis in Härle 1992.
3. The assertion that there is a 'clear lack of sensuality' ('deutliches Defizit an Sinnlichkeit'), a tendency in literature by women to characterize sexuality as the suppression of woman by man, and a tendency towards the transformation of physicalness 'into signs and digits' ('ins Zeichenhafte und Digitale') is the conclusion reached by Lieskounig 1999, esp. 231–237.
4. With reference to Walser cf. Jablkowska 1993, 105: 'Die schwülen Träume und Sex-Wünsche werden von den Helden Walsers entweder so weit verdrängt, daß sie überhaupt nicht in Erfüllung gehen können[,] oder sie gehen in Erfüllung, werden aber mit so schlechtem Gewissen praktiziert, daß sie zu abartigen Geschlechts-Übungen ausarten.' Interestingly enough, this does not hold good for Walser's latest novel *Ein springender Brunnen* (1999) in which he portrays the protagonist's sexual development as something normal. This is another text that would support my thesis of change.
5. With reference to the novel cf. the detailed study by Schlich 1994. With reference to the response to the novel cf. esp. 7–13.
6. An interesting selection of views can be found in Köhler/Moritz 1998.
7. With reference to the problem of literature and pornography cf. Glaser 1996.
8. A small selection from international literary history can be found in two anthologies. The first, Graeff 2000, falls victim to the misunderstanding that eroticism and the portrayal of sexual activity are the same. By contrast, the second, Arnold 1998, is based on a broad definition of eroticism, as it also includes texts containing no sexual activity but which can be best classified as 'love stories'; only the illustrations are clearly sexual.
9. It is superfluous to quote cheap novels and other banal texts which focus on sexuality in order to pander to the interests of their readers. It is, however, interesting to note that where sexuality constitutes a focal theme, it always occurs within the limits of the moral norms prevailing at the time of publication, i.e. that adulterers are 'punished' etc. This is

the only way a conflict, to use Freud's terminology, between the id and superego can be avoided.

10. 'Thomas Brussig's Roman *Helden wie wir* war *das* Medienereignis des Winters 1995 [/96]' (Zachau 1997, 387).

11. cf. Wedekind 1995, e.g. 42; Grass 1993, 33–34; Walser 2000, e.g. 205. With reference to eroticism in Grass's works in general cf. Jablkowska 1993.

12. cf. Durzak 1995. The term 'mittlere Generation' refers to authors who started writing in the late 1960s and 1970s, i.e. the generation after the Gruppe 47 authors.

13. 'Uwe Timms Roman ist eine Ästhetik, also eine Kunde darüber, wie man "die Dinge anders" sieht' (Ladenthin 1997, 169). With reference to Timm's works in general cf. Kesting/Ruckaberle 1998.

14. I refer to the 22 articles (reviews, reports on readings) about the novel which are located in the author's records at the Dortmund City Library.

15. 'Verlangen Sie nach Puk' (Johannisnacht 142). 'Shakespeare wußte das' (Johannisnacht 221).

16. This distinction is necessary. In a seminar I found that the majority of students initially did not understand that Tina is, in fact, a transvestite and the narrator disappears for this reason. My students were no less attentive in their reading than the critics, only some of whom recognized this connection. One even writes: 'Vor allzu intimen Einblicken scheut Timm jedoch zurück: Als sein aufgeregter Kartoffelforscher im Roman eine Liebesgeschichte mit jener Studentin beginnt, die ihr Geld mit Telefonsex verdient, läßt Timm ihn im letzten Moment heimlich durch den Küchengang verduften — der Roman bleibt "sauber". Schade, daß er diese Geschichten nicht weitergesponnen hat' (Pöpsel 1996).

17. Much the same is true of Woelk's first novel, *Freigang* (1992), which was awarded the Aspekte-Literaturpreis des Zweiten Deutschen Fernsehens, and his third novel *Amerikanische Reise* (1996). The reason for my choice of *Rückspiel* is that the portrayal of erotic scenes features more strongly both in terms of quantity and quality and contains more positive connotations than *Freigang*, while *Amerikanische Reise* contains even more sexual descriptions and reflections; sexuality could even be said to be the novel's focal theme. This latter would require a much more comprehensive analysis than can be achieved in the framework of this essay. Moreover *Amerikanische Reise* appears to me to mark a retrogression: the portrayals of sexuality are too explicit and concentrate too much on the male perspective. — With reference to the structure of *Freigang* cf. the intelligent analysis by Fitz 1998, 79–139.

18. Most major newspapers reviewed the novel. There was little criticism and a lot of praise, for example: 'Geht es um die Hoffnungsträger unserer jungen deutschen Literatur, so gehört Woelk ohne Zweifel dazu' (Steinert 1993).

19. 'Ein intelligenter Roman, der einen in der deutschen Literatur noch wenig beschriebenen Generationskonflikt auf den Punkt bringt' (Hummelt 1993). cf. Peitsch 1998.

20. 'Vielleicht wäre damals noch etwas zu ändern gewesen, hätte die ganze Geschichte eine andere Richtung nehmen können, aber im Laufe des Tages zerfiel mein Vorsatz, die Sache anzusprechen' (Rückspiel 236–237).

21. Other examples spring to mind. The spectrum ranges from Jurek Becker's underestimated, post-GDR love story *Amanda herzlos* (1992) to Felicitas Hoppe's 'stories' in her award-winning book *Picknick der Friseure* (1996) and Thomas Lehr's complicated philosophical novel *Nabokovs Katze* (1999). Even when eroticism and sexuality feature in a reserved (Becker) and alienated (Hoppe) manner, taboos are not used as points of orientation. Sexuality is simply a part of everyday life. However, there are other examples, following the tradition highlighted in my brief analysis of Jelinek's *Lust*. The best example I can think of is Thomas Hettche's novel *Nox* (1995). In *Nox* the portrayal of perversion is a symbolic comment on German unification (cf. Schmitz 2000).

The change in literary presentation of sexuality seems to correspond with a greater awareness of the topic in the media. A recent article in *Die Zeit* deals with the change in sexual consciousness and refers to several new publications about sexuality, even though the article's author notes pessimistically: 'Aber Zukunft und Erotik? Da bleibt nur noch der Weg in die Geschichte oder die Exotik' (Lütkehaus 2000).

Primary texts
Brussig, Thomas 1996: *Helden wie wir.* Roman. Berlin: Volk & Welt. (=Helden)
Grass, Günter 1993: *Katz und Maus.* Eine Novelle. Göttingen: Steidl.
Jelinek, Elfriede 1999: *Lust.* Reinbek bei Hamburg: Rowohlt.
Kinkel, Tanja 1991: *Die Löwin von Aquitanien.* Roman. Munich: Goldmann.
Timm Uwe 1998: *Johannisnacht.* Roman. Ungekürzte, vom Autor neu durchgesehene
    Ausgabe. Munich: dtv 1998 (1996).
Walser, Martin 2000: *Ein springender Brunnen.* Roman. Frankfurt am Main: Suhrkamp.
Wedekind, Frank 1995: *Frühlings Erwachen.* Eine Kindertragödie. Anmerkungen von Hans
    Wagner, Nachwort von Georg Hensel. Stuttgart: Reclam.
Woelk, Ulrich 1995: *Rückspiel.* Roman. Frankfurt am Main: Fischer.

Secondary literature
Anz, Thomas 1998: Literatur und Lust: Glück und Unglück beim Lesen. Munich: Beck
Arnold, Heinz Ludwig (ed.) 1998: Das erotische Kabinett. Munich/Zurich: Diana.
Barthes, Roland 1990: The Pleasure of the Text. Trans. Richard Miller. Oxford: Blackwell.
Brockmeier, Peter and Gerhard R. Kaiser (eds) 1996: Zensur und Selbstzensur in der
    Literatur. Würzburg: Königshausen & Neumann.
Deuse, Werner 1992: '"Besonders ein antikisierendes Kapitel scheint mir gelungen"':
    Griechisches in Der Tod in Venedig' in Härle 1992, 41–62.
Durzak, Manfred 1995: 'Ein Autor der mittleren Generation' in Durzak et al. (eds): Die
    Archäologie der Wünsche. Studien zum Werk von Uwe Timm. Cologne: Kiepenheuer
    & Witsch; 13–25.
Fitz, Angela 1998: 'Wir blicken in ein ersonnenes Sehen'. Wirklichkeits- und
    Selbstkonstruktionen in zeitgenössischen Romanen. Sten Nadolny — Christoph
    Ransmayr — Ulrich Woelk. St. Ingbert: Röhrig.
Freud, Sigmund 1999: Gesammelte Werke. (18 vols). Frankfurt am Main: Fischer.
Glaser, Horst Albert 1996: 'Die Unterdrückung der Pornographie in der Bundesrepublik —
    der sogenannte Mutzenbacher-Prozeß' in Brockmeier/Kaiser 1996, 289–306.
Graeff, Max Christian (ed.) 2000: Der verbotene Eros. Unstatthafte Lektüren. Ein Lesebuch.
    Munich: dtv 2000.
Grawe, Christian 1998: 'Die wahre hohe Schule der Zweideutigkeit: Frivolität und ihre
    autobiographische Komponente in Fontanes Erzählwerk', Fontane-Blätter 65–66,
    138–162.
Härle, Gerhard (ed.) 1992: 'Heimsuchung und süßes Gift': Erotik und Poetik bei Thomas
    Mann. Frankfurt am Main: Fischer.
Hielscher, Martin 1998: 'Literatur in Deutschland — Avantgarde und pädagogischer
    Purismus. Abschied von einem Zwang' in Köhler/Moritz 1998, 151–167.
Hummelt, Norbert 1993: 'Von den Trümmern der Ideale', Kölner Stadt-Anzeiger, 28–29
    August 1993.
Jablkowska, Joanna 1993: 'Die (un)erotische deutsche Literatur' in Schneider 1993, 99–108.
Kesting, Hanjo and Axel Ruckaberle 1998: 'Uwe Timm' in Kritisches Lexikon zur
    deutschsprachigen Gegenwartsliteratur.
Köhler, Andrea and Rainer Moritz (eds) 1998: Maulhelden und Königskinder. Zur Debatte
    über die deutschsprachige Gegenwartsliteratur. Leipzig: Reclam.
Ladenthin, Volker 1997: 'Würfelspiel oder Sommernachtstraum?', Neue deutsche Literatur
    45, 165–169.
Lieskounig, Jürgen 1999: Das Kreuz mit dem Körper. Untersuchungen zur Darstellung von
    Körperlichkeit in ausgewählten westdeutschen Romanen aus den fünfziger,
    sechziger und siebziger Jahren. Frankfurt am Main: Peter Lang.
Lütkehaus, Ludger 2000: 'Liebe nur. Tyrannei der Lust. Renaissance des Begehrens und
    Kunst der Liebe: Neue Bücher über die sexuelle Lage und kein Wort zuviel', Die Zeit,
    3 February 2000, 47.
Peitsch, Helmut 1998: 'Communication, Generations, and Nation: Ulrich Woelk's Rückspiel"
    in Williams/Parkes/Preece 1998, 317–340.

Pöpsel, Hans Hermann 1996: 'Wundersame Erlebnisse eines Kartoffelforschers', Westfälische Rundschau, 12 November 1996.
Schaber, Susanne 1993: 'Wie der Lauf einer Waffe', Die Presse, 28 August 1993.
Schabert, Ina et al. (eds) 1992: Shakespeare-Handbuch. Die Zeit — der Mensch — die Nachwelt. Mit einem Geleitwort von Wolfgang Clemen. Stuttgart: Kröner.
Schlaffer, Heinz 1971: Musa iocosa. Gattungspoetik und Gattungsgeschichte der erotischen Dichtung in Deutschland. Stuttgart: Metzler.
Schlich, Jutta 1994: Phänomenologie der Wahrnehmung von Literatur. Am Beispiel der Wahrnehmung von Elfriede Jelineks 'Lust' (1989). Tübingen: Niemeyer.
Schneider, Thomas (ed.) 1993: Das Erotische in der Literatur. Frankfurt am Main: Peter Lang.
Steinert, Hajo 1993: 'Doppelstern zwischen den Generationen', Focus, 15 November 1993.
Schmitz, Helmut 2000: 'German Unification as pornographic Nightmare: Thomas Hettche's Nox' in Williams/Parkes/Preece 2000, 213–227.
Shakespeare, William 1989: Sämtliche Werke in 4 Bänden. Ed. Anselm Schlösser. Berlin/Weimar: Aufbau.
Timm Uwe 1993: Erzählen und kein Ende. Versuche zu einer Ästhetik des Alltags. Cologne: Kiepenheuer & Witsch.
Walser, Martin 1997: Werke in 12 Bänden. VIII: Prosa. Frankfurt am Main: Suhrkamp.
Williams, Arthur, Stuart Parkes and Julian Preece (eds) 1998: 'Whose story?' — Continuities in contemporary German-language Literature. Bern: Peter Lang.
—— (eds) 2000: Literature, Markets and Media in Germany and Austria Today. Bern: Peter Lang.
Wittstock, Uwe 1995: Leselust. Wie unterhaltsam ist die neue deutsche Literatur? Munich: Luchterhand.
Zachau, Reinhard K. 1997: 'Das Volk jedenfalls war's nicht! Thomas Brussigs Abrechnung mit der DDR', Colloquia Germanica 30, 387–395.

REDUCTION, REGRESSION, SILENCE:
A CRITICAL LOOK
BEYOND THE CATEGORY OF THE PICARESQUE

TANJA NAUSE

Wir können auch anders
(Detlev Buck, 1994)

I 'Die Humoristen aus dem Osten' — Introduction

The recent appearance of works by German-speaking authors in both national and international best-seller lists is an unmistakable sign that the German-language literature is well and flourishing at present:

> Seit einiger Zeit verändert sich das Ansehen der deutschsprachigen Gegenwarts-literatur. Auf den Bestsellerlisten tauchen endlich wieder junge Autoren auf und können der internationalen Belletristik an die Seite gestellt werden; es geht sogar das Gerücht, daß ausländische Verlage wieder Lektoren für deutschsprachige Literatur einstellen. (BAB, Nr. 1)

Articles like Uwe Wittstock's 'Für die Lust an der Literatur. Ein Plädoyer' (1993; Wittstock 1995, 7–35), in which the advent of an entertaining German literature is still a distant hope, already seem out-of-date. German-language literature is popular and being increasingly bought and read again. Bookshops and publishers have brochures available, in which the new German writing is praised.[1] However, not altogether unexpectedly, this astonishing development has also triggered a few critical remarks. In an article about a meeting of young German writers, organized by Maxim Biller in Tutzing, Christof Siemes quotes the author Matthias Altenburg, who stated: 'Die neue Literatur ist wie Gervais-Frischkäse — die leichte Alternative' (Siemes 2000).

The first signs of the emergence of a new *Heiterkeit* and *Erzählbarkeit* may be detected in West German literature of the 1980s with the appearance of books like *Die Entdeckung der Langsamkeit* by Sten Nadolny and *Das Parfum* by Patrick Süskind — books which Wittstock mentions as examples of a happy marriage between entertainment and aesthetics, together with Austrian Robert Schneider's 1992 novel, *Schlafes Bruder*. The process became significant, however, with the year of the political *Wende*, 1989, when the way was opened for young writers from the former GDR to make their own distinctive contribution to the literature of the new Germany. The impact they made is to be sought not so much on a reader's level (what is read in the East is not necessarily read in the West)[2] — as in the feuilleton and in publishing houses. German critics reacted very enthusiastically to books like *Simple Storys* by Ingo Schulze, *Helden wie wir* by Thomas Brussig or *Der Zimmerspringbrunnen* by Jens Sparschuh, and German publishers may have realized that it is worth promoting young German writers again. With their activities, publishers have possibly helped to create the huge success of some of these novels.

In the feuilleton, it is a particularly striking feature of the relevant reviews that disproportionately many of these books were described by critics as 'picaresque': *Der Zimmerspringbrunnen* (1994), *Helden wie wir* (1995), *Simple Storys* (1998), Fritz Rudolf Fries's *Die Nonnen von Bratislava* (1994) and *Der Roncalli-Effekt* (1999), and Kerstin Hensel's narrative *Tanz am Kanal* (1996) were all seen as closely related to the *Schelmenroman*. Apart from the texts, critics also described protagonists (Kian in Christoph D. Brumme's *Tausend Tage*) or even the authors themselves as pícaros (Ingo Schulze).[3] Konrad Franke caught the mood when he stated: 'Daß eines Tages jemand kommen und schreiben würde: "Ich habe die Berliner Mauer umgeschmissen" — das war klar, auch, daß dieses Ich ein Simplicissimus sein würde' (Franke 1995)

In their comments, the critics seem to run true to form: 'for every new novel there is a critic waiting to find something picaresque in it' (Frohlock, cit. Dunn 1993, 3). Certainly, if novels and stories by east German authors after 1989 were 'picaresque', it might well mark a significant step towards a German-language literature that was 'popular' and 'international'. However, on closer examination, this statement appears to be superficial and grossly generalizing. It is reminiscent of an article by Willy Schumann (1966), in which he argues that the German-language literature of the twentieth century had already seen a 'return of the pícaro' as is to be expected in times of 'allgemeiner religiöser und weltanschaulicher Richtungslosigkeit' (Schumann 1966, 474). However, the appearance of three extremely different and heterogeneous German 'pícaros' in the 1950s (Felix Krull, Oskar Matzerath, Vigoleis) does not suffice to prove or even illustrate a genuine 'return'. By contrast, after 1989, at least the numbers of publications described as 'picaresque' were much higher. Although this verdict again will not bear close critical scrutiny, it does stress an important point: there really does seem to be something special about east German literature after the Wende, especially the way authors tell their stories. This article will attempt to establish a literary category which can help to describe a development for which critics have not yet found the right words. In the following, I will first deconstruct the topos of the 'picaresque' by showing why the novels and narratives cited are anything but Schelmenromane. I will then suggest the term 'adopted naive perspective' as an appropriate literary category which can shed light on the originality of these works. In my conclusion, I will suggest an answer to the question why of all places it is the former GDR where this writing has emerged.

II A critical look beyond the 'picaresque'

In an important study on the picaresque genre, Claudio Guillén proposed eight main characteristics of a genuine Schelmenroman. Briefly, a 'picaresque' text is characterized by: an outsider born into the lower classes and occupying a marginal position in society; an autobiographical narrative perspective with a one-dimensional point of view; the narrator's retrospective critical judgement of his life; an emphasis on the material sphere in contrast to the world of ideas; a criminal environment; a movement of the pícaro horizontally through space and vertically through society; and, lastly, an episodic narrative style. It can be ponted out at once that some of these crucial elements do not occur in the narratives and novels under scrutiny here. Firstly, the social origin of the protagonists is never particularly low. On the contrary, they seem to come from middle-class families of the GDR petty-bourgeois type.[4] Secondly, there is never any retrospective judgement. The traditional old pícaro looking back on his life in a spirit of regret and contrition cannot be found in these so-called Schelmen-romane. What is more, in novels and narratives written after 1989, protagonists never really move in a traditional criminal environment, they are anything but rogues. Likewise, the stories we encounter do not show charcters working their way through society by encountering many different environments. Thus, crucial elements of the picaresque genre are missing in the texts cited.

Nevertheless, there is some truth in the statement that there seem to be identifiable picaresque features in writing in the East after 1989. This has to do with the fact that picaresque literature, as noted above, is often linked with social crisis: the picaresque is said to flourish in times of social change. This thesis began to develop with books like *Thomas Manns Schelme* by Klaus Hermsdorf (1968) and, in particular, *Der Schelm als Widerspruch und Selbst-kritik des Bürgertums* by Dieter Arendt (1974), and it still survives today: 'Die Tendenz zur Entlarvung von Mißständen in der Welt durch eine der Gesellschaft entgegengesetzte Antifigur zeigt sich mit Vorliebe in Texten, die Zeitwenden oder Übergänge von einem Weltbild zum anderen markieren' (Aichmayr 1991, 42). This is important, since the pícaro is not only a literary character but, as such, also a social character ('sozialer Typus', Hermsdorf 1968, 9). The pícaro describes his path through society without criticizing it at first sight. Michael Aichmayr describes this technique as 'negative Didaxe' (1991, 77): the narrators often praise a society in order, by an ironic twist, to criticize it. This hidden critique has to be developed by the reader. However, some critics have suggested that this 'picaresque' critique always remains in a 'twilight zone'[5] because the novels never really question or challenge their contemporary society. The point is that the pícaro is dependent on the system he is criticizing; he takes advantage of this society and only survives because of it. Thus, the ultimate consequence, i.e. revolution, would mean the end of the pícaro. He knows this; this is why: 'er lieber eine Garküche auf[macht], als daß er den Umsturz der Zeiten oder die Reformation vorbereitete' (Fries 1988, 215). But still, looking back at his life, the pícaro reveals (through the reader) the miseries of society. It therefore becomes possible and potentially rewarding to relate narrative literature after 1989 to the 'picaresque' genre. On the one hand, authors could recount things from the past and assess their time in the GDR critically, on the other hand, it would also be possible to criticize post-unification Germany.

In addition to this, the 'pícaro' recounts his life in a memoir-like manner. This has been one of the clearest literary developments in east German literature since 1989. After the Wende, memoirs, autobiographies and diaries began to appear in large numbers. Fröhling's bibliography *Wende-Literatur* lists over a thousand autobiographical works which appeared in just five years after 1989, a 'publishing phenomenon' (Preece 1995, 349). It appears that, especially in times of social and cultural change, people want to preserve their memories and to maintain a knowledge of their past; there is, therefore, a particular need for autobiographical writing. Although not traditional autobiographical writing, 'picaresque' novels can be seen to follow this pattern: the picaresque novel is the autobiography of a fictional 'outcast' (Neumann 1970,168).

Leaving the main genre characteristics aside and considering only these last ideas, it becomes clearer why so many critics wanted to describe the new writing from the East as 'picaresque'. The genre does appear to be the ideal literary form in which to write today from an east German perspective. Critics like Stefan Sprang have noticed this: 'denn so gekonnt gemacht ist die kleine Schelmengeschichte der beste Weg, um dem Irrwitz in den Tiefen der alten und neuen deutschen Seelen auf die Schliche zu kommmen' (Sprang 1995).

This reference to the new social circumstances in Germany and the 'neue deutsche Seele' allows us to identify one further, important characteristic of the texts cited. The fact that so many of these books appeared as well as the texts themselves signify a general unhappiness with the way the GDR past is treated in the official discourse about unified Germany. In their texts, the authors express their critique by means of laughter and irony, not by means of lamentation and complaint. There is something special about these texts but, as yet, there is no altogether appropriate term to describe their originality. Whereas many factors link these novels with the picaresque tradition, a consideration of their narrative perspective suggests that it is inadequate. By concentrating on the way authors tell their stories, the perspective that is adopted in the texts, I intend to show that the concept of 'inszenierte Naivität' (Fischer 1992) is a much more adequate and fruitful description.

III The 'Naive Gaze'

A reading of texts by Sparschuh, Brumme, Hensel, Brussig, and Fries, which have all been described as 'picaresque', reveals common features. First, in none of them is the narrative perspective broken. The narrator keeps strictly to his or her point of view; commentaries outside this perspective are extremely rare. This creates a unidimensional perspective which is governed by the narrator. Thus, there are no meta-comments by distinct narrative authorities. Second, the narrative perspective is not just restricted to the point of view of the narrator. This narrator is also often 'naive', a rather odd person, a child, or an outsider. The scope for narrative complexity is, thus, even more restricted. Third, in many texts there is a strong use of dialect or colloquial language, which gives the narrative an 'oral' character. It stresses yet again the narrow world view of the person recounting the story. And, lastly, the relationships between the author, the protagonist and the reader are always marked by a pronounced distance. The characters at the centre of the stories are never really 'nice' because authors do not want to generate any false sympathy with the protagonist. Authors have to emphasise this distance because most readers will tend to sympathize with children, losers, and outsiders. These four elements seem to be constituents of a literary technique for which I propose to use the term 'adopted naive perspective'. This naivety is always created by the author and is, of course, by no means the author's own naivety — quite the opposite.

The use of the term naivety as a literary category is nothing new. André Fischer (1992) maps the various attempts to use and define this term in literary scholarship, identifying three main approaches. A first group of secondary literature attempts to define naivety as an anthropological fact that is necessarily linked to a certain kind of human being — in most cases children or women. Naivety is defined here (Schlüchterer, Donner, Keppel-Kriems, Appel) without taking into account the different historical or philosophical thoughts on the topic. In contrast, the second group (Henn, Jäger, Perels) applies these historical and philosophical concepts to define what naivety could be. Although Fischer does not place himself in this second group, his own definition is based to a great extent on Fridrich Schiller's *Über naive und sentimentalische Dichtung*. However, according to Fischer, the purely historical approach is only 'bedingt nützlich' because naivety is then not defined as a structuring principle of literature and writing today.[6] Hence, the third and most important approach to a definition of naivety is to grasp and describe it as a literary mode of writing, as a perspective that an author or narrator can adopt (Stierle). Or, as Fischer puts it: 'In literarischen Texten muß unter Naivität immer eine fingierte, relationale und inszenierte Naivität verstanden werden. Der Akt des Fingierens erfordert einen nicht-naiven Leser, der die Bezüge konstruktiv realisiert und konkretisiert' (1992, 30). One of the important aspects in Fischer's own definition of naivety draws on, in fact, Schiller's use of the term. Schiller defines naivety as 'Kindlichkeit, wo sie eigentlich nicht mehr erwartet wird' (Schiller 1962, 419) and states that naivety does not belong to childhood itself ('Kindheit in strengster Bedeutung'), but to a state of mind which can be described as naive, even though the age of naivety (childhood) has already been left behind. According to Fischer, this statement can be seen as the starting point for the definition of a modern concept of naivety where it relates to a literary technique. Fischer's argument concludes with the framing of naivety as an 'überraschende Reduktion von Komplexität' and, since it is an artificial perspective, a 'Verfremdungseffekt' (Fischer 1992, 87). Schiller's argument, of course, rested on the idea that naivety, as he understood it, was never something deliberately chosen or adopted; therefore Fischer's conclusion that Schiller paved the way for the modern definition of the term seems a little over-interpreted.

A completely different approach to 'naivety' can be found in Theodor W. Adorno's use of the term. This is already expressed in the different spelling: 'Naivetät'. Adorno uses this term, on the one hand, to refer to an uncritical attitude of authors towards the 'Kulturindustrie'. On the other hand, he also considers a critical potential in naivety by defining it generally as one of the last possible techniques of storytelling. The first aspect is mainly expressed in 'Frühe Einleitung' to the *Ästhetische Theorie* where Adorno criticizes: 'Was einst den Kunstwerken auf dem Piedestal ihrer Klassizität als ihr Tragendes nachgerühmt ward, die edle Einfalt, ist als Mittel des Kundenfangs verwertbar geworden' (Adorno 1998, 500). 'Naivetät', framed like this, amounts to little more than 'ein Stück Konformismus'. However:

Künstlerische Produktion, die in dem Impuls wider die Verhärtung des Lebens nicht sich beirren läßt, die wahrhaft naive also, wird zu dem, was nach den Spielregeln der

> konventionellen Welt unnaiv heißt und freilich soviel von Naivetät in sich aufbewahrt,
> wie im Verhalten der Kunst ein dem Realitätsprinzip nicht Willfähriges überlebt,
> etwas vom Kind, ein nach den Normen der Welt Infantiles. (500)

This argument leads to the second aspect of naivety, expressed in 'Über epische Naivetät' (1943). Epic naivety entails more than just a 'Lüge, um die allgemeine Besinnung von der blinden Anschauung des Besonderen fernzuhalten' (Adorno 1981, 36), it is also a form of critique: 'Aber nur solche Naivetät wiederum erlaubt es, von den unheilschwangeren Anfängen der spätkapitalistischen Ära zu erzählen [...] anstatt bloß von ihr zu berichten' (36). Naivety, thus, has a critical power because it enables authors to tell (simple) stories where others have already fallen silent or restricted themselves to the mere facts.

Apart from the critical potential of the naive gaze, this literary concept, of course, also owes much to irony. This is of fundamental importance; in fact, the adopted 'naive' view of the world and the concept of irony have very much in common. In the case of irony, a definition offered by Wolf-Dieter Stempel (1976) is extremely helpful. Apart from a pure linguistic definition Stempel points out that irony is also a relationship between the author and the object that is to be criticized. This relation is special because it is not explicitly present — it can only be realized by a third party, the reader, who has to decipher the hidden nods and winks of the author. The intentionally produced naive perspective shares the same initial constellation, again it is the reader who has to realize the author's intention. This is exactly the point where the humorous features come into play in texts which use naivety as a literary technique: irony, and self-irony, grotesque elements, and jokes. Fischer shows in his study that there can even be black humour and cynicism — but there is always irony. These comic elements make possible a position which enables authors to write about the past and the present without being lachrymose or sentimental. Thus, at the very centre of the adopted naive perspective we find tragicomedy with a kind of humour that does not hide social problems.

IV Authorial strategies

Once we have established these constituent elements of the literary concept of the naive gaze, it becomes possible to identify a whole range of varied attempts to create the naive perspective in literary texts. Apart from the empirical elements mentioned above, we have to answer the question about how authors actually construct this 'naivety' artificially. To anticipate the most important factor — there is always one main element in the naive gaze: reduction. This reduction can be found on very different levels of the text. The examples in this article show four types of pivotal reduction: the reduction of language and the view of the world of the protagonist, the reduction of the perception of history, the reduction achieved by means of regressive humour, and the deliberate self-reduction by the protagonist to a reduced level of knowledge — to silence. These different strategies are explored here on the basis of texts by Christoph D. Brumme, Kerstin Hensel, Thomas Brussig, and Fritz Rudolf Fries.

IVi 'Naive' protagonists

A first and obvious possibility to create the naive perspective in a literary text is to see the world through the eyes of a naive protagonist. Brumme's first novel *Nichts als das* (1994) employs this technique: it is the story of a boy and his childhood in Elend, a Harz village in the so-called *Sperrgebiet* in the GDR in the 1970s. Like his brothers, his sister and his mother, he suffers at the hand of his cruel father who beats his children, but whose aggression he eventually manages to overcome. The uncommon name of the main character, No, is of central interest. It is unlikely that this artificial name would be immediately particularly significant to a German reader. It enables Brumme to achieve the necessary distance between himself, the child character and the reader. However, in the course of the novel more clues emerge about this name. Since the novel revolves around the relationship between two people (No and his father) one could, firstly, think of the Japanese Nô theatre. Nô theatre is shaped by two male characters who play and fight with each other, who are fighting against each other, using traditional roles and masks. The novel *Nichts als das* is constructed quite similarly. It is a simple literary form which nonetheless evokes all the tragic problems of No's existence. A second aspect of the name points at Goethe and the geographical facts of No's origin: 'In der Gegend von Schierke und Elend waren Faust und Mephisto auf dem Besenstiel geflogen' (175). Mephisto is, as he states himself, 'der Geist, der stets verneint' (*Faust* Iiii, 1.1338). In this light, 'No' also stands for the boy's will to contradict. This rebellion is directed towards the father, but it does not always reach him and, because of No's subordinate situation, on many occasions it works against No himself.

The narrative strategy of limiting the perspective strictly to that of the young boy immediately creates the conditions for a fundamental 'naivety'. For example, it is never possible to decide whether events really happened the way No tells them; particularly, because No, in keeping with his programmatic name, tends constantly to contradict his own statements. When it comes to official GDR ideology, the power of the naive perspective becomes especially apparent:

Dafür waren bei den Russen die Städte ganz sauber, da lag nirgends Papier rum, und wenn da jemand eine Zigarettenkippe auf den Fußweg warf, dann hob ein anderer sie gleich auf und er sah den, der die Zigarettenkippe weggeworfen hatte, strafend an, und der schämte sich dafür und warf nie wieder eine Zigarettenkippe einfach auf den Fußweg. Das hatten sie im Russischunterricht gelernt. (49)

No's father, by contrast, is very critical of the GDR political system; he is fighting his own little war with the official ideology. Since this, too, is recounted from No's perspective, the father's grim attacks begin to appear ridiculous, simply because one unimportant detail after another about this little battle is given with a very serious 'face'.

The crucial device in constructing the 'naive' perspective in *Nichts als das* is, thus, a very restricted and simple language coupled with constant repetition of words and phrases. What is at stake behind this 'naivety' is credibility and truth: everybody around No is acting out different roles by telling different lies. No also tells lies — more obvious lies, and in fact he is often referred to as a 'liar'; but compared with the adult world around him his lies do not harm anybody — in fact, they reveal 'truth'. Significantly, the book has an open ending, there is no resolution, no catharsis; the reader is not liberated.

Brumme's second novel, *Tausend Tage*, follows on from his debut almost logically. It shows that a 'naive' protagonist does not have to be necessarily a child. This time, there is an 18-year-old, Kian, at the centre of the text. Again, the name of the main character is interesting for its symbolism: not only is Kian an anagram of the biblical Kain, but Kain also, read aloud, sounds like 'Kein', which refers back to No. Apart from the similarity of the two characters, there is also an explicit textual link between the two novels. In *Tausend Tage* Kian receives a letter from a cousin who turns out to belong to No's family, presumably this cousin is No's younger brother.

The narrative perspective in *Tausend Tage* is limited to the eye of the central character; thus it is quite similar to the technique in *Nichts als das*. But this time, as Brumme does not use a child figure, he has to construct something different. This, as I shall show briefly, is the topos of the literary *Sonderling*. As Herman Meyer first showed in 1943, while there is no concise definition of this type, there is a strong common motif that unifies different literary examples: the Sonderling always suffers from a strong dualism between 'Ideal und Wirklichkeit' (Meyer 1990, 19). The beliefs of the Sonderling never quite match reality. This is exactly the kind of dualism we find in *Tausend Tage*, where Kian's perception of things never seems to be close to other people's views. To start with, he always knows much less than other people in the same surroundings. Particularly in the context of his time in the Nationale Volksarmee, Kian's ignorance leads to constant misjudgements and misinterpretations of events; nevertheless he is convinced that he is the most important person in the army.

This dualism between Kian's world and reality is not only produced because of Kian's ignorance. Meyer (1990, 41) argued that another important element of the Sonderling is his preoccupation with a hobbyhorse that puts even more distance between the character's ideas and reality. Kian is obsessed with detective novels from the GDR. When he reads them, he interprets the banal thoughts of the characters as thoughts of wisdom and knowledge; in fact his own ideas are peppered with quotations from the books he reads.[7]

However, in both of Brumme's novels we also find first signs of a fractured naive gaze. This leads to an important new aspect of this literary technique: it is not only used but also indirectly commented upon. I will return to this point in more detail later. With Brumme's novels, these 'breaks' can be interpreted as a kind of rebellion of the characters against the narrator — as if Kian and No seek to escape the exaggerated naivety the narrator has created for them. At the end of *Tausend Tage*, Kian begins to 'awaken' from his naivety. He applies for a place at drama school and significantly chooses to perform a scene from Goethe's *Faust*, opting to play the part of Mephisto — Kian, like No, plays the 'Geist, der stets verneint'. Thus, it is the deliberately chosen masquerade which leads out of the naivety of No's and Kian's childhood and youth. It appears that to play-act was the only way to live in GDR society, and this, of course, did not change significantly when the state ceased to exist. The theatrical elements in both of Brumme's novels are, thus, not just a sign of how to live in a totalitarian world but of modernity in general. This speaks in favour of Brumme's analytical view, which is able to transcend the narrow world of the GDR, albeit from a post-unity perspective.

IVii Yellow and blue

In Hensel's *Tanz am Kanal* (1994) we find quite a different kind of attempt to create the naive perspective. Here, it is the literary technique of condensation and reduction of the perception of history which creates the naive gaze. The text revolves around a female narrator, Gabriela von Haßlau, who finds herself living under a bridge in the (fictional) town of Leibnitz. She starts writing her 'auto-biography'. The twenty-seven chapters of the narrative follow, on the one hand, a strict pattern of remembering the GDR past (Gabriela's own attempt at writing) and the present time of writing in 1994, on the other. The first and the last chapter are based in 1994. Moreover, the penultimate chapter draws a line back to the beginning: Gabriela's memories have caught up with the time of writing. Thus, the narrative circles twice and nearly everything happens twice, too.

This main motif is already introduced on the cover of the Suhrkamp paperback edition of *Tanz am Kanal* in quite remarkable fashion. There is a photograph of a street where two shopwindows belonging to GDR *Jugendmode* chain can be seen. Two *Trabis* are parked in front of these shopwindows: a yellow one and a blue one. The photograph shows a very symmetrical scene, yet the two halves are different. In the whole of the book there is always a tension between similar but not equal scenes, between repetition and contradiction.

The eponymous canal of the town Leibnitz stands for a first important contradiction. On the one hand, the canal symbolizes social decline, with the historical development becoming clear from the colours of the water. Whereas in GDR times the water was full of colours ('Rot, blau, grau und ocker floß er durch die Stadt, schluckte die Abwässer von Brauereien, Textil- und Maschinenbetrieben'; 31), the absence of colour in 1994 is indicative of the closure of factory after factory. Because of the dirt in and beside the canal it is also the place for social outsiders: In GDR times a woman used to live here with her mentally disturbed son, now it is the place for the homeless who live under the bridges. The canal signifies 'end' in a double sense: it is the end of the social 'ladder' and it is also the end of the town: 'Die Stadt endete am Kanal. Immer endet diese Stadt am Kanal' (64).

On the other hand, the canal is also the place of total freedom ('Tanz'). As a child, Gabriela came here with her friend Katka to be wild, solitary, and joyful. And after 1989, the narrator again sits beside the canal where she begins to write her life-story — an act which contrasts starkly with the fact that she is homeless and living under a bridge. When reading Gabriela's memoirs, the reader now faces the situation that many things Gabriela remembers occur again after 1989. The 'Jahrhundertsommer' of 1994, for example, the time when Gabriela begins her autobiographical project, is not the first 'Jahrhundertsommer' in her life. There was another 'Jahrhundertsommer' (95), back in the GDR, when Gabriela had to talk to two men from the Stasi who tried to persuade her to co-operate with them. Similarly, Gabriela is twice admitted to a mental asylum, and she is twice homeless. Most of the other characters also appear twice in the short text, as if they played double roles. In Hensel's narrative work, the reader often encounters the same characters in different stories. Policemen are called Paffrath, bar-owners Semmelweis-Märrie.[8] The free and sloppy artist is called Katka Lorenz.[9] These types of people return in Hensel's texts with no development whatsoever. This symmetry of similar yet changed situations and of similar people in different situations provides a 'roter Faden' in Hensel's narrative. It stresses the continuity of German history: situations of everyday life return with hardly any change, typical people occur in them again and again. What was the GDR is now Germany, with only superficial variations. This is, of course, a very reduced picture of history, but that is exactly the point of the artificially created naive perspective here. Gabriela von Haßlau perceives the world like this: there has only been superficial development. *Tanz am Kanal* thus criticizes the interpretation of the Wende as an event that has changed everything in Germany. People, that is at least one statement of the text, seldom change so dramatically.

IViii The joke in regression

> *Stop making sense*
> (Jonathan Demme, 1984)

With Brussig's *Helden wie wir*, one of the real literary surprises after 1989 and the novel that was most described as picaresque,[10] we find yet a different strategy to create a kind of naive gaze. At first sight, it might appear that it is again the protagonist who is mainly supporting the naive viewpoint. And undoubtedly, Klaus Uhltzscht is one of the most ill-informed persons in the whole literary scene after 1989. Like Kian in Brumme's *Tausend Tage* he never has any idea of the things that are going on around him. When he is still a child his misunderstandings are amusing — as soon as they begin to relate to his job within the Stasi they become seriously bizarre. Although Klaus breaks into a flat, kidnaps a child for an afternoon and unashamedly observes people, he still has a very romantic picture of the Stasi. Klaus, in his own mind a second James Bond, dreams of a secret mission that would send him to the United States or, at least, to West Berlin. His 'innocence' eventually culminates in a last great confusion. On 4 November 1989 he mistakes Christa Wolf, a speaker in Alexanderplatz, for Jutta Müller, the prominent GDR ice-skating trainer.

However, apart from Uhltzscht's pivotal ignorance we find another element of reduction at the centre of the text which is quite similar to the one in Hensel's narrative: a reduction of facts at the historical level. The Wende, in *Helden wie wir*, appears to be nothing more than 'a slip of the tongue' by Günter Schabowski and an act of grossly indecent exposure by Uhltzscht in front of some GDR border guards. And yet there is more to it. In contrast to Hensel's text, where the historical reduction contains all the author's irony and critique of issues relating to German unification, in Brussig's novel there is something different going on. Here, the historical reduction is part of a whole concept of humour which, in itself, is critical of the discourse in and about post-Wende Germany. I shall describe this concept of humour as 'regressive' and base my analysis on the article 'Infantilismus als Revolte oder Das ausgeschlagene Erbe — Zur Theorie des Blödelns' by Dieter Wellershoff (1976).

Wellershoff bases his thoughts on his observations of people telling jokes. First of all, to tell jokes and to laugh about them is a social activity which tends to define group boundaries. Laughter can be liberating; but it also binds people together. The group is here defined by those people who find the jokes funny and who are ready to tell other jokes. There are only two strategies available to those who want to criticize both the way the jokes are told and the level of humour. The obvious choice is to decide to drop out of the joke-telling group. But there is another, more subtle way to do this: it is the 'apparent joke'. On the surface, the apparent joke is a contribution, but, in essence, is not funny at all.[11] The level of jokes descends by deliberate choice, it is a reduction, a 'kaputter Witz' (337) — it is 'Blödeln':

> Unterhalb der Konvention des Witzeerzählens, die als deren erlaubte kurzfristige Aufhebung und Durchlüftung an die herrschende Rationalität gebunden bleibt, unterhalb eines Anspruchsniveaus, das Umkehrungen, Durchkreuzungen der Vernunft gestattet, aber nicht deren prinzipielle Aufweichung und Entformung, unterhalb der Normen des Ernstes und der etablierten Komik, hat sich eine anarchische Subkultur des Humors entfaltet: das Blödeln. (Wellershoff 1976, 338)

In *Helden wie wir*, 'Blödeln' as a strategy is employed on mainly two levels. Firstly, Klaus Uhltzscht, the anti-hero, 'blödelt' in his speech (he is 'ein mangelhaft sozialisierter, infantil gebliebener Mensch'; 338); his discourse shows him to be a very naive and also very silly person. Secondly, and more importantly, the whole novel can be seen as the author's regressive joke: *Helden wie wir* is not funny in a conventional sense, and Brussig is not a joke-teller. His novel has no real punch line, which is one of the five main elements of 'blödeln' that Wellershoff describes: on the level of the language, there are silly puns and frequent excursions into the absurd; on a rhetorical level there are constant transitions from free association to compulsive thinking and the blurring of punch lines; and, finally, at the level of content, there is the repeated disparagement of people or historic facts. *Helden wie wir* clearly possesses every one of these elements. Uhltzscht's attempts at linguistic humour, for example, are not funny at all: his numerous attempts at self-deprecation like 'Flachschwimmer' (Brussig 1995, 40, 92, 138), 'Toilettenverstopfer' (44), and the even worse 'Totensonntagsfick' (46) are not witty. On the author's level, the unpronounceable name 'Uhltzscht', of course, is also a joke. This leads already to the second feature of 'Blödeln': frequent excursions into the absurd. On the occasion of a break-in into the flat of a man observed by the Stasi Uhltzscht's train of thoughts runs:

> So wurde ich zum Einbrecher. Zum Einbrecher! Mit schlotternden Knien tappte ich durch die Wohnung von Individualist, ich halluzinierte Polizeisirenen, ich machte mir fast in die Hosen — aber ich wagte nicht, das Klo von Individualist zu benutzen, Sie wissen, mein Toilettenbrillenkomplex. [...] Wer weiß, wie das ausgeht! Jedes Kind weiß, das Einbrechen verboten ist [...] Ich war fast schon ein Mörder! [...] Ich werde lebenslänglich bekommen, ich werde wie der Graf von Monte Christo in meiner Zelle hocken und, im Stumpfsinn vor mich hin modernd, meine Arme mit Nixen tätowieren, ganz zu schweigen von den westlichen Gazetten! *SCHRAUBEN-SCHLÜSSEL-BESTIE: LEBENSLÄNGLICH!*. (224–225)

Apart from the absurd element, this quotation already shows the third aspect of 'blödeln': the transition from free association to compulsive thinking, especially if one continues to read beyond the passage cited above. The thought that he is about to become a murderer sticks in Uhltzscht's brain and leads to a strong wish to flee the flat, only to realize that there might be other obstacles in his way: 'Fliehende Einbrecher treffen immer auf einen Nachbarn, der sich verdutzt in den Weg stellt, worauf es Handgemenge und Treppenstürze gibt' (225). And Uhltzscht may not just end up in gaol: 'Die Familie am offenen Grab! Die Handschellen! Das Taschentuch der Witwe!' (225). Here, we slowly approach a climax which would lead to a punch line in a real joke — but here it is not used to trigger laughter and release tension, instead, everything is blurred and Uhltzscht will go on and on about it until the point of the joke is over:

> Zwar hatte ich keinen Schraubenschlüssel in der Hand, aber man kennt das ja aus den Krimis: Irgendeine Mordwaffe liegt immer in Griffnähe. Ich traf Vorsorge und griff in Panik nach dem erstbesten Gegenstand, der nicht tötet, wenn ich vor Angst die Kontrolle verliere [...]: ein Paperback, übrigens mit einem Säuglingsbildnis. [...] Als mich Grabs mit dem Buch sah, sagte er, baff vor Erstaunen: 'Dir entgeht aber auch gar nichts'. Die vermeintliche Stillfibel war nämlich ein Roman, *Garp — und wie er die Welt sah*, und Grabs glaubte, ich wolle ihm das Buch geben, weil ich an seinen Spleen mit den einsilbigen Vornamen, mit G beginnend, denke. (225–226)

Uhltzscht never pauses long enough to make a point out of a joke, instead, his uninterrupted flow of ideas and thoughts misses every possible or conventional pause for laughter. What is more, this lack of respect for convention extends, as we have seen, to historical facts and historical figures. The discourse in *Helden wie wir* is totally liberated from the 'adult' world, which is mostly represented by the generation of Klaus's 'mothers' Lucie Uhltzscht, Christa Wolf, and Jutta Müller with their sense of false harmony. *Helden wie wir* boycotts this world. The silly joke: 'Helden wie wir'! marks a step away from serious discourse; especially in relation to the Wende it appeared quite offensive. The provocation of *Helden wie wir* does not so much consist of the exaggerated sexual images, vocabulary, or onomatopoeic devices;[12] it is much more the case that it was its refusal to take anything related to the GDR seriously that proved provocative, not least to readers in the new *Bundesländer*.[13]

This is an authorial strategy which no longer depends on the main character of the novel, and it is precisely this that makes it interesting in our context. Instead of creating the naive gaze by means of a naive protagonist or a naive perception of history, the regressive humour leads to a naive perspective. This is an authorial attitude which, of course, should not be misunderstood. *Helden wie wir* is more than just a sad joke, it is a serious attempt to express a critical attitude towards the former GDR and the Wende, as well as towards today's situation in Germany. Uhltzscht's question: 'Irgendwo muß es ja abgeblieben sein, das Volk, das Mauern sprengen konnte — aber wo?' (6) is to be taken seriously. The critique in *Helden wie wir* is, thus, twofold: on the one hand, Brussig attacks the society that could create 'heroes' like Klaus Uhlzscht.[14] On the other hand, he also criticizes the process of the Wende and the way the GDR past is treated; or, as he remarked himself: 'daß ich [in *Helden wie wir*] sage, die deutsche Einheit ist derart mißraten, daß sie ohne weiteres einen solchen Urheber haben kann' (cit. Krekeler 1996).

Brussig's rebellion is a protest against an 'adult' world of hypocritical attitudes. One could say that this rebellion is, in general terms, a crucial device within Brussig's writing. In his new book *Am kürzeren Ende der Sonnenallee* (1999), as earlier in *Wasserfarben* (1994), his first novel, it is always a generation of 'angry young men' who rebel. In a recent article in *Die Zeit*, he said: 'Der Held meines besten, noch ungeschriebenen Romans ist neunzehn' (Brussig 1999). However, it remains to be seen whether he will ever reach the same level of regressive humour again.

IViv A clown is a clown is a clown

Finally, in my review of different authorial strategies to create the naive gaze, I come to a technique of which we have so far only encountered a few first signs: the 'naive gaze broken'. Our case study here is Fries's aptly named novel *Der Roncalli-Effekt* (1999).[15] In it we find a protagonist who is anything but naive, but who stages the naive gaze entirely by himself and for himself. This is the Kian of Brumme's *Tausend Tage* after he has put on his mask taken to the extreme: it is the character himself who takes control of the technique of literary naivety. What is more, the author himself then counteracts the strategy of the adopted naive perspective of his protagonist. The clown August puts on naive masks, but the author emerges from beneath this surface. It turns out that the points of August's reduced perspective are, at the same time, the points of the author's departure into an intertextual and intellectual universe of his own. Thus, *Der Roncalli-Effekt* embraces both the adopted naive perspective, i.e. the textual reduction, and its opposite, the departure into an open textual cosmos.

Fries is, in fact, one GDR author who has always been regarded as operating with forms very close to the picaresque. His first novel, *Der Weg nach Oobliadooh* put the author immediately into the 'picaresque' frame. This was not only because of Fries's personal origins (he was born in 1935 in Bilbao) but also because of numerous intertextual references in the novel itself. *Der Weg nach Oobliadooh* was very alien to the 'realism' of 1960s GDR literature — it was published in 1966 in the West, in 1989 (pre-Wende) in the East. It is a highly enjoyable, multi-layered text which put the author into a difficult situation because it cost him his job. From then on, the key word for Fries's writing became the Spanish term *desengaño*:[16] 'Das Moment des Desengaño als Erfahrung schockartiger Desillusionierung und frühzeitig erfahrener Verlassenheit sind für den frühen pikaresken Roman konstitutiv' (Bruns 1992, 72). The disillusionment, defined by this term, is a crucial device for all 'picaresque' writing.[17] Disillusionment is necessary, but it only becomes possible when we subject ourselves to further illusions. The process is continuous: dreams and ideals are constantly revealed as 'illusions', but this is not the end of the process: after the disillusionment we again have to 'delude' ourselves in order to go on living. Thus, the processes of creating illusions and disillusionment are constantly in play. This attitude is not only one of many of Fries's characters but of the author himself. The process of writing, for example, is described by Fries similarly: 'Gäbe es ein Rezept zum Schreiben, würde ich sagen, eine gewisse Naivität für den Anfang, als Anfangspunkt, von wo aus man dann den Prozeß *desengaño*, der Enttäuschung, zu beschreiben hätte und so Erfahrung vermitteln könnte. Alle wichtigen Romane der Vergangenheit, die mir einfallen, zeigen eine solche Verlaufslinie' (Fries 1988, 211).

Fries's latest novel allows us to examine more closely how the naive gaze is created. Here, the process becomes totally visible: instead of the author deciding for his characters that they should perceive the world naively, rather than his resorting to a narrative reduction of the perception of history or to regressive humour, here the main character himself adopts the naive gaze whenever he wishes to. This technique goes back to Grimmelshausen's *Simplicius Simplicissimus*, in which Simplex already did the same: once he had realized that he was treated with more respect when he acted like a fool, he made deliberate choices when to put on his donkey ears and act like a fool.[18]

August Augustin, whose name doubly reflects his role as a clown in the GDR 'State Circus', is put in prison because he is under suspicion of a murder committed in the circus in 1976. In gaol, everybody expects August to confess, and he does indeed begin to write his memoirs. This initial constellation seems typically 'picaresque', but by the end of the novel Fries will have inverted the pattern completely and August will not have confessed anything. He refuses to admit what he knows about the circumstances of the murder: 'Was hätte ich, ein simpler Clown, schon mitzuteilen gehabt. Die Geständnisse der Mitläufer sind die langweiligsten' (Fries 1999, 217). Against August's growing disillusionment with the legal system only the appearance of his children and the frequent conversations with his lawyer Tedeschi provide an opportunity for the relief of self-delusion. However, as August always anticipates, his own action of writing his memoirs will not influence the outcome of the trial. In the end, August decides to confess to the murder — and is released at the same moment because there are some new 'files' which appear in Berlin. Even August's final statement, 'Die Akten lügen' (253), cannot change this decision.

In his memoirs, the book we now read, August refuses to engage in any form of confessions. To justify this silence he pretends to know much less than he actually could reveal. With impressive and sometimes bewildering skill he is able to 'stage' his knowledge and his former involvement with the GDR on different levels of the book in different ways. Talking to journalists, he does not reveal anything ('Am Ende schickten sie ihren Chefredakteur, der mich in die Paris-Bar einlud, die dicke Rechnung bezahlte, ohne etwas aus mir herausgeholt zu haben'; 14). Similarly, the prison governor is also dissatisfied with August's feigned willingness to reveal the things he is waiting for. The lawyer Tedeschi elicits rather more information about August's life; but he is still far from telling him everything ('Ich verschwieg ihm, daß Friederike Hohn auf der nächsten Biennale für Deutschland ausstellen würde. Verlierer haben einen seltsamen Stolz, Signori'; 193). August's children meet a nearly truthful father, and the reader gets all of August's memories — and yet, even then it is not the complete story. August himself, in fact, only knows his past because he is recreating, reconstructing it:

> Für wen, wenn nicht für Leser, schriebe ich diese Memoiren auf? Ein Irrtum, Signori. Schreiben ist die Flucht nach einem Verrat im Leben, ist die Befreiung von den anderen, die bekanntlich die Hölle sind. Was dabei herauskommt, ist vielleicht eine Begegnung mit mir selber. Und die Wette gilt, ob am Ende ich mich in diesen Papieren erkenne oder Sie mich. (31)

The authorial strategy of letting the protagonist stage the level of his knowledge according to the respective audiences stresses an important point of the critique in *Der Roncalli-Effekt*: every attempt to tell a story, every effort to remember things past, contains an element of falseness and falls short of the truth. This means that the whole attempt at recounting a biography is doomed to failure. This amounts to an authorial strategy which can be described as the conscious inversion of the picaresque: the silence of the pícaro.[19] Only the pícaro who refuses his life-story has liberated himself from the genre. The silence of the clown appears to be the deliberate absence of the biography and confession we expect. This, of course, refers back to the widespread auto-biographical discourse after 1989 and sets a degree of scepticism against the illusion that the East and the West could come closer together by telling each other their biographies.[20]

These points of August's deliberate silence are, at the same time, the points where the author Fries comes out of his text and breaks August's 'simple' worldview. He thus counteracts August's attempts at staging the naive gaze. Two examples may suffice to show this technique, which can be encountered on many more occasions in the novel. When the GDR-circus gives its last performance before its closure after the Wende, August realizes: 'Der Staatscircus zog die Flagge ein und funkte SAVE OUR SOULS. Erst jetzt begriff ich ein geflügeltes Wort meines akademischen Freundes Retard, wonach sich die Idee blamiert, immer wenn sie mit der Realität zusammenstößt' (238). The phrase referred to, of course, is not Retard's phrase at all — Ernst Bloch coined the expression. August does not know this, for him it is genuinely Retard's idea, which still remains within the frame of staged naivety. However, as the character of Retard is created as an *alter ego* of the author,[21] Fries is clearly visible behind this figure, breaking any naive perception of the author's own intertextual game. The same technique can be encountered a few sentences further on, when August meets an old friend, Falk, who has become a neo-Nazi. August remarks: 'Ein Autor, auf dessen Namen ich nicht komme, hatte leichtfertig geschrieben, Hitler habe am 10. November am Brandenburger Tor den Zweiten Weltkrieg gewonnen. Der Mann hat recht, sagte mir Falk später [...]' (239).

This is intertextuality as self-quotation; we find these words in Fries's previous novel *Die Nonnen von Bratislava* (1994, 194). In the reviews of *Die Nonnen*, critics often picked particularly on this passage because it seemed grossly 'leichtfertig' (e.g. Basse 1994, Sturminski 1994), as Fries now ironically repeats. These are the points where August's naive gaze is totally broken. It becomes apparent that it is no more than a mask which is penetrated by the author to show what is hidden behind the text: a much more complicated, multi-layered, intertextual level of the story; another text, or: 'Immer werden Sie einen noch kleineren Clown sehen, der aus der Hosentasche seines etwas größeren Kollegen schaut und der eine Tüte Niespulver zieht...' (14). A clown is a clown is a clown — or is he?

V 'Die Humoristen aus dem Osten' — Conclusion

Sollte ich jetzt vielleicht besser
auf die Ost-West-Schiene einschwenken?
(Sparschuh 1999, 127)

Finally, I want to examine briefly why it is that the concept of the naive gaze can be related specifically to east German writing and perspectives. It is no accident that especially texts by east German authors, or sometimes even the authors themselves, were described by critics as 'picaresque'. As shown above, this statement was mainly based on the evidence of three characteristics which are traditionally associated with the 'picaresque': the humorous aspect, the autobiographical element, and the point of social change. However, given that crucial elements of the genre are not in evidence, these three characteristics do not provide a case for the label 'picaresque'. They may merely indicate a general dissatisfaction with German issues in the East. Authors who depict the East with an exaggerated, restricted, or reduced perspective obviously want to stress the feeling that the East is still not an equal part of German society.

However, apart from these socio-political circumstances, there are other, more interesting elements in the texts under scrutiny. Thus, beyond the category of the 'picaresque', I have suggested the term 'inszenierte Naivität' to shed light on this phenomenon: the naive gaze as a strategy by the author to create a very special point of view. The main element of the naive gaze proves to be a process of constant reduction which operates on different levels of the texts examined. Firstly, naivety can be staged by the author using a 'naive' protagonist, as is the case with Brumme's novels, where we encounter a child character, on the one hand, and a Sonderling on the other. Secondly, the author can stage naivety on levels of the text which do not depend on the protagonist. Here, one possibility is to describe historical circumstances in an elliptical way, as was the case with Hensel's *Tanz am Kanal*.[23] A second possibility to stage naivety independent of the protagonist is the regressive humour which confronts us in *Helden wie wir*. This novel, with its elusive humour, is an extensive critique of the way the German–German 'discourse' after 1989 has been structured as well as of the need to create 'heroes' who had allegedly overthrown the socialist regime all by themselves. Thirdly, another way of creating the naive perspective is illustrated by Fries in *Der Roncalli-Effekt*. Here, the trick is to let the main character stage the naive gaze for himself. This leads, as I have shown, to a self-imposed silence at the level of the protagonist. At the author's level, this pivotal reduction is counteracted by the joyful departures of the author into the open and multi-layered space of the text. Thus, the naive gaze is finally broken, fractured, and made visible as a literary technique.

Reduction, regression and deliberate silence can, thus, be seen as elements of a special literary development in east German writing. Authors like Brumme, Hensel, Brussig, Fries and others (e.g. Schulze and Sparschuh) put on naive masks to tell their stories. The intentionally produced naive perspective creates a 'cold eye' which shows the social circumstances in 'mitleidloser Präzision' (Höbel 1998). We encounter the power of the 'komischen Literaturgenres, jenes falsche Pathos zu vernichten, das die Heuchelei des öffentlichen Massen-diskurses auszeichnet' (Ecker 1995). Judgements are never articulated clearly in these texts, they are always implicit and left to the interpretation of the reader. It is this special mixture of seriousness and laughter — the tragicomic — which creates the critical potential of this narrative perspective. It proves to be a powerful mask to put on and express criticism by means of laughter and irony. However, as particularly Fries's novel shows, behind this mask there is another world where reduction is no longer in place. What the texts cited leave us with, then, is a nod and a wink from the author in the hope that the reader will accept the responsibility offered and read the texts in such a way that the irony and the critique hidden by the masks will be revealed to the reader's curious gaze. This is the impact that east German authors can make and have already made on the literary scene in Germany. If this has helped to create a new German literature and if it helps its popularity flourish a little longer without renouncing its original critical view, then it is a real contribution to a literature which, one day, perhaps even soon, will be truly 'popular' and may even be 'international'.

Notes

The epigraphs *Wir können auch anders* and [*Talking Heads* —] *Stop making sense* are both film titles.

1. The bookshop *Hugendubel* published the pamphlet 'Neues Deutschland. Die neue Lust am Erzählen' with 45 books by contemporary German authors; the *Berlin Verlag* published *Berliner Autoren Blätter* in which five German authors are portrayed: Katrin Askan, Jan Peter Bremer, Elke Schmitter, Michael Roes, Ingo Schulze; and there are articles in magazines for booksellers, e.g.: *BuchJournal* 1/2000 where Nele Löw Beer writes about the new German literature: "Kopfüber in eine nicht mehr bunte Welt stürzen", 29–32.
2. A personal anecdote: before Easter 2000 I was talking to some friends in Munich (he works at a publishing house and she in a bookshop). They hadn't even heard the name Ingo Schulze.

3. The reviews referred to are: Biermann 1997, Bormann 1996, Hinck 1994, Judersleben 1997, Kraft 1995, Krause 1996, Löhndorf 1995, Lüdke 1995, Sprang 1995, Steinert 1998, Wille 1996, Zachau 1997.
4. This is the case with Hensel's protagonist Gabriela von Haßlau in *Tanz am Kanal*, Brumme's No in *Nichts als das* and Kian in *Tausend Tage*, as well as with Klaus Uhltzscht of Brussig's *Helden wie wir*.
5. Böttiger 1990: 'im milden Abendschein des Schelmenromans, in uneigentlicher Idylle'.
6. Jäger's book *Naivität* (1995) does mention early intentions to use naivety as a rhetorical figure which is 'technisch einsetzbar [...], wo immer bestimmte Wirkungen erzielt werden sollen' (101). However, she does not pursue this further. See pt I 'Der naive Stil', 13–129, and especially the chapters about the rococo period (16–41) and 'Naivität als Figur des Witzes' (90–100).
7. An interesting and, in the context, unusual feature is the fact that the titles of these detective novels are listed at the end of the book. Thus, the narrator restricts at least parts of the intertextual references deliberately to texts that are clearly marked as such. Naturally, Kian's reading is strictly limited to GDR publications, thus revealing indirectly but very precisely what is paradoxical about writing 'socialist' detective novels: in a society where people are supposed to live in peace and mutual understanding, where do crimes have their place? Kian, however, remains indifferent to these discrepancies; quality is not an issue for him.
8. Both in *Tanz am Kanal* and in *Im Schlauch*.
9. In *Tanz am Kanal* and in *Das Mittwochsmenü*.
10. See for example Löhndorf 1995, Kraft 1995, Krause 1996, Biermann 1996, Wille 1996, Zachau 1997.
11. Wellershof gives an example: 'Einmal habe ich erlebt, wie ein etwa sechzehnjähriger Junge, ein etwas mürrischer Außenseiter, von seinen Witze erzählenden Altersgenossen genötigt wurde, auch einen Witz zur Unterhaltung beizutragen. Er hatte sichtlich keine Lust dazu [...] Schließlich sagte er mit wegwerfender Kürze: 'Kommt ein Mann in eine Wirtschaft, bestellt 'n Bier und bekommt 'n Schaschlik'. Es entstand eine Pause [...] Er sah die andern an und sie ihn. Es war ein soziales Vakuum, ein völliger Mangel an Anhaltspunkten. Plötzlich begann er zu lachen und die anderen mußten auch lachen. Sie lachten mehr, als über die üblichen Witze. Sie hatten etwas unglaublich Komisches entdeckt, aber keiner konnte sagen, was es war.' (337)
12. See the essay by Stefan Neuhaus in this volume, esp. 158–159 above.
13. Another personal anecdote: when my mother read the book she said that only a writer from the younger generation could make fun of everything related to life in GDR so mercilessly. When I told her that the book was a huge success, she said: 'Yes, that's how the *Wessis* would like to see us — everything was very funny'.
14. In this context it is important to note that it was Brussig's intention to illustrate the themes of Hans-Joachim Maaz's *Der Gefühlsstau* (1990). According to Escherig 1995 and Lahann 1995, Brussig was very affected by Maaz's analysis of GDR society as mainly repressed and wanted to write a literary text that complemented Maaz's empirical analysis.
15. *Der Roncalli-Effekt* was voted 'Buch des Monats Januar' 2000 by a Darmstadt jury, see 'Kleine Meldungen', *Frankfurter Allgemeine Zeitung*, 5 January 2000.
16. See the main studies on Fries: Böttiger 1985, Bruns 1992, Albrecht 1988.
17. The first and best-known literary example is to be found in the picaresque novel *Lazarillo de Tormes*. Here, the main protagonist, for the first time in his young life, serves a master. When they stroll out of Salamanca, the master (who is blind) teaches Lazarillo a lesson: not to trust anybody, which he underlines by smashing Lazarillo's head against a stone statue. It is the first painful disillusionment which Lazarillo experiences.
18. This is the kind of 'naivety' Fischer describes in Grass's *Die Blechtrommel*, see chapter: 'Ludismus und Negativitätserfahrung in der *Blechtrommel*' (95–213).
19. Cervantes already used this in his novella *Coloquio de los perros* ('Gespräch zwischen Cipión und Berganza'), where Cipión not only criticizes Berganza's confessions and memoirs but liberates himself completely from the picaresque genre by not being part of

this discourse. See Viviana Díaz Balsera (1995): 'La verdadera conversión del pícaro es pues el silencio. El texto autobiográfico de Cipión, diferido para siempre, es la maniobra ejemplar de Cervantes más allá de la picaresca' (197) [The true conversion of the pícaro is his silence. The actual 'exemplary' work by Cervantes, beyond the picaresque, is Cipión's autobiographical text, which is for ever too late.]

20. This idea is expressed enthusiastically in Brigitte Burmeister's *Unter dem Namen Norma*, where the main character Marianne demands: 'laßt uns unsere Biografien erzählen!' (Burmeister 1994, 179). There also it is equally illusory: Marianne makes up her GDR biography (cf. Schmidt 1998, 221–228).

21. Dr. Alexander Retard is one character who appears in more than one of Fries's books. We first encounter him in *Alexanders neue Welten* (1984), then in *Die Nonnen von Bratislava* (1994). In GDR-times Retard worked for the 'Akademie der Wissenschaften' in East Berlin, Enlightenment Section. This is the job Fries himself had lost in 1966, when his novel *Der Weg nach Oobliadooh* appeared. After the Wende, Retard loses his job and becomes a freelance scholar, travelling and earning his living by giving papers at all sorts of places and conferences. Significantly, he also bears an uncanny resemblance to the author.

22. In this context, F.C. Delius's text *Die Birnen von Ribbeck* should also be mentioned. Here we find the attempt by a west German author to recount a story from an east German perspective. *Die Birnen von Ribbeck*, interestingly, also creates a very simple image of history since the narrator compares the times before, during and after the Third Reich in the 'Mark Brandenburg' and, effectively, nothing has changed very much. This situation makes both narratives comparable — which would be an interesting analysis on its own.

Primary texts
Brumme, Christoph D. 1996: *Nichts als das. Roman*. Frankfurt am Main: Fischer.
—— 1997: *Tausend Tage. Roman*. Cologne: Kiepenheuer & Witsch.
Brussig, Thomas 1995: *Helden wie wir*. Berlin: Volk und Welt.
—— 1997: *Wasserfarben. Roman*. Munich: dtv. (3rd edn).
—— 1999: *Am kürzeren Ende der Sonnenallee*. Berlin: Volk und Welt.
Burmeister, Brigitte 1994: *Unter dem Namen Norma*. Stuttgart: Klett-Cotta.
Fries, Fritz Rudolf 1988: 'Gespräch mit Friedrich Albrecht' in: *Bemerkungen anhand eines Fundes oder Das Mädchen aus der Flasche. Texte zur Literatur*. Munich: Piper.
—— 1994: *Die Nonnen von Bratislava. Ein Staats- und Kriminalroman*. Munich: Piper.
—— 1997: *Die Hunde von Mexiko-Stadt*. Warmbronn: Verlag Ulrich Keicher.
—— 1999: *Der Roncalli-Effekt*. Leipzig: Kiepenheuer.
Hensel, Kerstin 1989: *Hallimasch. Erzählungen*. Halle/Leipzig: Mitteldeutscher Verlag; Lizenzausgabe Frankfurt am Main: Luchterhand.
—— 1993: *Im Schlauch. Erzählung*. Frankfurt am Main: Suhrkamp.
—— 1997: *Tanz am Kanal. Erzählung*. Frankfurt am Main: Suhrkamp.
—— 1997: *Neunerlei. Erzählungen*. Leipzig: Kiepenheuer.
Schulze, Ingo 1998: *Simple Storys. Ein Roman aus der ostdeutschen Provinz*. Berlin: Berlin Verlag
—— 1998: *33 Augenblicke des Glücks*. Munich: dtv.
Sparschuh, Jens 1997: *Der Zimmerspringbrunnen*. Munich: btb (4th edn).
—— 1999: *Lavaters Maske*. Cologne: Kiepenheuer & Witsch.

Secondary literature
Adorno, Theodor W. 1994: 'Über epische Naivetät' in Adorno: *Noten zur Literatur*. Ed. Rolf Tiedemann. Frankfurt am Main: Suhrkamp, 34–40.
—— 1998: *Ästhetische Theorie*. Ed. Gretel Adorno and Rolf Tiedemann. Frankfurt am Main: Suhrkamp.
Aichmayr, Michael-Josef 1991: *Der Symbolgehalt der Eulenspiegel-Figur im Kontext der europäischen Narren- und Schelmenliteratur*. Göppingen: Kümmerle.

Appel, Sabine 1995: *Naivität und Lebenskunst. Thomas Manns 'Die Bekenntnisse des Hochstaplers Felix Krull.* Heidelberg: Winter.

Arendt, Dieter 1974: *Der Schelm als Widerspruch und Selbstkritik des Bürgertums. Vorarbeiten zu einer soziologischen Analyse der Schelmenliteratur.* Stuttgart: Klett.

Basse, Michael 1994: '...und die Gegenwart haben wir nie besessen', *Süddeutsche Zeitung,* 5 October 1994.

Berliner Autoren Blätter (BAB) 2000/1, Berlin Verlag.

Biermann, Wolf 1996: 'Wenig Wahrheiten und viel Witz. Wolf Biermann über Thomas Brussigs Roman *Helden wie wir'*, *Der Spiegel* 5/96.

Bormann, Alexander von 1996: 'Ein leise plätscherndes Nein. Über Jens Sparschuhs Roman *Der Zimmerspringbrunnen'*, *Gegenwart* (Wien), 291, April–June 1996.

Böttiger, Helmut 1985: *Fritz Rudolf Fries und der Rausch im Niemandsland. Eine Möglichkeit der DDR-Literatur.* Hamburg: edition Nachtcafé.

Bruns, Stefan 1992: *Das Pikareske in den Romanen von Fritz Rudolf Fries.* Frankfurt am Main: Peter Lang.

Brussig, Thomas 1999: 'Dieses Bild wurde auf dem Schulhof meiner Berufsschule gemacht', *Die Zeit,* 14 October 1999.

Díaz, Balsera Viviana 1995: 'Un diálogo Cervantino con la picaresca: Intertextualidad, desplazamiento y apropiación en el *Coloquio de los perros'*, *Crítica Hispánica,* 2/17, 185–202.

Donner, Wolf 1976: 'Der naive Typus als dramatische Figur bei Schiller, Kleist, Grillparzer und Wagner' (unpub. doctoral thesis, University of Cologne).

Dunn, Peter N. 1993: *Spanish picaresque fiction. A new literary history.* London/Ithaca: Cornell University Press.

Durrani, Osman, Colin Good and Kevin Hilliard (eds) 1995: *The New Germany. Literature and Society after Unification.* Sheffield: Sheffield Academic Press.

Ecker, Hans-Peter 1995: 'Jens Sparschuh: *Der Zimmerspringbrunnen'*, *Passauer Pegasus,* 26/13.

Escherig, Ursula 1995: 'Kommt jetzt der wilde Osten? Eine neue Stimme vom Prenzlauer Berg: der Schriftsteller Thomas Brussig, *Der Tagesspiegel,* 31 August 1995.

Fischer, André 1992: *Inszenierte Naivität. Zur ästhetischen Simulation von Geschichte bei Günter Grass, Albert Drach und Walter Kempowski.* Munich: Fink.

Franke, Konrad 1995: 'Der Sieger der Geschichte. Thomas Brussig stellt vor: Helden wie wir', *Süddeutsche Zeitung,* 11 October 1995.

Fröhling, Jörg et al. 1996: *Wende-Literatur. Bibliographie und Materialien zur Literatur der deutschen Einheit.* Frankfurt am Main: Peter Lang.

Grambow, Jürgen 1991: 'Gespräch mit Fritz Rudolf Fries', *Sinn und Form* 5/43, 880–891.

Gretschel, Hans-Volker 1993: *Die Figur des Schelms im deutschen Roman nach 1945,* Frankfurt am Main: Peter Lang.

Guillén, Claudio 1987: *The anatomies of roguery. A comparative study in the origins and the nature of the picaresque literature.* New York/London: Garland.

Henn, Claudia 1974: 'Simplizität, Naivetät, Einfalt. Studien zur ästhetischen Terminologie in Frankreich und in Deutschland 1674–1771' (unpub. doctoral thesis, FU Berlin).

Hermsdorf, Klaus 1968: *Thomas Manns Schelme. Figuren und Strukturen des Komischen.* Berlin: Rütten & Loening.

Hinck, Walter 1994: 'Simplizissima unter der Brücke. Kerstin Hensels Schelmenerzählung *Tanz am Kanal'*, *Frankfurter Allgemeine Zeitung,* 2 November 1994.

Höbel, Wolfgang 1998: 'Glücksritter auf Tauchstation', *Der Spiegel,* 2 March 1998.

Jacobs, Jürgen 1983: *Der deutsche Schelmenroman.* Munich/Zurich: Artmenis.

Jäger, Hella 1975: *Naivität. Eine kritisch-utopische Kategorie in der bürgerlichen Literatur und Ästhetik des 18. Jahrhunderts.* Kronberg/Ts: Scriptor.

Judersleben, Jörg 1997: 'Auch Schauspieler dienen des Absurden: Christoph D. Brumme berichtet von Tausend Tagen in DDR-Kasernen', *Die Welt,* 25 October 1997.

Keppel-Kriems, Karin 1986: *Mignon und Harfner in Goethes Wilhelm Meister.* Bern: Peter Lang.

Kraft, Thomas 1995: 'An der Charmegrenze der Provokation. Thomas Brussigs Realsatire über 20 Jahre DDR-Geschichte', *Freitag*, 13 October 1995.
Krause, Tilman 1996: 'Kleine Trompete, zur großen Tuba aufgeblasen. Götz Schubert als darstellerischer Tausendsassa [...]', *Der Tagesspiegel*, 29 April 1996.
Krekeler, Elmar 1996: '*Da war eine Sehnsucht*. Der Schriftsteller Thomas Brussig schreibt, was er lesen will', *Die Welt*, 27–28 April 1996.
Lahann, Birgit 1995: 'Der Gigant aus dem Gartenzwerg', *Stern*, 24 August 1995.
Löhndorf, Marion 1995: 'Wer hat die Mauer umgeschmissen? Thomas Brussigs Wenderoman *Helden wie wir*, *Neue Zürcher Zeitung*, 10 October 1995.
Lüdke, Martin 1995: 'Piter wie St. Petersburg', *Focus*, 16 October 1995.
Marckwort, Ulf-Heiner 1984: *Der deutsche Schelmenroman der Gegenwart*. Cologne: Pahl-Rugenstein.
Meyer, Herman 1990: *Der Sonderling in der deutschen Dichtung*. Frankfurt am Main: Fischer.
Neumann, Bernd 1970: *Identität und Rollenzwang*. Frankfurt am Main, Athenäum.
Perels, Christoph 1974: *Studien zur Aufnahme und Kritik der Rokokolyrik zwischen 1740–1760*. Göttingen: Vandenhoeck & Rupprecht.
Preece, Julian 1995: 'Damaged lives? (East) German memoirs and autobiographies, 1989–1994' in Durrani 1995, 349–364.
Preisendanz, Wolfgang (ed.) 1976: *Das Komische*. Munich: Fink.
Roskothen, Johannes 1992: *Hermetische Pikareske. Beiträge zur Poetik des Schelmenromans*. Frankfurt am Main: Peter Lang.
Schiller, Friedrich 1962: 'Über naive und sentimentalische Dichtung' in *Werke. Nationalausgabe*, XX: *Philosophische Schriften*. Weimar: Hermann Böhlaus Nachfolger, 413–503.
Schlüchterer, H. 1976: *Der Typus der Naiven im deutschen Drama des 18. Jahrhunderts*. Nachdruck der Ausgabe von 1910, Nendeln.
Schmidt, Ricarda 1998: '"The Gender of Thought": Recollection, imagination, and eroticism in fictional conceptions of east and west German identity' in Williams/Parkes/Preece 1998, 219–247.
Schumann, Willy 1966: 'Wiederkehr der Schelme', *PLMA* 81/66, 467–474.
Siemes, Christof 2000: 'Schwäne im goldenen Nebel. Was verbindet die neuen deutschen Literaten? Ein Autorentreffen in Tutzing', *Die Zeit*, 6 April 2000.
Sprang, Stefan 1995: 'Not eines Handlungsreisenden. Jens Sparschuhs irrwitzige Burleske *Der Zimmerspringbrunnen*', *Rheinischer Merkur*, 8 September 1995.
Stempel, Wolf-Dieter 1976: 'Ironie als Sprechhandlung' in Preisendanz 1976, 205–235.
Stierle, Karlheinz 1980: 'Epische Naivität und bürgerliche Welt. Zur narrativen Struktur im Erzählwerk Balzacs' in Gumbrecht et al. (eds) 1980: *Honoré de Balzac*. Munich: UTB, 175–217.
Striedter, Jurij 1961: 'Der Schelmenroman in Rußland. Ein Beitrag zur Geschichte des russischen Romans vor Gogol' (unpub. doctoral thesis, FU Berlin).
Wehdeking, Volker 1995: *Die deutsche Einheit und ihre Schriftsteller. Literarische Verarbeitungen der Wende seit 1989*. Stuttgart: Kohlhammer.
Wellershoff, Dieter 1976: 'Infantilismus als Revolte oder das ausgeschlagene Erbe — Zur Theorie des Blödelns' in Preisendanz 1976, 335–357.
Will, Wilfried van der 1967: *Pikaro heute. Metamorphosen des Schelms bei Thomas Mann, Döblin, Brecht*. Stuttgart: Kohlhammer.
Wille, Franz 1996: 'Entfesselt verklemmt! Thomas Brussigs Wenderoman *Helden wie wir* als Monodram im Berliner Deutschen Theater', *Theater heute* 6, 36–39.
Williams, Arthur, Stuart Parkes and Julian Preece (eds) 1998: '*Whose Story?*' — *Continuities in contemporary German-language literature*. Bern: Peter Lang.
Wittstock, uwe 1995: *Leselust. Wie unterhaltsam ist die neue deutsche Literatur?* Munich: Luchterhand.
Zachau, Reihard K. 1997: 'Das Volk jedenfalls war's nicht! Thomas Brussigs Abrechnungen mit der DDR', *Colloquia Germanica* 4, 387–395.

HOW SIMPLE

ARE

INGO SCHULZE'S 'STORYS'?

PETER GRAVES

I 'Dieses Buch ist ein Ärgernis'

> Das Buch 'Simple Storys' (warum nicht stories?) ist kein Roman. Es ist eine
> Aneinanderreihung von Geschichten, die in jeder beliebigen Reihenfolge gelesen
> werden können. Einzelne witzige Situationen und Einfälle werden in eine Fülle von
> unverständlichen Sätzen verpackt. Diese Konstruktion machte es mir unmöglich,
> einen Gang der Handlung und eine Entwicklung der Figuren zu entdecken [...]
> [D]ieses Buch ist ein Ärgernis.

Thus the thoughts of one Barbara from Rostock, posted on Amazon's German
website on 6 December 1998. Professional critics were more enthusiastic.
Judgments such as 'Empfehlenswert!' (Lorenz 1998), 'virtuos und [...] einfach
gut' (Hagestedt 1999), 'ein kompositorisches und atmosphärisches Meister-
stück' (Hillgruber 1998), reflected the widespread consensus on the quality of
Ingo Schulze's novel, while other reviews declared that he had produced 'den
Roman der Vereinigung' (Greiner 1998), 'den langersehnten Roman über das
vereinigte Deutschland' (Höbel 1998, 218), 'one of the best books dealing with
the events of recent years in Germany' (Stüdemann 1998). Yet it is striking that
the authors of the last three comments, for example, despite their fulsome
praise, evidently had their own individual difficulties with the text. Frederick
Stüdemann in the *Financial Times* referred to 'comic and almost joyous moments' in the novel and gave as an example 'the touching opening tale of a
couple's first trip to the West'. Considering that the male of the couple is a Party
stalwart (it is still only February 1990) whose principal experience on the trip is
a disturbing encounter with one of his former victims, and since there are also
hints at the end of this first chapter (later confirmed) that the couple in question
have now separated, neither 'touching' nor 'joyous' would seem the most
appropriate adjective here. It was the final chapter of the book that caused
Wolfgang Höbel to stumble in *Der Spiegel*. Describing the memorable closing
scene, where two of the characters dress in wet suits, snorkels and flippers to
publicize a fish restaurant only for one to be assaulted by a passer-by, he notes
that it takes place in Altenburg, the Thuringian town where most of the novel is
indeed set. This particular incident, however, occurs in an unspecified locale

'bei Stuttgart' (SS, 227),[1] the attack therefore exemplifying, not social conflict within the former GDR, but tensions between East and West (the victim specifically says of his assailant: 'Dem gefiel mein Dialekt nicht'; SS, 301). Faced with these and other such intricacies within the novel, no less an eminence than Ulrich Greiner, the literary editor of *Die Zeit*, threw in the towel and candidly admitted to his readers: 'ich gebe zu, daß ich zwei, drei Geschichten nicht verstanden [...] habe' (Greiner 1998). Barbara was clearly not alone.

It is not my purpose here to dispute that, whatever its other merits, Schulze's *Simple Storys* also constitutes 'schwierige, anspruchsvolle Lektüre' (Cosentino 1999). Its twenty-nine chapters, moving in seemingly random sequence from scene to scene, appear designed to produce the bewilderment (if not the misreadings) displayed above and so, one might have thought, would disqualify the book from the outset as a candidate for popularity of any sort, most of all international. Yet despite the obscurities, 'simple' is still an apposite description of the stories themselves, for they deal not with the complications of great events but with an assortment of unexceptional individuals engaged in largely unexceptional activities. It is precisely the contrast this generates between the immediacy of the personal sphere and the inscrutable backdrop against which it is set that creates the tension within the novel and makes its apparently perverse mix so convincing a portrayal of post-unification life in the Federal Republic's new *Länder*.

II 'Provinz [...] finsterste Provinz!'

Writing in May 1991, some seven months after the GDR was dissolved, Christa Wolf described 'die erfolgreichen jungen Männer mit den Aktenköfferchen', who had arrived from the West armed with the laws of the free market and the demeanour that declared, 'Provinz war das doch hier, finsterste Provinz!' (Wolf 1994, 50, 53). Rather than challenge that kind of image, *Simple Storys* appears to assent to it with its unambiguous subtitle, 'Ein Roman aus der ostdeutschen Provinz'. Deploying a cast of some twenty main characters and nearly thirty lesser ones, almost all of them former citizens of the GDR, the narrative remains firmly based in and around Altenburg, that unassuming town of some 48,000 inhabitants, thirty miles south of Leipzig, where Schulze himself lived and worked for five years before and after the *Wende*. When the location does briefly stray, the characters leave behind neither their East German biographies nor their provincial perspectives, and these continue to mould their experiences, whether they are in Berlin or Baden-Württemberg, on holiday in Italy or even New York. But whilst adopting the designation of Christa Wolf's sharp-suited young men, Ingo Schulze's text displays none of their lofty attitudes. The novel's subtitle does no more than state, without edge or irony, what is to come, for characteristic of this text from start to finish is its detachment of tone. Whether events are recounted anonymously or by one of the participants, the perspective remains stubbornly external, the narrative voice registering but refusing to evaluate, and certainly never engaging in advocacy or moralizing. One recalls Christoph Hein's rejection in 1989 of the writer's prophetic rôle when he famously defined literature as, 'wenn Proust mitteilt, wie er Tee trinkt' (Hein 1990, 193). There is only one example of this particular activity in *Simple Storys*, but it is a revealing one. The owner of a struggling taxi firm in Altenburg, barely able to make a living, is in conversation with a former employee, victim of a racial assault and now jobless, and offers him refreshment with the words, 'Was für Tee willst du? Mate, Grüner, Pfefferminz, Earl Grey, Wildkirsche, English Breakfast? Weihnachtstee hab ich auch' (SS, 95). In view of what has been gleaned from the preceding dialogue about the pressures both men are facing, the generous selection may seem anachronistic, or its inclusion irrelevant, but in juxtaposing images of social dislocation and consumer choice this brief cameo captures the very essence of the changes that have occurred since 1990.[2] Similarly, the observation that the boss of a local newspaper sits behind an office desk discarded from the old Stasi headquarters (31), while under her desk outside his secretary has discarded an empty vacuum-packed drink carton of Nesquick (128), sums up the conflicting ideological values this society is having to absorb; just as passing mention of 'die neue Ikea-Küche' (197) on which one of the characters spends all his money and of the stronger door locks on which others spend theirs (251) neatly conveys both sides of the new prosperity.

It is this accumulation of detail, often seemingly inconsequential, that creates the density of the world presented here. Considerable attention can be given, for instance, to the lost half of a pair of 'Relaxsocken', with full citation of the label that accompanies them (186), or to the brainwave of one character in cutting down a pack of size 4 coffee filters to fit the size 3 holder of her coffee machine (142). But then the present and tangible can be far more readily controlled than the opaque forces at work in a society which has been stripped of all its familiar structures and where people must learn to play by entirely new rules. As another character puts it: 'Hauptsache, Geld und Arbeit und Wohnung und EC-Karte und daß man sich auskennt mit Gesetzen und Formularen' (225). In his poem, 'die mauer', written in 1990, Reiner Kunze described one effect of the Wall's then recent collapse in the words, 'nun stehen wir entblößt / jeder entschuldigung' (Kunze 1998, 60). By the same token, the individuals depicted in *Simple Storys*, deprived of the GDR's watchful attentions, must now take responsibility for their own lives, past as well as present, this applying as much to the erstwhile art historian or the failed author as to the one-time border guard or Free German Youth leader. And they cope with these new lives by simply living them, the reader observing from outside as they move house, seek work, go fishing, overcome bereavement, attend parties, take holidays, fall in and out of love, get drunk, shovel coal, struggle to bring up children, and generally make the best of their ordinary, unheroic existences.

Much has been made by critics of Schulze's debt to the modern American short story, an influence he has acknowledged, and Simple Storys was itself written during a stay in New York.[3] Nevertheless, with its laconic style, its coolness of tone and above all its emotional distance, *Simple Storys* also sounds unmistakable echoes of Uwe Johnson, that dispassionate chronicler of an earlier phase of German division, whose novels, *Mutmassungen über Jakob* (1959) and *Das dritte Buch über Achim* (1961), evoked the mood of the GDR in the 1950s in the way that *Simple Storys* seeks to do for its successor-territory in the 1990s.

III 'Oft fühlt sich der Leser verloren'

When *Mutmassungen über Jakob* first appeared, it was deemed so obscure in the wilfulness of its form that the publishers printed a plot résumé on the dust jacket, a device that still failed to satisfy Peter Hacks, who dismissed the novel (albeit as much for political as aesthetic reasons) as '[e]in schlechthin unlesbares Buch' (Baumgart 1970, 14). No-one went quite that far in respect of *Simple Storys*, even though Greiner did confess that he would have appreciated 'ein Personenverzeichnis (wie in englischen Krimis)' (Greiner 1998).[4] Nevertheless it is the absence in Schulze's work of a linear narrative, let alone of an integrated plot, that first strikes the reader. One is confronted instead by what, on superficial acquaintance, may appear to be isolated chunks of human experience cut out of some larger block which itself remains hidden, the tendency of the narrative to enter *in medias res* adding to this sense of incompleteness.

It is therefore at least understandable that one review could describe the individual chapters as 'auf den ersten Blick miteinander unverbundene, unzusammenhängende, in sich abgeschlossene Geschichten' (Henderson 1999). However, whilst the reviewer added that connections do become apparent, albeit '[e]rst im Laufe des Buches', this fails to acknowledge that clues signalling the presence of links are in fact embedded in the text from the outset. The narrator of chapter two, for instance, Conni Schubert, shares her surname with a central character in chapter one, and she also alludes to an incident from that same tale; the narrator of chapter four, Martin Meurer, is obviously related to Renate Meurer, the narrator of chapter one, and he is also mentioned by (first) name on the novel's opening page; in addition, he refers in his contribution to someone called Danny, evidently his sister-in-law; this same Danny has already appeared as the narrator of chapter three. Through such associations the first four chapters are all loosely bound together, and the beginnings of a web are spun that eventually embraces the whole book. However, although there is certainly enough continuity to justify the designation of 'novel', it remains a web with numerous holes and many dangling ends, and it requires both a good memory (or an orderly notebook) to disentangle the threads which do interlock, and a refusal to be discouraged by those that do not.[5] In the face of such demands made by the text there is a certain wry satisfaction in noting that at one point the complexities trap even the author himself into a discrepancy, when one of the book's leitmotifs, the fatal road accident involving Andrea Meurer, is first dated 'Oktober 91' (SS, 101), but on subsequent mention has mysteriously advanced a year to 'Oktober 92' (224).

A further source of perplexity has been the book's title. Barbara's question, 'warum nicht stories?', seems a legitimate one, and others have similarly assumed that Schulze's version must either be 'deutsch–amerikanisch verballhornt' (Lorenz 1998) or a 'bewußt falsche Schreibweise der englischen Pluralform' (Cosentino 2000). According to Schulze himself, however, speaking at the London Goethe-Institut in October 1999, it is intended as perfectly good German, Duden confirming that 'die Story' in German adds a single 's' in the plural. Whilst this is obviously true, and it therefore seems appropriate to use the German pronunciation of the title rather than the English, the choice of such a formulation, as well as nodding in the direction of the American model, also betrays a mischievous desire to confuse, or at least mystify, just as the teasingly unhelpful summaries at the head of each chapter, by offering synopses which obfuscate rather than clarify, raise expectations which are subsequently not fulfilled. However, this also exactly mirrors the experience of the characters themselves, as they taste some of freedom's long coveted fruits but are disorientated by the system of relationships that produces them. In her review of *Simple Storys* Christine Cosentino wrote: 'Wenn man Ingo Schulze einen Vorwurf machen will, so ist es der des Wirrwarrs im Figurengeflecht. Oft fühlt sich der Leser verloren, und wie die Personen der Handlung verliert er den Halt' (Cosentino 1999). Quite, but that is the point.

IV 'Der einzige deutsche Autor unter den Top 15'

During the literary controversy which raged through the 1990s on how best to restore the flagging fortunes of the German-language novel, one side was urging the adoption of a new realism, on the British or American model, in order to produce 'Romane, die man in einem Ruck durchliest'.[6] Their opponents, on the other hand, warned against broadening literature's appeal at the expense of its aesthetic qualities, for instance through the import of alien techniques such as mimicking 'die Geschwindigkeit der Schnittechnik des amerikanischen Kinos'.[7] *Simple Storys* manages to breach both these injunctions simultaneously. The already formidable problems of reading it at any speed, let alone 'in einem Ruck', are further exacerbated by the rapid changes of perspective introduced at the start of each new chapter, a style, as many critics have pointed out, reminiscent of Robert Altman's 1993 film, *Short Cuts*, itself an adaptation of stories by Raymond Carver, one of Schulze's acknowledged influences.[8]

Despite so unequivocally ignoring the advice of both sides, however, Schulze's work has achieved a popularity and an international recognition that, among the newer generation of German authors, was exceeded in the 1990s only by Bernhard Schlink's *Der Vorleser*. When *Simple Storys* was published in 1998, it went to the top of the best-seller lists in eastern Germany, leapfrogging works by, among others, Brigitte Reimann, Daniela Dahn, Markus Wolf, Manfred Krug, Hans Modrow, and Gregor Gysi. As those names indicate, books by authors with strong GDR connections hold a natural appeal for readers who themselves also experienced life in that republic, and it is therefore perhaps unsurprising that a work like Schulze's, dealing so unashamedly with contemporary conditions in the East, should find ready acceptance there. Such topics, however, rarely interest western book-buyers. None of those names just cited made any significant sales impact in the West, where the lists were dominated by foreign authors such as John Grisham, Ken Follett, Peter Mayle and Arundhati Roy. The all-German success of *Simple Storys* is therefore all the more striking, leading one East Berlin bookseller to conclude: 'Da wollen viele gutwillige Altbundesbürger noch was dazulernen über die Befindlichkeit der Brüder und Schwestern' (Wittmann 1998). Whilst it is doubtless comforting to imagine western readers driven to the book by thirst for knowledge of their brethren in the East, at least as large a part was probably played by the straightforward attraction of compelling narratives told in a restrained and non-ideological manner. Whatever the explanation, *Der Spiegel* on 27 July 1998 (156) thought it sufficiently noteworthy to draw special attention to the presence of *Simple Storys* at number eight in its own list of best-selling fictional works: 'Mit seinen Geschichten aus dem Osten ist Schulze der einzige deutsche Autor unter den Top 15'.

While apparently carrying the flag for contemporary German literature almost single-handedly at home, Schulze's work was also gaining attention abroad. It is not unusual that German novels in their original language are reviewed in the *Times Literary Supplement*, as *Simple Storys* was in October 1998 (Graves 1998), but it is extremely rare for them to be discussed in a daily newspaper, even one as venerable as the *Financial Times*. In the United States, *The New Yorker* ran a feature in May 1998 on Europe's most promising young writers, and Ingo Schulze was one of the six chosen, this largely on the strength of the English translation of his first work, *33 Augenblicke des Glücks* (1995). *Simple Storys* too has now appeared in English, and translations in twelve other languages are either complete or in preparation.[9]

V '...eigentlich an Chaplin gedacht'

For an author whose work offers so many challenges, this swift rise to popularity, both at home and abroad, is remarkable, but it also suggests that the difficulties of *Simple Storys* should not be exaggerated. Its structural complexities are, after all, not gratuitous but help to create that sense of a pattern which, examine it as one might, still refuses to cohere; just as the relentlessly narrow focus (even the chapter set in New York, never leaves the apartment where the visiting couple are staying) implies the existence of an outer world whose perimeters are still too distant, or too threatening, to explore.

However, although the unsettling structure is an intrinsic part of the novel's effect, it is unlikely to have been the ultimate determinant of its popular success. Unquestionably the most affecting part of the book is the array of characters it presents, and despite the absence of warmth in the narrative itself, the picture that emerges is far from unsympathetic. This is especially apparent if one draws a comparison with some other 'simple stories', published in 1999 and also set in eastern Germany. Luise Endlich's *NeuLand*, sub-titled 'Ganz einfache Geschichten', is an autobiographically-based account of a doctor's family who move from Weststadt to Oststadt (understood to be Wuppertal and Frankfurt an der Oder respectively). Although the wife and narrator paints herself as open-minded and adaptable, life in the new *Bundesländer* is presented as an almost unrelieved catalogue of sloppy service, inflexible thinking, unfriendly behaviour and political nostalgia on the part of a largely disgruntled populace whose provincial attitudes are underlined throughout by the reproduction of their speech in dialect form. One irate east German reader, according to a report

in *Der Spiegel*, informed the publisher that her copy had been 'einfach in Ofen
jesteckt', although there were apparently others who wrote to say, 'Endlichs
Buch sei zu harmlos, die Wirklichkeit wäre viel schlimmer' (Broder 1999, 159).

The reality in Schulze's 'simple stories' by contrast, though it may be
equally inhospitable, is seen as the product of a socio-economic system visited
upon people unprepared for its demands, rather than as the fault of the individuals who must now operate under it. To be sure, there are those who quickly
learn how to turn it to their advantage, but by and large the lives depicted
display no greater aspiration than the desire to be, in the words of a character
whose dismissal from her job is compounded by an unstable emotional life,
'mal wieder glücklich' (SS, 172). And when so much post-Wende writing has
tended to portray eastern Germans as victims, the casualties of political systems
they have been powerless to control, among Schulze's cast there is a conspicuous lack of bitterness or self-pity. Life may lack meaning, but it must none the
less be lived, and although we encounter some who can take it no longer,
resulting in their breakdown or suicide, most are surviving and resisting the
sense of the absurd, even if in a sometimes naïve or tragicomic way. There is a
touching ignorance, for instance, in the former transport worker who, unaware
that his title of 'Dispatcher' was only used in the GDR, assumes that it will be
immediately familiar to others: 'Zumindest die Westdeutschen mußten es
verstehen. Es war doch englisch' (98). Having discovered his mistake, however,
he does not abandon the term but instead takes an impish delight in using it in
order deliberately to baffle visitors from the West.

It is such gestures of personal defiance, turning adversity into victory,
however small, that help restore some individual dignity to these characters and,
together with the gentle humour that infuses much of the narrative, in the end
redeem the otherwise bleak world presented here. And it is on such a note that
the novel concludes. Parodying the cinematic cliché of a closing shot with
receding figures, Schulze has his two characters disappearing from the final
scene side by side. These, however, are not bronzed riders heading into the
sunset but our two divers, in full frogman regalia, squelching their way out of
the pedestrian zone of a town in western Germany. Recovered from the assault,
they have decided to abandon the fish restaurant, and as others must take cover
from the now pouring rain, they are able to make their exit while remaining
snugly dry. It is, we read, as if the shoppers sheltering on either side of the
square are forming a guard of honour for the couple as, hand in hand, they
splash through the puddles with their flippers. Speaking in ZDF's *Aspekte*
programme (see note 9), Schulze said of this scene that he had 'eigentlich an

Chaplin gedacht'. Chaplin, of course, is the quintessential little man, simple even, yet one who through tenacity and resilience overcomes all the odds to triumph in the end. Recognizing *Simple Storys* as ultimately an affirmation of that kind of spirit might have made the book, for all its other complexities, acceptable even to Barbara from Rostock.

Notes

1. Renate Meurer, the mother of the male 'diver', Martin Meurer, has found a job 'bei Stuttgart' after her separation from Ernst, the Party man of chapter one, and Martin 'besucht seine Mutter hier' (SS, 299). Jenny, the female 'diver', is coincidentally in the same place because her boyfriend, Maik, comes 'aus Stuttgart' (258: the first time we meet him it is noted that he speaks 'mit einem schwäbischen Einschlag'; 162) and, as mentioned in chapter 26, he had been hitchhiking 'nach Stuttgart, zu seinen Eltern' (267).
2. I am informed that by the late 1980s some exotic teas were already available in certain specialist shops in the GDR. However, like Volvos and VW Golfs, they would have been imported for a small clientele to create an illusion of material prosperity that socialism itself could never provide. An extensive range of consumer products, by contrast, is capitalism's defining characteristic and was also, of course, the prime attraction which led to the 1990 vote in the GDR for swift unification.
3. In another display of his attachment to paradoxical juxtapositions Schulze, speaking in ZDF's *Aspekte* programme in January 1999, referred to the delight it gave him, 'dieses Buch mit Blick auf midtown Manhattan zu schreiben'.
4. Greiner's disorientation before this book seems to be showing itself again here, as he is surely confusing the English detective story with the Russian realist novel.
5. The explanation in footnote one above illustrates the process that is often necessary to assemble the scattered pieces into a complete (or semi-complete) picture.
6. Maxim Biller, 'Soviel Sinnlichkeit wie der Stadtplan von Kiel', *Die Weltwoche*, 25 July 1991, reproduced in Köhler/Moritz 1998, 62–71, here 71.
7. Roger Willemsen, 'Fahrtwind beim Umblättern: Über den Streit der jungen deutschen Literaten', *Der Spiegel*, 21 December 1992, reproduced in Köhler/Moritz 1998, 79–85, here 82.
8. Dagmar Lorenz, for instance, points out these links (Lorenz 1998), as does Katrin Hillgruber (Hillgruber 1998). Christine Cosentino deals with them in greater detail in her article (Cosentino 2000).
9. By July 2000, in addition to English, translations had been published, or commissioned, in Danish, Dutch, Finnish, French, Greek, Icelandic, Italian, Norwegian, Portuguese, Spanish, Swedish and Turkish. That number is likely to rise, not least because at the same date *33 Augenblicke des Glücks*, although lacking eight languages from that list, could still boast versions in Russian, Estonian and Korean.

Primary text

Schulze, Ingo 1998: *Simple Storys. Ein Roman aus der ostdeutschen Provinz*. Berlin: Berlin Verlag. (=SS).

Secondary literature

Baumgart, Reinhard (ed.) 1970: *Über Uwe Johnson*. Frankfurt am Main: Suhrkamp.
Broder, Henryk 1999: 'Aufruhr unter Bummelanten', *Der Spiegel*, 4 October 1999, 158–162.
Cosentino, Christine 1999: 'rezension: Ingo Schulze, *Simple Storys. Ein Roman aus der ostdeutschen Provinz* (Berlin: Berlin Verlag, 1998)', *glossen* 7, 1999 (www.dickinson. edu/departments/germn/glossen)

—— 2000: 'Wirres und Wahres in "einfachen" Geschichten aus der ostdeutschen Provinz: Ingo Schulzes "Simple Storys"', *glossen*, 10, 2000 (www.dickinson.edu/departments/germn/glossen)

Endlich, Luise 1999: *NeuLand. Ganz einfache Geschichten*. Berlin: :Transit Buchverlag.

Graves, Peter 1998: 'Disillusion in the West', *Times Literary Supplement*, 2 October 1998, 27.

Greiner, Ulrich 1998: 'Menschen wie Tauben im Gras', *Die Zeit*, 26 March 1998, Literaturbeilage 2.

Hagestedt, Lutz 1999: 'Von neuen Jobs und alten Seilschaften', *Literaturkritik* 1, January 1999 (www.literaturkritik.de).

Hein, Christoph 1990: *Die fünfte Grundrechenart*. Frankfurt am Main: Luchterhand.

Henderson, Heike 1999: 'Die deutsche Vereinigung im Spiegel der Literatur', *glossen*, 6, 1999 (www.dickinson.edu/departments/germn/glossen)

Hillgruber, Katrin 1998: 'A. — eine Stadt sucht ihre Würde', *Der Tagesspiegel*, 29 March 1998 (www.tagesspiegel-berlin.de).

Höbel, Wolfgang 1998: 'Glücksritter auf Tauchstation', *Der Spiegel*, 2 March 1998, 218–219.

Köhler, Andrea and Rainer Moritz (eds) 1998: *Maulhelden und Königskinder. Zur Debatte über die deutschsprachige Gegenwartsliteratur*. Leipzig: Reclam.

Kunze, Reiner 1998: *ein tag auf dieser erde*. Frankfurt am Main: Fischer.

Lorenz, Dagmar 1998: Review of *Simple Storys* on www.amazon.de.

Stüdemann, Frederick 1998: 'Heroes of the wall', *Financial Times*, 30–31 May 1998, 'Weekend FT', v.

Wittmann, Angela 1998: 'Im Leseland', *Die Zeit*, 23 July 1998, 13.

Wolf, Christa 1994: *Auf dem Weg nach Tabou. Texte 1990–1994*. Cologne: Kiepenheuer & Witsch.

WHITHER? AWAY!
REFLECTIONS ON THE MOTIFS OF
TRAVEL AND IDENTITY
IN
RECENT EAST GERMAN PROSE

ASTRID KÖHLER

I Preamble

> Versehen
> Mit guten Ratschlägen
> Geh ich im Kreis.
> (Heinz Czechowski 1974, 64)[1]

> Ich kann nicht.
> Ich kann nicht weitergehen. Nicht wirklich.
> Ich kann nicht sagen, was mich bewegt.
> (Irina Liebmann 1994, 149)

As these two quotations show, the notion of circularity plays a crucial role both in Heinz Czechowski's poem 'Notiz für U.B.' and in Irina Liebmann's novel *In Berlin*, yet the two are worlds apart. The effect could not be more different. The potentially distressing resignation of the treadmill is opposed to something more existentially distressing: a centrifugally driven, inexorably accelerating dispersion into incomprehensible space. 'Es rutscht alles weg' (*Berlin*, 106).

Liebmann's novel is one of those books which might be called 'post-GDR literature'. This controversial term refers to texts by authors who once lived and wrote in the GDR. It implies less a thematic link between the literary text and its author's experience of the GDR than a faithfulness to a conception of literature as a surrogate public sphere which was typical for that state. For while in contemporary, unified Germany this public sphere can indeed be said to exist, there seems to be no space in it for the kind of intimate communication which GDR writers enjoyed with their audience. The sort of slow, intense debate which used to be conducted between the lines of literary texts is simply no longer possible.

'Mir ist, als sondere ich ein Ferment ab, das alle Gewißheiten zersetzt, wenn ich mich ihnen nähere', says the first-person narrator in Christa Wolf's story 'Wüstenfahrt' (Wolf 1999, 152). The necessity of re-establishing a sense of the self and the difficulties which become apparent in the process are a central theme of east German prose in recent years. Very closely connected with it is the question of the role of space and time in the life of the individual and of society. Disruptions in the perception of space and time suffered by the protagonists (things begin to move at an uncontrollable speed towards an unknown destination) often point to the experience of loss of identity. Conversely, attempts to rediscover a sense of identity are often linked to a renewed search for certainty about times and places in which people have lived. A stable, unquestionable and unquestioned sense of the spatial and temporal coordinates of one's own career would appear to be a prerequisite for a valid sense of the self. The question 'Who am I?' is thus inextricably bound up with the double question 'Where have I been and where am I now?'. Any attempts at an answer must try to bring time, space and the subject into a fruitful relation with each other. And at first sight at least, one of the most promising means of doing so is travel.

The undertaking of journeys and the discovery of hitherto unknown realms (countries, regions) with their landscapes and cultures depend crucially on comparisons. The discovery of the new can therefore be assumed to shed light on what is familiar. It can lead to the reaffirmation of what is known, but it can also open up undreamt-of new perspectives on it. This process is most often described in terms of the relationship between the self and the other. Admittedly, this only makes sense if the two terms are more narrowly defined. This is particularly important as they both sound so temptingly obvious. For although the other can have the status of the foreign, yet it can lose it in the course of becoming known, without for all that relinquishing its otherness, the self (the individual subject in its social environment) can very often be or become alien.

It is therefore not surprising that, alongside various forms of autobiographical writing, various sub-genres of travel literature, and a fortiori travel as a motif, have been particularly prevalent in recent post-GDR literature. Nor is it by accident that the metaphor of the journey to the self is frequently to be found in, say, autobiographical texts.

This essay will demonstrate, on the basis of three exemplary texts of contemporary east German prose, how the motif of travel is harnessed to the quest for the rediscovery of the protagonists' sense of identity. The texts in question are: Liebmann's novel *In Berlin* (1994), Angela Krauß's story *Die Überfliegerin* (1995) and Thomas Rosenlöcher's book *Die Wiederentdeckung des Gehens beim Wandern. Harzreise* (1991). In the first text, the motif of travelling plays a role, although there are no grounds for regarding Liebmann's novel in any sense or form as travel literature — the designation most often used for it, apart from 'autobiographical novel', is 'post-*Wende* Berlin novel'. The other two texts do exhibit certain classic features of the genre of travel literature (especially of the travelogue, the book of impressions and the adventure story).

II Irina Liebmann: *In Berlin*

In October 1987 a woman, a writer by profession, flies back from Vienna to Berlin Schönefeld. She had been travelling 'on business' and at the same time pursuing very private ends: she has fallen in love with a man from West Germany. In the wake of various political events in the GDR and of this love affair she decides to apply for an exit visa, is granted one and in the early autumn of 1988 moves with her daughter to West Berlin. From then on border crossings in both directions multiply. The question of whether she belongs to one side or the other becomes acute and proves to be insoluble. On the western side, be it in Munich or on the Ku'damm, she feels like a foreigner; and yet she has severed all ties with the East.

Neither the move back to her old flat in Pankow after the fall of the Wall, nor the resumption of work on an old project to write the history of East Berlin's Mulackstraße, nor the attempt to come to terms with the history of her family can relieve a sense of rootlessness. The end of the novel shows the protagonist as a small particle in the midst of the endless, and endlessly varied, commotion of a city unified at the behest of the state.

Although, as in most travel literature, references to time and space in the novel are conscientiously exact, unlike in most travel literature, the protagonist is rarely allowed to say 'I'. Her memories are used less for the benefit of others than as a means of securing her own identity; and the rhythm of the language, far from being comfortable or communicative, is characterized by an increasingly existential breathlessness.

Moreover the motif of travel is developed here as a permanent contrast to the motif of stagnation. The latter is represented by the socalled 'buntes Cafe'. The 'buntes Cafe' forms a microcosm: there are the insiders ('die "Echten"') and outsiders ('die "Ahnungslosen"'; Berlin, 33). The place is relatively gloomy and conveys an impression of confinement and belonging. References to the claustrophobia of the GDR are unmistakable. Admittedly, it is easier to leave the café than the country, and in the final analysis the clientele of the café do exactly what many citizens of the country would presumably have done if it had been possible: they enter and leave, they go away and come back. The 'buntes Cafe' and its habitués symbolize a tendency to cling, for reasons which are hard to define, to one particular place. 'Ich bin immer hier, sagt Manne. Kleiner Kreis, ja, kleiner Kreis, der kleine Kreis isset! Die Heimat!' (36). Irina too, when she comes back from Vienna, has only really returned once she has been back there. Yet even something as familiar as this place cannot be owned as home. Instead, it not infrequently happens that people 'just drop in for a coffee' and stay to talk endlessly of leaving — for Irina is by no means the only person there whose application for an exit visa is 'being processed'. It is this ambivalence of the desire to leave and the feeling of belonging which allows the café to stand as a microcosm for the country — though admittedly always with the proviso that the country regarded any attempt to leave as treachery and usually forbade return.

> Tritt aus. Gehst du pinkeln oder was? Tritt aus wie Schweiß oder Blut, aus, [...] raus muß das heißen, raustreten aus dem Verband, dem Verein und wieder rein, nein, heraus, heraus, [...] weinen gleich, weil wir nicht wollen, nicht draußen sein, nicht heraustreten, nicht treten, reten, reden, retten, doch retten, lieber retten den Körper, raus, rüber, probeweise mal, Herr Lehrer, ich muß mal austreten, raustreten aus dem Schlangenei hier, dann wär das ja Haut, aus der du trittst, klar, daß das wehtut. (77)

Once the protagonist has crossed the border, the routine of departure and return is broadened to encompass circularity:

> Es steht die Victoria golden wie immer im Tiergarten über dem Kreisverkehr, Berlin unterwegs, alles dreht sich, das kleine versperrte Berlin in den Mauern bewegt sich an dieser Stelle als Rad um die Frau herum, die Autos glänzen, auch wenn der Himmel bewölkt ist, sie glänzen, sie fahren in alle Straßen rein, so und so, so rum, so rum, ist alles nicht schlimm. (85).

With the opening of the border, however, the speed of the movements, their pull and centrifugal force increase to such as extent as to lead to sheer disorientation: 'Bruch und Gong, eine Schleuder, erst langsam, dann schneller, und zuerst drehn sich wohl diese weißen Kleider, bis alles in Fetzen und Stücken herumfliegt als ein Saturnring, (und) die Bilder verklumpen' (103).

'Es rutscht alles weg' (106) — there is no longer any point which the heroine can hold on to, let alone arrive at. This inability to arrive anywhere develops exponentially into an inability to stand still, a compulsion to move on. The question then is: where to? 'Ich kann nicht./ Ich kann nicht weitergehen. Nicht wirklich./ Ich kann nicht sagen, was mich bewegt./ Es ist etwas/ Schreckliches geschehen, aber ich weiß nicht, was' (149).[2]

In comparison with the other characters, Irina is shown to be especially affected and disoriented. Her daughter has adapted extremely well to life in the West; Eva, formerly one of the waitresses in the 'buntes Cafe' and also waiting for permission to leave the country, is now running a bar in Wedding; Manne, the café regular and invoker of the intimate circle, is now deeply involved in the politics of the east German CDU. 'Andere haben so längliche Wege, sind schon nicht mehr zu sehen am Horizont, und die rennt nur im Kreis und am Ende hierher, dreh dich um, und was siehst du — den Osten, ich kann dir nicht helfen' (109).

The 'buntes Cafe' loses its character and becomes a faceless bar. A little way down the street the newly opened 'Cafe Himmelblau' is light and empty, and the few guests set up tables and chairs for themselves in front of it. The 'Cafe Himmelblau' has succeded the 'buntes Cafe' in the sense that the latter is the western version of the first: the microcosm has been dissolved.

The final chapter of the novel provides, in short, disjointed and linguistically repetitive sequences, constantly changing images of the new 'open' Berlin.[3] In the middle of it all and in constant motion: the protagonist. The chapter is introduced with the question : 'Und nun, Liebmann, wie geht es weiter?' (165). There is no answer. The person addressed is in no position to provide one. Liebmann the author, however, writes and publishes a book in true travelogue manner: *Letzten Sommer in Deutschland. Eine romantische Reise.* But rather than accompanying Liebmann on this new journey, we shall follow the fortunes of our two other representative contemporary east German travellers. The first of them, Angela Krauß, sets out in the year which saw the publication of *In Berlin* : 1994.

III Angela Krauß: *Die Überfliegerin*

'Plötzlich faßte ich mit zwei Fingern den Zipfel der Tapete unter der Zimmerdecke und riß sie von oben nach unten herunter. Ich stieß das Fenster auf./ Fliegen wäre schön.' So begins *Die Überfliegerin* (9). The text is divided into three main sections. The second and third sections both begin with the words: 'Fliegen ist schön' (Überfliegerin, 53, 93).

Before the subjunctive becomes an indicative, the reader makes the acquaintance of a heroine who admits:

> Das hätte ich mir in meinen Alpträumen nicht ausgemalt, wie es sein wird, wenn ich eines Morgens aufwache, aus dem Fenster schaue, hinunter auf die Fabrikhallendächer, die Schornsteine und Kabelbäume, die Laderampen und Lagerschuppen, auf das Weichendrehkreuz und die liegengelassenen Ölkannen, auf die verlorene Putzwolle, und das alles steht in einer fremden Welt. (10)

The astonishing thing is: the most banal, ordinary details, in this case the dreariness of the area around the goods yard in Leipzig, which the heroine has been used to looking out on from her window for years, come to seem unrecognizably strange. The same is true of the other inhabitants of the house, with whom she has been living under the same roof for exactly the same length of time. It seems to her that changes of this kind to her social environment can only be answered with a drastic change in her own life. But what is to be done? What is the decisive deed and when is the right moment to carry it out? — Always assuming, of course, that it isn't already far too late. Preoccupied with these questions and anxieties, the protagonist has already embarked on a course of incessant action. She dismantles the world in which, up to this point, she has lived: tears the wallpaper from the walls of her room, layer by layer; saws up her antique sofa, a family heirloom; sends her beloved away: 'Wenn ich mich wieder zusammengesetzt habe, möchte ich ihm wiederbegegnen' (32). The self and the world, the inner and the outer are to be stripped down to their individual parts and put back together again in order to reach a new understanding of how they hold together. Only then, if at all, is the idea of a future conceivable.

However, this apparently linear decisiveness is undermined in the text by a constant tendency towards circularity. The device of self-quotation or quasi self-quotation recurs with striking frequency. The same questions, the same observations, the same helplessness in endlessly new variations come round again and again:

> Eines Morgens wachte ich auf an einem mir unbekannten Ort, der mit einigen vertrauten Zeichen sich stellte, als sei es der alte. Ein Verwirrspiel, das bereits fünf Jahre zurückliegt, und das zu durchschauen mir bis heute nichts genützt hat. Die Zeitungen betreiben und entlarven es. Meine Lage bleibt davon völlig unberührt. Wie alle habe ich ein paar Figuren eingeübt, die die Außenwelt über diese Tatsache täuschen. In Wahrheit taste ich, die Augäpfel nach oben gerollt, mit einem Stöckchen die Bordsteinkanten ab. (39)

The journeys in the second and third parts of the story are thus undertaken in the hope that it may, after all, be possible to escape from the endless vicious circle and in spite of everything to avert the ultimate failure of the search for the self. For according to the resolution of the protagonist: 'Meine Zukunft irrt durch die weite Welt. Ich muß sie erst wieder einfangen' (53). The railway station on her doorstep does not tempt her; she must fly, must literally take off.

The look back at the airfield, at the tracks made by the aeroplanes, in which 'alle Anspannung der letzten Sekunden vor dem Verlassen der Erde gepreßt ist', does not exactly bode well for her enterprise: 'Ein einziger Krampf, von oben gesehen' (53). But once the 'Überfliegerin' is airborne, this existential tension gives way to a scarcely bearable lightness of being.

The first flight takes the heroine in a westwardly direction, to that country which likes to think of itself as the freest in the world. On the plane, she shares her blanket for the night with a woman who has just been back, after fifty years, to visit the city of her birth, Berlin — she is a German Jew now living in America. The first place the protagonist visits is Minnesota, more precisely a house in the forest two hours by car to the south of Minneapolis. Madison is next, and after that San Francisco. There she meets, respectively, tireless do-gooders (in the house in the forest), workaholics (in Madison, suggesting a pun on 'mad' which would not occur to native speakers of English), and a woman who is expecting the world to end any day now (in San Francisco). She sees extraordinary wide open landscapes, experiences American fitness fanaticism and sits in on a lesson in which the schoolchildren talk about the Berlin Wall in terms that could scarcely be more simple-minded. When she herself is asked to report on the state of Germany, she cannot respond: 'Ich hatte, seitdem ich in Amerika gelandet war, aufgehört, über komplizierte Zusammenhänge nachzudenken' (66).

In a sleep reminiscent of, say, Orlando or Rip van Winkle, the protagonist transposes onto her own life the notion of America as the country without a past: 'Ich schlief immer weiter, und nach sechs Tagen wachte ich das erstemal nicht mehr nachts auf, um für den Fortgang des früheren Lebens gewappnet zu sein./ Am Morgen war es in ein Loch gefallen und verschwunden' (62). Moreover she 'discovers' in one of San Francisco's second-hand clothes shops, where the shop assistants are transvestites, a world of possibilities that had escaped her at home: you are who you want to be — by means of disguise. It's as simple as that.

At this point the American part of the travelogue breaks off and we find the heroine once again on the plane, this time on the way to Moscow. There she is the guest of a Russian penfriend she has known since her childhood. The chief impression of this journey is that of ahistorical synchronicity: from the Tsarist period through the Soviet era to the cowboy capitalism of the 1990s. Everything is to be had in one Moscow apartment block — and that with a notably restricted personnel: with apparent effortlessness almost all the inhabitants play several roles at the same time. You are the person that, according to the situation, you need to be. It's as simple as that.

The traveller leaves behind her, after only a short stay, both the West and the East, both the new and the unfamiliar, the old and the formerly familiar, both the country which is innocent of the past and the country which is redolent of it. The return to Germany is hinted at, the circle symbolically closed. The whole world has been airily circumnavigated — and at the same time a pilgrimage made to the geographical, historical and cultural sources of her ideological being. However, the zest for life postulated at the end and the 'neue Art von Begeisterung' (124) which accompany the thought of her home town and the arms of her beloved come as a complete surprise.

The utopia thus conjured is deliberately not realized in the text itself; we are not able to judge whether it is anything more than wishful thinking on the part of the protagonist. Once again, however, the title of the novel and the figure of the circle within it appear to give some indication. As we have seen, circular movements are described at various different levels of the story (plot: round trip, technique: repetition of self-quotation, even the dust jacket has words in the form of a circle). And yet these means seem to serve opposing ends. In the first part, the circularity of the language and the plot serves to help articulate the helplessness of the heroine in the face of her new situation. In the second and third parts, in conjunction with the travel motif, it is meant to point the way out of precisely this helplessness. The very neatness of the closure of this second circle makes it suspect in the light of the first. At the very least, therefore, the novel suggests a countercurrent to its own utopia.

IV Thomas Rosenlöcher: *Die Wiederentdeckung des Gehens beim Wandern. Harzreise.*

Rosenlöcher's walker is already armed with a comparable awareness when he sets out — which is why, from the outset, travelling to distant places seems superfluous. You don't need to go very far to discover that travel is not a suitable route to self-discovery — especially when a short trip can throw up so much that is generally regarded as strange. In this book, too, the notion of travel implies travelling back in time, though less with reference to an autobiographical framework than to literary history. Thus it is not only the figure of the traveller in general, but particularly that of the travelling writer and his work which is subjected to critical scrutiny. In this sense the very title of the book, with its prolix apparent paradox and its disingenuous referentiality, is programmatic: something classical is being elaborately attempted in full awareness of its classicality.

The journey begins on 1 July 1990, the day of the currency union between the FRG and the GDR, on which the protagonist, a Dresden writer (like Rosenlöcher himself) sets out by train for Quedlinburg. From there he is due to continue on foot through the Harz mountains, a region which, since it formed part of the border between the two German states, was, especiallly at this time, a popular holiday destination with countless tourists from East and West. However, the motive and motif of comparison which might therefore be expected to inform Rosenlöcher's book are constantly frustrated by the the text itself. The categories such a comparison would have had to invoke prove invalid from the start. At the same time, the chances of successfully finding a way back to oneself are also called into question by the protagonist right at the beginning of the journey: 'Als ob, wer ein anderer war, sein Anderssein wahrnahm' (Harzreise, 11). That is why a decisive final push from outside had been necessary: his wife had literally sent him away. And that is also why he needed to equip himself in advance with so many letters of reference addressed to fellow Harz mountaineers and other assorted poets and thinkers (Luther, Klopstock, Humboldt, Seume, Goethe, Heine, Brecht etc etc etc etc...).

Encounters on the way with representatives of both Germanies could not but strengthen the sense of foreignness, and not just on the western side, but even before that 'im eigenen Land, das mir freilich auch nie gehörte' (10). The occasions when this feeling arises change once he has crossed over the border, but not the reason why this happens: again and again it turns out to be the ways in which the details of human behaviour (including his own) adjust to the new social conditions. Whereas the scenes set in the East in each case present something long familiar over which something new (i.e. western) is superimposed like a patina, the encounter with the West evokes the so-called 'alien gaze'.[4] Thus the behaviour of the inhabitants of Goslar on the occasion of the football World Cup final in 1990 is described in the manner of an ethnologist:

> Schon war der Marktplatz besetzt von rhythmisch Springenden, die, im Takt mit dem Hupengedröhn, alle auf englisch sangen. Und hinter dem Marktplatz bildeten sie auf- und niederhüpfende Haufen, durch die die Autos hindurchfahren mußten. Derart, daß die Autos dicht umringt wurden und ihnen auf die Dächer geklopft und ihr Glanz mit den Händen gestreichelt. Und da sich die Chromschiffe Meter um Meter durch die Massen durchschoben, wurde zum Abschluß noch eine riesige Fahne über das Chromschiff gezogen, so daß die Fahne das Chromschiff nach und nach bedeckte und zärtlich von vorn bis hinten bestrich. Und der Glanz und die Rufe, die Fahne, das Blech einander begatteten. Und sie den Namen SUPER, ihres Gottes, anriefen, das omni-potente Ich, das mit einem kurzen Okay seiner Braue die Elektronen der Welt dirigierte. Und immer neue Fahnen kamen [...] Ich aber schlich mich beiseite, diesen mir völker-kündlich merkwürdigen Abend zu notieren. (87)

As is well known, the game was won by the team from Germany, and German patriotism, on this day, reached one of its high points — to put it mildly. Doubtless a comparable scene, with minor differences of detail could have been experienced anywhere in the East, even at home in Dresden.

The technique of the alien gaze is preceded in the text by other alienation techniques. Through the use of metonymy and metaphor, Rosenlöcher (or his protagonist) constantly and consciously reduce what is seen to known types: 'die Aktentasche', 'der Kohlenmann', 'die Hundenase', 'der Apotheker', 'Jesus', 'das Chromschiff' etc. These types are however never to be associated exclusively with one of the two countries:

> Schon heulte der Motor dicht hinter mir./ Schon konnte ich die Stoßstange spüren. Ver-zweifelt versuchte ich noch, die Internationale zu pfeifen, oder die Marseillaise. 'Hier geh ich und kann nicht anders', sprach ich, 'und wären alle Apotheker der Welt in ihren Chromschiffen hinter mir her.' Da aber, ein fanfarisches Blöken [...] und schon fuhr das Chromschiff vorüber. So, an die Hauswand gelehnt, wand ich dem Apotheker mein schreckensbleiches Profil in seiner Sterblichkeit zu. Indes auch das Apothekergesicht

etwas Sterbliches hatte, da er aus dem Chromschiff schaute und im Vorüberfahren noch
das Gespräch mit mir suchte, indem er sich erstaunlicherweise meiner Landessprache
bediente. 'Blödnischel!' sagte er. Der plötzliche Auftritt von Ostapothekern machte
mein Weltbild noch komplizierter. (24–25)

It is symptomatic that one of the key sentences used by the west German
'Apotheker' on their visit to Quedlinburg: 'Was haben die hier aus unserem
Deutschland gemacht!' (21), is uttered by the protagonist himself on his trip to
Goslar: 'Was hatten die hier aus unserem Deutschland gemacht!' (89). The
meanings of the word 'unser' could scarcely be more multivalent. To start with, it
is used to refer to two apparently quite different things. But when it is then taken
up by a group of west Germans in the East and subsequently by the (isolated)
protagonist in the West, it is shown in both cases as referring to something in the
past which thereby is claimed to be identical: the Germany which existed before
partition. The relationship between the two phrases 'unser Deutschland' thus lies
somewhere (and the text does not specify where) between the congruent and its
converse.

The plethora of literary references in Rosenlöcher's book points to a
phenomenon which, if one compares the life cultures in the two German states
after 1949, is doubtless more typical of the GDR: travelling in one's head by
means of literature. Occurring from the very beginning only in distorted form,
these intertexts are inexorably compounded into satire and pastiche. Where there
is nothing original to be said, the text, if it is to continue, has no choice but to rely
on extensive quotation. 'Da ging man nun in den Harz, um zu sich selber zu kommen, aber was hörte man? [...] Aber was hörte ich? Nur meine eigene Seelen-
kahlheit. Ich hatte mir nichts zu sagen' (55).

In several of the passages already quoted we have seen glimpses of
Rosenlöcher's treatment of the bourgeois literary canon. But the two texts to
which he refers most extensively are the *Harzreisen* of Goethe and Heine. Like
Heine's, Rosenlöcher's prose text can be classified as a succession of 'impressions'. Needless to say, halts are made at at least some of the same places, and
certain specific experiences, such as the loss of a shoe, the injury to a leg, or the
encounter with old friends at the chalet on the Brocken are 'repeated'. Much more
important though is the way that Rosenlöcher, in describing the situation in 1990
rather than 1825, adopts Heine's ironic manner of storytelling and takes it even
further. This means, for example, that Rosenlöcher (actually a poet) does not feel
able to include any lyrics among his impressions; that the only erotic experience
vouchsafed his travelling protagonist consists of an intensely amorous dream of
his wife ('so daß ich am Morgen danach endlich wußte, warum sie mich in den
Harz geschickt hatte'; 88); that the experience of unsullied nature is no longer to

be had even for a second; that nowhere are traces of a projected simple rural idyll to be seen; and that ultimately the length of the journey is reduced from 4 weeks to 3 days.

It is Goethe, though, the classical German author par excellence, who has a particularly hard time of it — incidentally not entirely without the support of Heinrich Heine, who also slipped a few snide references to Faust and Mephisto into his account of climbing the Brocken. Goethe made three journeys through the Harz mountains (in 1777, 1783 and 1784), to which inter alia his hymn 'Harzreise im Winter', but also passages from the *Farbenlehre*, parts of his collection of geological samples, and drawings etc bear witness. His visits to the Harz apparently offered Goethe the chance to experience (again) the feeling of being at one with nature and with himself. Rosenlöcher invokes Goethe less as text than as a person, in a kind of parodic identification of his protagonist with the historical figure of Goethe as represented in one of the most familiar clichés drawn from contemporary portraits: Goethe standing erect with his hands behind his back.[5] 'Im Gehen zu denken, Goethe zu sein, brachte mich leidlich voran' (Harzreise, 45); 'Zumal ich meine Arme wie er hinter dem Rücken verschränkte. Und mich auch sonst bemühte, auf die Johann Wolfgangsche Art klar und frei dreinzublicken' (44); 'Noch immer hielt ich die Arme hinterm Rücken verschränkt. Noch immer schaute ich drein, als ob ich Goethe wäre' (45) — this sentence is repeated in numerous variations. Moreover Goethe in his capacity as 'Geheimrat des Waldes' (46) is besought on the journey for advice, comfort and encouragement. As one might expect, however, no answer is forthcoming from this conspicuously successful precursor.

It is scarcely surprising that the classic, inherently catharctic experience of nature is not one which our Harz mountaineer ever shares. What Goethe could richly claim for himself, and Heine could still enjoy in certain inspired moments, remains completely hidden from the hiker of 1990. As a literary device particularly this topos is so irredeemably hackneyed, that it is only available as burlesque. And that is what Rosenlöcher makes of it:

Am Wegrand ein Baumstumpf. Auf dem Baumstumpf ein Unkenntliches, so daß der Stumpf als Postament des Unkenntlichen diente. Und ich noch einmal umkehrte, eingehend das Phänomen zu betrachten. Und leider feststellen mußte, das es ein Scheißhaufen war. 'Woher diese Schwärze', sprach ich, 'hat dich der Teufel geschissen' — So mich im Prozeß des Verwunderns ein wenig darüberbeugend, um selbst noch dem Unheimlichsten gefaßt ins Auge zu sehn, hob sich vor meinen Augen der Scheißhaufen vollständig auf. Und warf sich, ein Sirren grünglitzernder Flügel, mir rings um das Haupt hin, in ekligem Zickzack, so daß ich, im Gegenzickzack, hin und her sprang, als ob ich der Waldkasper wäre. Und klagend, 'Oh Furien aus fliegender Scheiße', mit

deutlich verfinsterter Brille entfloh. 'Es gibt noch Momente', sprach ich. Dann hielt ich
das Ereignis im Notizbuch fest. (46)

In the course of the journey it becomes increasingly obvious that walking
as a means of locomotion is completely anachronistic: too tiring and above all too
slow. It is only in the form of hiking or trekking that it can still eke out a
questionable existence. Questionable to the extent that this form of walking only
appears to be an alternative to driving — for ultimately what matters in both is
only distance covered and speed. Thus what the protagonist witnesses while
walking is not pedestrianism as he understands it, but competition. The upshot is
that he votes with his feet: 'Drei Tage war ich bis hierher gewandert und fünf
Minuten von hier fuhr ein Bus' (90).

'Du kannst machen, was du willst, die Harzreise bleibt Fragment.' (88).[6]
And the text that remains is a set of (marvellously funny) variations on one
theme: the vanity of the enterprise: see above.

V Travellers from nowhere: conclusion

Having accompanied three literary characters on their various journeys and
undergone with them processes of loss of and search for identity, let us pause for
a moment to consider the success of the venture. 'Es ist ja ein Scheitern im
Grunde' says an old friend of Liebmann's, when she tells him about her attemtps
to find herself (Berlin, 140; my italics, AK). This seems to me to be a symptomatic expression of a tendency perceptible both in the three texts presented here
and in other texts of recent east German prose writing: travelling with a view to
finding oneself turns out to be a vain undertaking.

The reasons for this are spelled out particularly by Liebmann, but also
hinted at by Krauß and Rosenlöcher: namely that the place which used to be
home and ought to be familiar has changed or is changing beyond recognition.
Thus the character Liebmann literally has the ground taken away from under her
feet when the border is opened, and the protagonists of Rosenlöcher and Krauß
already have the feeling of being in a foreign country before they set out on their
respective journeys. However, the central figures in In Berlin and Die Überfliegerin both try with varying degrees of intensity to exploit movement and travel as
a means of opening the path to self-discovery. Rosenlöcher for his part caps it all
by establishing the senselessness of the enterprise at the outset.

In other words, all three texts more or less consciously implicate a paradox.
For in order to be properly open to the 'other' and to derive from it insights which
can be of help in understanding the self, it is necessary already to possess a sense
of that self which is at least firm enough to form the basis for a comparison. As

noted earlier, this sense of the self relies upon definite spatial and temporal coordinates. With the loss of a familiar environment and a defining history, travel is reduced to tautology, burlesque or compound disorientation.

Clearly when from one year to another a state simply ceases to exist, this loss must necessarily be felt in a particularly acute form. It is therefore not surprising that it should be thematized with particular intensity in post-GDR prose. As with much else, though, the question needs to be asked whether this experience was unique to the GDR, or whether a process which has been taking place gradually in the West over a number of years did not simply occur there in an accelerated form. But that is a question to which neither Irina Liebmann, nor Angela Krauß, nor Thomas Rosenlöcher provides an answer.

Notes
Translation by Robert Gillett.
1. cf. the same author's later, eponymous poem from *Was mich betrifft* (Czechowski 1981, 17).
2. This sequence occurs in several places, with variations which in each case illuminate the situation: 'Ich kann nicht. Ich kann nicht weitergehen. Nicht wirklich. Es ist etwas Schreckliches passiert, aber ich weiß nicht, was. Ich kann mich nicht erinnern' (Berlin, 155).
3. 'mit dem Kind [...]/ mit der Mutter [...]/mit den Jungs [...]/ mit den Kindern [...]/ mit den Mann [...]/ mit dem Krüppel [...]/ mit der Frau [...]// mit den Hunden [...]/ mit dem Fahrrad [...]/ mit dem Motorrad [...]/ // und der Hund [...]/ und die Frau [...]/ und die Kinder [...]/ und der einsame Mann [...]' (Berlin, 168–169).
4. 'Alien gaze' ('fremder Blick') refers to texts such as Montesquieu's *Lettres persanes* and Voltaire's *L'Ingénu*. The English term is borrowed from Shklovski (cit. Dickinson 1969, xxi).
5. See, for example, Schmeller's painting *Goethe seinem Schreiber John diktierend*; Rauch's statuette of Goethe from 1828, and Döpler's engraving *Felix Mendelssohn Bartholdy bei Goethe*.
6. 'Die Harzreise ist und bleibt Fragment', Heine wrote, 'und die bunten Fäden, die so hübsch hineingesponnen sind, um sich im Ganzen harmonisch zu verschlingen, werden plötzlich, wie von der Schere der unerbittlichen Parze, abgeschnitten. Vielleicht verwebe ich sie weiter in künftigen Liedern, und was jetzt kärglich verschwiegen ist, wird dann vollauf gesagt' (Heinrich Heine: *Die Harzreise* in *Heines Werke in fünf Bänden*. Berlin/Weimar: Aufbau-Verlag, 1986, II, 209–279, here 275). Rosenlöcher for his part nowhere holds out the hope that he may take the threads of his 'Fragment' up again elsewhere.

Primary texts
Czechowski, Heinz 1974: *Schafe und Sterne. Gedichte*. Halle/Saale: Mitteldeutscher Verlag.
—— 1981: *Was mich betrifft. Gedichte*. Halle/Leipzig: Mitteldeutscher Verlag.
Krauß, Angela 1995: *Die Überfliegerin*. Frankfurt am Main: Suhrkamp. (=Überfliegerin)
Liebmann, Irina 1994: *In Berlin*. Cologne: Kiepenheuer & Witsch. (=Berlin)
—— 1997: *Letzten Sommer in Deutschland. Eine romantische Reise*. Cologne: Kiepenheuer & Witsch.
Rosenlöcher, Thomas 1991: *Die Wiederentdeckung des Gehens beim Wandern. Harzreise*. Frankfurt am Main: Suhrkamp. (=Harzreise)
Wolf, Christa 1999: *Hierzulande. Andernorts*. Munich: Luchterhand.

Secondary literature

Arnold, Heinz Ludwig (ed.) 1999: *Die deutsche Literatur seit 1945. IV: Augenblicke des Glücks 1990–1995*. Munich: dtv.

Brenner, Peter J. 1990: *Der Reisebericht in der deutschen Literatur: ein Forschungsüberblick als Vorstudie zu einer Gattungsgeschichte*. Tübingen: Niemeyer.

Blackbourn, David 1999: *A Sense of Place. New Directions in German History*. The 1998 Annual Lecture. London: German Historical Institute.

Bode, Christoph 1994: 'Beyond / Around / Into one's own: Reiseliteratur als Paradigma von Welt-Erfahrung', *Poetica* 26, 1/2, 70–87.

Dickinson, Keith A. 1968: *Bertolt Brecht: Fünf Lehrstücke*. London: Methuen.

Döring, Christian (ed.) 1995: *Deutschsprachige Gegenwartsliteratur wider ihre Verächter*. Frankfurt am Main: Suhrkamp.

Erb, Andreas (ed.) 1998: *Baustelle Gegenwartsliteratur. Die neunziger Jahre*. Opladen/Wiesbaden: Westdeutscher Verlag.

Wehdeking, Volker 1995: *Die deutsche Einheit und die Schriftsteller. Literarische Verarbeitung der Wende seit 1989*. Stuttgart/Berlin/Cologne: Kohlhammer.

BRIDGING THE CULTURES:
GERMAN CONTEMPORARY *JUGENDLITERATUR*

SUSAN TEBBUTT

I Orientalism, otherness and Jugendliteratur

'A place of romance, exotic beings, haunting memories and landscapes, remarkable experiences' (Said 1995, 1). Is this a description of the world of children's literature, with its *Arabian Nights*, *Grimm's Fairy Tales*, *Struwwelpeter*, *Treasure Island*, *Journey to the Centre of the Earth*, and *Momo*? In fact, the writer, Edward Said, is referring in *Orientalism* (1995) to the Orient. He argues that the Orient is largely a European construct, a material part of European civilization, which has helped to define Europe and the Occident. He sees Orientalism, both the study of the East and the approach to that study, as a 'style for dominating, restructuring, and having authority over the Orient' (Said 1995, 3). When Said poses the question: 'How does Orientalism transmit or reproduce itself from one epoch to another?' (15), he hopes that scholars will continue its analysis, arguing that 'as time passes and as more information is accumulated, methods are refined, and later generations of scholars improve upon earlier ones' (202).

It is in this spirit that I want to take the concept of Orientalism as identified by Said and explore ways in which aspects of it can throw light on the definition and study of children's or young people's literature. Just as parallels have been drawn between Orientalism and anti-Semitism, and later with anti-Gypsyism,[1] I would like to argue that children's literature and the study of it may also be approached by means of similar insights. It, too, can be seen to have been marginalized, and many of Said's comments on the hierarchical relationship between the Orient and Occident can be interpreted as mirrored in the traditional relationship between adults' and children's literature:

> Along with all other peoples variously designated as backward, degenerate, uncivilized, and retarded, the Orientals were viewed in a framework constructed out of biological determination and moral-political admonishment. The Oriental was linked thus to elements in Western society (delinquents, the insane, women, the poor) having in common an identity best described as lamentably alien. Orientals were rarely seen or looked at; they were seen through, analyzed not as citizens, or even people, but as problems to be solved or confined or — as the colonial powers openly coveted their territory — taken over [...] Since the Oriental was a member of a subject race, he had to be subjected: it was that simple. (207)

The world of children's literature remains for many a construct, a view of a world which bears little resemblance to the contemporary social reality of its

readers or writers, eternally rooted in the mysterious, fantastic and exotic. Similarly, the study of children's literature is rarely elevated to the status accorded to
the study of literature aimed primarily at those who are no longer chronologically young. There is thus a romanticization of children's literature which
goes hand in hand with romantic notions of the child as noble savage, as
innocent creature unsullied by the harsh realities of the everyday world. Just as
the 'Orient' did not speak up for itself but was represented by others, so the
world of children's literature was traditionally defined and characterized by
works produced by adults; few young people were in a position to create such
works themselves or to have them published.

Although the history of *Jugendliteratur*[2] can be traced back to the Middle
Ages and there are numerous academic studies of the field,[3] even today there is
a certain stigma attached to this literature, which is for many academics
'lamentably alien'.[4] In his article entitled 'Kinder- und Jugendliteratur im
Ghetto?' Klaus Doderer (1981, 9–17; here 10) hypothesizes that the isolation of
European children's literature was due in no small part to the move away from
the oral tradition:

> In vielen außereuropäischen Kulturen, bzw. bei manchen Minoritäten wie Zigeunern,
> Indianern, afrikanischen Stämmen, in denen orale Traditionen vorherrschen, existiert
> ebenfalls kein kulturelles Ghetto für Kinder. Offensichtlich ist die Einsperrung der
> Kinderliteratur das Ergebnis einer 'Lesegesellschaft' und in Zusammenhang mit der
> technischen Entwicklung, der Industrialisierung, den damit verbundenen Kommuni-
> kationsveränderungen vom mündlichen zum schriftlichen Verkehr, mit einer Ver-
> schulung der Jugend, mit einer Explosion des bürgerlichen Lesepublikums zu sehen.

These observations on the parallels between reactions to children's
literature and other, supposedly more primitive, cultures strengthen the case for
applying theories of Orientalism to the traditionally marginalized field of children's literature. My goal here is to examine the extent to which images of
foreigners within the field of contemporary German Jugendliteratur are 'Orientalist' constructions. After looking at attempts to create institutional 'bridges' in
the immediate post-war period, particularly the work of Jella Lepman, I shall
first assess the representation of foreigners in novels of the 1960s, 1970s and
1980s, secondly, contrast this with more oblique approaches to promoting an
appreciation of other cultures, and finally explore the depiction of right-wing
extremism and xenophobia. I shall conclude by returning to the global comparison of Jugendliteratur and the Orient, exploring writing *by* young people *for*
young people, including writing by foreigners as well as Germans, which
creates new spaces in which they can construct their own self-image rather than
be members of the 'subject race' (Said 1995, 207).

II *Die Kinderbuchbrücke* and institutionalized 'bridges'

At the end of World War II when Germany's cities were in ruins, its people struggling to find food, shelter and relatives, and its culture inextricably associated with the barbarous excesses of Nazism, it was particularly important to make its children aware of the richness of the international literary heritage as an antidote to narrow, nationalist thought-patterns. For one German returning from exile in America, Jella Lepman, children's literature held the key. In the *Kinderbuchbrücke* (1964) she explains her vision of a new, more harmonious Europe, a new era of cultural understanding and cooperation between nations. Central to this vision was Jugendliteratur, since children could travel effortlessly in their imagination to the landscapes real and fantastic created by writers from other nations. The Germanness of Struwwelpeter, the Englishness of Robin Hood or Gulliver, the Indianness of Kim, or the Americanness of Uncle Tom were immaterial, for the children 'hatten sie adoptiert und ihr Ursprungsland vergessen' (Lepman 1964, 83). Lepman thus arranged for books from many countries to be sent to Munich to form part of an exhibition in Munich, which was to act as a 'Bote, der Berge und Flüsse, ja sogar Meere überwindet und hingeht ans andere Ende der Welt, um dort Freundschaften zu werben. Jedes Land gibt, und jedes Land empfängt; unzählbar sind die getauschten Werte; und so entsteht in dem Alter, da wir unsere ersten Eindrücke empfangen, die Weltrepublik der Kinder' (Paul Hazard cit. Lepman 1964, 11).

Lepman's efforts did not go unnoticed in the literary world. Carl Zuckmayer, in the introduction to the volume (9), praises her energy and vision:

> Sie hat, single-handed, würde man auf englisch sagen, im Alleingang wie ein Alpenbezwinger, gegen den 'Dienstweg', gegen Kaltherzigkeit, Gleichgültigkeit, Phantasielosigkeit gekämpft, sie hat es geschafft, ihren schönen und noblen Gedanken zu verwirklichen, und was sie geschaffen hat, die 'Erste Internationale Jugendbibliothek' und das 'Internationale Kuratorium für das Jugendbuch', mögen mehr für die Verständigung der Völker und die Ausrottung des Hasses bedeuten als viele Sitzungen und Beschlüsse höchster politischer Instanzen und Körperschaften. Ein Werk echter Menschlichkeit — das Werk eines großen Herzens.

In his *Nachwort* to *Die Kinderbuchbrücke*, Andreas Bode, the then director of the International Youth Library, highlights Lepman's pioneering work (214):

> Kinder, meinte Jella Lepman, haben ein natürliches Zusammengehörigkeitsgefühl. Für sie lohnt es sich, Brücken zu anderen Kulturen zu bauen; die 'Kinderbuchbrücke' war als Investition in die Zukunft gedacht. Es ist faszinierend zu verfolgen, wie die weltumspannende Idee einer Frau, die sich eine internationale Bibliothek für die Kinder erträumte, wider alle Wahrscheinlichkeit langsam Wirklichkeit wird.

The legacy of Lepman's work can be seen in three key interrelated areas. Firstly, the International Youth Library in Munich holds one of the largest collections of primary and secondary literature in the field and plays host to researchers, teachers and children from all round the world. Secondly, the Institute for Research into Children's Literature in Frankfurt has, from its inception, had a strong focus on the international dimension. Finally, the setting up of numerous literary prizes in the German-speaking world has served to promote the cross-fertilization of the literary world at a structural level. The earliest of these include the Friedrich-Gerstäcker-Preis (1947), the Austrian Staatspreis für Kinder- und Jugendliteratur (1955), which was established to highlight works which have insights into faraway places, the German Children's Literature Prize (endowed in 1956),[5] and a variety of prizes for translations of children's books into German.

III Orientalist images of foreigners

Bridges between the nations came into being not only at institutional level; they can also be seen to emerge with the publication of individual works of literature. With the rise in popularity of socially critical literature in the 1960s, the representation of the so-called *Gastarbeiter* and their children took its place alongside representations of issues such as drugs, pregnancy and generation conflicts.[6] As in the world of adult *MigrantInnenliteratur*, the early works present the 'peculiarities' of the foreign culture to a German readership, but these cultural insights are usually limited to short references to language, food, or religion (cf. König/Straube/Taylan 1985 and 1988). The well-intentioned authors, mainly white, middle-class, female German teachers, produced novels which John Stephens (1992, 120–157) would classify as 'time out' texts in which the emphasis is personal and familial rather than political.[7]

In works such as Hans-Georg Noack's *Hautfarbe Nebensache* (1960) and *Benvenuto heißt willkommen* (1973), Ruth Herrmann's *Wir sind doch nicht vom Mond: Klein-Istanbul an der Elbe* (1975), and Sigrid Schuster-Schmah's *Staatsangehörigkeit: griechisch* (1978) the chief protagonist is a foreign child (usually Greek, Italian, Spanish, Moroccan or Turkish) in a German milieu (cf. Feid 1983; Banscherus 1985; Fiechtner 1986). Some problems arise as he or she gradually makes a few German friends, who then find themselves defending their new foreign chum against the less enlightened, but all is well that ends well. The German culture is seen as the norm against which others are measured. The narrative perspective resembles the colonialist-style promontory gaze, in which the landscape is surveyed from on high, i.e. is described from the point of view of the conqueror, the superior.

This 'Orientalist' gaze is particularly apparent in the condemnation of the patriarchal attitudes of Turkish men and the support for those Turkish or Moslem girls who try to break out from within the constraints of their own culture, as seen in Annelies Schwarz's *Hamide spielt Hamide: Ein türkisches Mädchen in Deutschland* (1986). Although it and similar works are marketed as promoting cross-cultural understanding, they fall short of their aim because they over-emphasize the ethnicity, exoticness, otherness of the foreign protagonists.[8] And even when the prejudice encountered by asylum seekers in the 1980s is placed in a historical context in order to underline the continuity of persecution, it does not necessarily diminish the 'Orientalist' tendency. The Berlin-based Grips-Theater's adaptation for the stage of Leonie Ossowski's *Stern ohne Himmel* (1978) under the title *Voll auf der Rolle* (1984) is a case in point. Whereas in the novel it is a Jewish boy in the Third Reich whom a group of German children hide, in the stage version the victim of racist persecution is a young Turkish asylum seeker. In both cases the critique of institutionalized discrimination is counterbalanced and relativized by the positive roles played by the young German protagonists.[9]

At the beginning of the twenty-first century most of these works from the 1960s to the 1980s depicting cross-cultural relationships in Germany seem dated and lack sparkle. They are peopled by cardboard foreigners whose generally inferior living conditions and strange, generally patriarchal culture are presented as undesirable. Harmony requires a loss of identity and is achieved only as a result of assimilation and integration into what by inference is the more sophisticated, progressive, German culture.

IV Less is more: non-Orientalist images of other countries and cultures

A discussion of three very different works will show how a less direct emphasis on nationality can result in more differentiated images of other cultures. Thus Austrian writer Karl Bruckner's internationally acclaimed novel *Sadako will leben* (1961) is set in Japan and deals with the devastation, both physical and human, caused by the dropping of the atomic bomb on Hiroshima. It tells the story of Sadako, a young girl who survives. With great skill, Bruckner interweaves accounts of different people's lives at the time the bomb was dropped, from the pilot carrying the bomb to a man fishing in the river. The geographical location is literally oriental, since the novel is set in the East; however, the focus is not on the ethnicity of the characters but on the universal theme of the evil of war and the suffering it causes to innocent victims. It is the bombing which is criticized rather than the nation which perpetrated it. And in choosing a young girl as the central figure of the novel, Bruckner is inviting his readers to identify with young people round the world who are threatened by war.

A similar appeal for understanding of global issues can be perceived in a work of non-fiction aimed at young teenagers, Reinhardt Jung's *Kleine Hände — Kleine Fäuste: Der Kampf der Kinder in Lateinamerika* (1983). These interviews with young children working as shoe-shiners, brick-makers, lottery ticket sellers or scrap metal sorters, employed in mines, plantations or quarries, may be seen as a Jugendliteratur counterpart to the *Dokumentarliteratur* and *Reportagen* of writers such as Max von der Grün, Günter Wallraff and Erika Runge in the 1960s, 1970s and 1980s.[10]

A work which stands at the borders of documentary reportage, autobiography, and oral history is *'Da wollten wir frei sein!': Eine Sinti-Familie erzählt* (1983), recorded, transcribed and edited by Michail Krausnick. Along with the Danes, Frisians and Sorbs, the Sinti are one of Germany's few autochthonous minorities, but have been noticeable by their almost complete absence from the world of Jugendliteratur.[11] However, Romany culture is almost exclusively an oral culture and, as Doderer pointed out (1981, 10; see 222 above), oral cultures do not view children's literature as inferior in the same way that most other European cultures do. It is thus particularly interesting that one of the very first autobiographical accounts of Romany life to be produced in Germany was in fact published as a work for teenagers. Here four generations of a Sinti family tell of their experiences of persecution as Romanies on ethnic grounds; and they also narrate their day-to-concerns and aspirations from an individual, personal standpoint. The members of the family are not analysed or portrayed by Gadjos, or non-Romanies; they are empowered, speak for themselves, offer alternative images to set against the all-too-pervasive, judgmental images of Romanies which are in common currency throughout Europe (Tebbutt 1998, ix–16).

In all these works the foreign protagonists are not seen as empty constructs, but as real people with real concerns. Whether they are seen as victims or as empowered individuals, their ethnicity is never exoticized.

V Rebuilding broken bridges: exposing extremism

The third step in my discussion of 'Orientalism' and multi-culturalism in recent Jugendliteratur takes us to the opposite end of the spectrum from where we started, to the portrayal of prejudice and right-wing extremism in a number of works. Arguably the authors help to rebuild the broken bridges between the nations. Readers are presented with what Stephens terms 'transgressive' texts

(1992, 147–155), i.e. texts in which taboos are broken, themes such as brutality and aggression are treated frankly, and the ending remains open.

The culmination of right-wing violence in the series of attacks on hostels for asylum seekers and immigrant workers in the late 1980s[12] and early 1990s forms the background to the publication of works such as Margret Steenfatt's *Haß im Herzen* (1992), Marie Hagemann's *Schwarzer, Wolf, Skin* (1993),[13] Gunter Preuß's *Stein in meiner Faust* (1993) and Günter Saalmann's *Zu keinem ein Wort* (1993).[14] These are works which bring the simmering undercurrents of racism in German society to the surface. The abrasive tone of these works is very different from the earlier novels about cross-cultural friendships. Rather than beginning with the potential for racial harmony, the authors give shocking insights into the range of factors associated with right-wing attacks. Commitment to extremist causes is shown to result even in murder and mutilation.

The autobiographical work *Die Abrechnung: Ein Neonazi steigt aus* (1993) by Ingo Hasselbach, born 1967, written together with journalist and film-producer Winfried Bonengel, is aimed at a teenage readership.[15] It is presented in the form of an extended letter to Hasselbach's natural father, in which he explains the reasons for his disillusionment with and departure from the neo-Nazi scene, in which he was a leading figure for many years. It is a hard-hitting account of his time in prison, his involvement with neo-Nazi groups and his participation in demonstrations, street fights and the production of propaganda material. Having lived for a time in England and Italy, he now realizes how isolated foreigners can feel and how dangerous neo-Nazism can be.

Far from serving as blueprints to those members of society with right-wing inclinations, these texts are intended to highlight the need for vigilance. They show how quickly young people can become swept up in the fervour of gang activities. The reader is offered the opportunity to re-examine his or her own attitudes and take a closer look at the causes and consequences of right-wing extremism.[16]

VI The new bridge builders: foreigners and young people

A brief survey of works published in the 1990s written by young people will show that foreigners and young people are themselves the new bridge-builders, the 'post-Orientalist' creators of a new wave of 'popular' German-language Jugendliteratur at the end of the twentieth century. A need for such works had been pinpointed by Winfried Kaminski and Gerhard Haas in their 1984 survey of children's literature dealing with contemporary social and political issues:

> Wünschbar wären für die Zukunft jedoch Bücher von Autoren der jeweiligen anderen Nationalität und Kultur, die authentischer, als das deutschen Autoren in der Regel möglich ist, die Lebensvorstellungen, spezifischen Denk- und Fühlweisen sowie die Erwartungen und Ängste der Fremden in unserer Gesellschaft zur Darstellung zu bringen vermöchten. (Haas 1984, 102)

There are many parallels between these works and the travel writing produced by women in the mid-nineteenth to early twentieth century. In her study of the discourse of difference, Sara Mills argues that

> even when women's writing seems to consist of similar elements to men's, it is judged and categorized differently. Thus, the difference is not a simplistic textual distinction between men's writing on the one hand and women's writing on the other, but rather a series of discursive pressures on production and reception which female writers have to negotiate, in very different ways to males. (Mills 1991, 5–6)

She argues persuasively that critics 'lack an overall perspective of the role of women's travel texts and the discourse of Orientalism, since they insist on treating these women's texts as expressions of personal endeavour and individualism rather than as part of a larger enterprise' (Mills 1991, 34). In my view similar observations apply to the writing of young people, which has to be taken as a body of work as well as the sum of its individual parts, and is to be seen as humanizing in the same way that the women's travel writing opened up new literary vistas. Further similarities exist in the autobiographical, self-revelatory nature of many of the texts, and in the vulnerability of the authors to sweeping condemnation of their works as trivial and too focused on personal relationships and domestic details.

Ich bin, was ich bin, ein Jude (Brum et al., 1995), the result of an initiative by the *Pädagogisches Zentrum der Zentralwohlfahrtsstelle* of Jews in Germany, was published against a background of right-wing attacks on Jewish cemeteries and memorials in 1992–1993. It is a collection of short texts, stories and poems by Jewish young people aged 7 to 18, selected from over 150 entries. It may be seen as a form of 'travel' writing in that the writers are describing journeys into a different culture. The late Ignatz Bubis argues in the foreword (8) that the texts offer:

> die Chance, in eine für viele noch unbekannte Welt hineinzublicken, die mitten in Deutschland existiert und doch kaum wahrgenommen wird. Dieses Buch birgt auch die Aufforderung zur Toleranz in sich, einmal hinzuschauen und das Fremde nicht als etwas Bedrohliches auszugrenzen, sondern als Bereicherung einer Kultur zu sehen, die in ihrer Geschichte durch vielfältige Einflüsse geprägt wurde.

Cultural boundaries are not synonymous with national boundaries, and some of the authors are German, others from the former Soviet Union, some from Israel. There are personal themes (such as explanations of the reasons for leaving their country, delight in possessing a secret language for use in the playground, and participation in or exclusion from religious education lessons), contributions tracing cultural roots (such as the account of the Warsaw ghetto, grandparents' recollections of the war and concentration camps), and a local history account of the Jewish cemetery in Neuß. Each piece reflects an individual agenda. Fourteen-year-old Hadar points out that not all foreigners are Jews, and not all Jews are foreigners, and observes:

> Zu meiner Verwunderung habe ich bemerkt, daß auch manche Ausländer eine Art von Nazis sind. Zum Beispiel kenne ich ein Mädchen, das aus Iran kommt. Sie haßt Deutsche und die deutsche Sprache. Ich habe ihr schonend versucht beizubringen, daß es nicht stimmt, daß alle Deutschen Nazis sind, oder, daß Deutschland ein Naziland ist. (Brum et al. 1995, 29)

The diversity of the experience of different cultural groups in Germany is also emphasized by two Turkish teenagers living in Berlin, Ayse and Devrim, in *Wo gehören wir hin?: Zwei türkische Mädchen erzählen* (1983), which could be loosely categorized as travel writing, casting the ethnographic gaze both on the home country and the new homeland. Ayse, for example, writes about what she calls her two faces: 'Das eine Gesicht war türkisch und das andere deutsch. Mit meinem türkischen Gesicht konnte ich es vereinbaren, wie eine Türkin zu leben, aber das deutsche wehrte sich dagegen. Wie und wann sich die einzelnen Gesichter zeigten, stellt man fest, wenn man weiß, wie der Tag bei mir ablief' (Ayse und Devrim, 1983, 33–34).

Although the title of *Wir leben hier: Ausländische Jugendliche berichten* (Holler/Teuter 1992) may stress the first person plural, the anthology of articles by over thirty young people from Europe and beyond, some born in Germany, some with a German passport, is as varied as their backgrounds. The families originate from countries in Europe and Africa, the Soviet Union, Iran, Afghanistan, Pakistan, and Cuba. One black girl born in Darmstadt talks about her experiences of discrimination, which changed once she reached puberty: '"Jetzt war das Exotische dran", sagt sie, "von den Jungs wurde ich wegen meiner Hautfarbe ausgesucht, im Schwimmbad bewundert. Ich betrachtete das als Kompliment, es war die Anerkennung, die langersehnte. Über mehr dachte ich damals noch nicht nach"' (Holler/Teuter 1992, 19–20).[17]

Given Germany's multicultural society, it is not surprising that in the anthology *Kinder sehen ihre Stadt: Hamburg* (1997), some of the 11–15-year-old contributors are not native Germans, but come from other parts of the world. Chosen from some 400 entries to a competition, the articles range from one about a friend who was found dead in an S-Bahn tunnel because he had been 'surfing' on the roofs of the trains, articles on skateboarders, BMX bikers, graffiti, harbour life, the fish market and the Dom, and imaginative pieces on Hamburg from the perspective of the Elbtunnel or a Jack Russell terrier. Journalist Anne Buhrfeind, one of the jury, comments in the introduction to the volume (10) on the skill of the writers' approach: 'Wir in der Jury waren überrascht, wie genau sie hingucken – und zwar aus den verschiedensten Blickwinkeln [...] genau. Nicht durchs Panoramafenster, nicht wie Junior-Texter aus der Werbeagentur, nicht mit der Affenliebe der Erwachsenen'.

A similar variety is also at the heart of Anne and Abraham Teuter's two anthologies *Ich mit Dir: Geschichten über die Liebe von jungen Autorinnen und Autoren* (1996) and *Du gegen Mich: Geschichten über Gewalt von jungen Autorinnen und Autoren* (1997) and Regina Rusch's *Gewalt* (1993), an anthology of writing by young people on the theme of violence, be it physical or verbal, experienced live or seen on television. Judging from the contributions, the writers clearly do not see the world as an exotic fairy-tale realm, and this impression is backed up by Harry Böseke and Bernhard Wagner's anthology published in the aftermath of the Chernobyl accident, *Sind es noch die alten Farben?* (1987),[18] Regina Rusch's *So soll die Welt nicht werden: Kinder schreiben über ihre Zukunft* (1989),[19] and Steff Rohrbach and Hans Saner's *Utopien: Träume der jüngsten Generation* (1991), written by seventeen to nineteen-year-olds in Switzerland. Topics range from major questions of disarmament, the environment and new technology to the importance of sport in schools, yet the balance between reality and dreams is stressed. One contributor, Marianne Koch, hopes: 'Vermeintliche Träume Wirklichkeit werden zu lassen, an Unmögliches zu glauben, ohne die Sensibilität für die Realität zu verlieren' (Rombach/Saner 1997, 10).

Yet these children and young people have not become adults prematurely. They retain their youth-specific identity and perspective. And this, somewhat perversely, can still place them in a framework to which the term 'Orientalist' may apply. *Blume ist Kind von Wiese* (Glantschnig 1992), an alphabetically arranged collection of children's responses to the world, edited by a teacher of German as a second language in Vienna, might be seen as a classic case of Orientalism. Although it is written by young people, it has been published as a work for adults.[20] In the introduction to this extended alphabet book (9), Ernst Jandl claims that the children:

[sind] zu einer Art von Sprachkünstlern geworden.
Das werden sie mit zunehmender Beherrschung der deutschen Norm-Sprache immer weniger sein und zuletzt überhaupt nicht mehr.
Eben deshalb erscheint es wichtig, diese vorübergehende Phase naiver Sprachkunst

festzuhalten, nicht zuletzt zum Vergnügen all jener Leser, die der Sprache mehr
abgewinnen können als ihren rein utilitaristischen Zweck.

Their definition of 'Kunst', for example, is 'Wenn nicht echt ist, ist Kunst. Ist
oft ein bißchen Chemie. Coca-Cola zum Beispiel ist nur Kunst oder Kaugummi
und Gummibären. Kunst ist nicht gut für Körper' (Glantschnig 1992, 64).
'Wahrheit' is defined as, 'Ist immer mit ohne Fehler, wenn alles ist richtig, ganz,
ganz richtig. Nichts Gelügtes' (124). The editors have deliberately not corrected
the errors in the German, which gives the work its feeling of spontaneity and
immediacy. It is unlikely, however, that many children would read the work,
other than those whose words are quoted, and for adults the pleasure is in the
superior reader position, in the laughter generated by the naive, 'other', exotic
slant on the world around them. Arguably, however, the work offers glimpses of
a fresh perspective and thus indicates why a more open-minded view than that
of the classic 'Orientalist' may yet prove rewarding.

VII Conclusion

Traditionally regarded as the poor relation, as 'trivial' or inferior, Jugendliteratur is now becoming a subject for serious academic investigation. Young
people are no longer merely the exotic 'other', no longer seen and not heard;
they are treated as people with rights and responsibilities. As I have shown, the
phenomenon of 'Orientalism' within Jugendliteratur is particularly clear in
works of the 1960s, 1970s and 1980s about foreign children in Germany. These
works tend to be too explicitly educational and moralizing to actually present
differentiated images of foreigners. In the non-Orientalist works analysed
earlier the prime focus lies on war, poverty and human rights. Thus, in the
1980s and 1990s there is a clear development away from the Orientalist construction of the foreigner who is radically different from but learns to make
friends with Germans, to a new construction of a more challenging nature.
Paradoxically, the works which deal with right-wing extremism are more
successful in illuminating the need for bridges across cultures, and these
provocative 'transgressive' texts allow readers to read between the lines and
reappraise the origins of prejudice and intolerance.

The increase in works of Jugendliteratur by young people makes this
literature 'popular' in the literal sense, being 'of the people'. Their paramount
concerns are not with the exotic, the romantic, the idealized eternal, but with
everyday issues, discrimination, life-style, individuality. With the exception
perhaps of *Blume ist Kind von Wiese*, all these works fulfil an empowering role

by allowing young people to speak directly to their peers and to present their highly personal, heterogenous images of the world.

The new Jugendliteratur by young people may offer what Said calls 'haunting memories and landscapes, remarkable experiences' (Said 1995, 1), but the wheel has come full circle. The haunting memories relate to the strength of the voice of the young person, not to an Orientalist construction of what adults/others may wish to associate with young people. It is the young people who build the bridges to their own and other cultures for other young people and, indeed, adults.

Notes

1. See Wippermann 1997 for a wide-ranging comparison of anti-Semitism and anti-Gypsyism from the Middle Ages to the present day and Tebbutt [2000] for a study of the ways in which the concept of Orientalism may be applied to anti-Gypsyism.

2. While Jugendliteratur is a collective term for fiction and non-fiction for young people, it is also the collective term for books for very young children (Kinderliteratur) and what in English is now referred to as teenage or young adult fiction. It can be variously defined as works marketed specifically for young people, as all the works actually read by young people, or as works written by young people themselves. In this essay I omit newspapers, magazines and comics from the survey. See Tebbutt 1994, 13–76 for a detailed discussion of the perception of Jugendliteratur and changes in the study of it.

3. See Wild 1990 for an extensive, accessible overview of the history of German children's literature from the Middle Ages to the present day. Doderer's lexicon (1975–1981) brought together information on the breadth and depth of the research; it remains the major reference work in the field.

4. See Dahrendorf 1980, 148–157 for an analysis of the arguments claiming that *Kinder- und Jugendliteratur* is inferior, and therefore to be classified as 'trivial', and also his 1988 article 'Kinder- und Jugendliteraturforschung in der Bundesrepublik Deutschland', in which he differentiates three phases of research into West German children's literature up to the 1980s, the idealist research up to the 1960s, Marxist materialist literary theories in the 1970s and an increased emphasis on theories of childhood and the history of civilization at the end of the 1980s.

5. See Peetz/Liesenhoff 1996 for a full list of the prize-winning works (1956–1995), together with seven articles on aspects of the prize, its jurors and its impact.

6. Gudrun Pausewang's *Und dann kommt Emilio* (1974) was commissioned by the publisher (personal communication from the author; ST). See Tebbutt 1995a for a study of social critical German teenage literature.

7. In the chapter entitled 'Ideology, carnival and interrogative texts', Stephens distinguishes between two main types of interrogative text: 'time out' and 'transgressive'. From an examination of aspects such as structure, ending, mood, focus, register, and chacters, he concludes that 'transgressive' textual strategies discourage unquestioning identification with the main characters and situate the reader firmly outside the text. The 'transgressive' text is more openly critical of authority than the 'time out' text.

8. In this respect Ranka Keser's first novel, *Ich bin eine deutsche Türkin* (1995), is unusual. Keser, who has lived in Germany since she was three years old, is actually from Croatia, and so the novel is not directly autobiographical, although she has experienced many similar situations to that of her heroine. The novel is in the form of a diary from July 1993 to February 1994, and revolves round the life of Ferda, a fifteen-year-old Turkish girl. Key issues are emancipation, the role of women, xenophobia and a sense of being between two cultures. She takes a very balanced view of the problems: 'Türkei und Deutschland sind zwei Extreme. Wie Schwarz und Weiß. Die türkischen Frauen

müssen sich noch immer sehr oft dem Mann unterordnen. Aber die deutschen Frauen sind auch unzufrieden, obwohl sie gleichberechtigt sind. Ich weiß, daß es hier ebenso Ungerechtigkeiten gegenüber Frauen gibt und daß in Deutschland auch nicht alles perfekt ist mit der Gleichberechtigung'.

9. A notable exception is Lutz van Dick's novel about the Gulf War, *Feuer über Kurdistan* (1991). It is about asylum seekers living in Hamburg and is a good example of a work which is more concerned with outlining the situation in Kurdistan and the plight there than with relationships between German and Kurdish children. van Dick is certainly not presenting the Germans in an unambiguously superior light. In a complicated debate about the Iran/Iraq war Anna points out, for example, that the poisonous gas used in Iraq comes from German firms.

10. There are two distinct strands to this writing. Firstly, there are the accounts of the world of work not traditionally portrayed in depth, such as Wallraff's *Industriereportagen* (1970), *Neue Reportagen* (1972), *13 unerwünschte Reportagen* (1975), *Der Aufmacher* (1977) and *Ganz unten* (1985). Here the author provides pen-portraits of the exploitation, injustice and corruption of the work-place. Secondly, there are the 'protocols' produced from transcripts of actual tape-recordings, such as von der Grün's *Menschen in Deutschland* (1973) or Runge's *Bottroper Protokolle* (1968) and *Frauen: Versuche zur Emanzipation* (1970).

11. One of the very few exceptions is Alex Wedding's novel *Ede and Unku* (1931). See Krausnick 1998 for an overview of the representation of the Gypsy in German children's literature.

12. This was not an exclusively German phenomenon. See Björgo/Witte 1993 for accounts an analyses of racist violence in a number of European countries including Germany, Scandinavia, the Netherlands, Sweden, Britain, Turkey, Romania, and France.

13. Hagemann (a pseudonym adopted by an author subjected to threats in the course of research for the novel) based her work on authentic incidents in the Federal Republic in the 1980s and early 1990s.

14. Interesting comparisons might be made between the portrayal of the mutilation of a young girl in this novel and in Kerstin Hensel's *Tanz am Kanal* (1994). Both are set in the former GDR and highlight the aura of secrecy and the unwillingness of officials to acknowledge in public the existence of violence.

15. Hasselbach was 26 at the time of publication, and might therefore be considered still a 'young person', given that in Germany surveys generally count those under 30 as young. It is, however, debatable whether the work can be regarded as 'Jugendliteratur'.

16. See Tebbutt 1995b for a more detailed discussion of these works.

17. *Hier war ich ein Niemand* (Förg et al. 1992) is a similar collection, but includes both articles by foreigners and those by Germans who had visited developing countries. See also Norbert Ney's *Sie haben mich zu einem Ausländer gemacht* (1984), which was one of the first Jugendliteratur anthologies of work by writers of foreign origin living in Germany, several of whom have since become firmly established in the German literary world, such as Alev Tekinay, Fakir Baykurt and Jusuf Naoum.

18. This collection includes articles, short prose passages and poems by children, students, teachers, and a number of other people who responded to the call for contributions. By publicizing the appeal on children's radio, in newspapers and via Bürgerinitiativen the editors managed to reach a wide range of people.

19. Rusch selected the works from over 550 letters submitted in response to a call for entries to the fourth IG Metall children's writing competition (1998).

20. Vera Leon's *Ohne Liebe wär' ich futsch* (1995), a collection of short comments by children on alphabetically arranged topics, is also aimed primarily at adult readers.

Primary literature
Ayse und Devrim 1983: *Wo gehören wir hin? Zwei türkische Mädchen erzählen.* Bornheim: Lamuv.
Banscherus, Jürgen 1985: *Keine Hosenträger für Oya.* Würzburg: Arena.

Böseke, Harry and Bernhard Wagner 1987: *Sind es noch die alten Farben?* Weinheim/
Basle: Beltz & Gelberg.
Bruckner, Karl 1961: *Sadako will leben.* Vienna/Munich: Jugend und Volk.
Brum, Alexa et al. (eds) 1995: *Ich bin, was ich bin, ein Jude: Jüdische Kinder in Deutschland
erzählen.* Cologne: Kiepenheuer & Witsch.
Cumart, Nevfel 1999: *Generation 3000.* Munich: dtv.
Dick, Lutz van 1991: *Feuer über Kurdistan.* Ravensburg: Otto Maier.
Engelmann, Reiner 1993: *Morgen kann es zu spät sein: Texte gegen Gewalt — für Toleranz.*
Würzburg: Arena.
Feid, Anatol 1983: *Achmed M im Bahnhofsviertel.* Mainz: Matthias Grünewald.
Fiechtner, Urs 1986: *Mario Rosas.* Baden-Baden: Signal.
Förg, Artur et al. (eds) 1992: *Hier war ich ein Niemand...: ...vielleicht nur ein Regentropfen,
der auf die Erde gefallen ist; Kinder und Jugendliche schreiben ein Buch über das
Zusammenleben mit Ausländern.* Marburg: Schüren.
Glantschnig, Helga 1996: *Blume ist Kind von Wiese: Oder Deutsch ist meine neue Zunge.*
Freiburg/Basle/Vienna: Herder.
Grün, Max von der 1973: *Menschen in Deutschland (BRD).* Darmstadt/Neuwied: Luchter-
hand.
—— 1975: *Leben im gelobten Land. Gastarbeiterporträts.* Darmstadt/Neuwied: Luchterhand.
Hagemann, Marie 1993: *Schwarzer, Wolf, Skin.* Stuttgart: Thienemann.
Hasselbach, Ingo and Winfried Bonengel 1993: *Die Abrechnung: Ein Neonazi steigt aus.*
Berlin/Weimar: Aufbau.
Hensel, Kerstin 1994: *Tanz am Kanal.* Frankfurt am Main: Suhrkamp.
Herrmann, Ruth 1975: *Wir sind doch nicht vom Mond!: Klein-Istanbul an der Elbe.* Reinbek
bei Hamburg: Rowohlt.
Holler, Ulrike and Anne Teuter (eds) 1992: *Wir leben hier!: Ausländische Jugendliche
berichten.* Frankfurt am Main: Alibaba.
Jung, Reinhardt 1983: *Kleine Hände — Kleine Fäuste: Der Kampf der Kinder in Latein-
amerika.* Vienna: Langbrunnen.
Keser, Ranka 1995: *Ich bin eine deutsche Türkin.* Weinheim/Basle: Beltz & Gelberg.
*Kinder sehen ihre Stadt: Hamburg. Die schönsten Geschichten aus dem Hamburger Erzähl-
wettbewerb.* Weinheim/Basle: Beltz & Gelberg. 1997.
König, Karin, Hanne Straube and Kamil Taylan 1985: *Merhaba... Guten Tag.* Rev. edn. Born-
heim: Lamuv (1st publ. 1981).
—— 1988: *Oya: Fremde Heimat Türkei.* Munich: dtv.
Krausnick, Michail (ed.) 1986: *'Da wollten wir frei sein!': Eine Sinti-Familie erzählt.* Weinheim/
Basle: Beltz (1983).
Leon, Vera (ed.) 1995: *Ohne Liebe wär' ich futsch.* Munich: dtv.
Ney, Norbert 1984: *Sie haben mich zu einem Ausländer gemacht... ich bin einer geworden:
Ausländer schreiben vom Leben bei uns.* Reinbek bei Hamburg: Rowohlt.
Noack, Hans-Georg 1960: *Hautfarbe Nebensache.* Baden-Baden: Signal.
—— 1973: *Benvenuto heißt willkommen.* Baden-Baden: Signal.
Ossowski, Leonie 1978: *Stern ohne Himmel.* Weinheim/Basel: Beltz & Gelberg.
Pausewang, Gudrun 1974: *Und dann kommt Emilio.* Ravensburg: Otto Maier.
—— 1993: *Der Schlund.* Ravensburg: Ravensburger.
Preuß, Gunter 1993: *Stein in meiner Faust.* Ravensburg: Ravensburger.
Rohrbach, Steff and Hans Saner (eds) 1991: *Utopien. Träume der jüngsten Generation.*
Basle: Lenos.
Runge, Erika 1968: *Bottroper Protokolle.* Frankfurt am Main: Suhrkamp.
—— 1970: *Frauen: Versuche zur Emanzipation.* Frankfurt am Main: Suhrkamp.
Rusch, Regina (ed.) 1989: *So soll die Welt nicht werden: Kinder schreiben über ihre Zukunft.*
Kevelaer: Anrich.
—— (ed.) 1993: *Gewalt: Kinder schreiben über Erlebnisse, Ängste, Auswege.* Frankfurt am
Main: Eichborn.
Saalmann, Günter 1993: *Zu keinem ein Wort: Ein Kriminalfall.* Berlin: Der Kinderbuch-Verlag.

Schüler der Klasse 10a der Ferdinand-Porsche-Realschule Wolfsburg 1994: *Was ist denn schon dabei?* Weinheim/Basle: Beltz & Gelberg.
Schuster-Schmah, Sigrid 1978: *Staatsangehörigkeit: griechisch.* Baden-Baden: Signal.
Schwarz, Annelies 1986: *Hamide spielt Hamide: Ein türkisches Mädchen in Deutschland.* Munich: dtv.
Steenfatt, Margret 1992: *Haß im Herzen.* Reinbek bei Hamburg: Rowohlt.
Teuter, Anne and Abraham 1996: *Ich mit Dir: Geschichten über die Liebe von jungen Autorinnen und Autoren.* Frankfurt am Main: Alibaba.
—— 1997: *Du gegen Mich: Geschichten über Gewalt von jungen Autorinnen und Autoren.* Frankfurt am Main: Alibaba.
Wallraff, Günter 1970: *Industriereportagen.* Reinbek bei Hamburg: Rowohlt.
—— 1972: *Neue Reportagen, Untersuchungen und Lehrbeispiele.* Reinbek bei Hamburg: Rowohlt.
—— 1975: *13 unerwünschte Reportagen.* Reinbek bei Hamburg: Rowohlt.
—— 1977: *Der Aufmacher. Der Mann, der bei 'Bild' Hans Esser war.* Cologne: Kiepenheuer & Witsch.
—— 1985: *Ganz unten.* Cologne: Kiepenheuer & Witsch.
Wedding, Alex 1931: *Ede und Unku.* Berlin.

Secondary literature
Björgo, Tore and Rob Witte 1993: *Racist Violence in Europe.* Basingstoke: Macmillan.
Dahrendorf, Malte 1980: *Kinder- und Jugendliteratur im bürgerlichen Zeitalter.* Königstein/Taunus: Athenäum.
—— 1988: 'Kinder- und Jugendliteraturforschung in der Bundesrepublik Deutschland', *The Germanic Review*, 63, 1/1988, 6–12.
Doderer, Klaus 1975–1981: *Lexikon der Kinder- und Jugendliteratur.* 3 vols + suppl. vol. Weinheim/Basel: Beltz & Gelberg.
—— 1981: 'Kinder- und Jugendliteratur im Ghetto?' in Doderer (ed.): *Ästhetik der Kinderliteratur.* Weinheim/Basle: Beltz & Gelberg; 1–17.
Durrani, Osman, Colin Good and Keith Hilliard (eds) 1995: *The New Germany: Literature and Society after Unification.* Sheffield: Sheffield Academic Press.
Fischer, Sabine and Moray McGowan (eds) 1997: *Denn du tanzt auf einem Seil: Positionen deutschsprachiger MigrantInnenliteratur.* Tübingen: Stauffenburg.
Fuchs, Anne and Theo Harden (eds) 1996: *Reisen im Diskurs.* Heidelberg: Winter.
Haas, Gerhard (ed.) 1984: *Kinder- und Jugendliteratur. Ein Handbuch.* Stuttgart: Reclam.
Jordan, James and Peter Barker (eds) 2000: *Minorities in German-speaking Countries: Aspects of social and cultural experience.* (Modern German Studies 2). London: CILT.
Kaminski, Winfried and Gerhard Haas 1984: 'Zeitgeschichte und politische Kinder- und Jugendliteratur' in Haas 1984, 88–109.
Krausnick, Michail 1998: 'Images of Sinti and Roma in German Children's and Teenage Literature' in Tebbutt 1998, 107–128.
Lepman, Jella 1964: *Die Kinderbuchbrücke.* Frankfurt am Main: Fischer.
Mills, Sara 1991: *Discourses of Difference: An analysis of women's travel writing and colonialism.* London/New York: Routledge.
Peetz, Heide and Dorothea Liesenhoff 1996: *40 Jahre Deutscher Jugendliteraturpreis.* Munich: Arbeitskreis für Jugendliteratur e.V.
Said, Edward W. 1995: *Orientalism.* London: Penguin (1st edn 1978).
Stephens, John 1992: *Language and Ideology in Children's Fiction.* London: Longman.
Tebbutt, Susan 1994: *Gudrun Pausewang in context: socially critical 'Jugendliteratur': Gudrun Pausewang and the search for utopia.* Frankfurt am Main: Peter Lang.
—— 1995a: 'New directions in socially critical German Jugendliteratur 1970–1995', *New Comparison*, Autumn 1995, 106–117.
—— 1995b: 'The representation of right-wing extremism in post-unification German Jugendliteratur' in Durrani/Good/Hilliard 1995, 302–320.

—— 1996: 'Das Südamerikabild in Gudrun Pausewangs sozialkritischen Jugendromanen' in Fuchs/Harden 1996, 188–198.

—— 1997: 'Bild und Selbstbild türkischer Jugendlicher in der zeitgenössischen deutschsprachigen Jugendliteratur' in Fischer/McGowan 1997, 165–177.

—— (ed.) 1998: *Sinti and Roma: Gypsies in German-speaking society and literature*. New York/Oxford: Berghahn.

—— 1999: 'Kreatives Schreiben und Jugendliteratur von Jugendlichen', *Deutsch: Lehren und Lernen* 20, 14–21.

—— [2000]: 'Die Sinti und Roma, Antiziganismus und Orientalismus' in Jordan/Barker 2000, [forthcoming]

Wild, Reiner (ed.) 1990: *Geschichte der deutschen Kinder- und Jugendliteratur*. Stuttgart: Metzler.

Wippermann, Wolfgang 1997: *'Wie die Zigeuner': Antisemitismus und Antiziganismus im Vergleich*. Berlin: Elefanten Press.

STAGING EXOTICISM AND DEMYSTIFYING THE EXOTIC: GERMAN-ARAB *GRENZGÄNGERLITERATUR*

UTA AIFAN

Mit einer Weisheit,
die keine Tränen kennt,
mit einer Philosophie,
die nicht zu lachen versteht,
und mit einer Größe,
die sich nicht vor Kindern verneigt,
will ich nichts zu tun haben.
(Gibran 1991, 16)

I Crossing the border between triviality and humour

The term 'Orientalism' subsumes not only what is generally understood in Germany by the term 'Arab', but also the discourse around the Arab world and the Arab people. Since the publication of Edward Said's *Orientalism* in 1978 the reputation of European images of the Orient has been tarnished, even though Said concedes that the Germans are a special case because of their limited, somewhat sporadic colonial history under Wilhelm II.[1] The fact remains, however, that we Germans are influenced by French and British Orientalism and must therefore look critically at our image of the Arab. Yet at the heart of this extensive debate sparked off by Said's theory of Orientalism there is a completely different issue to be faced, at least within the world of literary scholarship. Just as in the case of the German *Literaturstreit*, we are facing fundamental questions about the essence of literature, and whether political commitment in literature necessarily means forgoing the intrinsic nature of its impact on readers. Literary history dictates that German writers are in the difficult position of having to opt for the stance of one or other of Germany's two most famous writers, Goethe and Schiller.[2] On top of this, for quite some time now researchers into the psychology of perception have questioned the links between concepts and reality on account of their cyclical nature.

In order to track down the Arab element in the German literary landscape it is therefore preferable to look primarily at actual representatives of that ethnic group living in Germany — in other words at authors who came to Germany from the Arab world. Since all literary translations extend and complicate the three-way relationship between author, text and reader by a further dimension, namely the subjective interpretation of the translator, it seems sensible to limit the study to those authors who, by their own admission clearly want to make a contribution to German-language literature. Within the field of German studies those authors are referred to as 'deutschsprachige Autoren nicht-deutscher Herkunft', or more recently as 'Migrantenautoren' (Suhr 1989),[3] but specialists in the field are still not happy with this terminology.[4] It seems much more appropriate to me to use the paradigm of 'deutsch-jüdische Literatur' and refer to these authors as *deutsch-arabische Grenzgängerautoren*, since they have to find their own routes between the worlds of German-language and Arab-language literature. Of course this is by no means a new phenomenon; one only need think of Canetti. Yet there was originally a small group of these 'intercultural crossover' writers in contemporary literature who had a different goal, namely to produce a fifth German-language literature which would take its place alongside East German, West German, Austrian, and Swiss literature.[5]

Although the authors may operate as individuals, border-crossing literature has two distinctive features. Firstly, the German language is deliberately chosen as the medium for the literature, and secondly the experience of two or more[6] cultures and languages is reflected in the work.[7] The order of the adjectives reflects the cultural commitment of the authors. 'Deutsch' refers to the impact of the immediate environment of the literary creative process, and 'arabisch' relates to the influence of the country of origin on the writers, whose lives are inextricably linked to both cultures.[8] Rafik Schami's statements are typical of the way in which the cultural background affects the production and reception of works.

> 'Es regnet' ist ein einfacher Satz. Was hat dieser Satz für einen Stellenwert in der Stimmungsskala eines Zuhörers? In diesem Land wird jeder wahrscheinlich stöhnen und seufzen 'Schon wieder!', während in meinem Dorf in Syrien mit einem erleichterten 'Endlich!' zu rechnen ist. Der Regen ist derselbe, aber der Ort ist verschieden. Literatur ist komplizierter als Regen, ihr Stellenwert noch abhängiger von der Warte, von der aus sie beurteilt wird. (Schami 1996, 55)

In this article I am thus not concerned with the origin of the author as a factor in making literature international, but with the claim of a number of these authors to be producing important works of literature. The article focuses on the ways in which the authors produce entertaining literature with a view to making their German readers revise or at least question their image of Arabs. In other words, entertainment is deployed to inform and enlighten. Furthermore, I am interested in establishing to what extent a possible regeneration of German-language literature can be traced back to the fact that we are dealing with authors who belong to the modern phenomenon of German-Arab *Grenzgängerliteratur*. We are now moving into in an area of literary studies which is the traditional domain of image studies, or rather intercultural or hermeneutic studies, the analysis of images of one's own world and that of outsiders, national stereotypes and clichés, self-images and hetero-images.

Yet there is an important element missing from the existing methodology, which is why I have decided to adopt a different strategy. I would like to draw on Frei's terms (1989, 222): 'Selbstbild' (i.e. one's concept of one's own culture) and 'Gegnerbild', which I shall rename 'Fremdbild' (i.e. one's concepts of others and their cultures), and introduce a further category, 'Metabild' (i.e. my concept of how others perceive me).[9] The larger the discrepancy between others' perceptions of me and my assumptions about their perceptions, the harder it is to establish any form of communication which is free from mis-understandings (cf. Aifan 1997, 1998). This is precisely the fascination of the literary images of Arabs produced by German-Arab authors. In their literature they react both to literary images of Arabs and to anti-Arab prejudices which they perceive and encounter in the real world.

The following statement by Schami, who has succeeded in becoming a best-selling author and is the most famous of the twelve German-Arab authors, may be seen as typical of the group. Schami, who has a PhD in chemistry, was born as Suheil Fadel in Damaskus in Syria on 23 June 1946. He came to Germany in 1971 and published his first German-language volume of short stories in 1978 (*Andere Märchen*). In the following passage he describes how his first impression of Germany was dominated by a negative image of Arabs, the intensity of which he could not have anticipated:

> Eine weitere negative Überraschung war für mich die Aggression der offiziellen Medien gegen die Araber. Weder Afrikaner noch Inder oder Indianer werden *bis heute* so oft beleidigt wie die Araber. Das hat komplizierte, politische und historische Gründe und ist absolut verwerflich. Der Haß gegen die Araber ist ein Zwillingsbruder des Antisemitismus, doch leider ist dieser Zusammenhang vielen klugen und bornierten Intellektuellen nicht klar. (Schami 1998; 63)

And he sums up the clichés associated with this hostile image of the Arab thus:

> Wenn ich vom Araber im Zusammenhang der Feindseligkeit spreche, dann meine ich genau das Klischee, das in den Köpfen fest verankert ist. Es ist die sorgfältig erzeugte Karikatur eines häßlichen Menschen, der über Macht (Erdöl, Geld und Waffen) verfügt, sehr sinnlich lebt (Freßorgien und Harem), gewalttätig ist (krummes Messer und Säbel; Alternativen: Handgranaten und Raketen) usw.
> Daß man darin den puren, aber straffreien Antisemitismus wiederfindet, macht jede Begründung dieser Darstellungen, sei es in Bild, Film oder Witz, unglaubwürdig. (Schami 1998, 67)

The typically Arab elements cited by Schami, such as 'unverdiente Macht', 'maßlose Sinnlichkeit' and 'unberechenbare Gewalttätigkeit', all point to a person whose life is dominated by the emotions rather than characterized by rationally controlled actions. Schami is not the only person to hold this opinion and in their works many of the German-Arab authors want to focus on or even attempt to change this negative image of Arabs.

This brings me to the techniques used by the authors. I shall limit the study to those authors who steadfastly resist the categorization 'trivial' by the way they produce exciting, humorous, at times even satirical or cynical works of literature. The genres and literary forms used by the German-Arab authors cover a wide spectrum, ranging from the essay to the socially critical novel to poetry (Khalil 1996, 151–153). In this article, however, I am focusing exclusively on those works which deliberately ignore German Studies' traditional criteria for high literature and take what Tanja Nause (173–196 above) would term a 'picaresque' approach.

II Staged exoticism

In their public statements not all authors use their background in a foreign culture as a justification of why they write as they do. Schami is the most important and best-known representative of those German-Arab authors who employ, and simultaneously attack, German sterotypical images of Oriental literature in a deliberate and challenging way. Time and time again he emphasizes the Arab roots of his narrative style and his concept of literature. This Arab dimension should not, however, confuse the reader into thinking that Schami is writing for a fictitious Arab reader, as the following quotation would imply:

> Erkenntniswert und Modernität, so Martin Lüdke, sei sein Maßstab für gute und schlechte Literatur, und Rafik Schamis Erzählungen [...] hätten keinen modernistischen Gehalt. Seine Märchen handelten von vorindustriellen Welten, sie seien abgestanden wie 'der Mief aus unseren Wohnküchen in den 50er Jahren'. Schamis Geschichten hätten weder Relevanz für die Leser und Zuhörer in den arabischen Ländern noch für die hier lebenden Araber. Denn die Welt sei weitaus komplexer. (Burkhard 1990)

This would-be cutting criticism is based on criteria which clearly construe the relevance of the work in terms of Arab and not to German readers. Yet Schami cannot be considered an exile author in the classical sense. He is writing for German readers and is very successful in this respect:

> Rafik Schami kann sich vermutlich als einer der letzten aufklärerischen Autoren erfolgreich (sein letzter Band 'Erzähler der Nacht' hat es auf 130 000 Exemplare gebracht) behaupten, weil seine 'Befreiungsbewegung von unten' *nicht mit deutscher* Gründlichkeit im moralischen Zwangsanzug daherkommt, sondern sich auf Samtpfoten strategisch einschleicht, meistens mit einem Lächeln im Mundwinkel. Das sind Siege, die nicht müde, sondern Spaß machen. (*Börsenblatt* 1992; my emphasis, UA)

His success with his readers is explained by the reviewer as lying in his 'un-German concept of literature', and this to some extent inadvertently testifies to the success of his poetological strategy. Schami is staging a literary form of exoticism which allows him, under the guise of the outsider in the literary industry, to go against established aesthetic conventions of literary history. Schami's storytelling seems to evolve so casually and spontaneously, but is in fact meticulously planned with particular aims in mind, as is confirmed by statements like the following:

> In Deutschland haben Literaturkritiker aber eine besondere Vorliebe für Literatur, die viel Arbeit und weniger Vergnügen bereitet. Anscheinend liegt die Ursache dafür in den Selbstzweifeln der Kritiker an der Berechtigung ihres Berufs. Der Leser soll nicht die Literatur lieben, sondern überzeugt werden, daß der Umgang mit ihr Knochenarbeit bedeutet. (Schami 1994a, 18)

This idea becomes even clearer in his novel *Der ehrliche Lügner* (1992), in which he allows his protagonist to describe which element of his literature has Oriental roots:

> Es war seine bittere Weisheit, die er wie viele Orientalen mit einer witzigen Schale umhüllte. Überhaupt bin ich fest davon überzeugt, daß nichts auf der Welt mehr unterschätzt wird als das leicht, witzig und virtuos Daherschwebende, und nichts auf der Welt wird mehr überschätzt als aufgeblasene, von Belehrung triefende Worte, die zudem todernst vorgetragen werden.
> Das Witzige, Leichte und nicht Seichte, das die Herzen kitzelt und vor den Augen der Kenner Abgründe aufschlägt, in die hineinzuschauen einen schwindlig macht, liebe ich. (Lügner, 418–419)

His readers approve of the way in which Schami makes what literary critics see as a provocative distinction between popular fiction and entertainment and they even defend his works against the critics. They argue that he is satisfying human needs instead of 'auf Kosten der Menschlichkeit immer Neues produzieren zu müssen', and Schami accuses German literary critics of 'quasi zwangsneurotisch nach "E" und "U" [ernste und unterhaltende] Lektüre zu unterscheiden' (Burkhard 1990). In so doing he is participating in the debate which raged in the 1990s about the death of German literature, the need for humour and the return of the pícaro, all seen against the topos of the aestheticism of the so-called ivory-tower literature.[10] Light and witty literature should make 'bittere Weisheiten' palatable to the reader. What is unusual about Schami's case is that he describes not only his techniques but also the defamiliarized genre as being of explicitly Oriental origin:

> Realismus kam [in die arabische Welt] erst um die Jahrhundertwende durch den Einfluß Europas. Das heißt, Märchenerzählen war bei uns immer tiefer und verwur-

zelter als das realistische Erzählen. In dieser Gegend sind Märchen tatsächlich eine erprobte, der kulturellen Entwicklung entsprechende Erzählweise, die lange Jahrhunderte oder Jahrtausende hinter sich hat. (Schami cit. Tantow 1985)

Once again Schami uses the writing traditions of his Arab culture of origin to explain why he makes a further break with German-language literary traditions as well as deliberately disregarding the traditional distinction made between great and trivial literature:

> Ich bin ein Prosaschriftsteller, ein Erzähler ohne Zusätze, also weder ein Märchenerzähler noch ein Kinder- und Jugendbuchautor. Ich hoffe immer, daß mein allerschönstes Buch für Erwachsene gerade gut genug für Kinder ist. Ich kann solche Begriffe nicht teilen, weil es sie in meiner Kultur nicht gibt. Bei uns werden Geschichten im Kreis erzählt, und wenn Kinder da sind, wird Rücksicht auf sie genommen, indem man die Geschichte etwas spannender macht. (Schami in Wehrle 1992)

Schami expands the concept of literature, as do many German-Arab writers, to include not only written texts but the oral dimension:

> Schami vermißt in Deutschland einen Gegenpol, die deutschen Schriftsteller erzählten nicht, ausgenommen Süskind; in Lateinamerika gebe es noch Erzähler. er hätte hier gerne das Erzählen weitergelernt, anderen beigebracht. Hier aber gebe es keine literarischen Abende mit Erzählgut, nur Lesungen mit wichtigen Texten — das erinnere ihn an Predigten von der Kanzel. Woher die Armut? Hunger und Not als Quelle des Erzählens, nein, das ist ihm zu einfach. Vielleicht liege es daran, daß an den Menschen jetzt das Leben zu schnell vorbeirausche, denn ein guter Erzähler benötige ein langes Gedächtnis. (Wagner 1990)

Schami's preferred form is 'fabulieren', the spinning of yarns, i.e. Oriental storytelling or fairy tales (cf. James Jordan, 255–268 below). With this topos he is also able to exploit his target audience's concepts of the Orient. He is working with the image of the cunning but sympathetic Oriental. In short, his entertaining literature, which he himself explicitly terms 'Oriental', can be summed up in his phrase: 'Phantasie *spürt* man um so weniger, je besser sie *durchdacht* ist' (Schami 1994b, 152; my emphasis, UA. cf Stolz, 19–30 above). But his crossing of borders has had to become increasingly refined: 'Beim Inhalt ist es am schwierigsten, meine Meinung hineinzuschmuggeln, ohne daß die Leser es spüren. Und nur wenige, die mich gut kennen, können meine Geschichten trotz ihrer unterhaltenden Tarnung aufknacken. Ich bin ein ziemlich erfahrener Schmuggler geworden' (Schami 1998, 152). If the message is to be smuggled effectively into the hearts of his readers, the educational nature of a literary work must not be presented in a teacherly fashion. Similarly, this concealed message of the author should not be misunderstood as part of a mission to improve the world: 'Die Literatur kann nur leise und schüchtern Alternativen anbieten. Das Problem liegt aber darin, daß diejenigen, die aufzuklären sind, weder mich noch Gabriel Garcia Marquez, noch Albert Camus, Peter Hoeg oder Franz Hohler lesen' (Schami 1998, 154).

Despite this scepticism there is evidence in the literary reception of his works that the author is successful in his strategy. As Birgit Dankert notes (1987): 'Die Bäckerläden, die schattigen Innenhöfe, die fliegenden Händler im Basar, die staubig-geheimnisvollen Buchläden, die selbstbewußt-geduldigen Frauen, auch die bedrückende Allgegenwärtigkeit des Militärs gibt es ebenso noch wie die pfiffigen Jungen, die mit kleinem Taschengeld von großer Zukunft träumen'.[11] The familiar elements of the Arab cliché are all there, from the 'Basar' to the 'Frauen' to the 'Militär'. Yet we are not talking here about oppressed women but about patient and self-confident women, not talking about cheating, swindling traders but about mysterious shops. This other way of looking at the world is in fact nothing new. It goes back to the tradition of the image of the Orient in the Romantic period, an image frequently found in Hauff's fairy tales or in Heine's work. The latter's *Poesie-Orient* takes shape when 'das Märchenhafte das Exotische mit sich vereint, wenn die Realität des "ernsten Abendlandes" durch die phantastische farbige Welt des sinnlichen Morgenlandes, und wenn der 'kalte Norden' von dem "warmen Süden" verdrängt wird' (Seuss 1995). And, indeed, in the colour supplements of German newspapers contemporary reviews of German-Arab authors take as their starting point not a poetic Orient, but an expectation that first-hand information will be provided about life in the Arab world. Schami's figures break down the Orientalist cliché: 'Wer Rafik Schami gelesen hat, sieht sie nicht nur als Ambiente, als Objekt touristischen oder politischen Kalküls, sondern als Subjekte, als Menschen im Mikrokosmos Damaskus der großen, geschundenen Vielvölker-Region in Nahost' (Fendri 1980, 150).

It is a particular indication of Schami's success that even critics who do not have any time for his concept of literature can accept his work by according him the status of an outsider. This means they are then no longer obliged to use their conventional aesthetic criteria to evaluate his work:

> Wie leicht zu erkennen ist: Wir haben es hier mit einem Stoff zu tun, aus dem Träume sind, aber auch Drehbücher zu deutschen Vorabendserien. Das könnte einem das Lesen verleiden, wenn man mit dem Anspruch an die Lektüre ginge, ein stilistisch durchdachtes, auf das Wesentliche konzentrierte Stück Literatur zu verzehren. Aber nein, der Leser erfährt sehr bald, daß er sich nicht in einem geschliffenen Werk belletristischer Prosa befindet, sondern in einem arabischen Caféhaus zwischen zwei Buchdeckeln. (Seuss 1995)

We must remind ourselves, however, that there is, in fact, a difference between the Arab concept of high literature and Schami's pronouncements.

Since the Middle Ages poetry has been considered the crowning glory of high literature (Walther 1988, 881) and this has allowed prose fiction room for experimentation, as long as it did not limit itself by imitation of and strict adherence to European literary traditions. Yet here too Arab contemporary literature is developing in a different direction.[12] With reference to folk literature, however, Schami correctly points out that the boundaries between literature for adults and literature for children are not valid in this case, and that literature conveys its insights by means of edification.

> Um Rafik Schamis Dichtung zu verstehen, muß man seine Texte von der europäischen Form des Märchens abgrenzen. Mit der knappen, konzentrierten und zusammenfassenden abendländischen Erzählweise haben seine häufig langsam im Gespräch wachsenden, auf Abschweifung bedachten Geschichten wenig gemein. Seiner Meinung nach wirken die aus der Perspektive eines rechtschaffenen Konservativen erzählten abendländischen Märchen eher heilend und problemverdeckend, während die aus dem Blickwinkel eines listigen Unterlegenen vermittelten, auf konkreten Erlebnissen beruhenden und somit gesellschaftliche Verhältnisse einfangenden Geschichten des Orients rebellisch sind. (Tantow 1988, 2)

Schami is thus working both with the topos of Oriental storytelling and the motif of the cunning Oriental. He is playing on the expectations of his readers, which include their expectation that the stories will be entertaining. Just like Schami, other German-Arab authors also resort to this technique[13] of making self-criticism into a statement for the readers. The latter can accept the criticism as they are not being accused of having any bad intentions but merely of being ignorant about the feelings of foreigners. Yet Schami goes further than this by defamiliarizing the situation as he takes the criticism of false perceptions arising from preconceived ideas and relocates it firmly in the Arab world. Once again this gives rise to irony here in that, on the one hand, it is Arabs who attribute to the narrator the Arab cliché of spinning yarns, or, to put it more bluntly, lying, whilst, on the other hand, he transforms his criticism of the Germans into a criticism of the Arabs. All readers will, however, identify with the idea of clinging on to familiar ways of looking at the world, and since they are not being criticized directly, they will be able to reflect on their own behaviour.

The paradoxical title of the novel *Der ehrliche Lügner* can be explained as a combination of appearance and reality. 'Mein Name bedeutet der Ehrliche, doch in meiner Gasse hatte ich einen anderen Ruf' (Lügner, 39). Schami called his novel 'Der ehrliche Lügner' and not 'Der lügende Ehrliche', which would have been a possible combination given that the name 'Sadik' means 'the honest man'.[14] This would seem to suggest that the adjective 'ehrlich' describes an actual quality of the protagonist, whereas the noun 'Lügner' is not to be seen as an 'Eigenname' in the literal sense but as a description and as a term applied by others based on how they perceive him. The adjective thus represents reality, whereas the noun represents appearance. This interpretation is backed up by Sadik's description of how he arrived at his reputation of being a liar:

> Meine erste Freundin hieß Aida.. Ich habe sie als Kind sehr geliebt und wollte nur noch mit ihr spielen [...]
> Durch Aida erfuhr ich schon mit fünf, daß ich ein großer Lügner war. Das lag an meiner Langsamkeit, denn wenn ich als Kind durch irgend etwas auffiel, dann durch meine Langsamkeit. In allem war ich langsam [...]
> Auch beim Sprechen war ich unendlich langsam. Ich dachte viel nach und fand eine Pause mitten im Satz gar nicht so übel. Und da passierte es. Ich wollte Aida imponieren und erzählte ihr, daß ich von einem Berg zum anderen fliegen könnte. Ihre Augen weiteten sich vor Entsetzen. 'Du lügst, ja!' rief sie und rannte davon, bevor ich die Zeit fand, ihr zu sagen, daß ich das könnte, wenn ich ein Vogel wäre.
> Bald machten halbe Sätze von mir die Runde in der Gasse, die vollständig die harmlosesten Aussagen der Welt bedeutet hätten. Aber halb ausgesprochen hörten sie sich wie die dicksten Lügen aller Zeiten an [...]
> Ob alt oder jung, alle Nachbarn, Freunde, Verwandten und Schulkameraden wußten schon im voraus, daß ich lügen würde, sogar wenn ich auf eine Frage nur den Kopf schüttelte. Wenn ich den Mund aufmachte, war es sowieso sicher. Seit dieser Zeit heiße ich: Sadik, der Lügner. (Lügner, 39–40)

The twin themes of the novel[15] are the thin line between half-truths and lies and the way in which other people's perceptions are determined by their expectations. Sadik speaks so slowly that his truth turns into a half-truth.[16] Because this happens fairly frequently the people around him begin to expect that he will make things up. Once the slow statement has been interpreted as a half-truth people expect that Sadik will make things up (Lügner, 134), or even lie. The narrator attributes an Arab cliché, slowness, to himself, but in the end he is also addressing the theme of the way in which Arabs and Germans live together. He is looking at the ways in which German people misinterpret Arab rhetoric or Arab ways of conversing as fanciful flights of the imagination which are devoid of any meaning. He argues that if the Germans lose patience they tend to presume that the speaker has finished his delivery, when in actual fact he may be just working up to the climax of his speech. Here too the reader can accept the criticism of the author because it is not directed at him personally.

III Demystifying the exotic

Ethnologist Salem Alafenisch is the best known exponent of an alternative way of dealing with the exotic. Like Schami, he too incorporates the motif of appearance and reality. Born the son of a Bedouin Sheikh in the Negev Desert in 1948, he grew up within this traditional community. Although he did not learn how to read and write until he was 14, he then completed his schooling as a mature student and gained entry to university, including a period of study in the

Federal Republic, where he has lived since 1973. In 1988 he published his first German-language volume of stories, *Der Weihrauchhändler*. Whereas Schami emphasizes the Arab nature of his work, other German-Arab authors like Alafenisch speak in more general terms of 'literature' without differentiating between a German or German-Arab approach, and point to the supra-national importance of literature. Thus, in an interview in 1996, Alafenisch said: 'Literatur hat viele Aufgaben, von diesen Aufgaben ist [eine], etwas aufzuklären, etwas mitzuteilen, und ich möchte gerne etwas mitteilen, was wirklich stimmt. Wie die Leute das aufnehmen, [...] kann ganz verschieden sein' (Interview). He sees himself as providing entertaining enlightenment through literature. Rather than emphasizing the Arab tradition of entertaining literature, he highlights his own subjective personal viewpoint: 'Als Leser habe ich auch meine Ansprüche. Wenn ein Buch langweilt, dann lese ich das Buch nicht' (Interview).

Reviews of his work provide ample evidence that his different approach has not gone unnoticed. Even if his work is frequently regarded against the background of the Arab narrative tradition of story-telling as bordering on the trivial, he is nevertheless granted a special status between the cultures:

> Wenn er in seinem neuesten Buch, 'Die Nacht der Wünsche', anfangs offen die Erzählstruktur von 'Tausendundeiner Nacht' aufgreift, dann tut er es mit jenem ironischen Augenzwinkern, das uns ein solches Zitat allein erträglich macht. Man ist auch literarisch amüsiert, wenn der grausame und hartherzige Sultan zu seiner jüngsten Frau Zarah kommt, mürrischer denn je, da er 'nicht seine Wachtel verspeisen' konnte wie jedesmal, wenn er zu einer seiner Frauen ging, worauf Zarah ihn in bewährter Manier mit dem Erzählen von Geschichten beruhigt. Alafenischs Spott ist deutlich spürbar, wenn er schildert, wie der Sultan mangels Wachteln auf Äpfel umsteigt und Zarah daraufhin überlegt, daß nun wohl die Obstpreise steigen werden.

The explanation follows: 'Es sind die erstaunlich selbstverständlich gezogenen Querverbindungen von Tradition zur Moderne, von der arabischen Welt zu unserer, die die Weite und Offenheit, ja Weisheit dieser Geschichten ausmachen' (Soldat 1996).

Alafenisch communicates the Bedouin perspective by defamiliarizing foreignness to such an extreme that he locates events in situations which are all too familiar to the reader.[17] 'Das versteinerte Zelt' revolves, on the one hand, around that well known problem in the western world, being up to one's eyes in debt with a mortgage; on the other hand, it deals with a topic which is less current in the western hemisphere, namely the impact of compulsory settlement on the Bedouins' social system. Once he is no longer confined within the four walls of a house, Musa, the chief protagonist, for the first time for a long time, again begins to dream. He relishes the stillness:

Musa drehte sich auf den Rücken und lauschte in die Nacht. Nur das Rascheln der Maus und die gleichmäßigen Atemzüge des Gastgebers waren zu hören. 'Diese Stille der Nacht habe ich lange nicht mehr genossen', dachte er. Und während er durch das Zeltloch die Plejaden betrachtete, versank er wieder in tiefen Schlaf. Der Alte träumte von der Zeit, als das erste Radio im Stammeslager auftauchte.
Es war ein unvergleichliches Ereignis, als Abu Hassan den großen Kasten auf dem Eselsrücken ins Zeltlager brachte. Als Händler hatte er oft auf den Märkten der Städte zu tun, und so kam er in Berührung mit dieser Neuheit. Er hatte schon viel davon berichtet und die Zeltbewohner neugierig gemacht. Das Radio könnte sprechen, singen, Koranverse rezitieren und noch vieles mehr, erzählte er.
Musa fütterte gerade seinen Esel, als sich die Nachricht von der Ankunft dieses sonderbaren Gerätes im Zeltlager verbreitete.
'Wer das Radio sehen will, kann in das Zelt von Abu Hassan kommen!' hieß es.
Innerhalb kürzester Zeit hatte sich Abu Hassans Zelt gefüllt, vor dem Zelteingang drängten sich Duzende von Kindern. Der Lärm war so groß, dass man sein eigenes Wort nicht hören konnte.
In der Mitte des Zeltes hatte Abu Hassan den Kasten aufgestellt. Das Radio spielte Musik, die von brummenden Tönen untermalt wurde. 'Wo versteckt sich diese Musikgruppe?' wollte ein Greis wissen. (Zelt, 94–95)

It is precisely the peace and quiet Musa so cherishes that has been lost from Abu Hassan's tent with the arrival of the modern world, symbolized by the radio. This illustrates how closely the framing narrative and the story within it are interrelated. The concept of peace and calm as the antithesis of the hectic pace of life today set out in the framing narrative (symbolized by the contrast between the quietness of the night of dreams and the desperate endeavours of Musa and his wife to pay off their debts) is extended through into the secondary story. Abu Hassan, who is a trader, brings the first radio into the Bedouin camp on the back of his donkey: 'Von diesem Tag an riß der Besucherstrom nicht mehr ab. Bis spät in die Nacht war Abu Hassans Frau damit beschäftigt, die Besucher mit Tee und Kaffee zu bewirten. Am frühen Morgen glimmte noch die Glut vom Feuer der vergangenen Nacht. Es war vorbei mit der Ruhe in Abu Hassans Zelt' (96). The only way that Abu Hassan can reconcile his need for sleep with the demands made on his hospitality is by establishing yet another social obligation. The radio is personalized and thus, like everyone else, gains the right to hospitality, which includes the right to peace and rest. At night Abu Hassan switches off the radio and tells his visitors, 'es sei schlafen gegangen' (96). Thus he manages to satisfy people's demands that he be hospitable by using a trick which is based on an honourable intent. He is paying his respects to the traditional customs. In this episode it becomes clear that Alafenisch's concept of truth should in fact be interpreted as truthfulness.

In a society with strong social groupings and codes of conduct there are two truths, society's and that of the individual, and in order to reconcile the two it is necessary to strike a happy medium between people's own needs and respect for the rights of others. This rule affects not only the relationships between the sexes[18] but all relationships. People feel comfortable with Abu Hassan's solution because he uses the idea of the radio as his guest as a way of offering a familiar explanation for a new phenomenon. When the radio's battery is going flat people suspect it is 'müde' or 'krank' (97) and in the end they finally surmise that 'es sei verstorben' (98). Even the owner of the shop he takes the radio to resorts to the notion of personification, this time referring to the radio as an animal: 'Je mehr das Radio spricht, umso mehr Futter braucht es' (98). In view of the increasing cost of the batteries together with hospitality for the guests Abu Hassan decides to abandon the radio. Since he does not feel he can reveal these egoistic considerations to his guests he announces to those in the camp that 'das Radio sei nicht mehr wiederzubeleben' (99).

By omitting to mention the cost-factor the half-truth is turned into a compromise between the truth of the individual and the truth of the tribe. In this society respect is based on a different concept. Whereas people in Germany show respect by being honest or by keeping strictly to the rules, Alafenisch's Bedouins do this by keeping up appearances. Individuality, which is generally regarded in western industrial states as what distinguishes the modern world from tribal societies, is presented provocatively by Alafenisch who locates it within just such a traditional society, showing how individuality is never taken to the extreme but is framed within a compromise with society. He does not want simply to depict phenomena, but to probe behind them. That is why he elevates the everyday to the level of the special, and familiar images appear as if they are being viewed for the first time. On the surface a situation is being described. At a deeper level the radio stands for the destructive influence of the modern in a world of tradition. This influence is so strong precisely because people are open to new impulses. They are drawn 'magically' towards and under the spell of the 'sprechenden Kasten'. They draw close to it again and again even when the weather forecast is not correct and the stock of tea and sugar is dwindling and the stories fall silent.

IV Conclusion

As has been demonstrated, German-Arab authors play with the expectations of their readers with respect to literature by authors from the Arab world. They instrumentalize the meta-image. In other words, they communicate a serious message which is only accepted by the readers because they are not prepared for it. The usual defence mechanisms (emotional value systems and stereotypical arguments about Arabs) are not deployed because this literature is only read for entertainment. Yet this relationship only works in as far as it exploits the outsider role within German-language literature; in other words, when an author of Arab origin uses Arab characters, plots and settings within a genre which, even when it is not reminiscent of fairy tales, at least evokes memories of Arab narrators. It is true that this is susceptible to the argument that this type of literature is communicating the notion of an apparent stasis in the Arab world and is trivializing social problems. However, we must not forget that the authors are completely aware of the limited impact of literature; they are not just writing for their readers, they are writing also for themselves. As my discussion of German-Arab literature has shown, these German-Arab authors are not producing formulaic works of trivial literature wrapped up in an exotic new guise which have no place in German-language literature and can be simply dismissed. Schami and Alafenisch both use the literary strategy of presenting German clichés of the Arab, which they instrumentalize either explicitly (Schami) or implicitly (Alafenisch), in order to communicate their message in a gentle but entertaining way. We can reject the criticism that they are trivial and ask instead whether they represent a new topos of *Heiterkeit* in German-language literature?

In order to answer this question it is necessary to take a somewhat wider view. The reception of these *Grenzgängerautoren* differs from that of other authors in one fundamental respect. What, in Said's terms, may be seen as an Orient which exists only in the imagination of the writer and his readers, which is unrealistic only there to be celebrated, is accepted as 'ein Bedürfnis für den "Nordmenschen"' and explained in terms of 'Sehnsucht nach Vergangenem und Fernen' (Fendri 1980, 178 and 175). Since Heine makes a clear distinction between reality and the Orient of poetry, he avoids the accusation of being trivial. His poetic Orient fulfils the function of expressing his innermost thoughts, which is why it cannot exist and why (at least professional) readers do not expect to find the real world there.

By contrast, quite different expectations are invested in the image of the Arab in the work of German-Arab *Grenzgängerautoren* — both by the authors of the works and by their recipients. Intrinsically expected of the 'message' of these works is that they will communicate 'the' truth about the Arab world to their German readers. But, as we have seen, truth here does not stand for objectivity but for a very subjective form of truthfulness from the point of view of the authors. It is precisely these truths that their readers expect of these authors. The new Heiterkeit is not a phenomenon which is limited to German-Arab authors, it is a general trend within modern German-language literature, yet these authors use the clichés of the happy bright Arab world to their advantage — or, like Schami, even invent some of their own. Thus, on the one hand, we are dealing with a particular type of new staged exoticism, and, on the other hand, with new exotic figures whose everyday banality robs them of their fantastical magic. The exotic nature of the locations, of the character combinations and narrative techniques facilitate the access of the authors, as outsiders, to a space which places them beyond the criteria of classical literary criticism. Triviality is a criterion which cannot be applied to them because, while we are dealing here with German-language literature, we are not dealing with German authors in the classical sense. Thus the new Heiterkeit of the literature must be seen as part of a general phenomenon, whereas the new exoticism is a phenomenon which originated in *arabisch-deutsche Grenzgängerliteratur*.

Literature would not be literature if it did not continue to evolve. This is why the Austrian author Barbara Frischmuth opens her novel *Die Schrift des Freundes* [19] with the words: 'Es war einmal, es war keinmal...', the classical opening formula of the fairy tale and the yarns spun over 'A thousand-and-one Nights'. Whereas German-Arab authors distance themselves clearly from this masterpiece of world literature, despite the fact that the Heiterkeit of their works is learned from it, an author of European provenance can let the wheel spin a little further. Frischmuth can replicate and adapt the traditional formula, for it is hardly possible to doubt the seriousness of her literary production and pass her off as just a 'narrator of fairy tales'. Frischmuth's work could never be cited as proof that Arab literature had been in stagnation for centuries. In the final analysis it is all a question of perspective.

Notes

The essay deals with aspects of my doctoral thesis 'Araberbilder im Werk deutsch-arabischer Grenzgängerautoren der Gegenwart', supervised by Professor Horch at the RWTH-Aachen. UA.
Translation by Susan Tebbutt.

1. Germany did admittedly try to become a colonial power under Wilhelm II but was never particularly successful in this endeavour. This is why the literary discourse about the Orient developed under different conditions to those, for example, which prevailed in Great Britain. Said points out that German authors, including Goethe, owe a debt to French and English literature and what he terms colonialist Orientalism, but his interpretation of this writing is significantly different, since in the case of Germany there was no direct contact between the two cultures in terms of power relationships and colonial pretensions.
2. As Helmut Peitsch's essay on Uwe Timm (131–152 above) demonstrates, this is not a phenomenon which is limited to migrant literature. Uwe Timm also contravenes aesthetic conventions by deciding to write entertaining literature for his readers. In the land of Shakespeare he received formal recognition, whereas in Germany he was mainly acclaimed by his readers. cf. also Sefan Neuhaus above, esp. 159–164)
3. The literature of German-language writers of foreign origin is generally subsumed under the term 'Migrantenliteratur' (previously 'Gastarbeiterliteratur' and 'Ausländerliteratur'). This terminology does not, however, do the literary phenomenon full justice, because it reduces it to the socio-political dimension.

4. In the introduction to their volume, the editors decide to use the term 'migrant writing', even though in the same breath they acknowledge its inadequacy (Fischer/McGowan 1997, 9).
5. In the 1980s Franco Biondi, Jusuf Naoum, Suleman Taufiq and Rafik Schami founded the PoLi-Kunst-Verein and published literary theory essays on 'Gastarbeiterliteratur', which was the provocative term chosen by the authors themselves. In addition they published anthologies of German-language texts written by authors of non-German origin as part of the so-called *Südwind* series. cf. Burns 2000, esp.127–128.
6. cf. Tekinay's assertion that the increased academic recognition of German language border-crossers in the Anglo-American world opened up a 'third "I"' to authors and the third language opened the door to a new phase in their life (Tekinay 1997, 29–30).
7. By contrast authors of exile literature either write for readers of the country from which they have been exiled, or they present their experience of exile in the language of their former home country.
8. The term Arab-German literature can be used for the literature of German-speaking minorities in the Arab world.
9. The term 'meta-image' was coined by Daniel Frei within social science research into images of the enemy (Frei 1989, 222).
10. On the return of the picaro see Tanja Nause (esp. 173–175 above), and on ivory tower aestheticism: Kiedaisch 1996, Schneider 1989, Weinrich 1986.
11. It should be noted that the reviewer works in the field of children's and young people's writing, which also has a special position within literary criticism and therefore can be more flexible in its response.
12. Hartmut Fähndrich, a translator of Arab literature, stated at a literary event in Munich on 13 April 2000 that modern Arab contemporary literature is moving away from being national literature which helps to create a group identity and opting instead for greater subjectivity.
13. This is the view of the sociologist Wadi Soudah, who was born in 1948 in Palestine. Soudah has been living in the FRG since 1979. cf. Soudah 1991, 103.
14. By naming his protgaonist 'Sadik', Schami is also referring to Voltaire's 'Zadig' and thus to Said's criticism of European perceptions of the Orient.
15. *Der ehrliche Lügner* was written when the Gulf War and the German media's militaristic, propagandistic coverage of it were still fresh in Schami's mind. Because of the local censorship in operation he was not able to conduct on-the-spot research and thus focuses on the relationship between appearance and reality. At a time when truth and reality are uneasy bedfellows, the honest man has to lie to survive. This refers not only to life in Syria in the 1960s under a series of dictators, the time at which the novel is set, but also to the image of the Arab in the western media during the second Gulf War.
16. Sten Nadolny also operates with the idea of slowness and misinterpretation of intention or intelligence in *Die Entdeckung der Langsamkeit* (1983) and with related concepts in *Selim oder Die Gabe der Rede* (1990). cf. Tebbutt 1998.
17. A similar narrative technique is adopted by the Germanist and expert on Islam and film, Huda Al-Hilali, who was born in 1947 in Baghdad. She lived with her family in West Germany between 1959 and 1964 and settled there for good in 1976. The only woman among the German-Arab writers to be published in Germany, her career began in 1984 with storytelling evenings which she described as 'One Woman Theatre'. Her first German-language volume of short stories was published in 1992 under the title *Von Bagdad nach Basra*.
18. As in *Die verkaufte Braut, Der Weihrauchhändler* (1988) and *Die acht Frauen des Groß-vaters* (1989).
19. Frischmuth explains in a speech made in Vienna that she has had extensive discussions with writers who are 'by nature' *Grenzgänger* (1999, 72).

Primary texts
Alafenisch, Salim 1988: *Der Weihrauchhändler*. Berlin: Arabisches Buch (quoted from 1991 edn. Zurich: Unionsverlag).

—— 1989: *Die acht Frauen des Großvaters*. Zurich: Unionsverlag (quoted from 19991 edn.)
—— 1993: *Das versteinerte Zelt*. Zurich: Unionsverlag. (=Zelt)
—— 1996: Interview with Uta Aifan, 15–16 August 1996 in Heidelberg (=Interview)
Schami, Rafik 1978: *Andere Märchen*. Bonn: PDW.
—— 1986: 'Eine Literatur zwischen Minderheit und Mehrheit' in Ackermann/Weinrich 1986, 55–64.
—— 1992: *Der ehrliche Lügner. Roman von tausendundeiner Lüge*. Weinheim/Basle: Beltz & Gelberg (quoted from the 1995 edn). (=Lügner)
—— 1994a: *Der brennende Eisberg. Eine Rede, ihre Geschichte und noch mehr*. Frauenfeld: Verlag im Waldgut.
—— 1994b: *Zeiten des Erzählens*. Ed. Erich Jooß. Freiburg im Breisgau: Herder.
—— 1998: *Damals dort und heute hier. Über Fremdsein*. Ed. Erich Jooß. Freiburg im Breisgau: Herder.

Secondary literature
Ackermann, Irmgard and Harald Weinrich (eds) 1986: *Eine nicht nur deutsche Literatur: Zur Standortbestimmung der 'Ausländerliteratur'*. Munich: Piper.
Aifan, Uta 1997: 'Balanceakt auf dem Drahtseil. Theorie, Analyse und didaktische Behandlung von Stereotypen und Vorurteilen im Unterricht an Hochschulen' in Breuer/Sölter 1997, 265–286.
—— 1998: 'Fremdwahrnehmung und Emotionen im Fremdsprachenunterricht' in Wolff/Eggers 1998, 416–423.
Al-Hilali, Huda 1992: *Von Bagdad nach Basra. Geschichten aus dem Irak*. Heidelberg: Palmyra.
Börsenblatt 1992:'Ein neuer "Schami" ist da', *Börsenblatt*, 28 August 1992, 53.
Breuer, Ingo and Arpad Sölter (eds) 1997: *Der fremde Blick. Perspektiven interkultureller Kommunikation und Hermeneutik. Ergebnisse der DAAD-Tagung in London, 17.–19. Juni 1996*. Innsbruck/Vienna: StudienVerlag.
Bullivant, Keith (ed.) 1989: *Englische Lektionen: Eine andere Anthologie deutschsprachiger Gegenwartsliteratur*. Munich: iudicium.
Burkhard, Angelika 1990: 'Voll vom "Mief der Wohnküche"?: Rafik Schami und Martin Lüdke diskutieren über gute und schlechte Literatur', *Frankfurter Rundschau*, 10 November 1990, 18.
Burns, Rob 2000: 'Between market assimilation and cultural resistance: The migrant writer in the work of Alev Tekinay' in Williams/Parkes/Preece 2000, 127–138.
Dankert, Birgit 1987: 'Tagebuch aus Damaskus', *Die Zeit*, 10 April 1987, 27.
Fendri, Mounir 1980: *Halbmond, Kreuz und Schibboleth: Heinrich Heine und der islamische Orient*. Hamburg: Hoffman und Campe.
Fischer, Sabine and Moray McGowan (eds) 1997: *Denn du tanzt auf einem Seil: Positionen deutschsprachiger MigrantInnenliteratur*. Tübingen: Stauffenburg.
Frei, Daniel 1989: 'Wie Feindbilder entstehen: Drei Elemente der gegenseitigen Einschätzung' in Wagenlehner 1989, 222–226.
Frischmuth, Barbara 1998: *Die Schrift des Freundes*. Vienna/Salzburg: Residenz.
—— 1999: 'Löcher in die Mauer bohren' (March 1998) in Frischmuth: *Das Heimliche und das Unheimliche: Drei Reden*. Berlin: Aufbau, 55–76.
Gibran, Khalil 1991: *Lieder, die der Wind schrieb: Anstiftung zum Frieden*. Ed. Wolfgang Poeplau. Wuppertal: Peter Hammer.
Kiedaisch, Petra 1996: *Ist die Kunst noch heiter? Theorie, Problematik und Gestaltung der Heiterkeit in der deutschsprachigen Literatur nach 1945*. Tübingen: Niemeyer.
Khalil, Iman O. 1996: 'Arabisch-deutsche Literatur' in Lützeler1996, 149–164.
Lützeler, Michael (ed.) 1996: *Schreiben zwischen den Kulturen: Beiträge zur deutschsprachigen Gegenwartsliteratur*. Frankfurt am Main: Fischer.
Said, Edward 1994: *Orientalism*. New York: Vintage Books (1979 edn with 1994 afterword by Said).
Schneider, Michael 1989: 'Wie vernünftig kann Literatur sein?' in Bullivant 1989, 197–214.

Seuss, Siggi 1995: 'Alle guten Geister der vereinigten Morgenländer', *Süddeutsche Zeitung*, 8 January 1995, XII.

Soldat, Hans-Georg 1996: 'Sanft fabulierender Wüstensohn: Salim Alafenisch verbindet in seinem neuen Buch die Traditionen von Orient und Okzident', *Berliner Zeitung*, 12–13 October 1996, 50.

Soudah, Wadi 1991: *KAFKA und andere palästinensische Geschichten*. Frankfurt am Main: Brandes & Apsel.

Suhr, Heidrun 1989: '"Ausländerliteratur": Minority Literature in the Federal Republic of Germany', *New German Critique*, 46/1989, 71–104.

Tantow, Lutz 1985: 'Abenteuer in der deutschen Sprache. Die List der Märchen. — Interview mit dem Erzähler Rafik Schami', *Süddeutsche Zeitung*, 22 February 1985, 2.

—— 1988: 'Rafik Schami' in *Kritisches Lexikon der deutschsprachigen Gegenwartsliteratur*. Munich: edition text + kritik.

Tebbutt, Susan 1990: 'Borderlines and communication: Sten Nadolny's *Die Entdeckung der Langsamkeit*' in Williams/Parkes/Preece 1990, 51–65.

Tekinay, Alev 1997: 'In drei Sprachen leben' in Fischer/McGowan 1997, 27–33.

Wagenlehner, Günther (ed.) 1989: *Feindbild: Geschichte — Dokumentation — Problematik*. Frankfurt am Main: Report-Verlag.

Wagner, René 1990: 'Von Damaskus nach Kirchheimbolanden: Der aramäische Syrer Rafik Schami. Fabulieren war dem Chemiker wichtiger. Der Wahrheit verpflichtet', *Frankfurter Allgemeine Zeitung*, 1 September 1990, 7.

Walther, Wiebke 1988: 'Die Arabische Literatur' in *Kindlers Neues Literaturlexikon*, XIX, 881. Munich: Kindler.

Wehrle, Beate 1992: '"Man sollte die Deutschen nicht so oft und laut belehren": Gespräch mit dem Schriftsteller Rafik Schami', *Saarbrücker Zeitung*, 18/19 November 1992, 11.

Weinrich, Harald (ed.) 1986: *Literatur für Leser: Essays und Aufsätze zur Literaturwissenschaft*. Munich: dtv. [1971]

Williams, Arthur, Stuart Parkes and Julian Preece (eds) 1998: *'Whose Story?' — Continuities in contemporary German-language Literature*. Bern: Peter Lang.

—— (eds) 2000: *Literature, Markets and Media in Germany and Austria today*. Bern: Peter Lang.

Wolff, Armin and Dietrich Eggers (eds) 1998: *Lern- und Studienstandort Deutschland, Emotionen und Kognition, Lernen mit neuen Medien*. Materialien Deutsch als Fremdsprache 45. Regensburg: Fachverband Deutsch als Fremdsprache.

OF FABLES AND MULTICULTURALISM:
THE *FELIDAE* NOVELS OF AKIF PIRINÇCI

JAMES JORDAN

I Preamble

In an edition of the *Literarisches Quartett* Akif Pirinçci, invited originally to give his opinions on the works of other authors, bemoaned to Marcel Reich-Ranicki the fact that his own works had never been considered worthy of discussion in the programme. Reich-Ranicki, defending his decision to include Pirinçci as a commentator but not as an author, began his reply with the words: 'Wenn Sie mal ein gutes Buch schreiben...'. Two elements of this interchange are striking. The first is Pirinçci's status in Reich-Ranicki's eyes as an author well enough known to the audience of the *Literarisches Quartett* to merit inclusion in the programme, but whose work does not match the cultural expectations of the presenter. The second is Pirinçci's desire to be taken seriously by Reich-Ranicki and his audience, despite the fact that his work is unashamedly populist and in certain respects dismissive of the 'bildungsbürgerlich' aspirations of the viewers.

Pirinçci is best known for his three novels featuring the feline detective Francis: *Felidae* (1989), *Francis* (1993) and *Cave canem* (1999). All of these have topped best-seller lists, with *Felidae* achieving sales of over one million in Germany shortly after its publication, and all have been reviewed positively in broadsheet feuilletons. The publishing success of the novels is easily explicable in terms of the pace, originality and unstuffiness of the subject matter and style, but the approbation of some of the more serious critics, such as Stephan Bauer in *Die Horen* (1992), is a phenomenon which merits further consideration.

After a brief review of the *Felidae* novels hitherto published, this essay will examine two aspects of them which suggest that they are more than *Unterhaltungs-* or *Trivialliteratur*, namely the use of the animal fable and the relationship to the detective-story genre. Using Pirinçci's highly autobiographical debut novel *Tränen sind immer das Ende* (1980) as a reference point, it will then be argued that his close self-identification with the feline detective Francis arises from his own experience of social marginalization. By enlisting perspectives from multiculturalism and the study of cultural identity, the exploration of the experience of marginalization in the novels will be made fully apparent.

II The *Felidae* novels

Nearly a decade elapsed between *Tränen* and the publication of Pirinçci's second and hitherto most famous novel *Felidae*, a detective novel related from the perspective of the cat world. Francis and his owner — or, as the cats refer to them, 'Dosenöffner' — move into a new neighbourhood in which there has been a history of serial killings of specific members of the feline population. Francis, the self-styled 'Klugscheißer', embarks on an investigation of the mystery with the aid of the crippled Blaubart and the terminally ill, but highly intelligent, Pascal, amongst whose many gifts is the ability to operate computers. Francis discovers that the local cats have formed a sect based on the martyr figure Claudandus, a cat horribly maltreated in experiments designed to create a treatment for open wounds. Ultimately, Francis realizes that Claudandus is in fact his clever friend Pascal who, having survived such appalling mistreatment at the hands of humans, has kept the local population in subjugation through the cult of Claudandus and has been murderously cleansing the feline gene pool in his ambition to establish a master-race of cats which will establish world domination at the expense of human beings. In a desperate struggle Pascal/Claudandus perishes, but Francis survives and settles back into peaceful coexistence with his still entirely unsuspecting owner.

Felidae was remarkably successful, topping the best-seller charts and giving rise to a film version in 1994. It was reviewed widely and favourably in the popular press but also caught the attention of the literary world. Bauer described it as an 'erstklassigen Kriminalroman' and placed it in the tradition of E. T. A. Hoffmann and Edgar Allan Poe (Bauer 1992). *Felidae*'s popularity led to the reprinting of *Tränen* and to two further Francis novels.

In the sequel *Francis*, the eponymous hero leaves the comforts of his 'Dosenöffner' Gustav in order to avoid the imminent prospect of his being neutered. Washed by a torrential storm into the sewer system, he encounters a horde of cats who have adapted to the dark conditions in the hope of avoiding a series of murders being carried out on cats in the world above. True to his curious nature, he sets about investigating the mystery and uncovers a failed attempt to reintroduce wild cats bred in captivity into their (formerly) natural woodland habitat. No longer able to hunt other prey, these cats are obliged to attack the weaker domestic cats, and their activities are concealed by the highly intelligent Siamese Ambrosius, who perpetuates the myth of a psychopathic renegade cat working in murderous harmony with a Great Dane. In a conflation of animal rights and broader environmental concerns, the wild cats leave the polluted and dying woods in order to seek better fortune in Scandinavia.

Pirinçci's hitherto latest novel, *Cave canem* (1999), begins with Francis in semi-retirement after a distinguished detective career, enjoying the comforts of his maturity. After the murder of his most recent mate, he is drawn reluctantly into the mystery of a series of savage murders of dogs and cats in the neighbourhood, which threatens to break the uneasy truce between them and precipitate war. Francis is obliged to work with Hektor, an aging Alsatian who has seen service with the UN in the Balkans. His attitude to Hektor develops through grudging admiration into genuine affection and, after the dog's death, Francis reveals the murderer as a psychopathic academic allergic to animals who has been attempting to draw the cats and dogs into mutual annihilation.

Neither the transposition of the detective story to an unusual context (cf. Eco's *The Name of the Rose*) nor the anthropomorphic use of animals is particularly original; the combination of the two, however, accounts for the success of the *Felidae* novels. Their literary quality requires more examination. I shall now consider how distinctive Pirinçci's use of the animal fable and the detective story is before exploring the broader thematic implications.

III The *Felidae* novels as animal fables

The basic strategy of the Aesopian fable is to endow animals with particular human characteristics and, through their interaction with other animals or with people, to make apparent a moral message concerning desired behaviour. The strategy of overlaying human characteristics on to animals, or of identifying their instinctive behaviour with human traits, serves to crystallize and simplify the issues involved — the reader or listener thus has no need to speculate about complex human motivations. The European fabulist tradition stems back to the tales of the sixth-century B.C. slave turned sage; Aesop's wisdom is said to have gained him his freedom. In the Middle Ages, figures such as Maître Renard and Reinecke Fuchs, as well as characters from Chaucer's *Canterbury Tales*, were used to comment not merely on human behaviour but also on social mores. The use of animal figures, by that time a standard convention, provided opportunities to criticize the social order which, while they were transgressive in nature, were sanctioned by custom and practice.

This gently subversive use of the animal fable has been a feature of the work of late twentieth-century migrants writing in German. The tales of the Lebanese Jusuf Naoum (e.g. *Die Kaffeehausgeschichten des Abu el Abed*, 1987; *Nacht der Phantasie*, 1994), use animals in the Middle Eastern fabulist tradition to depict attitudes consonant with the author's Marxist leanings. Emine Sevgi Özdamar in *Das Leben ist eine Karawanserei* (1992) interweaves narrative and fable in her examination of Turkish society in the 1950s and 1960s. By far the most successful fabulist is the Syrian Rafik Schami, the most extensively published Middle Eastern author writing in German. His fables are either narrated directly, as in *Das Schaf im Wolfspelz: Märchen und Fabeln* (1989), or they are contained within a framework in which an older member of the community relates tales to a younger audience, for example Onkel Salim in *Der Fliegenmelker und andere Erzählungen: Geschichten aus Damaskus* (1985). The fables are informed by Christian moral values, but also promote tolerant modes of behaviour in a Middle Eastern setting which are directly applicable to relations between the German and migrant communities.

The twentieth century has also seen a use of animal fables for explicitly political ends. George Orwell's *Animal Farm* (1945), for example, used the genre for political allegory, encoding figures and positions from Soviet Communism in specific animals and their characteristics. More recently Azouz Begag, born in 1957 in France of Algerian parents, has used the animal fable for political purposes in *Les chiens aussi* (1995), which overlays on to the canine principal characters themes and concerns relating to the political and social position of the working class and of immigrants. Because Beur writers are French citizens, albeit of North African origin, their work concentrates more on social and economic exclusion than the denial of civic rights and integration, which forms the focus of the work of migrant writers in Germany.

Pirinçci's use of animals, and in particular cats, is not part of the trend towards political use of the animal fable. He even denied intending to write a fable at all: 'Keine Fabel, kein Walt-Disney-Kitsch, kein Kindermärchen, sondern ein Roman, der dem Tier sowohl von seinem Verhalten her als auch auf einer philosophischen Ebene gerecht wird' (Pirinçci 1994, 10). This disavowal may hold true for Pirinçci's intentions, but several aspects of the *Felidae* novels place them clearly in the fabulist tradition. The cat figure in Aesop and in Turkish folklore may be associated with deviousness, cruelty and laziness, but it is also used to comment on the weaknesses of others. Francis comments throughout on the pretensions and foibles of humans in general and of German middle-class society in particular. One notable target is his owner Gustav's methodical but ultimately inept attempts to renovate the delapidated house they move into and to create a chic living environment. The superior perspective of the cat-narrator throws these efforts into ironic relief every bit as skilfully as the more direct satirical assaults of other migrant writers in Germany, for example Osman Engin, a Turkish satirist based in Bremen and an acute observer of German mores in works such as *Alle Dackel umsonst gebissen* (1989).

The character of the cat has become much more subtle since the time of Aesop, latterly it has enjoyed much higher status on account of its perceived independence, intelligence and self-reliance. This shift in perception probably results from the transition from a largely agrarian to a largely urban society: in this latter environment the cat is a model of the instinct for survival and for the defence of the individual's interests in indifferent, if not hostile, circumstances. Seen from this perspective, one can appreciate the confluence of experience and interests between Pirinçci as author and Francis as his chosen hero. Both have been transplanted to a foreign and initially inimical environment; both are street-wise and (at least overtly) cynical; and both achieve admiration and recognition by their peers in their adopted environment through the demonstration of their superior intelligence and gifts. This close identification of Pirinçci with Francis will be now extended to include the latter's role as detective.

IV The *Felidae* series as self-conscious crime novels

> Der Detektiv, der mir vorschwebte, mußte viele Eigenschaften in sich vereinen. Er sollte die Bildung und Belesenheit eines Geisteswissenschaftlers besitzen, die sportliche Gelenkigkeit eines Hochleistungsathleten, die Kombinationsgabe eines Genies, die Liebesfähigkeit eines Don Juan und die ethische Gesinnung eines Moraltheologen. Vor allem jedoch mußte er umwerfend sympathisch sein, ein Kerl, den man einfach liebhaben mußte. Kein Wunder, daß dafür kein Mensch in Frage kam. (Pirinçci 1997, 11)

The intelligence and independence of the cat, in Pirinçci's view, suited it admirably to the role of detective. *Tränen*, published nearly a decade before *Felidae*, demonstrates an enduring fascination with the detective novel (and film) and the crime mystery. Frequent references to Raymond Chandler show Pirinçci to be well acquainted with him and his work. Stephen Knight, in his analysis of Chandler and his novels, sums up the author's detective hero thus:

> [...] Marlowe is a marginal bourgeois, below the professional classes, educated above the workers, but insisting on a freelance position to replicate his alienated attitude. He appears to have had a college education, but to be guarded about it; education is not allowed to become a way of life, but merely validates the hero's superiority. The alienated persona is also shown in, and protected by, the deliberately unostentatious life-style, the neutral, potentially hostile public manners and the secret domestic pleasures like chess and coffee making: all these features confirm Marlowe's position as an archetype of the educated urban alien. (Knight 1980, 161)

Although he does not share Marlowe's bourgeois status and formal education, the first-person narrator of *Tränen* (who is actually called Akif Pirinçci), is similar in many respects: he is freelance, he vaunts his autodidactic knowledge to demonstrate his superiority over others (particularly German university students), and his life-style is demonstrably, though necessarily, simple. Whether these characteristics go beyond mere similarity to deliberate stylization is arguable, but Chandler's novels have undoubtedly influenced Pirinçci. The first-person narrators in *Tränen*, *Felidae* and *Der Rumpf* (1992) all adopt the hard-boiled, cynical, wise-cracking tone of Marlowe. Frequent references to works by Agatha Christie and others demonstrate just how conversant Pirinçci is with the detective genre both in film and literature. Francis even has a penchant for music (Mahler), echoing the musical sophistication of Sherlock Holmes.

This affinity for the detective genre would seem to stem from Pirinçci's self-identification with the heroes of such works. The detective is almost invariably a loner, either foreign to the environment in which he operates or in some other way alienated from it, for example excluded from the conventional police force in the case of Philip Marlowe. Knight argues of Chandler's hero: 'The pressure of the form and the content suggests that an isolated, intelligent person, implicitly hostile to others and basically uninterested in them, can verify his own superiority by intellectual means and create a defensive withdrawal' (Knight 1980, 138). The private detective is characterized by superior intelligence and quick-wittedness which stands in stark contrast to the dullness of his more conventional colleagues.

It is not difficult to see the relevance of this role model for Pirinçci. As the son of immigrants coming to Germany at a time when he would expect to have established firm childhood friendships in Turkey, he immediately became the outsider. If we can accept the autobiographical accuracy of *Tränen*, this rejection led to self-exclusion as a positive act of self-definition against an indifferent society. Rejecting the conventional career paths which a university education might offer, Pirinçci assumed that most marginal of occupations, the freelance writer. In this area it was his ambition to demonstrate his superior intelligence and gifts over those who had been socially integrated and had enjoyed the benefits of that status.

The *Felidae* novels, however, go beyond the conscious adoption of an established genre. Once the reader has progressed beyond the first few pages and ingested the inversions and ironies which a feline narrator brings with it, he or she soon forgets the abnormal aspects of the situation and settles comfortably into the internal logic of the device, accepting quite happily that cats can communicate with each other as well as humans do, that they have social structures and conventions which run parallel to those of humans, that they can read as humans do and that they are fully aware of human cultural traditions and achievements. The considerable comic potential of the device is left largely unexploited to help the reader suspend disbelief. Occasionally, though, Pirinçci reminds the reader of the fiction-within-a-fiction he has created. The final confrontation between Francis and Claudandus in *Felidae* mirrors, for example, the final scene of a Bond movie: the arch-villain, having been tracked down by the skilful investigator, takes the opportunity to impress on him the megalomaniac grandeur of his plans. When Francis requests Claudandus to fill in for him the last details of the plan he has uncovered, Claudandus answers: 'Ach, du meinst, die berühmte Geschichte, die der Mörder dem Detektiv anvertraut, bevor er ihn umbringt — oder umgekehrt?' (*Felidae*, 256).

This reminder of the bizarre logic of the novel which the reader has been persuaded to accept subverts, albeit in a genial way, the conventions of the detective genre by introducing this comic irony at a time which is traditionally the most tense, namely the showdown between hero and villain. To this extent, *Felidae* moves beyond the frame of reference of Trivialliteratur by explicitly adopting a set of cultural conventions and then adapting and subverting them.

V *Felidae* as a multicultural fable

Pirinçci was born in Istanbul in 1959 and came to Germany as a ten-year-old child with his guest-worker parents, but in interviews and personal statements he has consistently denied any thematization of his Turkish–German status in his work and rejected any suggestion that he is a migrant author rather than part of the German literary mainstream. In an interview for *The Independent* in 1993 for example he insisted 'I just entertain' (cit. Crawshaw 1993). While relations between the German majority community and the Turkish minority do not feature explicitly in any of his later novels, they do arise in *Tränen*, and the high autobiographical content of this novel is the key to understanding the role his perceived social status plays in *Felidae*.

Tränen relates the love affair of a young Turk with a German girl. The central figure, the 18-year-old Akif Pirinçci, has been thrown out of his parents' home and moves to Cologne to achieve success as a writer. His circle of friends consists of off-beat Germans and non-Germans marginalized by their ethnicity. Akif's relationship with Christa founders on his obsessive need for reassurance, his antagonism towards her student friends and his adoption of behaviour designed to test her commitment to the limits. When she finishes the relationship he attempts suicide, is reconciled with his parents and resolves to commit the story of their relationship to writing.

The parallels with *Die Leiden des jungen Werther* are obvious, and Petra Fachinger has convincingly documented the relationship with Plenzdorf's *Die neuen Leiden des jungen W.* (Fachinger 1997). The crucial element of Akif's insecurity arises not solely from adolescent role- and identity-seeking but also from his marginal status in German society. His choice of occupation (freelance writer) both confirms and augments this marginalization, and is compounded when he falls in love with a German girl and thus enters a mixed-race relationship. Akif senses and responds aggressively to the lack of esteem in which Christa's friends hold him, and at a student party conspicuously drinks himself to illness. Christa's anger at his behaviour leads him significantly to seek refuge in a *Kneipe* frequented by Turks, where a fatherly friend offers him advice based on Turkish emigrant mores and expectations.

Pirinçci may be correct in his disavowal of any intention to make a general statement about migrant and post-migrant experience, but this is quite different from suggesting that his experiences as a youth displaced from one society, language and culture to another cannot recur as themes in later works which do not apparently have such a close biographical connection. And what was valid for him as an individual also holds good for a considerable number of children (the so-called 'Seiteneinsteiger' arriving at awkward stages in the school system) required to make similar fundamental adjustments and exposed to similar difficulties and disadvantages. The response in *Tränen* is the depiction of apparently extreme individualism and cynicism towards the adopted society; by reference to *Felidae* we shall see that, ten years on, Pirinçci's attitudes towards the experience of social alienation had mellowed.

I have already evinced Pirinçci's close identification with the figure of Francis as both cat (and thus a symbol of independence) and freelance detective (with the self-assurance and innate superiority this status brings). Francis is also close to Pirinçci's own position in his youth: he is moved from a secure environment in which he is fully acquainted with locations and routines; he enters a new locality in which he is initially subjected to aggression by those already living there; he wins his assimilation into the new feline community by demonstrating his superiority over its inhabitants.

Thus far there would appear to be little development from Pirinçci's debut novel. However, the clash between Francis and his friend and mentor-cum-enemy Pascal/Claudandus, which comes to a head in the final scene, does mark a significant step forward. Commissioned by a pharmaceutical firm, a scientist has been working on a substance which would promote healing by stimulating the closure of the wound. As his work begins to falter and the number of experiments he is permitted to carry out on cats (by cutting them open and comparing rates of healing) is reduced, he begins to collect up strays from the neighbourhood. One of these reveals a genetic mutation which enables him to heal rapidly — hence Claudandus, derived from the Latin 'claudere', 'to close'; he thus holds the key to the scientist's work. In his desperation to uncover the secret of Claudandus's extraordinary powers of healing, the scientist redoubles his savage mutilation of the cat. One evening, Claudandus is able to escape and manages to kill his tormentor by biting him through his neck.

Claudandus hides his real identity and resolves to breed a super-race of cats closer to the original hunter-killer instincts of the species, which will then at some future point kill off human beings and assume dominance in the order of creation. Having identified a particularly suitable breed, he kills all those cats in the neighbourhood who try to breed with the females and thus unwittingly pollute the gene pool. Simultaneously he promotes the myth of the martyr Claudandus in order to lull the local cat population into superstitious submissiveness. Claudandus is, however, dying and identifies the clever newcomer Francis as a suitable successor, but allows him to follow his own investigative path towards the truth.

If we step back from the specific nature of Claudandus's views and interpret them instead as social visualizations, then a new dimension becomes apparent. Claudandus is a member of a species which has a subaltern place to the dominant species, humankind. Furthermore, he has been exploited and badly mistreated. His response is to campaign for the racial integrity of the feline species and to work towards domination over humans and the rest of creation. He thus wishes to invert the original power relationship in favour of his own species, i.e. to replace one form of oppression by another. His opponent in this is Francis, who is not only a member of the subaltern species but also an individual with experience of isolation and exclusion within that species, and who therefore has a deeper insight into mechanisms of exclusion and domination than Claudandus. He therefore rejects the replacement of one form of tyranny by another, accepts the desirability of interbreeding, and argues for a future vision of a society in which all animals (including humans) are equal and live in mutual tolerance and friendship.

If we transpose these positions into models of multi-ethnic society, the significance of their conflict becomes clear. Claudandus rejects both assimilation and multiculturalism as social models, preferring instead to perpetuate a society where power is concentrated in the hands of a dominant majority which excludes and disenfranchises all other communities. The social embodiments of these views would be either societies based on racial supremacism, such as South Africa under apartheid, or those which have undergone fundamentalist revolutions which restrict power to a religious-political elite, as is the case in Afghanistan. Francis, by contrast, frequently acknowledges with approval the variety of breeds in the neighbourhood and the characteristics which make them particular, but does not view any individual breed as superior to another. He advocates a multicultural society based on tolerance and the rights of the individual in which subscription to a liberal consensus will, over a period of time, render group allegiances token and perhaps even redundant. In essence, Francis's views of society accord with those of the philosopher Charles Taylor who, in his influential essay 'The politics of recognition' (1994), argues that the inclusive flexibility of liberalism is the key to absorbing otherwise conflictual group-specific identity needs.

VI *Felidae* and the politics of cultural identity

Along with debates concerning multiculturalism, and in some senses growing out of them, there has come an increasing focus on the question of identity and the political consequences which flow from it. A frequent criticism of liberal multiculturalism is its reliance on the assumption that ethnic communities are discrete and possess clear boundaries. All individuals ascribed to a community are assumed to have identical interests and social needs. These assumptions begin to break down under conditions of globalization in studies of transnational communities and of second- (and third-) generation migrants with multiple cultural allegiances (Werbner 1997). Multicultural theories designed to describe processes of inter-community regulation cannot be meaningfully applied to these situations, more differentiated analytical concepts relating to cultural identities are required. These include essentialism (the proposition that there are fixed racial, ethnic and cultural characteristics which apply to all members of a community) or hybridity, the deliberate or inadvertent fusion of two or more distinct cultural influences.

If we assume the perspective of the politics of identity, the split between the protagonists in *Felidae* is once again quite clear. Claudandus holds to the concept of the indivisibility of identity, seeing interbreeding as a threat. From this essentialist perspective group identities are amenable neither to negotiation nor to change. Francis, on the other hand, sees the relative group identities as being capable both of mutation and integration and of producing new hybrid identities within the feline species and in terms of inter-species relations — he describes with relish the moments of abandon he enjoys with a female of the new super-race. Thus Francis's victory over Claudandus can be seen to demonstrate definitively the author's own preferences. The victor is an individual who is comfortable in the company of humans, able to re-establish himself in a new environment, moving easily between sectors of society. He has no absolute allegiance to any group and rejoices in the freedom this bestows on him, trusting to his own abilities and the opportunism of a society which offers the prospect of meritocratic advancement. In order for this exceptional individual to function to his full potential, he requires an environment of individual freedom and tolerance. In this way, Francis's attitudes, the ideas he opposes together with his vision of a desirable environment define the society which his alter ego, the author, wishes for himself. The close self-identification of the author with the feline hero permits us to read into this figure his own self-perceptions, attitudes and aspirations. Even if, therefore, Pirinçci did not consciously set out to include an allegorical or metaphorical element, the proximity of narrator and author suggests its existence.

VII The sequels to *Felidae*

Francis: Felidae II, the sequel to *Felidae*, was published four years later, shortly before the opening of the cartoon version of the first novel. It is a Gothic tale of the failed introduction of an endangered species from captivity into woodland. The background to the events is the issue of *Waldsterben* and is thus a calculated appeal to Pirinçci's environmentally conscious German audience. He is able to include more personal concerns with animal welfare and with human-animal relationships. While the thematic focus is clearly no longer relations between groups and individuals in multi-ethnic society, the use of the cat detective has a clear thematic function and the story is not intended merely to entertain.

The third, and hitherto last, Francis novel *Cave canem* reverts to the question of relationships between communities in mixed societies. Francis is now many years on from his move to his adopted neighbourhood — in essence, therefore, he is a first-generation migrant growing old in the adopted community. His passive prejudices against and contempt for dogs, an old reflex, surface when he is required to work with a dog to solve a series of murders and to avert a feline-canine conflict. Through his collaboration with Hektor, Francis's prejudices are at first challenged and then overcome. His growing awareness of the untenability of his views is highlighted when he saves an ailing dog from attack by a group of young cats which includes his own son. The final step in Francis's conversion occurs when Hektor dies saving him:

> Hektor war mein Beschützer gewesen und mein Freund — und ein Kläffer. Wie töricht doch meine Feindseligkeit gegenüber seiner Rasse vor unserer Begegnung ge-

wesen war, wie widerlich meine Vorurteile [...] Doch während ich Hektor zwischen
meinen Pfoten beschnupperte, ihn mit meinen heißen Tränen wusch, ihn leckte und
küßte, hatte ich im Gegensatz zu den anderen Kriegslüsternen im Geiste einen Trost:
Ich war geheilt! (*Cave canem*, 268)

Eventually, Francis and his son Junior are reconciled, but on the basis that
Junior now accepts the validity of his father's new-found tolerance.

Written during (and published just after) the Kosovo conflict, the novel is
intended as a comment on the inhumanity of ethnic cleansing and conflicts
between communities which have previously inhabited common areas peace-
fully. It is also clear, though, that many of the attitudes criticized in the work are
also apparent closer to Pirinçci's own situation, namely in the divergence of
attitudes between first- and second- or third-generation migrants. Francis's
initial position is that of the migrant who has chosen to remain within his own
community and has built up a stock of prejudices against other communities
which grow and remain unchallenged as a result of the lack of contact with the
other community. Francis's realization after the death of Hektor is that the effort
to integrate, not necessarily to assimilate, on the part of the migrant community
would reduce the tensions between both communities and further the cause of
mutual respect without undermining cultural integrity.

Junior represents the post-migrant generation which, faced with the
prospect of trying to integrate into a perceived hostile society, retreats into an
exaggerated version of their parents' cultural identity. This defensive mechan-
ism is depicted by Feridun Zaimoglu in *Kanak Sprak: 24 Misstöne vom Rande
der Gesellschaft* (1995) and *Abschaum: die wahre Geschichte von Ertan Ongun*
(1997), which reveal a Turkish–German youth sub-culture created in opposition
to a forbidding and uncaring German society. Junior's eventual rejection of the
sub-culture and acceptance of his father's belated tolerance make Pirinçci's
fears about the divergence of first and subsequent generations clear. Most
interesting, however, is the acknowledgement by Francis that the cultural
isolationism of his own generation is responsible for creating and sustaining the
aggressive antagonisms of subsequent generations towards integration.

VIII Conclusion

Pirinçci's innovative use of the animal fable and detective genre, and his highly
original combination of the two, explain in large measure why the *Felidae*
novels have been such a success as Unterhaltungsliteratur and have also been
taken seriously by the critics. However, although he wishes to be considered a
mainstream writer and for his ethnicity not to be taken into account, much of his
initial success is also due to his status as a Turk writing German detective best

sellers, a novelty which has also worked to the advantage of Jakob Arjouni, though in a rather different way. Arjouni has written a series of detective stories (*Happy birthday, Türke!*, 1987; *Mehr Bier*, 1987; *Ein Mann ein Mord*, 1991) featuring the sleuth Kemal Kayankaya, a Turk brought up by Germans after the death of his parents in migration. Arlene Teraoka (1999) has examined the manner in which Kayankaya's elusive status enables Arjouni to probe the need of German society to attach clear essentialist ethnic labels to individuals. She has also demonstrated how Arjouni's studied vagueness regarding his own ethnic background has forced critics to try to attach ethnic labels to him in an attempt to apply clear categories to author and work, seemingly unaware that his intention is to disclose the untenablity of such labels and categories in societies which have undergone substantial immigration.

Both Arjouni and Pirinçci disavow any intention of thematizing multiculturalism or identity. In his interview in *The Independent* Pirinçci complained about the reception of *Felidae*: 'The reviews are all too serious. They took the book apart, as though I meant something special' (cit. Crawshaw 1993). The unwillingness of the authors to be pigeon-holed as representatives of a socially critical *Migrantenliteratur* is understandable both from an artistic and a commercial point of view. It is, however, obvious that their work has a great deal more to say about the position of migrants and post-migrants in German society than they either intended or, more likely, have been prepared to concede. In her essay on *Tränen* Fachinger stresses the qualitative difference between this and the 'Literatur der Betroffenheit' written by migrants to Germany which preceded it: 'Koffer und Bahnhöfe beherrschen nicht länger die Vorstellungswelt der Schriftsteller nichtdeutscher Herkunft; vielmehr machen die Hybridität und Intertextualität der Texte von Autoren der zweiten und dritten Generation eine neue Standortbestimmung dieser Literatur notwendig' (Fachinger 1997, 150).

What was true of *Tränen* has been exceeded by the sophistication of the *Felidae* novels, but there is a further aspect in which Pirinçci has developed from that time. Migrantenliteratur remained marginalized because, amongst other reasons, it was the victim of certain ambiguities and contradictions. A literature which explored split cultural allegiances was addressed to a society which defined its cohesion in terms of distinguishing itself racially, through the 'ius sanguinis', from that which it was not. Equally, a socially critical literature which required a wide audience in order to effect change failed to reach that audience because of the narrowness of its concerns. Pirinçci's work trancends these contradictions by following Aristotle's enjoinder to both entertain and educate.

Primary texts
Pirinçci, Akif 1980: *Tränen sind immer das Ende*. Munich: Goldmann.
—— 1989: *Felidae*. Munich: Goldmann.
—— 1992: *Der Rumpf*. Munich: Goldmann.
—— 1993: *Francis. Felidae II*. Munich: Goldmann.
—— 1994a: *Felidae. Der Katzenkrimi mit den schönsten Bildern aus dem neuen großen Kinofilm*. Munich: Goldmann.
—— 1994b: 'Über ein Buch mit dem Titel *Felidae*' in Pirinçci 1994a, 7–20.
—— 1999: *Cave canem*. Munich: Goldmann.

Secondary literature
Aesop 1996: *Aesop's Fables*. Trans. Jack Zipes. London: Penguin.
Arjouni, Jakob 1987: *Happy birthday, Türke!* Zurich: Diogenes.
—— 1987: *Mehr Bier*. Zurich: Diogenes.
—— 1991: *Ein Mann ein Mord*. Zurich: Diogenes.
Bauer, Stephan 1992: 'Francis contra Claudandus', *Die Horen*, 37/165, 173–176.
Begag, Azouz 1995: *Les chiens aussi. Roman*. Paris: Éditions du seuil.
Crawshaw, Steve 1993: 'Feline fantasies', *The Independent*, 18 September 1993, 29.
Engin, Osman 1989: *Alle Dackel umsonst gebissen: Satiren*. Berlin: TÜ–DE Kultur-Austausch GmbH.
Fachinger, Petra 1997: 'Ohne Koffer: Renan Demirkan und Akif Pirinçci' in Howard 1997, 139–151.
Gutmann, Amy (ed.) 1994: *Multiculturalism: Examining the Politics of Recognition*. Princeton: Princeton UP.
Howard, Mary (ed.) 1997: *Interkulturelle Konfigurationen: zur deutschsprachigen Erzähl-literatur von Autoren nichtdeutscher Herkunft*. Munich: iudicium.
Knight, Stephen 1980: *Form and Ideology in Crime Fiction*. London: Macmillan.
Naoum, Jusuf 1987: *Die Kaffeehausgeschichten des Abu el Abed*. Frankfurt am Main: Brandes & Apsel.
—— 1994: *Nacht der Phantasie*. Frankfurt am Main: Brandes & Apsel.
Özdamar, Emine Sevgi 1992: *Das Leben ist eine Karawanserei / hat zwei Türen / aus einer kam ich rein / aus der anderen ging ich raus*. Cologne: Kiepenheuer & Witsch.
Orwell, George 1945: *Animal Farm: A Fairy Story*. London: Secker & Warburg.
Schami, Rafik 1997: *Der Fliegenmelker und andere Erzählungen: Geschichten aus Damaskus*. Munich: dtv. (Originally 1985)
—— 1998: *Das Schaf im Wolfspelz: Märchen und Fabeln*. Munich: dtv. (Originally 1982)
Spieß, Otto (ed.) 1967: *Türkische Märchen*. Munich: Eugen Diederichs.
Taylor, Charles 1994: 'The Politics of Recognition' in Gutmann 1994, 25–73.
Teraoka, Arlene 1999: 'Detecting Ethnicity: Jakob Arjouni and the case of the missing German detective novel', *The German Quarterly* 72/3 (Summer 1999), 265–289.
Werbner, Pnina 1997: 'The dialectics of cultural hybridity' in Werbner/Modood 1997, 1–26.
—— and Tariq Modood (eds) 1997: *Debating Cultural Hybridity: Multi-Cultural Identities and the Politics of Anti-Racism*. London/New Jersey: Zed Books.
Zaimoglu, Feridun 1995: *Kanak Sprak: 24 Misstöne vom Rande der Gesellschaft*. Berlin: Rotbuch.
—— 1997: *Abschaum: Die wahre Geschichte von Ertan Ongun*. Berlin: Rotbuch.

'DEN AMIS IN HOLLYWOOD EIN FÜR ALLEMAL DAS LEBENSLICHTLEIN AUSBLASEN!' ASPECTS OF TEXT AND FILM IN THE LATE 1990s

COLIN RIORDAN

I Culture and intermediality

Although beating American popular culture at its own game has been a European aspiration since the early twentieth century, the constraints of commercial imperatives do not always sit easily with the European artistic tradition. Moreover, the techniques demanded by the visual and aural media through which much popular culture is disseminated are frequently not congruent with those which have shaped the literary tradition. The consequence of this can be a kind of intermedial conflict which has interesting implications in an age in which technological change seems likely to alter the way both high and low culture are produced and consumed. DVD technology allows films to be viewed in much the same way that we read a book; it is now more convenient than with VHS video to move about in the text and view at our own pace. The growth of the internet and the concomitant supplanting of paper-based by screen-based consumption of information seem likely to further exacerbate the blurring of the line between traditional reading and the use of aural and visual media.

In this essay I wish to explore the way in which the boundaries between the print medium and the screen medium are being renegotiated. The reason for such renegotiation, I would suggest, is not merely the shift to screen-based consumption which characterizes the turn of the century, but also the desire, in contemporary German-language culture, to break parochial boundaries and recognize the global nature of all information-based fields of human endeavour. By its nature this effort implies a simultaneous erosion of the boundaries between high and low culture. The elitism which has long been a feature of German-language culture is becoming less sustainable in the face of international competition. It has now become a commonplace to point out that *Der Spiegel* best seller lists are dominated by literature in translation, but the point is nevertheless an important one. In an age of global markets and global media, the question of whether German-language culture is or can be both popular and international may well be one of long-term survival.

These considerations have informed the choice of texts to be discussed in this essay. The focus falls particularly on the Swiss writer Urs Richle's novel

Hand im Spiel (1998), for which he had support from the Drehbuchwerkstatt München, and on *Rossini*, a film made in Munich in 1996. The latter was directed by Helmut Dietl, who also wrote the screenplay together with Patrick Süskind; it was then published in book form with an essay by Süskind in 1997. The choice of these two works rests on more than their shared association with the 'bayerische Filmmetropole'. Admittedly, *Hand im Spiel* is a gritty urban thriller, a tale of murder, high finance, the diplomatic elite and the criminal underworld on the streets of Geneva, while *Rossini*, by contrast, is a comedy drama, a fantasy set in a Munich restaurant frequented by the film and literary 'Schickeria'. Nevertheless the points of contact are striking. In each the conflicting demands of art and commerce are part of the theme, and each is clearly designed to undermine any impression of elitist parochialism in their treatment of violence, sex, death, and the drama of high finance. The novel and the film both explore the interplay between the written word and filmic representation, and in both several individual stories are interwoven in a way which deliberately eschews the hero narrative. And these points of contact extend beyond merely thematic and structural similarities: both also challenge assumptions about the nature of German-language cultural production in the information age.

II *Hand im Spiel*: filmic antecedents

Hand im Spiel, it has to be said, is a text which is hardly likely to be popular; it is not an easy read and is unlikely to be widely read. Part of this lies in the novel's origins as a film (of which more below). The narrative owes as much to the cinematic technique of the storyboard as it does to traditional literary storytelling. Moreover, the plot is so complex that it is only by leafing backwards and forwards and comparing several descriptions of the same scene that it is possible to assemble a comprehensible picture of events. Indeed, this is a novel which positively invites re-reading.

Richle's thriller is a complex of stories all of which hinge on coincidence, misunderstanding and confusion. The book is divided into five unnumbered chapters with one-word headings, which are themselves sub-divided into further sections. In the opening and closing chapters the subsections are given headings indicating where the action takes place. All other subsections indicate which characters are involved. Essentially, a Middle Eastern diplomat who is being blackmailed is murdered when a bag containing his payment is accidentally taken by an old man suffering from senile dementia. Instead, a similar bag is delivered to the blackmailers who find only clothes inside; the confusion is further heightened by the appearance of a third bag. Crucial to the plot, then, is the mixing up of three leather bags which are visually identical. The novel thus depends for its structural integrity on the operation of visual cues which, though integral to a storyboard teatment, can only awkwardly be represented in the form of prose fiction. The misappropriation of the bags could be rendered in a few shots on film; in the novel, cumbersome explanation or excessive complexity is the result. These complexities are confronted in the text by an attempt to render filmic techniques such as camera perspectives, the framing of shots, lighting effects and sound effects. As a closer examination of particular passages will make clear, the complexity of scene changes and the detail of description give the sense of a visual and aural medium being rendered purely linguistically.

This is apparent at its most basic level in repeated reference to lighting conditions, as one example will illustrate: 'Das schummrige Licht dringt bis in den Flur. An der Wand der Schatten der Fensterkreuze. Der Glanz der Strassen-laterne auf dem schwarzen Leder' (HS, 67). Such nods in the direction of the *film noir* do lend the novel a certain atmosphere appropriate to a *Krimi*, but there is more to it than this. Much use is made in the text of detailed description in the present tense, adopting perspectives which are equivalents of long, medium, and close-up shots. The complexity of the scene changes and the detail of description also seem more suited to a visual medium:

> Nur ein paar Meter hinter dem Opel, auf der anderen Strassenseite, am Eingang zum Bains des Pâquis steht ein alter verwirrter Mann, hält eine Tasche in die Luft, schaut suchend um sich, ruft etwas. Sein Rufen ist im Lärm des vorbeirauschenden Verkehrs nicht zu hören. Ein Motorrad fährt in der ins Stocken geratenen[1] Kolonne Slalom. Aus einem Sportwagen dröhnen stampfende Technorhythmen, eine blausilbrig gestreifte Krawatte wippt im Rhythmus dazu.
> Blick auf die Uhr: es ist neunzehn Uhr, siebenundvierzig Minuten und sechzehn Sekunden. Ein uniformierter Arm mit Streifen am Ärmel, eine falsche Rolex, jetzt auch die Schulter mit Streifen, ein blauschwarzer Pullover, ein Büro, ein Telefon, zwei weitere kahlgeschorene Herren in der gleichen Uniform, Füsse auf dem Pult, überein-andergeschlagen, hin und her wippend. Ein Fernseher läuft in einer Ecke, einer geht ans Fenster, das mit breitrandigen Lamellen verhängt ist, schiebt sie zur Seite und wirft einen schnellen Blick hinaus, lässt die Lamellen wieder los, die in ihre senk-rechte Stellung zurückfallen. (132)

The first paragraph is strictly inessential, merely reinforcing what we know already. In fact, the description is an element of film narrative: a medium estab-lishing shot of a busy city street centering on an old man whom, by now, we would recognize. The second paragraph is even more pointedly filmic, allowing us to reconstruct the shots that would be used. The sequence starts with an ex-treme close-up of the watch, so that we can read the numerals from the perspec-tive of the wearer, then the camera pulls back to the arm (note 'jetzt auch'), then the owner of the arm, finally cutting to a view of the whole room with the action taking place. This kind of detailed description, always dwelling in as objective a way as possible on the visual impression, and adopting frames and perspectives reminiscent of the cinema, is characteristic of the whole text.

There is also an attempt to render the soundtrack. For example, at one point we know that during a kidnapping a character has been hiding on the balcony unbeknown to the kidnappers. The passage (or perhaps sequence) depicting her terrified departure when all is quiet, and the subsequent arrival of another character on foot, takes place almost entirely through descriptions of sounds, which would, of course, in a film be sound effects:

> Auf dem schmalen Balkon im fünften Stock ist ein Rascheln zu vernehmen, wie von Laub, dann wie von Stoff, einige klirrende und scheppernde Geräusche folgen, dann ist eine Nuance eines Schattens sichtbar, ein Huschen und Verschwinden, danach dringt das Knirschen von Glassplittern nach aussen, dann nichts mehr. Es dauert eine ganze Weile, bis Schritte in der Ferne zu hören sind, die dann aber schnell näher kommen und zwischen den Fassaden der Wohnblöcke hallen, als renne jemand durch ein Museum. (234)

This kind of aural description, complementing the highly visual narratives, does allow the reader almost to run a mental film whilst reading the text. The technique throughout is to present us with scenes viewed externally with little or no authorial comment,[2] using language which is determinedly unpoetic. Only at a later stage are we given an explanation of the plot (e.g. 144–145), which then allows us to piece together events in their context. Occasionally more conventional literary techniques are used such as the internalized account of Lucie's state of mind entitled 'Lucies Kopf' (255), but even then the detailed sequencing of events is maintained.

There is a literary and structural sense to this approach. As noted above, the plot hinges on a series of occasions where people leap to wrong conclusions and misunderstand each other. In itself, this is the very stuff of a commercial film plot (except that, in this case, there is no satisfactory resolution). But the advantage is that the filmic perspective allows us to see why the characters fall victim to misunderstanding. The evidence, as conveyed to external observers by the camera-like registration, is bound to lead them to those conclusions. All of us are highly trained in this method of perceiving a story; the use of the camera perspectives shows us how the misunderstandings occur which lead to so many disastrous outcomes for the characters.

This is, of course, a familiar literary technique as much as a filmic one, and indeed there is nothing new about the idea of literature which adopts the perspective of a camera, or which borrows heavily from cinema (John Dos Passos's *Manhattan Transfer* would be an obvious venerable example). In this novel, however, the process is so striking that the text seems to be located somewhere between a novel and a screenplay, as though the bones of a screenplay have been taken and a novel constructed on the basis of a storyboard. And indeed, as it transpires, this may be quite close to what actually happened, for the novel also exists in the form of a screenplay under the title *Transit Café* (which is probably the Café du Rond Point in the novel, where some of the bag handovers take place). The rights were sold in 1997, but, contrary to early optimistic declarations, the film has not so far been produced.[3] This, of course, is the fate of the great majority of film concepts and of screenplays. The success of Richle's attempt to render a screenplay as a novel without entirely losing the effect of a film remains debatable; it does, however, express at least an uneasiness with the limitations of prose fiction in an age of global media.

III The globalization of culture

Although the action of *Hand im Spiel* takes place in Geneva, there is a fairly clear attempt to break the bounds of Swiss literature, Swiss culture and traditional Swiss concerns and to write a novel which acknowledges the global nature of modern capitalism, the internationalization of culture and the fragmented perception of reality in a multimedia world. It is worth noting that some of Richle's previous work, particularly *Mall oder das Verschwinden der Berge* (1993) and, to some extent, *Das Loch in der Decke der Stube* (1992), has fallen squarely into a Swiss literary tradition of mountain landscapes, isolation and reflection. His earliest works are also noticeably indebted to Max Frisch (e.g. *Der Mensch erscheint im Holozän*) in terms of narrative techniques.

Yet in *Hand im Spiel* there is a constant effort to place the action in a world beyond Switzerland. The complex web of criminal intrigue which underlies the plot relies on a connection with a Middle Eastern arms deal, adding an international dimension which is in any case easy to evoke in Geneva, a city which is also a world centre of diplomacy. The seamy urban setting itself seems like a deliberate gesture of distancing from the rural or small-town setting so characteristic of Swiss literature, including Richle's own earlier work. The characters are also a bewildering range of nationalities, while the framework of references is pointedly multicultural. The two ways in which the multicultural elements emerge most prominently are through language and music.

The inability of Juanita, the Filipino maid, to speak French or German leaves her at the mercy of her employer, the Arab diplomat Ali, who keeps her a virtual prisoner. She is disempowered by her linguistic ignorance, cut off through linguistic disadvantage. And language is indeed the clearest possible indicator of multiculturalism. At a party, one of the characters (Lucie) notes the cultural diversity expressed in an array of languages:

> Das Internationale an dieser Truppe gefällt ihr, François ist Franzose, Marjam Irane-rin, Valentin Deutschschweizer wie sie und Herbert kommt aus Dortmund, eine Stadt, die ihr auch nach nächtelangen Schilderungen und Beschwörungen Herberts so fremd bleibt wie Diepoldsau oder Würenlos. Lucie macht der Sprachmix unter ihnen nichts aus, im Gegenteil, sie geniesst es, von einer Sprache in die andere überzugleiten, sich auszudrücken, gerade wie es ihr in den Sinn kommt. Manchmal helfen französische Ausdrücke im Englischen, englische Wörter im Französischen und Deutschen. Nur ihren Zürcher Dialekt versucht sie so wenig wie möglich zu benutzen. Es ist ihre ganz private Sprache geworden. (HS, 147–148)

The role of Swiss dialect is relegated to the private sphere; moreover, we discover that she associates it also with the past. A mixture of languages is, then, redolent of the future. Swiss tradition, it seems, is irrelevant to contemporary concerns. This echoes an almost traditional complaint of Swiss and indeed Austrian writers since the 1960s and forms part of a more general campaign against parochialism in the novel, summed up in the lament 'alles so langweilig und bieder wie eh und je, die ewige Wiederkehr des Gleichen' (218). Interculturality is distinctly more desirable, as the regular references to popular music also underline.

The characters' choice of music accentuates both the multicultural nature of modern society and the globalization of the media. Car radios are the main source as the characters listen to such culturally varied music as rap, 'französischen Schlager' (105), 'orientalischer Schlager' (121), and classic American jazz (142). Music is a marker both of individual taste and for regional or national affiliation, but it also fulfils its traditional role as an indication of rebellion against established mores by the young. Opera, for example, is dismissed by one of the characters as mere bourgeois affectation: 'Was willst du denn in der Oper? Sekt trinken für zehn Franken das Glas und sich mit den Leuten über Krawattenmuster unterhalten?' (206). By contrast, the underground scene in Geneva is described as a 'neue Welt', a paradoxical haven of chaos amid the orderliness of the Swiss city. When Georg, Fred and Eliane enter an illegal bar, there is a rare glimpse of authorial preference: 'Eine wärmende Ruhe geht von diesem Chaos aus, als liege darunter ein urzeitlicher Malstrom' (212). How a primeval maelstrom might engender feelings of calm is not further explained, but it is clear that the music emanating from the enormous loudspeakers is at least partly responsible: 'Der Bass ist so hart und so laut, dass die Brustkörbe zittern und die Zwerchfelle flattern, die Wände beben. Das Blech der Bierdose vibriert in der Hand' (213). Music, along with film, is appropriated as a means of defining an identity separate from that of Switzerland in its international profile. It is a means of joining forces with global youth in the common effort to break free of the bonds of the bourgeois establishment. A young Irishwoman called Vicky runs the bar; she has (somewhat unlikely) plans to make a film, the screenplay for which she has already started: 'es sollte ein Film mit soviel Kraft und spritziger Wut werden, wie sie in dieser Musik liegt, ein Film wie eine Techno-scheibe, ein Film wie ein Hirnriss mitten im bornierten Spiessertrott' (215). Although we can safely conclude that this film is unlikely to be made, Richle's plans for *Transit Café* may well have originated in similar ambitions.

The important role of music is likely, at least in part, to be a legacy of the novel's genesis as a screenplay, and the attempt to compensate for the missing aural stimulus reveals the limitations of the printed text in the multimedia world. Snatches of dialogue transcribed from the Arabic (166) and of music from all over the world would certainly work better on film, and many of the coincid-ences and confusions would also be more suited to a visual medium. This is a narrative which is conceived in filmic terms; its expression as a novel has its drawbacks. That said, the expression of a narrative as film brings its own prob-lems, as an examination of Helmut Dietl's film *Rossini* will demonstrate.

IV *Rossini* and the syntax of film

If *Hand im Spiel* is a filmic novel that was never made into a film, then *Rossini oder die mörderische Frage, wer mit wem schlief* is a successful film about a film of a novel that is never made. But both grapple with the same problem: how to tell a story. Richle's novel is a thinly disguised attempt to use language to cover the gaps left by missing images; Süskind, in his long essay on the writing of *Rossini*, laments precisely the inadequacy of the language of film when compared with that of the novel:

> Gelobt sei die Prosa, verflucht sei der Film als erzählerisches Medium! Diese teuflische Wirklichkeitsvorspiegelungsmaschine kennt keinen Nebensatz und kein Konditional, kein à propos, keine Einschübe, nicht die simpelste rhetorische Figur, keine Zeitenfolge, kein 'wenn', kein 'während', kein 'sowohl-als-auch' — nichts als dieses primitive, undifferenzierte, grobschlächtige 'Hier-bin-ich' des Bildes auf der Leinwand... (R, 227)

Admittedly, Süskind does later recant, allowing that the 'syntax' of film is equally sophisticated, though in a different way. However, this part of his commentary focuses on a structural difficulty common to both works: how to combine many strands of narrative, in effect several stories which are intercon-nected but separate, each with its own main characters.

Three main stories are intertwined in *Rossini*, which is set in the Munich restaurant of that name, where movers and shakers of the German film and literary scene are almost part of the furniture. The first of these stories, which I sketch here in no particular order, concerns the efforts of Oscar Reiter, a film producer, and Uhu Zigeuner, a director, to obtain the rights to a world-wide best-selling novel called *Loreley. Geschichte einer Hexe*. They need to persuade its author, their publicity-shy friend Jakob Windisch, to sign a contract, although he has always insisted he will not allow it to be filmed. A sub-story here concerns Windisch's relationship with an attractive waitress, Serafina. The second story shows a love-triangle between the beautiful Valerie, Reiter, and Bodo Kriegnitz, a poet, which ends in the suicide of Valerie. The third concerns the efforts of a young actress, known only as Schneewittchen, to get the part of Loreley in the putative film. She goes about this by seducing, in true Lorelei fashion, first, Rossini himself, then Zigeuner and then Reiter. The *Loreley* project never comes to fruition, it seems; though the film closes with the characters discussing another idea for a film which is obviously akin to *Rossini* itself.

V Art versus commerce

The fraught relationship between art and commercial pressures is a prominent feature of the film. Though there is a serious undertone, the main thrust is parodic. Reiter is deeply in debt and needs to make the film for commercial reasons. Windisch, however, regards himself as an artist and is unwilling to allow his novel to be debased, even though it has apparently had sales exceeding 300 million world wide. Kriegnitz, the poet whose sales we can safely assume are considerably less, is scathing about such literary pretensions. He regards *Loreley* as a licence to print money and sees the three of them as 'Großkunstfabrikanten' (R, 79). Reiter's response is 'Geh, Bodo, was verstehst denn du von Literatur, du Lyriker!' (80). The satire is clear enough, particularly when Reiter, on reading the contract agreed between Zigeuner and Windisch, feels he has been betrayed. In an access of self-pity, he portrays himself as a misunderstood 'Künstler [...] tief in meinem Herzen', in contrast to other producers, who are 'Arschlöcher' (97). Moments later he flies into a rage at the antics of 'die Herren Künstler' (97). In a scene dripping with irony, Freddy, Reiter's chauffeur, writes a false dedication into a copy of *Loreley*. It reads: 'Wir beide wissen Bescheid um das Heikle der Verfilmung von wirklicher Literatur' (94). Yet despite the satire, even parody, there is a serious point at issue here. The conflict between the demands of popular success, or at least critical acclaim, and art is one which has long plagued German-language literature and film. Like *Hand im Spiel*, *Rossini* tells a sophisticated complex of stories which is not immediately accessible. The film is so elliptical that at times elements of the story risk being lost. Why Zigeuner appears at the end of the film looking as scratched and battered as the formerly perfect Maserati he has borrowed from Rossini is not explained. It is left to the viewer to deduce that his external appearance is representative of his internal state. Yet despite such relatively demanding devices, unusual in films which sell well, it was deemed both a commercial and an artistic success (a trick which Süskind, at least, seems able to achieve effortlessly).[4]

The reasons for the popular and critical success are not hard to find. Despite the serious themes of love, sex, relationships, and suicide, this is a comedy drama (or 'Melodramödie', as Dietl calls it; 278) which moves at a brisk pace, with scenes of a slower and more contemplative nature, some of them wordless, interspersed. 'Bloß keine Intellektuellenfilmkunst!' (205) says Süskind in his essay, yet this really is a film on two levels. Thus, at one level, Valerie's constipation, apparently caused by the love-triangle, allows lines such as: 'Ich will wieder scheissen können, wie früher auch' (113). Yet a scene of her in a state of distress on the lavatory, unable to do so, allows a reprise near the end of the film in which we see her once again in the bathroom, but this time dead in the bath, leading the more discerning viewer to detect a parallel between Valerie and art itself, snuffed out by the selfishness of the central male characters. Alternately treated like a prostitute and a princess by her suitors, it is Valerie who suffers from the macho power-play of Reiter and Kriegnitz.

Despite the serious treatment of male–female relations, Dietl is not above a little cheap slapstick, with Uhu Zigeuner sweeping out of a room in a rage, but catching his coat absurdly in the door on the way out; similarly, the owner Rossini in his white suit is covered in food by a careless waiter, and shortly afterwards his tie catches fire. The language too is entertainingly rich, never more so than in the baroque insults hurled by the characters at each other, especially by Oskar Reiter. But those among the audience with any knowledge of German literature and film will also find much to amuse them. Quite apart from the allusions to Heine's poem 'Die Loreley', many viewers would recognize Patrick Süskind in the figure of Jakob Windisch: a secretive but immensely successful author of whom no photograph exists and who refuses to sell the film rights to his bestselling novel. In order to leave no room for doubt, he is given lines such as 'Windisch, Windisch [...] sei nicht kindisch!' (74), and his novel is scornfully dismissed by Kriegnitz as 'seine parfümierte pseudoliterarische Quarkspeise' (79), and as a 'parfümierter Pudding' (130). And some might also recognize the poet Wolf Wondratschek in the figure of Bodo Kriegnitz: if they do not, then the credits will tell them that there are several quotations from the work of Wondratschek, including the film's subtitle. Oskar Reiter is a thinly disguised version of the producer Bernd Eichinger, whilst Uhu Zigeuner is clearly Dietl himself. All of these people were customers of the restaurant Romagna Antica in Munich in the 1980s (and some still are), which was the model for the set. In a strange case of art becoming life, some of the set is now part of the décor of the restaurant. As one might expect from a screenplay co-authored by Süskind, there is much intertextuality, and the whole premise of the film is almost aggressively self-referential.

Yet at the same time Dietl makes strenuous efforts to avoid too direct an impression of gritty realism, and, indeed, attempts to imbue the film with a fairy-tale quality. Using the pretext that Valerie wishes her fortieth birthday to be celebrated by candlelight, a large portion of the film takes place in a flickering semi-darkness which has nothing to do with the tradition of the *film noir*. Although filming exclusively by candle-light causes extensive technical problems, it was deemed necessary in order to create an atmosphere bordering on fantasy. And the roles of Schneewittchen and Zillie add a further ironic layer to this approach. They act in a *Märchentheater*, and Schneewittchen's real name is never betrayed; instead, she is transformed into Loreley by the end of the film, replacing Valerie in the characters' affections as the interchangeable vamp. The almost mystical power of Schneewittchen to charm, seduce and ruthlessly discard the male characters (who with their misogynistic macho posturing deserve nothing less) does seem to suggest that she is the witch rather than Snow White, a suspicion borne out by the subtitle of Windisch's book, *Geschichte einer Hexe*. The choice of the Loreley legend, and the allusion to Heine which it incorporates, are of particular interest in the present discussion, for this brings us on to the whole question of internationality.

It seems clear that one reason for the phenomenal popularity of Windisch in Germany is because *Loreley* is seen as restoring pride to the German nation and German literature to its rightful place in the world pantheon. Dietl and Süskind go to some lengths to make this point, sacrificing precious screen minutes to a scene in which the notoriously reserved Windisch is cornered by two fans who express their outrage at the way in which Reiter, angered at the terms of the contract to secure the film rights, has been publicly disparaging both Windisch and his novel. They assure him of their deepest respect:

> *Ledersteger*: Die deutsche Literatur hat durch Sie wieder Weltgeltung errungen. Wir werden es nicht zulassen, das Ihr Name mit Schmutz beworfen wird. Die Loreley ist uns heilig [...] Meine Frau und ich, wir wissen schon, wie Sie's gemeint haben! Ende der Bescheidenheit! Wir sind wieder wer. Respekt! Und entschiedenen Gruß! (R, 101)

From the screenplay (in a section omitted from the final film), it seems possible that the couple has decisively misunderstood the novel, for it is described by another (though equally unsympathetic) character as 'ein knallharter Schlag vor den Latz des deutschnationalen Spießertums' (75). In a further layer of irony, anybody who knows Süskind's work would be aware that *Das Parfum* could not be further removed from some sort of celebration of German folk heroes; nor could the rest of Süskind's work. Be that as it may, the notion of renewed national success is paralleled and parodied in the way in which the deeply provincial financial backers of the planned film express their obviously absurd hopes that the project will outdo the competition from Hollywood:

> *Weich*: ...dann wird das ganz zweifelsohne, Oskar, ein solcher Riesenmega — — äh... Super — Riesenhammer, mit dem wir...zweifelsohne...
> *Reiter*: ...den Amis in Hollywood ein für allemal das Lebenslichtlein ausblasen!
> Er holt tief Luft und bläst Weich ins Gesicht.
> *Reiter*: Und zwar weltweit!
> *Melk*: (im Einsteigen): Wird höchste Zeit, daß wir Deutschen es den Amis mal endlich zeigen, wo's langgeht!
> *Reiter*: Genau, Melk! In den Staub... mit allen Feinden Brandenburgs! (95)

Again this is heavily ironic. This ambition stands in stark contrast to the shambolic state of Reiter's finances, and to the farcical contract which is being drawn up as he speaks, including the limiting proviso that 'Das Drehbuch kann eigentlich gar nicht, und wenn überhaupt, dann nur unter der Regie von Uhu Zigeuner verfilmt werden...' (92), and that Reiter, as producer, is to be prohibited from visiting the set or even seeing the film.

Again there is a serious point to the satire, for despite the claim of *Die Weltwoche* that *Rossini* is 'Endlich ein deutscher Film im Weltformat',[5] in fact it is inward-looking, the opposite of international and at times heavily reliant on undermining both national stereotypes (provinciality, *Spießertum*) and regional identity. Thus a scene where three obviously unsuitable actresses are trying to persuade Zigeuner to cast them as Loreley relies for its comic effect on their respective Rheinisch, Bavarian, and Hungarian accents. Indeed, the very choice of Loreley as the subject for a putative film, with all the associations and connotations it has for 'deutsches Volksgut', would preclude this film from a wide international audience. In one sense, it could be regarded as profoundly elitist, the German film industry contemplating its own navel. Even if this judgement is unfair, as a German satire the film is naturally constrained by its targets. It was certainly a hit in Germany — contrasting strongly with the more modest success of novel *Hand im Spiel*.

VI Popular? International?

It seems safe to conclude that Hollywood film moguls can sleep easy in their beds in the face of competition from films like *Rossini*. The international success of Süskind's *Das Parfum* is likely to remain unique; even if Süskind were to sell the film rights, genuine world-wide popular success could only be achieved if the result were made in English, almost certainly in Hollywood. And a film of *Hand im Spiel* would not have much chance in the international market, even if one reviewer did have this to say about the novel: 'Daß die Straßen von San Francisco in Sachen "action" um nichts nachstehen, versucht der 1965 geborene Schweizer Autor Urs Richle in seinem fünften Roman "Hand im Spiel" zu zeigen. Es gelingt ihm recht passabel' (Kretzl 1999). But while the suggestion of the same reviewer that Joyce's *Ulysses* may have been a model for Richle is rather overstating the case, there is no doubt that *Hand im Spiel* does have artistic merit, as does *Rossini*. In common with many products of contemporary German culture the works discussed here are successful within their own ambits. Yet popular and international in the broadest sense they are not. Even though there is clear enough evidence of an awareness of the challenges facing German-language culture, there seems little notion of how, in an age of global media, those challenges might be met.

Notes
1. A typographical error has been corrected.
2. Except on one occasion, when a comment is passed on the reasons for the continuing illegality of cannabis (HS, 214).
3. The firm was restructured and the rights returned to Richle, according to the author himself (e-mail to me dated 10 March 2000; CR).
4. The positive tone of Andreas Kilb's review (1997) is typical: 'Der Film ist zum Brüllen, weil es stimmt'. Cinemagoers agreed; a respectable three million saw the film on its release.
5. Quoted on the cover of the video copy.

Primary texts
Richle, Urs 1998: *Hand im Spiel*. Berlin: Eichborn (=HS)
Dietl, Helmut and Patrick Süskind 1997: *Rossini oder die mörderische Frage, wer mit wem schlief*. Zürich: Diogenes (=R)

Secondary literature
Kilb, Andreas 1997: 'Helmut Dietl's Triumph über die deutsche Filmkomödie: "Rossini oder die mörderische Frage, wer mit wem schlief"', *Die Zeit*, 24 January 1997.
Kretzl, Helmut 1999: 'James Joyce gab das Muster vor', *Salzburger Nachrichten*, 16 January 1999.

ACCESS DENIED.
WERNER SCHWAB, THE EXPLOSION OF CHARACTER
AND
THE COLLAPSE OF THE PLAY-WITHIN-A-PLAY

DAVID BARNETT

I Schwab's Theatricality

Werner Schwab wrote almost all his plays between 1989 and 1993. On New Year's Day 1994, he drank himself to death. In this short time he produced fifteen full-length dramas, all of which were either being performed or were to be premièred posthumously in Austria, Germany or Switzerland. Christian Seiler (1994, 43) reports 35 productions across Europe in 1992, 45 in 1993 and 50 in 1994. The impressive rate of increase reflects a heightened awareness of Schwab beyond the German-speaking world in the period before his death. Helmut Schödel, in an article written five years later, shows that national and international interest in Schwab has shown no sign of abating (Schödel 1999, 33), and in a letter of 28 February 2000, Eva Feitzinger, Schwab's literary agent, told me that performance rights to Schwab's plays were still being withheld from amateur and student groups in the German-speaking countries. This indicates that interest in Schwab is still strong enough to be economically viable without granting any rights at all to the undoubtedly enthusiastic amateurs of Austria, Germany and Switzerland. The sustained engagement with Schwab's dramas in the broader European context, well after the flurry of attention around his untimely death, would seem to indicate that the playwright may well be considered 'popular and international'. This essay, however, proposes that Schwab's degree of accessibility diminishes over time as, amongst other things, his concept of character undergoes a fundamental redefinition. Brecht's assertion that 'Theater theatert alles ein, also muß man ständig dem Theater etwas in den Rachen schieben, was das Theater nicht verdauen kann' (cit. Müller 1990, 47) supports the relationship between 'avant-garde' dramaturgy and problematic realization, which is the basis of my argument. By amplifying difficulty, Schwab is reducing his own marketability by challenging both directors and actors in a money-fixated world where inaccessibility cannot pay for itself. It is important to note that the plays performed in German-language theatres and abroad do not usually extend beyond the earlier, problematic but less complex ones collected as the *Fäkalien-*

dramen.[1] I shall be examining the evolution of Schwab's dramaturgy under the lens of its increasingly intricate investigation of human identity. In doing this, I shall be adducing an ever-proliferating complexity which precludes easy assimilation either within or beyond the German-speaking theatre.

The young writer's much staged dramas share two main features. First, Schwab's stage worlds are mostly inhabited by unpleasant characters. They and their actions can be violent and disturbing. Spectators are invited into a milieu which is extreme and unreal yet uncannily recognizable, a noxious distillation of modern society. The second, possibly more striking feature of Schwab's plays is the language he employs. Ludicrous compound nouns, verbs with erroneous prefixes, distorted adjectives, and inappropriate showers of adverbs are the conduits for the darkly comic grotesques on stage. Both form and content confer on Schwab an alluringly repulsive quality unparalleled in the contemporary theatre. Both elements also point to an overt theatricality that runs through his work.

It is difficult to watch one of Schwab's plays without acknowledging the rift between the nightmarish lives of his characters and the workaday world of the spectator. Yet as well as repugnant scenarios and contorted linguistic signs Schwab is also wont to employ more conscious references to the theatrical frame that seems to enclose his world. He frequently acknowledges the tension between the external world and that of the stage, something which is often referred to as 'metatheatre'. Metatheatre, put simply, is theatre within theatre and/or theatre about theatre. One of its many functions is to make connections between the stage and the auditorium, suggesting that the two are more closely related to each other than the dividing proscenium arch might imply. Schwab often activates the play-within-a-play, a device that frames one theatrical event within another. Role-playing and spectatorship become foregrounded motifs which, by extension, heighten awareness of the theatrical process and affect the audience's reception of the dramatic event as a whole.

The play-within-a-play has a long history, from the metatheatre of the Greeks, through the more conscious employment of the device in the Renaissance, to the modernist and post-modernist experiments of the likes of Pirandello, Lorca and Stoppard in the twentieth century. An almost constant feature of the device is its contrastive function: in presenting a play-within-a-play, the dramatist is offering (at least) two levels of dramatic discourse that demarcate themselves and may serve as a vehicle for a more considered evelution of the means and ends of the theatre by the spectator. The play-within-a-play also becomes a device through which the ontology of character may be investigated; the relationship between the characters presented in the stage world and the

characters playing characters in the staged performance can probe issues of identity. This essay will show how Schwab's evolving treatment of the device signals
an attack on the conventional tension between the dramatic levels and leads to a
radical reconsideration of character inside and outside the theatre, because metatheatre asks questions about 'the theatrical' in our own existences, too.

In the following discussion, I shall be referring to the play-within-the-play
as the inset, and the play in which it takes place as the frame. Schwab used the
play-within-a-play three times in his short career; each play displays a changing
attitude to the relationship between the theatre and its frame, and between the
theatre and the spectator.

II *Die Präsidentinnen*

Schwab's first major play, *Die Präsidentinnen* (première Vienna, 13 February
1990), is set in a 'hideously kitschy' (13) flat owned by Erna, an obsessively
religious pensioner. The first two (of three) scenes feature no overtly metatheatrical discourse, although the second touches on the theme of the relationship
between fiction and reality. Two unappealing old women, the aforementioned
Erna and her flirtatious friend Grete, together with the more sympathetic
Mariedl, turn their backs on their lowly existences and dream of a beer festival
far away. Mariedl's fantasy leads to disaster for the other two and provokes the
most violent of responses. Erna and Grete cut off Mariedl's dreamy head in the
most matter-of-fact fashion. The fictional discourse, the fantasy, has brought
forth a real murder. What follows, however, contextualizes this action, which
never once broke its frame with an aside or a direct reference to the theatre.

A stage is erected on the stage and we see an inset audience with its backs
to the audience in the auditorium watching a play. Three pretty, young actresses
present *Die Präsidentinnen* '*bösartig, übertrieben und kreischend*' (P, 58). Only
after a while do we notice that Erna, Grete and Mariedl are a part of the inset
audience, something made plain when they try to leave the over-the-top
performance in high dudgeon. Once they have left, the performance is to
continue '*noch eine geraume Zeit*' (58). Schwab's play-within-a-play functions
in a fairly conventional way in that it allows the audience to view and to contrast
a dramatic fiction presented twice.[2] Schwab throws a play we have already
experienced into relief by having it performed a second time in an obviously
inappropriate manner. Jörg Henning Kokott, in his book on the technique, plays
off the unsuccessful performance of a play-within-a-play (cf. Pirandello's *Six
Characters in Search of an Author*) against the dramatist's demands and expectations of the theatre (Kokott 1968, 9). The second performance of *Die Präsi-*

dentinnen, with its unsuitable actresses and acting styles, suggests that Schwab privileges the style of acting employed in the first presentation. We are effectively asked why the second style is less fitting than the first. The grotesque women of the frame play, who storm out of the performance of the inset, are dramaturgically contrasted with the exaggerated histrionics of the inset. The play-within-a-play thus retains its more conventional function, without necessarily affecting the philosophical or aesthetic issues raised by the *mise en abîme* itself.

At this early point in his short writing career Schwab is already trying to suggest a more problematic and unsettling link between what seemed a deformed version of reality and the world of the spectator. This possible convergence between a clearly stylized dramaturgy and its (to quote Artaud) 'double', life, is pushed to the limit in the two dramas that press the play-within-a-play into service again. *Endlich tot Endlich keine Luft mehr* (première Saarbrücken, 23 September 1994) and *Troiluswahn und Cressidatheater* (première Graz, 25 March 1995) both depict theatrical processes in action. From the evidence currently available,[3] *Endlich tot* was written before *Troiluswahn*, and I shall be arguing that the former makes certain discoveries which paved the way for the radical implications of the latter.

III *Endlich tot Endlich keine Luft mehr*

Very briefly, *Endlich tot* charts the realization of a play written by the dramatist Mühlstein, rehearsed under the director Saftmann. When Saftmann criticizes his four actors too harshly, they walk out and he recruits three more from the local old people's home. The pensioners, led by the theatre's cleaning lady, Frau Haider,[4] have the set-builder, Rubens, beat Saftmann to death with a plank of wood. They then install Frau Haider on a throne, using the crown from a previous production of *Richard III*. The play continually raises issues of theatricality and its relationship with reality. The functions, means and the state of the theatre pervade the dialogues, and all these concerns relate to the three inset scenes taken from Mühlstein's text.

The first inset scene is set in an erotic art exhibition. A very large sign tells us 'DIESES BILD WIRD IHNEN DEN ATEM VERSCHLAGEN' (E, 240); under it we see a picture which is so small that it is only visible up close. The actress Manuela Schrei looks at the picture and can no longer catch her breath; she is patted on the back by the museum attendant and exits with thanks. The attendant takes a good look at the picture himself and can only shrug his shoulders. The actor Robert Kuß then enters and falls to the ground gasping for air. This time the attendant starts kicking him. Saftmann immediately compares the performance with Mühlstein's text in a line typical of Schwab's linguistic excess: 'Na, Mühlstein, na, Dichter, wie geht es Ihnen am realpolitischen Fleischtheater mit Ihrem festgeschriebenen Schreibtischzimmertheater?' (242). This question about authorial intentionality and its realization in the communicative process between transmitter and receiver echoes the action we have just seen. In the inset play, a painting is unable to translate itself into its desired effect universally: the attendant barely bats an eyelid, whilst Schrei and Kuß are both winded. Saftmann's question acknowledges the two extremes of the efficacy of art and points to a fundamental problem within the theatre: theatre with an intentional agenda is doomed to failure. Here the inset scene helps to illustrate a point by comparing itself with an argument in the frame. The two worlds of frame and inset are clearly demarcated here, and the play-within-a-play's contrastive function is successfully employed as it was in *Die Präsidentinnen*.

The second inset scene portrays, as Saftmann puts it, 'die Wiederholung der Wiederholbarkeit der Wiederholung. Die Liebesszene also' (E, 251). Unlike the first, this inset requires different qualities from Saftmann's actors, namely a 'double awareness' that acknowledges the artifice of the performance. Saftmann instructs his actors, 'wir müssen uns also die Liebe als eine amnesiebegabte Schülerhaftigkeit vorbildern, die sich jeden Tag frischfleischig einbildet, neu in der Lebensklasse zu sein' (251). The scene has an altogether different quality from the first. Kuß and Schrei sit '*steif in Positur*' (256) and, according to the stage directions, the dialogue on love is to be delivered neutrally. Once the inset has ended, Saftmann comments that the performances were 'zu gefühlsaufgebracht' (258). This provokes Mühlstein to throttle the director for his deadpan demands, which, he contends, pervert the script. The scene comments on the cleft between text and performance but here a more dynamic interaction between the inset and the frame is involved. Whereas the first inset demarcated itself from the frame, the second engages in a dialogue between the two: in the Brechtian style, the actors are encouraged to comment on their texts whilst acting. The second scene suggests a theatrical mode that acknowledges its frame whilst retaining the inset. The actors thus occupy a more problematic space, somewhere between the reality of the stage and the illusion it seeks to generate.

The third inset takes place towards the end of the play and features the new actors, Frau Edith, Frau Krimhild and Herr Adolf, who perform another of Mühlstein's texts, this time as a three-voice chorus. Their lines are continually interrupted by Saftmann, whose commentary consists of the line 'und das ist ein Scheißdreck' or minor variations of it (290–291). Saftmann, the figure exterior to the inset, blurs his role with his unceasingly regular interjections. His contribution becomes an element of the inset play whilst still remaining a part of the frame. The delineation of the first inset and the attempt at mediation in the second is supplanted by a more generally ambiguous relationship between inset and frame in the third.

The inset scenes, which explore the relationship between theatrical presentation and its context, are made more problematic by the ubiquitous discourse on the theatre that surrounds them. Opinions which are at times sententious and contradictory are bandied about by all the characters. The many perspectives articulated make the business of deciphering a 'message' impossible. The problematization of communication finds a useful ally in the theatrical medium. This link is made explicit in Saftmann's comments on a theatre that deals with issues or tries to put across messages. He says, 'ich bin längst abgewirtschaftet als Meinungsträger [...] Mein Aussagerepertoire dunstet als Schadstoff im ranzigen Fett des Theaterkulturkörpers' (E, 247). The repudiation of a theatre of argument opens up the freedom to generate a plethora of meanings which ultimately trump even The Great Leveller: Mühlstein contends, 'der Tod sieht sich vor lauter Spieltriebhaftigkeit mißachtet' (242). The redefinition of the theatre's values places playfulness as its most hallowed quality, one which is even able to cheat death of its majesty. The first two inset scenes with their attack on authorial intentionality point to the primacy of play. The third extends the scope of the theatre to its frame and thus tars 'life' with the brush of theatrical playfulness. The danger to the theatre (and, by extension, to life) is seriousness, the force that seeks to reduce the polyvalent to a single meaning.

Seriousness is personified in the character of the Minister for the Family and the Environment, who visits the theatre in the fourth scene. In her first speech she declares, 'das Theater ist selbstsicher unverständlich die größtmöglichste Errungenschaft der menschlichen Menschheit und der redlichen Redlichkeitsmaschine' (269). Humanism and honesty, expressed tautologically by Schwab, are the death of the theatre. The inset scenes have already pointed to the essentially ironic nature of the theatrical process. The Minister's nostalgic faith in an art form that can deliver truth and humanity is radically undermined by Schwab's increasing destabilization of the inset scenes

The ultimate test of such an all-pervading playfulness (which need not be equated with 'frivolity')[5] is how it is to be deployed in the face of the death it so brazenly mocked. At the end of the third inset scene Frau Edith discards her text and complains that the pensioners should be engaging with the subject of death rather than the scene's theme of unfulfilling sex. Saftmann retorts, 'aber ein

Rollenspiel ist ein Angriff auf Ihre Altersverfestigung' (293). If role-playing is to have this liberating effect, then one must re-evaluate its ontological status. Traditionally, role-playing has assumed that 'a self' dons a mask and pretends to be something it is not; this is implicit to many plots which involve the disguising of a character.[6] Schwab proposes that role-playing alters the self in a way that echoes Brecht's understanding of character in the *Lehrstück*.[7] Old age is consequently a discourse that has trapped Frau Edith. Saftmann encourages her to explore as yet uncharted possibilities for existence by playing a different part. The advocate of the theatrical exploration and extension of the self is put to the test himself soon after his remark.

By the conclusion of the scene Saftmann is forced to test his contention that all is play. The pensioners decide to end Saftmann's life. Saftmann concurs and adds 'ich muß als meinige Person aber mitnichten getötet werden müssen' (295). The connective between the 'ich' and 'meinige Person' suggests that Saftmann does indeed view his life as an ever-expanding set of roles which will soon be augmented by his last, that of the corpse. The power of the theatre (and its implications for human existence) over life and death is located in the scene's curtain line. The theatre is raised to the status of the Almighty when the set-builder Rubens says, 'ja die Wege des Theaters sind unergründlich' (296). The blur between theatre and its frame, signalled in the third inset, is affirmed.

The final and shortest scene depicts Saftmann's murder and the triumph of Frau Haider. Saftmann does not speak in this scene and seems to have accepted the role that he assented to. Once Saftmann is dead, Frau Haider wears an ambivalent signifier, the crown of Richard III. Her victory is just as theatrical as Saftmann's death. Frau Edith then sniffs around Saftmann's corpse and says she cannot detect a soul. Frau Krimhild deduces that it was not murder if he had no soul. The soul, 'the ghost in the machine' in Descartes's dualistic philosophy, is abandoned in favour of a non-essentialist reading of human identity.

The inset scenes chart the movement from theatre as distinct from life in the art exhibition, through an attempt to negotiate the route between the actor and the acted in the second, to a vertiginous blurring of the edges in the third. The demarcation of boundaries is challenged earlier, in the third scene, when Saftmann threatens Frau Haider with a replica revolver. Initially she has no fear: 'haha, der ist ja eh nicht echt. Wir leben ja am Theater unser uneigentliches Theaterleben'. Saftmann replies, 'das Theater durchblutet sich großplötzlich und verwandelt die unechten Gegenstände in echte Gegenstände' (E, 262–263) and gives Kuß a signal to knock over a vase when he shoots with the replica. Frau Haider is terrified. Rubens, suspecting a trick, comforts Frau Haider and takes the gun from Saftmann. As proof of the gun's inauthenticity, Rubens puts it to his own head, a theatrical gesture which backfires on him when he cannot bring himself to pull the trigger. The category of the playful undermines certainty. Saftmann's relationship with reality is one that fails to accept an essential link between perception and truth: 'ich spiele noch nur die Wirklichkeit mit der Wirklichkeit' (278). Frau Krimhild later shows how experience in a theatrical frame shapes reality when evaluating Saftmann's directorial style as obsolete. Her qualification for the decision is that the situation is 'erprobterweise wirklich' (284). Schwab stresses the root of 'proben', 'to rehearse', in his formulation to reinforce the convergence of life and theatre, and the effects that such a *modus vivendi* implies.

Schwab's subtitle to *Endlich tot* is 'ein Theaterzernichtungslustspiel', and by its conclusion, one may surmise that the idea of theatre as a discrete entity has been destroyed. The subtitle could, however, be considered more appropriate to Schwab's final drama that exploits the play-within-a-play.

IV *Troiluswahn und Cressidatheater*
This piece portrays a rehearsal of Shakespeare's *Troilus and Cressida* from its optimistic beginning to its helpless conclusion over five acts. Schwab's prefatory note on his characters amply sets the scene:

> Eine Person ist hier freilich keine Person im üblichen Herkömmlichkeitswahn mehr. Jede Personenhaftigkeit ist VOLLKOMMEN verloren, verloren von einer Rolle in die andere und davongeglitscht in eine weit weg herumliegende: auf und hinweg: und retour. WAS aber keinerlei ältliche Rollenspielvorstellungsscheiße aufkommen lassen darf, weil eben bei keiner Person eine originärindividuelle Anwaltschaft vorausgesetzt werden kann. Die wirkliche Wirklichkeit ist schließlich das gleich große Arschloch wie die Theaterwirklichkeit.
> Es gibt nichts ALS DAS ERLEBNIS. (TC, 8)

These rather grandiose assertions are realized with the most accomplished rigour in the text that follows. Schwab employs a variety of means to undermine all the characters that appear and one of his most interesting is the manipulation of the play-within-a-play device.

The play opens with the Prologue's first three lines from *Troilus and Cressida*, as rendered in German in a translation by Michael Wachsmann. The Prologue is directed to speak '*schwärmerisch*' (TC, 9), a theatrical sign to the audience that what is being played is not only a performance, but is also part of the inset play. Yet before he has a chance to continue, the actor playing Pandarus interjects that he always considered the actor playing the Prologue to be a man who would rather rush to the epilogue. Pandarus goes on to refer to the actor as

'Herr Epiprolog' thus distorting the 'Folgerichtigkeitsmerkmale' of the play (9). The Prologue's identity is swiftly plunged into confusion — Pandarus's biographical critique raises questions about the relationship between actor and character that force the Prologue onto the defensive. The Prologue tries to argue his way out of the impasse by resorting to a convoluted, but still character-based exposition of the art of the actor. He alludes to Stanislavskian ideas of an actor's identification with a role before returning to his heroic pose and continuing his declamation. The Prologue's opening speech is not, however, the place to deploy such an approach to acting. The lines, still a translation of the Shakespearean original, are metatheatrical: they overtly draw attention to the themes of the play and are spoken directly to the spectators. The Prologue's realization prompts an embarrassed 'um' midway through the speech (10), the only, but telling, divergence from the original. Identity problems, postulated through the interaction of frame and inset, are thus raised from the play's first speeches. Matters are further complicated when the Prologue returns only a few pages afterwards as the Trojan warlord Aeneas.

One of Schwab's strategies to undermine linear characterization of one actor to one role is the enforced doubling of roles. The scheme, as set out in the *dramatis personae*, is deliberately obtuse. Pairings one might expect to find are few and far between. The actor playing Agamemnon also plays Priam — both are the heads of their respective armies. Elsewhere, however, Pandarus and Thersites, two characters who offer commentary in *Troilus*, are oddly doubled in *Troiluswahn*. Pandarus is yoked to Diomedes, a strange choice in a conventional theatre, because Pandarus concludes Shakespeare's III ii and Diomedes enters in III iii. The costume change is thus forced onto the stage, and the preparation usually required for an actor to change role is no longer available. Thersites is doubled with Ulysses, which offers a thematic conflict between a lowly, deformed slave and a noble Greek general.

The idea of doubling is an ancient one: Athenian tragedians had only three actors at their disposal for their sometimes broad range of characters. Sigrid Löffler emphasizes Schwab's clever dramaturgical touch in the casting of *Troiluswahn*: 'die Taktik, herkömmliche Rollenfixierungen aufzulösen und mit wechselnden Identitäten von Bühnenfiguren zu spielen, ist zwar weder besonders neu noch sonderlich schwer zu verstehen, doch Schwab macht daraus ein Vorhaben von bombastischer Bedeutsamkeit' (Löffler 1995, 14). This is because Schwab's role-playing is not simply a case of seamlessly switching from one character to another. Character construction in *Troiluswahn* involves the amalgamation of several characters in one actor, something which is no longer commensurate with the single body that broadcasts the conflicting signals.

A feature of the characters' textures is their inability to differentiate between the world of *Troilus* and the outside world of the actor. An early indication of this is found in one of Troilus's first speeches, taken from Shakespeare's I i, where the actor playing Troilus unconsciously exchanges the word 'Frauenträume' for 'Frauenträne' (TC, 12–13). Pandarus picks up on the slip, but it is not long before a more radical and less detectable form of convergence starts to emerge. Troilus has to change costume rapidly to play the role of Cressida's servant, Alexander. Cressida follows the Shakespearean text, 'und wohin gehen sie?' (TC, 17), yet Alexander replies by mixing together his own reactions to his off-stage hunger and paraphrases of the speech he is supposed to be delivering (I ii, 4–11) in Schwab's distinctive linguistic style. The speech becomes a peculiar intermingling of worlds that do not seem to belong together:

> auch dieses ist mir eine Weltwurstverachtung als Abwesentheitsmerkmal. Was kümmerts meinen Hungerhausdiener, daß selbst dem Hector die Schlacht die Stahlseilnerven anfrißt, daß er selbst seiner Hauswirtschaft den Krieg erklärt, indem er seinem Knecht das Kreuz umkreuzigt und Andromache über einen gut geführten Ziegenvergleich in ein genervtes Abseits hinwegverunglimpfte? (TC, 17)

This dense mixture of styles permeates the play as a whole. Speeches like these are problematic for an audience, which is confronted with semblances of several worlds. The play-within-a-play starts to break down as it becomes more difficult to ascertain who is actually speaking and what is actually being spoken.

The relationship between the theatre and the actors becomes increasingly fraught. Any attempt to differentiate between the worlds fails, sometimes immediately after it is made. At one point, for example, Agamemnon calls for 'Ruhe im Stück' and asserts straight after, 'ich spiel das Stück, bis das Stück mich spielen kann...' adding, 'selbst wenn ich den Theatervorhang spielen müßte' (all TC, 25). His desperate attempt to gain mastery over his role swiftly crumbles: he returns to his lines from Shakespeare only to comment on one of Ulysses's new strategies using metaphors from modern consumer life, couched in 'Schwab-isch'. Pandarus, too, often tries to marshal the rehearsal but finds the collision of dramatic worlds too violent.

The failure of characters to distinguish between their own range of roles extends into an inability to follow the unstable identities of the others, too. In the fourth act, for example, Andromache storms in, is mistaken by the actor playing Menelaus and Achilles for Helen, and has to assert that she is indeed Andromache. 'Menelaus/Achilles' throws down his Menelaus props believing he is better off in this situation as Achilles. But Ulysses soon suggests, with reference to *Troilus and Cressida*, that that may not have been the right decision. In addition to this, roles within the inset play start to be undermined by roles played by the actors in the past. Cressida remembers the actress playing Helen and Andromache playing Ophelia in Vienna, and Agamemnon addresses the actor playing Nestor and Calchas as Feers from Chekhov's *Vishnevii Sad* (*The Cherry Orchard*). As well as Chekhov, and later Ibsen, Beckett also makes an appearance. Agamemnon, often seen trying to impose order in the rehearsal process, describes III iii as an 'Endspiel' (TC, 60),[8] a direct reference to *Fin de Partie* (*Endgame*). Shakespeare's play-within-a-play takes its place in the nomenclature of great drama and acknowledges the innumerable associations it generates in performance. The dramatic text travels through time influencing other works while creating new connections which cannot be ignored by either the play's actors or its spectators.

Troiluswahn starts out as the attempt to stage a play-within-a-play but soon reveals that this has now become an impossibility. The division between actor and role, past and present, and surface and depth becomes obscured. Commentaries are given in and out of character, the Shakespeare text is delivered in verse and is adulterated by paraphrasing in 'Schwab-isch', anecdotes and material from the characters' biographies appear, the time scheme breaks down and before long the play-within-a-play is forced to defer to the idea of performance without end. With great dramatic irony, Schwab orchestrates a telling acknowledgement of this recognition at the point of traditional climax in a five-act structure, that is, at the end of the third act. Pandarus strikes a pose and asks the other actors, 'wollt ihr das totale Theater, sodaß wir scheinbar nicht mehr am echten Theater sein müssen?', to which all the assembled cast replies, 'jaaa' (TC, 55–56). The paraphrase merges Joseph Goebbels and Erwin Piscator and applies the idea of a ferocious, all-encompassing theatricality to the wildly assenting cast. The total theatre reaches out of the traditional theatre (ironized by the use of the word 'echt'), but only seemingly so: the 'scheinbar' refuses to guarantee the change of status and leaves the rousing line, its speaker and audience hanging somewhere in no-man's-theatre.

The play-within-a-play has become untenable — the contrastive distinction between art and life can no longer sustain itself. The flood of impulses that permeates the actors in *Troiluswahn* undermines any sense of fixed identity, either as an individual or as a brace of differentiated characters in a play. The actors switch between different worlds accepting text from wherever they can, demonstrating that the inset play is merely one more source for the make-up of their personalities. Human agency is inverted in a condition that Schwab had sought to dramatize from the outset as a playwright, namely that, 'die Leute nicht sprechen, sondern gesprochen werden' (Schwab in Koberg and Nüchtern 1992, 4). As Julian Preece observes, 'language is so powerful a force that it crushes the distinctions between individuals rather than enabling them to express their own distinctions' (Preece 1996, 270).

Their personalities are, as Schwab states in his opening note, beyond their control. They struggle in vain to gain mastery. The attack on human agency is signalled by an important omission in the *dramatis personae*. One of the most conspicuous absences from the more conventional play-within-a-play format is that of a director. There is no Saftmann, but, as we have already noted, this moribund figure already foreshadowed the decline of directorial authority when he consented to his own death at the end of *Endlich tot*. We have seen that certain characters try to establish order, but this always fails. The absent director is an allegory of the characters' own unchecked selves. The switches between the Shakespeare text, a character's paraphrase, and commentary takes place without explanation. There is no director left in the theatre; there is no-one to organize the many texts. The collapse of the play-within-a-play device becomes a metaphor for the inability of any of the characters to differentiate between the many compartments of their lives.

V Conclusion

The associative leaps between one text and another in *Troiluswahn und Cressidatheater* points to a radically deconstructive agenda. The linguistic sign is given free rein in this play and acknowledges its protean nature. The failure to control the different textual sources points to the possibility that it *is* in fact the texts that are playing the actors and not vice versa. The play-within-a-play is no longer demarcated into sections; it emerges briefly only to be challenged by alternative texts. It is forced to defer to the theatre of the actors' lives. The conclusion drawn from *Endlich tot*, that the theatrical informs and constructs the texts of our lives, is dramatized in *Troiluswahn*. The play-within-a-play breaks down. Its conventional contrastive and illuminating functions, found in *Die Präsidentinnen* and the first two inset scenes in *Endlich tot*, are illusory. The distinction between the theatre and the external world has imploded as the signs used in theatrical production become confused with those of their frame.

Schwab fundamentally criticizes the play-within-a-play as a device that can separate dramatic levels and parodies its potential for communicative enlightenment. His strategy has the effect of making *Troiluswahn und Cressidatheater* not only an incredibly difficult piece to follow, but also one which presents a welter of performative problems.[9] Over time, Schwab has made the business of navigating and understanding the concept of character increasingly obscure. The quirky yet unified figures of the *Fäkaliendramen* give way to 'landscapes of consciousness' in the later works. Characters constitute themselves by verbalizing internal impulses, giving the impression that they are continually thinking aloud. Again this signals an escalation that pervades Schwab's development as a dramatist. Preece notes that, 'when someone says "I could murder you", or words to that effect [in Schwab's plays], he means the threat and is probably about to carry it out' (Preece 1996, 276). The movement from voicing one's intentions to performing the vast array of the mind's associative impulses demonstrates Schwab's radicalizing direction. Schwab challenges our understanding of character in drama to such an extent that acting and spectating strategies are forced into unknown realms. This progression in Schwab's work is at odds with both audience understanding and, by extension, commercial success. Schwab has always been an avant-garde writer. His first major work, *Die Präsidentinnen*, was rejected by the Burgtheater as 'nicht aufführbar' (cit. Schödel 1995, 120), an evaluation it would later regret when the play was staged there to great acclaim under Peter Wittenberg in 1994. *Die Präsidentinnen*, now an eminently performable 'modern classic' of the German repertoire has been assimilated by the theatre. *Endlich tot* and *Troiluswahn* have proved less 'digestible', to quote Brecht. It would seem, then, that the globalization of culture may well have reckoned without the theatre of Werner Schwab.

Notes
1. The most popular plays abroad are *Die Präsidentinnen, ÜBERGEWICHT, unwichtig: UNFORM* and *Volksvernichtung oder meine Leber ist sinnlos. Mein Hundemund*, also a *Fäkaliendrama*, is a play with the more parochial subject matter of rural life in Austria and has not found the international recognition of the others.
2. The same occurs in Luigi Pirandello's *Six Characters in Search of an Author* and Sam Shepard's *Cowboys #2*, to name but two examples.
3. An article in *Profil* asserts that *Endlich tot* was written in early 1992, 'unter dem Eindruck seiner [Schwab's] ersten Erfahrungen mit dem Theaterbetrieb' (Kralicek 1994, 100). In *Die Weltwoche* (late autumn of 1992), Schwab reports that he has 'einen Shakespeare neu geschrieben' (Hammerstein 1992, 69). Precisely how long the manuscript had been completed is uncertain, but the failure to announce the new play earlier may indicate that it was indeed written after *Endlich tot*.
4. Schwab, who was well aware of Jörg Haider, used the name in an earlier play, too. Herr and Frau Haider appear in *Mesalliance aber wir ficken uns prächtig* (where Herr Haider is a long-distance lorry driver and local councillor). Although neither depiction is a brash political attack, both succeed in debunking the politician's aspirations.
5. Donatella Fischer raises the question whether the postulate that 'all the world's a stage' reduces, misses or dismisses the urgency of political problems (Fischer 1994, 5). I would suggest that such an all-encompassing theatricality provides the context for serious issues, without which the issues may not be fully addressed. The equation of playfulness and frivolity is based on a false premise that undervalues the implications of playfulness.

6. cf. Schlueter 1979, 14, where she talks of 'the rift between the essential self (the actor) and the role-playing self (the character)' in modern drama. Schwab's understanding deconstructs this opposition and expands the remit of 'the actor'.
7. The *Lehrstück* was a theatrical form in which the actor/audience division was abolished in favour of drama as a rehearsal for real moral and political problems. The form is defined thus by Brecht: 'diese Beziehung gilt nur für die Stücke, die für die *Darstellenden* lehrhaft sind. Sie benötigen kein Publikum' (cit. Steinweg 1976, 61). The learning function of the form depended on the experience of fiction as a catalyst for real change in the actors. Acting is seen as a modification of the self.
8. The reason for this particular epithet for the scene may lie in the short section that deals with role-playing. Between III iii 280 and 300 Thersites impersonates Ajax.
9. To my knowledge, the play has only ever been produced once. Yet even the first production lay in the wake of an abandoned attempt to perform the piece by the highly accomplished Hamburger Schauspielhaus (cf. Kruntorad 1995, 9 and Melzer 1995, 22). My research has also failed to find a second production of *Endlich tot*.

Primary texts
Schwab, Werner 1991: *Die Präsidentinnen. Drei Szenen* in Schwab: *Fäkaliendramen*. Graz: Droschl, 11–58. (=P)
—— 1992: *Endlich tot Endlich keine Luft mehr. Ein Theaterzernichtungslustspiel* in Schwab: *Königskomödien*. Graz: Droschl, 237–300. (=E)
—— 1995: *Troiluswahn und Cressidatheater. Ein Spiel nach TROILUS UND CRESSIDA von William Shakespeare in der deutschen Übersetzung von Michael Wachsmann* in Schwab: *Dramen III*. Graz: Droschl, 7–74. (=TC)
Shakespeare, William 1998: *Troilus and Cressida*. Ed. David Bevington. Walton-on-Thames: Thomas Nelson (The Arden Shakespeare).

Secondary literature
Fischer, Donatella 1994: 'A Study of Metadrama in the Selected Plays of Edward Bond' (unpub. doctoral thesis, University of Leeds).
Hammerstein, Dorothee 1992: 'Beulen, Wülste, Wucherungen', *Die Weltwoche*, 1 October 1992, 69.
Koberg, Roland and Klaus Nüchtern 1992: 'Vernichten, ohne sich anzupatzen', *Falter*, 2–8 October 1992, 2–5.
Kokott, Jörg Henning 1968: *Das Theater auf dem Theater im Drama der Neuzeit. Eine Untersuchung über die Darstellung der theatralischen Aufführung durch das Theater auf dem Theater in ausgewählten Dramen von Shakespeare, Tieck, Pirandello, Genet, Ionesco and Beckett*. Cologne: University of Cologne.
Kralicek, Wolfgang 1994: 'Wie ein Bäckermeister', *Profil*, 19 September 1994, 99–100.
Kruntorad, Paul 1995: 'Kraftmeierei', *Frankfurter Rundschau*, 29 March 1995, 9.
Löffler, Sigrid 1995: 'Shakespeare rächt sich', *Süddeutsche Zeitung*, 28 March 1995, 14.
Melzer, Gerhard 1995: 'Minidramen der Sprache', *Neue Zürcher Zeitung*, 27 March 1995, 22.
Müller, Heiner 1990: *Gesammelte Irrtümer 2*. Frankfurt am Main: Verlag der Autoren.
Preece, Julian 1996: 'The use of language in the plays of Werner Schwab: Towards a definition of "Das Schwabische"' in Williams/Parkes/Preece 1996, 267–282.
Schlueter, June 1979: *Metafictional Characters in Modern Drama*. New York: Columbia UP.
Schödel, Helmut 1995: *Seele brennt. Der Dichter Werner Schwab*. Vienna: Deuticke.
—— 1999: 'Eine Piste fürs Genie', *Die Woche*, 15 January 1999, 33.
Seiler, Christian 1994: '"Gern gelebt hat er nicht"', *Die Weltwoche*, 27 January 1994, 43.
Steinweg, Rainer 1976: *Das Lehrstück. Brechts Theorie einer politisch-ästhetischen Erziehung*. Stuttgart: Metzler (2nd exp. edn).
Williams, Arthur, Stuart Parkes and Julian Preece (eds) 1996: *Contemporary German Writers, their Aesthetics and their Language*. Bern: Peter Lang.

GERMAN POP LITERATURE:
ROLF DIETER BRINKMANN AND WHAT CAME AFTER

CARSTEN ROHDE

I There is Pop and there are Pop intellectuals

We are not talking about Pop, of course; we never are — at least not mainly about Pop, but about what artists and intellectuals think about Pop. In this essay I would like to call those intellectuals and artists who do think thoughts to themselves on this subject 'Pop intellectuals'. Essentially what makes the Pop intellectual different from Otto Average-pop-consumer is his ability for contemplative thought. My friend Torsten, for example, who, like me, loves Pop and even Techno but who is not an intellectual, would presumably react to the following disquisitions with incomprehension. He would think that any utopian musings on rave society were — well, a load of rubbish. He does not *think* about Pop and Techno, he just experiences them directly or at least witnesses others doing so.

It is the contemplative powers of the Pop intellectuals that we have to thank for the debate on Pop, indeed that there is something we might call a 'discourse' on the subject: Pop discourse — something, which is after all alien to it, a contradiction in terms, or, to quote Rolf Dieter Brinkmann: 'Zuviele Wörter / Zuwenig Leben' ('Der Tierplanet'; FiW, 159).[1] The main areas of controversy in Pop discourse tell us a great deal about its nature. Society itself is the first bone of contention, or rather society in its current, what we might call 'Pop-modern' guise. In contrast to the non-intellectuals (in vulgar terms: the masses) who are only interested in 'Pop culture' for reasons of entertainment, Pop intellectuals, adapting principles they learnt in seminars on the philosophy of history, want to interpret the spirit of the age through its cultural manifestations. Evidence can easily be misconstrued. Those on the theoretical Left in particular look for signs of rebellion, subversion and emancipation. When they find them, they conclude that the language of Pop culture could lead us on the path to the liberated society. It is not surprising that at every stage of its history Pop discourse has had its chief theoreticians and favourite philosophers. This was the case in the 1960s during the first wave of Pop when Pop intellectuals lapped up the works of Marcuse, Reich and McLuhan whose ideal society had been liberated by the senses, sex, or even electronics. In the 1990s, the second wave of Pop and Pop discourse, the Pop intellectuals took up the theories of post-structuralism with great enthusiasm. The idea of social change played an important role here too, since as far as post-structuralism is concerned it is the structures of power and hegemony in western capitalist civilization which stand in the way of social liberation. It was Pop, however, in all its shimmering superficiality which, in the opinion of Pop intellectuals, could help to pulverize the ideological superstructure, viz. western logocentrism. The Pop icon Madonna, whose ever-changing image defies categorization according to the principles of discursive logic, is a Blochian anticipation (*Vorschein*) of a general anarchy of signs and meanings which would have social implications — that was roughly what they had in mind when they set out to transport the 'liberation movement' into the Pop world.

II Rolf Dieter Brinkmann

In Rolf Dieter Brinkmann we have a Pop poet whose works from the end of the 1960s originated unmistakably in a unique historical moment despite his attempts to create a pure aesthetics of the surface, ostensibly devoid of meaning. Inspired by the mood of social renewal, Brinkmann was interested in redefining literature as Pop Literature: no small undertaking. The title of a radio broadcast hints as much: 'Einübung der neuen Sensibilität', a clear echo of Marcuse's widely-circulated idea that the liberation of society must have a sensual element: to adapt Schiller's famous phrase, that the route to freedom was through the senses.[2] By siding with the multifaceted world of American Pop culture Brinkmann advocated an aesthetics of the surface, completely dependent on the experience of the passing moment. In his own words: 'wir leben in der Oberfläche von Bildern, ergeben diese Oberfläche, auf der Rückseite ist nichts — sie ist leer' ('Die Lyrik Frank O'Haras'; FiW, 215). The primacy of superficiality in his aesthetics, which he shares with Pop, is more important than his adaptation of Pop material and motifs, which Leslie A. Fiedler once propagated in his essay, 'Cross the Border, Close the Gap' (1969). It is only through this superficiality and impermanence that Pop culture contains a promise of happiness: that of innocence. By denying the objects in the world of Pop any depth of meaning, they are made free for poetry. Working material derived from the late-modern Pop civilization is turned into dream material, the experiential substratum of a second, imagined reality: 'Die alltäglichen Dinge werden vielmehr aus ihrem miesen, muffigen Kontext herausgenommen, sie werden der gängigen Interpretation entzogen, und plötzlich sehen wir, wie schön sie sind' ('Notizen 1969 zu... Silverscreen'; FiW, 251).

Pop as sensual liberation could thus be defined as the poeticization of everyday life under Pop civilization. The omnipresent images from advertising provided one obvious source:

> Das Licht wird
> seine Wärme voll
> zum Ausdruck bringen und läßt
> es in einer angenehmen Farbe schimmern.

Thus Brinkmann versifies an unprepossessing advertising text in 'Make-up-Reklame von Revlon' (ES, 153). Investing the everyday world with poetry presupposes, of course, a fundamentally affirmative attitude to the everyday world of late modernity, which is saturated with Pop. This is why Brinkman demands a 'vorbehaltsloses Sicheinlassen auf Leben, Umwelt, Dinge, Bewegung', insisting that the objects of a contemporary poem should be 'Teil des Verkehrslärms' ('Die Lyrik Frank O'Haras'; FiW, 213). The goal is the 'totale Verklammerung von subjektivem Interesse und objektiven Gegebenheiten zu einer durchgehenden *Oberfläche*' (210). Instead of speaking of 'clamping' the two together ('Verklammerung'), one could say they had to melt into a unity: subject and object, ultimately I and world. The utopian impulse of Pop aesthetics expresses itself through precisely such time-honoured ideas of the expansion and obliteration of the self (*Entgrenzung*): by being joined to the flow of objects from the 'Großzivilisation', which themselves have been poeticized by the subject, one comes to be, this is the hope, 'endlich im Zentrum der Dinge glücklich' ('Notizen 1969 zu... "Silverscreen"'; FiW, 250).

The poetic transformation of the everyday world of late-modernity fails, however, at the moment where the present is experienced as being so catastrophic that its encoding into a Pop aesthetics is no longer possible. Criticism of a civilization which destroys the senses can already be found in poems Brinkman wrote before 1970. But here it is more a case of him aligning himself with so-called *Schocker-Pop*, a pose which does not exactly see the present as catastrophic but merely holds the ways desire is chanelled in modern society to be inhibited and distorted. *Schocker-Pop* looks for ways of employing anarchy and obscenity to exaggerate the repressive mechanisms in the economy of desire in a bid to overcome sensuality which has been thus distorted.[3] In anticipation of a general social upheaval in the name of Pop, a sense of euphoria begins to take over, euphoria predetermined by a belief in new forms of sensuality, art and literature.

This all changes for Brinkman in the 1970s when he feels his subjectivity, no longer euphoric, is under threat and he seeks refuge in radical social criticism and violent polemic. Why? What are the causes of this turn-around which has puzzled all his readers? Why can he no longer invest the civilization of late modernity with poetry, no longer encode it anew as fantasy material for a liberation of the senses? In my view, it is because his exuberance for the flood of signs in the Pop world led to self-deception when it came to the relationship between signifier and signified. This has been described as arbitrary since Saussure. Modern cultural semioticians, usually schooled in post-structuralism, took up this idea and applied it to contemporary Pop culture, declaring that signs and signifiers swirled around anarchically without any signifieds. But Brinkmann shows that you cannot deal with the 'things', the objects of the material world, quite so simply. The things, irrespectively of whether or not they have been invested with poetry, recoded or subjected to any other semiotic strategy, retain a materiality which defies interpretation. In short: the civilization which, before 1970, Brinkmann thought he could recode by means of Pop aesthetics in order to bring about a sensually liberated society proved in its materiality and facticity, in its concrete and sensory effect on the subject, to resist all such attempts. There were some *hard facts*, social and cultural structures, not to mention anthropological constants such as birth and death, which cannot be easily interpreted away with Pop aesthetics. Just because you call everything Pop does not mean that everything is Pop — not by a long chalk. That is the misapprehension that has preoccupied Pop discourse to this day.

At the beginning of the 1970s Brinkman bade farewell to an idealistic understanding of modern Pop, which he had explored extensively in the essays of the late 1960s. He may still articulate the vision of a different society in 'Unkontrollierte Nachwort zu meinen Gedichten', but tangible reality has been left behind: 'Ich stelle mir eine Stadt mit schattigen Bäumen und stillen Boulevards vor. Ich stelle mir eine Stadt mit Dichterlesungen vor, Wandzeitungen mit Gedichten, Gedichte, die an Haltestellen morgens verteilt werden'. This is a town with 'Rock 'n' Rollkonzerten auf entspannten Plätzen' and 'warme, lässige Sommerabende, an denen die Gesichter entspannt sind' (UN, 240). This town exists beyond and outside any Pop-saturated, post-modern civilization; it is a town 'ohne Reklamewände', 'ohne Illustriete', 'ohne Verkehr' and 'ohne die miesen Namen in Neonschriften an den Hauswänden' (239). The poems in *Westwärts 1&2* are no longer proud to be part of the 'Verkehrslärm', on the contrary, this noise is now presented as a component of the general environment of destruction in which the lyrical I now finds himself caught. Nonetheless there are a few poems in this collection which part company with this 'Todesterritorium' (W, 62) inhabited by violence and death, poems such as 'Einen jener klassischen' and 'Die Orangensaftmaschine'. These are are usually classified as *Alltagslyrik*, but they can also be read as Pop verse. In what way? What is Pop about them?

To begin with there is an emphasis on the immediacy of the present, an attention to the sensuality of the moment, which in itself is typical of Pop. In 'Einen jener klassischen' (W, 25) he writes of this moment explicitly:

> ein Wunder: für einen Moment eine
> Überraschung, für einen Moment
>
> Aufatmen, für einen Moment
> eine Pause in dieser Straße,
>
> die niemand liebt und atemlos
> macht, beim Hindurchgehen.

This emphasis on the moment should not be confused with the high-flown utopian theorizings on the subject by the authors of High Modernism, such as Benjamin, Proust, Joyce and Musil. They accorded the single moment experienced as epiphany, a redemptive function within a grand framework of the philosophy of history (Braun 1986; Bohrer 1981). Brinkmann's 'Moment' poems, on the other hand, are all the lighter for being free of any such eschatalogical ballast. In the simple diction of everyday life they report on the sensory beauty of a moment. In German philosophical terms the moment is pure appearance (*Schein*), not an anticipation (*Vorschein*) of messianic redemption. Abjuring anything as weighty as the philosophy of history, Brinkman's Pop poems come into their own all the more forcefully through the precise noting down of what can be perceived on the surface by the senses. He does this most successfully, in my opinion, in 'Die Orangensaftmaschine', his Pop poem par excellence.[4]

> Die Orangensaftmaschine
>
> dreht sich & Es ist gut, daß der Barmann
> zuerst auf die nackten Stellen eines
> Mädchens schaut, das ein Glas kalten
>
> Tees trinkt. 'Es ist hier heiß,
> nicht?' sagt er, eine Frage, die
> den Raum etwas dekoriert,
>
> was sonst? Sie hat einen kräftigen
> Körper, und als sie den Arm
> ausstreckt, [...]
>
> [...]

> einen schwitzenden, haarigen
> Fleck unterm Arm, was den Raum
>
> einen Moment lang verändert, die
> Gedanken nicht. [...]
> (W, 24)

Here we have the concentration on the moment and the transcription of the feelings which floated at large in the room during that moment. It is this floating, this poetics of the moment, which the Pop poem tries to capture, that 'zärtliche Ton des Nebenbei' (ES, 150), 'das Flair des Nebenbei, die Zärtlichkeit des Zufälligen' (FiW, 230), as Brinkmann had already postulated in his essays of the late 1960s. In poems such as 'Die Orangensaftmaschine' he demonstrates what he means by this — in the barman's stolen glance 'auf die nackten Stellen eines / Mädchens'. The lyrical I also notes the 'schwitzenden, haarigen / Fleck unterm Arm' of the girl and with other similar details (the barman's causal question: 'Ist hier heiß, / nicht?') evokes the high erotic tension, which pertains at this moment in this room between the barman, the girl, and the first-person lyrical observer. The erotically charged atmosphere is evoked delicately through the understated poetics of the moment, which take physical shape in the quiet humming of the ventilator, articulated formally in the relaxed nonchalance of the poetic phrasing: 'nach einer langen / Pause, in der nur der Ventilator / zu hören gewesen ist wie / immer'. 'Die Orangensaftmaschine', one might be entitled to conclude, takes place on just such a warm, laid-back summer evening he had described in 'Unkontrolliertes Nachwort'. In its idiomatic rhythmic flow it recalls the catchy simplicity of a Pop song, anything but heavy, it is gentle, even serene.

'Ich hätte gern viele Gedichte so einfach geschrieben wie Songs', Brinkmann wrote in the Foreword to *Westwärts 1&2* before immediately explaining why this was not possible: 'Leider kann ich nicht Gitarre spielen, ich kann nur Schreibmaschine schreiben, dazu nur stotternd, mit zwei Fingern'. 'Stuttering' is to be understood metaphorically, an image for Brinkmann the raging social critic, manically hammering away at the contemporary world. And yet there is a 'but' at the end of this thought: 'Vielleicht ist mir aber manchmal gelungen, die Gedichte einfach genug zu machen, wie Songs, wie eine Tür aufzumachen, aus der Sprache und den Festlegungen raus' (W, 7). 'Die Orangensaftmaschine' is just such a poem with the simple beauty of a song.

Moments of reconciliation, are, of course, rare, never more than brief suggestions of sensual happiness in a present which is felt to be destructive and catastrophic. The opposite of the happy moment is designated also in 'Einen jener klassischen', which immediately extinguishes the 'miracle' of this moment 'in der verfluchten / dunstigen Abgestorbenheit Kölns' (W, 25). This tension is constitutive of Brinkmann's poetry. It is only the negative reflection of a civilization experienced as destructive which can illuminate the moment of reconciliation. And only the reader who has worked his way through the painful urgency of his dark despair and the page-long tirades of contempt (in his notebooks stuffed with collages, for instance) can properly appreciate the beauty of this illumination.

'Einen jener klassichen' and 'Die Orangensaftmaschine' are by no means the only poems by Brinkmann which deserve to 'last', even under the criteria of Pop aesthetics. Elements of Pop are to be found in other poems, such as 'Oh, friedlicher Mittag' or in 'Canneloni in Olevano'. But the marrying of Pop and everyday lyricism is nowhere managed with such virtuoso nonchalance as it is here. And it is only here that we see what Pop can be, what the nature of the happiness is which Pop promises and sometimes supplies: that is participation in the beauty of the everyday. A beauty which is dazzling precisely on account of its chance creation and its uninsistent presence. A beauty furthermore which is inextricably bound up with urban civilization. It is thus not the case that poetry takes refuge in some distant natural idyll in its pursuit of the beautiful. For once at least we find that a constellation of people and things in space and time is possible which is not possessed by the Brinkmann triad of 'Sex, Geld, Tod' (RB, 234). For once, at least, there is the moment of total sensual happiness or, if not that, then a contentedness with what is and with how it is — even if it is, was, always just for a brief, passing moment. But that's the way it is with Pop. Pop is always short, that much is signalled through its own single monosyllable. Even a Pop song only lasts a few short minutes.

III After Brinkmann — Rainald Goetz?

After Brinkmann, who died in 1975, what became of German Pop Literature? Because the word Pop can be used to mean so many different things and because it is always hard to assess literature without the benefit of hindsight, this is difficult to establish. Here and there and especially in the review sections of the newspapers attempts are made every now and then to sort the wheat from the chaff.[5] Yet what Pop Literature and the new Pop generation are supposed to be exactly is still unclear. For that reason it will be useful to list, in no particular order, the many authors and genres commonly categorized as Pop and linked with Brinkmann. We could start off with the Pop underground with its love of the trivial and the obscene, which experienced recently a renaissance in the poetry of Slam (cf. Neumeister/Hartges 1996); there is then *Alltagslyrik*, a few poems by Nicolas Born and Wolf Wondratschek, of course, who understand, like Brinkmann, how to capture the poetry of an everyday situation;[6] we could then move on to the Pop hype and Pop discourse of the 1990s, the Pop theoreticians, Diedrich Diedrichsen and Ulf Poschardt, the so-called New German Pop Literature by Rainald Goetz and Thomas Meinecke and the young stars like Benjamin Lebert and Benjamin Stuckrad-Barre, who are genuinely 'pop' in the original sense of the word, that is they are popular, their works best sellers;[7] finally there is the latest branch of Pop, the internet, and so-called hypertext literature, a development of Brinkmann's notebook collages, if you like. What links all these apart from material and motifs from Pop and media, in themselves hardly unusual any more, is a subject for further research. But measured against their own high pretensions, against all the claims made by the practitioners, what they have actually produced is meagre. We have been waiting in vain for the Pop equivalent to the great state-of-the-nation novel, what Rainald Goetz called the 'geiler Realreißer aus der Technowelt' (Goetz 1993b, 386). What's more Pop Literature is rarely popular in the sense that it is commercially successful. On the contrary, the claim to avant-garde status always seems to entail that any artistic movement in the modern epoch will be appreciated by a tiny minority: 'Pop für Ultrawenige' (Goetz 1999, 83).

For reasons of time and space and others listed above, I propose to limit myself in the final part of this essay to one of these authors. The choice is not quite arbitrary as his name was ubiquitous in the Pop discourse of the 1990s. He wrote a great deal too, a weighty oeuvre in terms of quantity if nothing else, several thousand pages, most recently a five-volumed *Geschichte der Gegenwart*, a Pop title if ever there was one (cf. Schalk 1996). Declaring Rainald Goetz to be the successor to the man who in his time was called the 'chief pilot' of German Pop Literature will raise a few eyebrows (Asche 1968). Goetz has produced absolutely nothing in the genre where Brinkmann excelled: verse. And yet there is, especially with respect to the 'late' Brinkmann of the 1970s a meeting of minds, a spiritual affinity even. Their way of living and writing is similar and not limited to their shared love of provocative appearances on the stage of German literary life. Brinkmann and Goetz represent the poetic type of 'Rauschkopf', an expression Brinkmann used of himself in *Rom, Blicke* (RB, 162). The 'Rauschkopf' wants the present all the time, for him that is the only place happiness can be found: 'jetzt, jetzt, jetzt, jetzt, jetzt, ad infinitum!' (Brinkmann; Erk, 240). Or as Goetz put it:

Umhüllt von Gegenwart.
Die Irgendwie-Welt, strukturell latent, verborgen von der gütig-gnädigen Dunkelheit,
der großen, heiligen, ewigen Nacht des Jetzt. — Halleluja. (1999, 219)

For the 'Rauschkopf' the stress on contemporaneity goes hand in hand with the stress on sensuality, the happiness in the moment is always a happiness of the senses and the body. The 'Rauschkopf' exists only in the close connection of art with life; for him literature becomes a transcription of life, everyday life a vitalistic work of living art. As this life takes place in the midst of highly complex sign and image systems, he practises a discontinuous, fragmented narrative style, interspered periodically by montages juxtaposing image and text. Goetz follows Brinkmann in trying to appropriate elements from the popular media. While Brinkmann always experimented with photographic and cinematic writing techniques, then declared the rhythmic ideal of the Pop song for his poems, at the end of the 1980s Goetz found his favourite popular medium on the dancefloor in Techno music. Since then he has been slaving at his one big project of making writing into Techno prose. This is underscored by modern literature's secret wish to do away with itself. Literature does not want to be literature because it suffers from its own peripherality and the inadequacy of abstract expression. This causes the flight to something else — in other supposedly more sensual arts, to nature, to 'simple' folk, to religion, to politics. Goetz's writing would only then be quite completed if, in what appears to be a paradox, it stopped being literature, as he states in the foreword to *Celebration*: 'Immer auf der Suche nach Formen des Schreibens, näher dran am Leben, als die Schrift von sich aus, freiwillig, automatisch sein möchte. Auch auf der Suche nach einem Buch, das man eigentlich nicht mehr lesen muß. Das einfach so rum liegt, in dem man bißchen blättert, das einen angenehm anweht, fertig' (Goetz 1999, 4).

It is not just a matter of copying the sound of Techno into words but of transforming all the social practices of the subculture with its own specific forms of communication into literature.[8] The result is something like this:

Gehalten vom Gehämmer.
Dann sah ich, wie sie mir ihr —
Und drehte mich —
Und lauter neue Blicke. Ich lachte, weil —
Ich weiß nicht so genau —
Und drehte mich um. 'Was ist denn?'
Ach so, ja, ja. Gut.
Okay.
Hinter ihm, über ihm, um ihn: da waren jetzt ganz groß die Sound-Gewalten aufgestanden, diese riesigen Geräte, die in ihm ineinander donnerten, übermenschengroß. Er schaute hoch, er nickte und fühlte sich gedacht vom Bum–bum–bum des Beats.
[...]

Vom Rand her kamen die Beine und Lichte, auf Füßen, in Flashs, die Schritte und
Bäße, die Flächen und das Gezischel, die Gleichungen und Funktionen einer höheren
Mathematik.
Er war jetzt selber die Musik.
(Goetz 1998b, 18–19)

This is informed even more clearly than Brinkmann's Pop works from the end
of the 1960s by age-old fantasies of the subject merging with his environment.
The aim is unconditional surrender to the music, the abolition of the individual
body in the happy collective of dancers, in the 'Kirche der Ununterschied-
lichkeit' (Goetz 1999, 217). Goetz tries repeatedly to express this merging process in literary terms. The question of whether or not he has succeeded, whether
he has located a suitable aesthetic medium for the world of Techno touches on
another question which in turn leads back to the connection between art and
life, which is so central to both Brinkmann and Goetz. Because the association
of art and life is so close the reader demands both an aesthetic *and* an ethical
judgement. It is never just a question of the 'right' art but always also a question
of the 'right' life.

People react dismissively to Goetz's Techno poetry not only on grounds
of aesthetics. They may find the whole scene he celebrates simply alien; they
may reject it altogether because they take a Spenglerian view of the uninhibited
hedonism of the society of fun, seeing it as an indication of cultural decline. But
might there not be an element of envy of someone who apparently flouts
bourgeois convention, goes to drug-induced extremes and in so doing overcomes his alienation and achieves authentic experience? Don't we all yearn for
that? Yet, at the same time, we have to distinguish between the world of Techno
in which Goetz lives and which he describes and the ways in which he does so,
which are literary, in the form of books. Especially as he deals with themes
which have belonged to the realm of art since time immemorial, such as
happiness, intoxication, love, and appreciation of music. An aesthetic judgement is thus nonetheless permissible, as long as we refrain from damning
something on the grounds that it is not what we ourselves are used to.

The core intention of the Goetz's Techno prose is to transpose the sound
and the social praxis of Techno into letters, true to the slogan, 'the texts is my
party' (Goetz 1993b, 297). Only the problem is simply that the text can be any
number of things, but not a party. The text is and remains a collection of
abstract letters which can be arranged in any number of ways to produce particular reading experiences. These experiences may even have a physical dimension. But none of that has anything to do with the concrete physicality and
sensuality of a Techno party; they are two quite different categories of experi-

ence. It is no use reverting to a breathless rhythm in time with some imaginary drum 'n' bass: words per minute are not the same as beats per minute. It is no more possible to bridge the gap between event and language with these aesthetic means than it is to convey to the reader the various states of nocturnal happiness and delirium. All that happiness, all that non-stop euphoria are just too good to be true. What is missing in other words is that tension which was characteristic of Brinkmann's late Pop verse between individual moments of happiness and the negativity of a world which would not permit that happiness for very long — for whatever social, anthropological or individual reasons. With Goetz it is all the other way round. He is mainly manic and euphoric and only sometimes depressive, but his depressive states occur within a context of 'Exzeß und Erschöpfung' (Goetz 1999, 59). He seems to accept them as going with the territory, rather like a self-discovery trip in the name of Bataille with his theorem of giving one's uttermost. Exceptions prove this rule. Lutz Hagestedt concludes in a review of *Jeff Koons* and *Rave* that the thread of dialogue devoted to 'Fun und Feiern' contrasts with the 'Begleitspur des Todes und der "Auslöschung"'. He contends that the poet of Techno warns of the 'immense Gefahren dieser Welt' (*Frankfurter Rundschau*, 2 May 1998). That seems an exaggeration to me. That desperate and sometimes paranoid autism which characterized Goetz's prose of the 1980s in novels such as *Irre* and *Kontrolliert* is virtually nowhere to be found in the Techno pieces of the 1990s. Robin Detje described the transition in a review of *Rave* (*Berliner Zeitung*, 6–7 February 1999) as the change from 'innere Hirnmaschinenradadadadad' to the 'Genuß eines von außen hereindröhnenden Musikmaschinenradadadadad'. In interviews Goetz is quite aware of the difference, as he shows, for example, in an answer to the question which raves in which city he likes the best:

> Für mich ist es eigentlich immer da am schönsten, wo ich gerade bin. Jeden verstehe ich, mit allem bin ich einverstanden, alles ist toll. Für Außenstehende wirkt das, merke ich oft, leider ziemlich penetrant. Ich versuche dann zu denken: ich bin so ein dauernder JA-SAGER ja nur, weil ich in Wirklichkeit, daheim allein bei mir im stillen Kämmerlein, so ein notorischer NEIN-DENKER bin. (Goetz 1999, 86)

'Komm her, Sternschnuppe' — writes Goetz in wonderful lyrical vein on the cover of *Rave*. But what becomes of this desire for happiness when shooting stars are falling from the sky like rain? After all, shooting stars are only beautiful because all around them it is deepest night. And the happiness which comes from Pop would always be like a shooting star against a dark background, a fleeting flickering lasting minutes, if not seconds. In the writing of Rainald Goetz such moments are rare as he follows the thumping Techno beats. It is rather the moments of silence and listening, as in *Katarakt* or the final image of *Jeff Koons*, which enchant the reader with their poetic beauty. Instead of preaching happiness, intoxication and redemption at maximum speed, Goetz then seems to have his finger on the pulse of the world and, with child-like surprise and dread, to be tuned in to the buzz of life. Have you seen what the world has to offer! And how different and complex it all is! How beautiful and terrible at the same time. Goetz the astronaut, looking down at the earth from his capsule hurled into the fourth dimension beyond time and space, astonished at the beauty he beholds and terrified by the loneliness of man in the cosmos. At that point the tension returns. Derived from the tension the happiness both in the moment itself and from the surface of a scene before his eyes. Then the wonder returns at all the possibilities and realities which are in the world. Goetz often finds beguilingly beautiful images for this wonder, for this richness in the world, but images of mourning and melancholy too, images of fury at the threat to beauty from hatred and violence. These passages, which often snake their way through pages and pages of lyrical meanders, have to be read in context; it is the only way their expressive power can be appreciated.

The opening of the monologue *Katarakt* gives a hint of this technique:

> ALTER
> hören Sie das?
> Moment
> jetzt
> haben Sie das gehört?
> faszinierend
> wenn man sich sonst nicht bewegt
> hört man sogar das Öffnen und Schließen
> der Augenlider
> vor allem das Öffnen
> das scheint lauter zu sein.
> Wunderwerk der —
> Unsinn.
> (Goetz 1993a, 251)

The break in the lines is not the only source of lyricism in this passage. But doesn't that disprove my contention that Goetz has no lyrical talent? What is worth noting is that Goetz succeeds in writing his poetically most impressive lines when he keeps away from the noisy world of Pop and Techno. A bad omen for Pop Literature?

Notes

This essay is an expanded version of a paper delivered to the Rolf Dieter Brinkmann Symposium in Vechta, 15–18 May 2000.
Translation by Julian Preece.
1.   On the development of the discourse on Pop in the 1980s and 1990s, see Geer 1995.

2. Marcuse 1969, 272: 'die Revolution muß gleichzeitig eine Revolution der Wahrnehmung sein'.
3. Brinkmann's volume of poems *Godzilla* is a good example; on 'Schocker-Pop', see Hermand 1971, 95–97.
4. cf. the interpretation given in Hügel 1982. Hügel, like Zenke 1982 in his analysis of 'Einen jener klassischen', does not see the break between the 'early' and the 'late' Brinkmann and instead stresses the continuities. In my view this is wrong, as even though Brinkmann retains in formal terms his sensually intensive aesthetics of the surface, what he does with it is radically different. Stolz 1996 also comments inter alia on this poem.
5. See, for instance, Seibt 2000, writing on the appearance of the self-styled 'Pop-Cultural Quintett' and their book, *Tristesse Royale*.
6. cf. for instance Born's poem 'Es ist Sonntag' (from *Das Auge des Entdeckers*, 1972) or Wondratschek's 'Endstation' (from *Das leise Lachen am Ohr eines andern*, 1976). After the 1970s boom in 'Alltagslyrik', this genre is no longer as popular as it once was. When everyday subject-matter does enter poetry, it is distorted to such an extent through irony, fantasy or other means that one can no longer speak of 'Alltagslyrik' in the same sense as in the 1970s. See the anthology by Braun/Thill 1998.
7. cf. Poschardt 1997; Diedrichsen 1993. On recent German Pop Literature, Winkels 1999.
8. See comments Goetz has made in interviews, Goetz 1999, 86–88 and 262–263.

Primary texts

Brinkmann, Rolf Dieter 1975: *Westwärts 1 & 2. Gedichte*. Reinbek bei Hamburg: Rowohlt. (=W)
—— 1976: 'Ein unkontrolliertes Nachwort zu meinen Gedichten', *Literaturmagazin 5*, 228–248. (=UN)
—— 1979: *Rom, Blicke*. Reinbek bei Hamburg: Rowohlt. (=RB)
—— 1982: *Der Film in Worten. Prosa. Erzählungen. Essays. Hörspiele. Fotos. Collagen. 1965–1974*. Reinbek bei Hamburg: Rowohlt. (=FiW)
—— 1987: *Erkundungen für die Präzisierung des Gefühls für einen Aufstand: Reise Zeit Magazin. Die Story ist schnell erzählt. (Tagebuch)*. Reinbek bei Hamburg: Rowohlt. (=Erk)
—— 1995: 'Einübung einer neuen Sensibilität', *Literaturmagazin 36*, 147–155. (=ES)
Goetz, Rainald 1993a: *Katarakt* in Goetz: *Festung. Stücke*. Frankfurt am Main: Suhrkamp.
—— 1993b: *Kronos. Berichte*. Frankfurt am Main: Suhrkamp.
—— 1998a: *Jeff Koons. Stück*. Frankfurt am Main: Suhrkamp.
—— 1998b: *Rave. Erzählung*. Frankfurt am Main: Suhrkamp.
—— 1999: *Celebration. 90s Nacht Pop*. Frankfurt am Main: Suhrkamp.

Secondary literature

Asche, Gerhart 1968: 'Chef-Pilot der Pop-Lyriker', *Bremer Nachrichten*, 13 December 1968.
Bekes, Peter et al (eds) 1982: *Deutsche Gegenwartslyrik von Biermann bis Zahl. Interpretationen*. Munich: Fink.
Bohrer, Karl Heinz 1981: *Plötzlichkeit. Zum Augenblick des ästhetischen Scheins*. Frankfurt am Main: Suhrkamp.
Braun, Michael 1986: 'Der poetische Augenblick. Studien zu einem Fluchtpunkt der literarischen Moderne' in Braun 1986: *Der poetische Augenblick. Essays zur Gegenwartsliteratur*. Berlin: Vis-à-Vis, 16–30.
—— and Hans Thill (eds) 1998: *Das verlorene Alphabet. Deutschsprachige Lyrik der neunziger Jahre*. Heidelberg: Das Wunderhorn.
Diedrichsen, Diedrich 1993: *Freiheit macht arm*. Cologne: Kiepenheuer & Witsch.
Geer, Nadja 1995: 'Humus oder Löschkalk. Zum journalistischen (Unter-)Grund von literarischer Subversion am Ende der achtziger Jahre', *Jahrbuch für Internationale Germanistik 27/1*, 66–84.

Hermand, Jost 1971: *Pop International. Eine kritische Analyse.* Frankfurt am Main: Athenäum.
Hinck, Walter (ed.) 1982: *Gedichte und Interpretationen. VI: Gegenwart.* Stuttgart: Reclam.
Hügel, Hans-Otto 1982: 'Rolf Dieter Brinkmann. Die Orangensaftmaschine' in Bekes 1982, 44–68.
Marcuse, Herbert (1969): 'Versuch über die Befreiung' in Marcuse: *Schriften, VIII: Aufsätze und Vorlesungen 1948—1969. Versuch über die Befreiung.* Frankfurt am Main: Suhrkamp, 237–317
Neumeister, Andreas and Marcel Hartges (eds) 1996: *Poetry! Slam! Texte der Pop-Fraktion.* Reinbek bei Hamburg: Rowohlt.
Poschardt, Ulf 1997: *DJ-Culture. Diskjockeys und Popkultur.* Reinbek bei Hamburg: Rowohlt.
Schäfer, Jörgen 1998: *Pop-Literatur: Rolf Dieter Brinkmann und das Verhältnis zur Populärkultur in der Literatur der sechziger Jahre.* Stuttgart: M & P Verlag.
Schalk, Axel 1996: '"Trinken Trinken Trinken. Die Welt in Ordnung trinken": The language-fortification of Rainald Goetz' in Williams/Parkes/Preece 1996, 283–296.
Seibt, Gustav 2000: 'Aussortieren was falsch ist', *Die Zeit,* 2 March 2000.
Stolz, Dieter 1995: '"Zuviele Wörter/Zuwenig Lesen" oder "He, he, wo ist die Gegenwart?". Lyrik und Fotografie am Beispiel von Rolf Dieter Brinkmann', *Sprache im technischen Zeitalter,* 33/133, 98–117.
Williams, Arthur, Stuart Parkes and Julian Preece (eds) 1996: *Contemporary German Writers, their Aesthetics and their Language.* Bern: Peter Lang.
Winkels, Hubert 1999: 'Grenzgänger. Neue deutsche Pop-Literatur, *Sinn und Form* 51, 581–610.
Zenke, Thomas 1982: 'Der Augenblick der Sensibilität [zu: *Einen jener klassischen*]' in Hinck 1982, 387–393.

SELECT BIBLIOGRAPHY OF SECONDARY WORKS

Aichmayr, Michael-Josef 1991: *Der Symbolgehalt der Eulenspiegel-Figur im Kontext der europäischen Narren- und Schelmenliteratur*. Göppingen: Kümmerle.

Anderson, Perry 1998: *The Origins of Postmodernity*. London/New York: Verso.

Anz, Thomas (ed) 1995: *'Es geht nicht um Christa Wolf'. Der Literaturstreit im vereinigten Deutschland*. Rev. edn. Frankfurt am Main: Fischer.

—— 1998: *Literatur und Lust: Glück und Unglück beim Leser*. Munich: Beck.

Arnold, Heinz Ludwig (ed.) 1992: *Vom gegenwärtigen Zustand der deutschen Literatur*. Munich: edition text + kritik.

—— (ed.) 1995: *Ansichten und Auskünfte zur deutschen Literatur nach 1945*. Munich: edition text + kritik.

—— (ed.) 1998: *Das erotische Kabinett*. Munich/Zurich: Diana.

—— (ed.) 1999: *Die deutsche Literatur seit 1945. IV: Augenblicke des Glücks 1990–1995*. Munich: dtv.

Bachmann-Medick, Doris (ed.) 1997: *Übersetzung als Repräsentation fremder Kulturen*. Berlin: Erich Schmidt.

Baker, Mona (ed.) 1998: *Routledge Encyclopaedia of Translation Studies*. London/New York: Routledge.

Barret-Ducrocq, Françoise (ed.) 1992: *Traduire l'Europe*. Paris: Éditions Payot.

Basker, David (ed.) 1999: *Uwe Timm*. Cardiff: University of Wales Press.

Blackbourn, David 1999: *A Sense of Place. New Directions in German History*. The 1998 Annual Lecture. London: German Historical Institute.

Braese, Stephan (ed.) 1998: *In der Sprache der Täter. Neue Lektüren deutschsprachiger Nachkriegs- und Gegenwartsliteratur*. Opladen: Westdeutscher Verlag.

Braun, Michael and Hans Thill (eds) 1998: *Das verlorene Alphabet. Deutschsprachige Lyrik der neunziger Jahre*. Heidelberg: Das Wunderhorn.

Brauneck, Manfred (ed.) 1995: *Autorenlexikon deutschsprachiger Literatur des 20. Jahrhunderts*. Reinbek bei Hamburg: Rowohlt.

Brenner, Peter J. 1990: *Der Reisebericht in der deutschen Literatur: Ein Forschungsüberblick als Vorstudie zu einer Gattungsgeschichte*. Tübingen: Niemeyer.

Breuer, Ingo and Arpad Sölter (eds) 1997: *Der fremde Blick. Perspektiven interkultureller Kommunikation und Hermeneutik*. Ergebnisse der DAAD-Tagung in London, 17.–19. Juni 1996. Innsbruck/Vienna: StudienVerlag.

Briegleb, Klaus and Sigrid Weigel (eds) 1992: *Gegenwartsliteratur seit 1968*. Munich: dtv.

Brockmeier, Peter and Gerhard R. Kaiser (eds) 1996: *Zensur und Selbstzensur in der Literatur*. Würzburg: Königshausen & Neumann.

Bruns, Stefan 1992: *Das Pikareske in den Romanen von Fritz Rudolf Fries*. Frankfurt am Main: Peter Lang.

Bullivant, Keith 1994: *The Future of German Literature*. Oxford/Providence: Berg.

Caruth, Cathy (ed.) 1995: *Trauma: Explorations in Memory*. Baltimore: Johns Hopkins University Press.

Currie, Mark (ed.) 1995: *Metafiction*. London: Longman.

Delabar, Walter and Werner Jung (eds) 1993: *Neue Generation — neues Erzählen. Deutsche Prosa-Literatur der achtziger Jahre*. Opladen: Westdeutscher Verlag.

Döring, Christian (ed.) 1995: *Deutschsprachige Gegenwartsliteratur wider ihre Verächter*. Frankfurt am Main: Suhrkamp.

Durrani, Osman, Colin Good and Kevin Hilliard 1995: *The New Germany. Literature and Society after Unification*. Sheffield: Sheffield Academic Press.

Durzak, Manfred et al. (eds) 1995: *Die Archäologie der Wünsche. Studien zum Werk von Uwe Timm*. Cologne: Kiepenheuer & Witsch.

Eke, Norbert Otto (ed.) 1991: *Die erfundene Wahrnehmung: Annäherung an Herta Müller*. Paderborn: IGEL.

Emmerich, Wolfgang 1996: *Kleine Literaturgeschichte der DDR*. Rev. edn. Leipzig: Gustav Kiepenheuer.

Engel, Henrik D.K. 1997: *Die Prosa von Günter Grass in Beziehung zur englischsprachigen Literatur*. Frankfurt am Main: Peter Lang.

Erb, Andreas (ed.) 1998: *Baustelle Gegenwartsliteratur. Die neunziger Jahre*. Opladen/Wiesbaden: Westdeutscher Verlag.

Felman, Shoshana and Dori Laub 1992: *Testimony: Crises of Witnessing in Literature, Psychoanalysis, and History*. London: Routledge.

Fischer, André 1992: *Inszenierte Naivität. Zur ästhetischen Simulation von Geschichte bei Günter Grass, Albert Drach und Walter Kempowski*. Munich: Fink.

Fischer, Sabine and Moray McGowan (eds) 1997: *Denn du tanzt auf einem Seil: Positionen deutschsprachiger MigrantInnenliteratur*. Tübingen: Stauffenburg.

Fitz, Angela 1998: *'Wir blicken in ein ersonnenes Sehen'. Wirklichkeits- und Selbstkonstruktionen in zeitgenössischen Romanen. Sten Nadolny — Christoph Ransmayr — Ulrich Woelk*. St. Ingbert: Röhrig.

Förster, Nikolaus 1999: *Die Wiederkehr des Erzählens. Deutschsprachige Prosa der 80er und 90er Jahre*. Darmstadt: Wissenschaftliche Buchgesellschaft.

Friedlander, Saul (ed.) 1992: *Probing the Limits of Representation: Nazism and the 'Final Solution'*. Cambridge, Mass.: Harvard University Press.

Frizen, Werner and Marilies Spanken (eds) 1996: *Einführung: Patrick Süskind, Das Parfum*. Munich: Oldenbourg.

Fröhling, Jörg et al. 1996: *Wende-Literatur. Bibliographie und Materialien zur Literatur der deutschen Einheit*. Frankfurt am Main: Peter Lang.

Fuchs, Anne and Theo Harden (eds) 1996: *Reisen im Diskurs*. Heidelberg: Winter.

Fulbrook, Mary 1999: *German National Identity after the Holocaust*. Cambridge: Polity Press.

Görtz, Franz Josef, Volker Hage and Hubert Winkels (eds) 1996 [1997]: *Deutsche Literatur 1995 [1996]. Jahresüberblick*. Stuttgart: Reclam.

——, Volker Hage and Uwe Wittstock (eds) 1988 [–1995]: *Deutsche Literatur 1987 [–1994]. Jahresüberblick*. Stuttgart: Reclam.

Gretschel Hans-Volker 1993: *Die Figur des Schelms im deutschen Roman nach 1945*. Frankfurt am Main: Peter Lang.

Griotteray, Alain and Jean de Larsan 1999: *Voyage au bout de l'Allemagne*. Monaco: Éditions du Rocher.

Gutmann, Amy (ed.) 1994: *Multiculturalism: Examining the Politics of Recognition*. Princeton: Princeton UP.

Hage, Volker, Rainer Moritz and Hubert Winkels (eds) 1998 [1999]: *Deutsche Literatur 1997 [1998]. Jahresüberblick*. Stuttgart: Reclam.

Haines, Brigid (ed.) 1998: *Herta Müller*. Cardiff: University of Wales Press.

Hilfer, Tony 1990: *The Crime Novel. A Deviant Genre*. Austin: University of Texas Press.

Howard, Mary (ed.) 1997: *Interkulturelle Konfigurationen: Zur deutschsprachigen Erzählliteratur von Autoren nichtdeutscher Herkunft*. Munich: iudicium.

Husemann, Harald (ed.) 1994: *As Others See Us. Anglo-German Perceptions*. Frankfurt am Main: Peter Lang.

Jordan, James and Peter Barker (eds) 2000: *Minorities in German-speaking Countries: Aspects of social and cultural experience*. London: CILT.

Keenoy, Ray, Mike Mitchell and Maren Meinhardt (eds) 1997: *The Babel Guide to German Fiction in English Translation: Austria, Germany, Switzerland*. London: Boulevard Books.

Kiedaisch, Petra 1996: *Ist die Kunst noch heiter? Theorie, Problematik und Gestaltung der Heiterkeit in der deutschsprachigen Literatur nach 1945*. Tübingen: Niemeyer.

Knobloch, Hans-Jörg and Helmut Koopmann (eds) 1997: *Deutschsprachige Gegenwartsliteratur*. Tübingen: Stauffenburg.

Köhler, Andrea and Rainer Moritz (eds) 1998: *Maulhelden und Königskinder. Zur Debatte über die deutschsprachige Gegenwartsliteratur*. Leipzig: Reclam.

Köhnen, Ralph (ed.) 1997: *Der Druck der Erfahrung treibt die Sprache in die Dichtung: Bildlichkeit in Texten Herta Müllers*. Frankfurt am Main: Peter Lang.

Kraft, Thomas (ed.) 1996: *Edgar Hilsenrath: Das Unerzählbare erzählen*. Munich: Piper.

Kramer, Sven (ed.) 1996: *Das Politische im literarischen Diskurs. Studien zur deutschen Gegenwartsliteratur.* Opladen: Westdeutscher Verlag.

LaCapra, Dominick 1994: *Representing the Holocaust: History, Theory, Trauma.* Ithaca: Cornell University Press.

—— 1998: *History and Memory after Auschwitz.* Ithaca: Cornell University Press.

Langguth, Gerd (ed.) 1997: *Die Intellektuellen und die nationale Frage.* Frankfurt am Main: Campus.

Lieskounig, Jürgen 1999: *Das Kreuz mit dem Körper. Untersuchungen zur Darstellung von Körperlichkeit in ausgewählten westdeutschen Romanen aus den fünfziger, sechziger und siebziger Jahren.* Frankfurt am Main: Peter Lang.

Lodemann, Jürgen (ed.) 1995: *Die besten Bücher. 20 Jahre Empfehlungen der deutsch-sprachigen Literaturkritik. Die 'Bestenliste' des Südwestfunks.* Frankfurt am Main: Suhrkamp.

Lottmann, Joachim 1999: *Deutsche Einheit.* Zurich: Haffmans.

Lützeler, Paul Michael (ed.) 1994: *Poetik der Autoren. Beiträge zur deutschsprachigen Gegenwartsliteratur.* Frankfurt am Main: Fischer.

—— (ed.) 1996: *Schreiben zwischen den Kulturen: Beiträge zur deutschsprachigen Gegen-wartsliteratur.* Frankfurt am Main: Fischer.

Malchow, Helge and Hubert Winkels (eds) 1991: *Die Zeit danach. Neue deutsche Literatur.* Cologne: Kiepenheuer & Witsch.

Meyer, Herman 1990: *Der Sonderling in der deutschen Dichtung.* Frankfurt am Main: Fischer.

Mills, Sara 1991: *Discourses of Difference: An analysis of women's travel writing and coloni-alism.* London/New York: Routledge.

Negt, Oskar (ed.) 1996: *Der Fall Fonty.* Göttingen: Steidl.

Neuhaus, Volker 1993: *Günter Grass.* 2nd edn. Stuttgart: Metzler.

Nünning, Ansgar (ed.) 1998. *Metzler Lexikon Literatur- und Kulturtheorie. Ansätze — Per-sonen — Grundbegriffe.* Stuttgart, Weimar: Metzler.

Peetz, Heide and Dorothea Liesenhoff 1996: *40 Jahre Deutscher Jugendliteraturpreis.* Munich: Arbeitskreis für Jugendliteratur e.V.

Poschardt, Ulf 1997: *DJ-Culture. Diskjockeys und Popkultur.* Reinbek bei Hamburg: Rowohlt.

Roskothen, Johannes 1992: *Hermetische Pikareske. Beiträge zur Poetik des Schelmen-romans.* Frankfurt am Main: Peter Lang.

Roussel, Danièle 1995: *Der Wiener Aktionismus und die Österreicher. 50 Gespräche.* Klagenfurt: Ritter.

Sartorius, Joachim (ed.) 1996: *In dieser Armut — welche Fülle! Reflexionen über 25 Jahre auswärtige Kulturarbeit des Goethe-Instituts.* Göttingen: Steidl.

Schäfer, Jörgen 1998: *Pop-Literatur: Rolf Dieter Brinkmann und das Verhältnis zur Populär-kultur in der Literatur der sechziger Jahre.* Stuttgart: M & P Verlag.

Schlant, Ernestine 1999: *The Language of Silence: West German Writers and the Holocaust.* London: Routledge.

Schlich, Jutta 1994: *Phänomenologie der Wahrnehmung von Literatur. Am Beispiel der Wahrnehmung von Elfriede Jelineks "Lust" (1989).* Tübingen: Niemeyer.

Schneider, Thomas (ed.) 1993: *Das Erotische in der Literatur.* Frankfurt am Main: Peter Lang.

Schödel, Helmut 1995: *Seele Brennt. Der Dichter Werner Schwab.* Vienna: Deuticke.

Stefan, Cora 1993: *Der Betroffenheitskult. Eine politische Sittengeschichte.* Berlin: Rowohlt.

Stephens, John 1992: *Language and Ideology in Children's Fiction.* London: Longman.

Süssmuth, Hans (ed.) 1993: *Deutschlandbilder in Dänemark und England, in Frankreich und den Niederlanden.* Baden-Baden: Nomos.

Symons, Julian 1992: *Bloody Murder. From the Detective Story to the Crime Novel: A History.* London: Faber and Faber.

Tebbutt, Susan 1994: *Gudrun Pausewang in context: socially critical 'Jugendliteratur': Gudrun Pausewang and the search for utopia.* Frankfurt am Main: Peter Lang.

—— (ed.) 1998: *Sinti and Roma: Gypsies in German-speaking society and literature.* New York/Oxford: Berghahn.

Venuti, Lawrence (ed.) 1992: *Rethinking Translation: Discourse, Subjectivity, Ideology*. London/New York: Routledge.
—— 1995: *The translator's Invisibility: A History of Translation*. London/New York: Routledge.
Wehdeking, Volker 1995: *Die deutsche Einheit und ihre Schriftsteller. Literarische Verarbeitungen der Wende seit 1989*. Stuttgart: Kohlhammer.
Weniger, Robert and Brigitte Rossbacher (eds) 1997: *Wendezeiten – Zeitenwenden*. Tübingen: Stauffenburg.
Werbner, Pnina and Tariq Modood (eds) 1997: *Debating Cultural Hybridity: Multi-Cultural Identities and the Politics of Anti-Racism*. London/New Jersey: Zed Books.
Wild, Reiner (ed.) 1990: *Geschichte der deutschen Kinder- und Jugendliteratur*. Stuttgart: Metzler.
Williams, Arthur and Stuart Parkes (eds) 1994: *The Individual, Identity and Innovation. Signals from contemporary literature and the new Germany*. Bern: Peter Lang.
——, Stuart Parkes and Julian Preece (eds) 1996: *Contemporary German Writers, Their Aesthetics and Their Language*. Bern: Peter Lang.
——, Stuart Parkes and Julian Preece (eds) 1998: *'Whose Story?' — Continuities in contemporary German-language Literature*. Bern: Peter Lang.
——, Stuart Parkes and Julian Preece (eds) 2000: *Literature, Markets and Media in Germany and Austria Today*. Bern: Peter Lang.
——, Stuart Parkes and Roland Smith (eds) 1990: *Literature on the Threshold. The German novel in the 1980s*. Oxford: Berg.
——, Stuart Parkes and Roland Smith (eds) 1991: *German Literature at a Time of Change, 1989–1990. German unity and German identity in literary perspective*. Bern: Peter Lang.
Wippermann, Wolfgang 1997: *'Wie die Zigeuner': Antisemitismus und Antiziganismus im Vergleich*. Berlin: Elefanten Press.
Wittstock, Uwe (ed.) 1994: *Roman oder Leben. Postmoderne in der deutschen Literatur*. Leipzig: Reclam.
—— 1995: *Leselust. Wie unterhaltsam ist die neue deutsche Literatur?* Munich: Luchterhand.

INDEX

The categories in this index are intended to be broad and, in most cases, include both the English and the equivalent German terms.

NOTES ON CONTRIBUTORS

Uta Aifan has just completed her doctoral thesis on German-Arab *Grenzgängerliteratur* at the RWTH Aachen where she also gained her MA (in German Studies and Political Sciences). She works mainly in the areas of stereotypes and perceptions of foreigners and is currently teaching at the University of Stuttgart.

David Barnett is a Lecturer in Theatre Studies at the University of Huddersfield. He has published a book on the dramaturgy and theatrical realizations of Heiner Müller's later work, *Literature versus Theatre* (1998), and continues to work on contemporary German dramatists and metatheatre.

Peter Graves is Senior Lecturer in German at the University of Leicester. He has published extensively on post-war German writers from both East and West, in particular Christa Wolf. He is a regular contributor on contemporary German literature to the *Times Literary Supplement* and has recently co-edited *From Classical Shades to Vickers Victorious: Shifting Perspectives in British German Studies* (1999).

Silke Hassler studied Comparative Literature and German in Vienna (Magister) and London. She currently combines freelance writing with work as librettist at the Neue Oper, Vienna, and as Dramaturgin, mainly for plays by Peter Turrini whose collected works she has edited. Apart from publications on Turrini and the Neue Oper, she has written on Jakov Lind, Austrian theatre, Jewish themes, and both contemporary and *Exilliteratur*.

Christopher Jones is Senior Lecturer in German at Manchester Metropolitan University. His research interests are in the field of popular culture with a particular focus of crime fiction. He is currently working on projects relating to Swiss crime fiction and to women's crime fiction.

James Jordan is Senior Lecturer in German at Nottingham Trent University. He is co-editor (with Peter Barker) of *Minorities in German-speaking countries: Aspects of social and cultural experience* (2000) He has also completed a critical edition of the unpublished poetry of Ernst Toller.

Astrid Köhler lectures in German at Queen Mary and Westfield College in the University of London. Her main fields of research are the cultural history of classical Weimar and the east German Literature of the 1990s.

Jonathan Long holds a Lectureship at the University of Durham where his main fields of research embrace literary theory, narratology. historiography and biography. He has published recently on Thomas Bernhard, Dieter Kühn and Wolfgang Hildesheimer.

Tanja Nause is currently completing her PhD at the University of Bradford on aspects of the picaresque in recent east German writing. She studied German and Cultural Studies at the Humboldt University, Berlin (MA) and has several articles in press in the area of her doctoral research.

Stefan Neuhaus is a Wissenschaftlicher Assistent at the University of Bamberg. Apart from the contemporary period, his interests span German Romanticism and the work of Fontane. His recent publications include: *Fontane-ABC* (1998), *Ernst Toller und die Weimarer Republik. Ein Autor im Spannungsfeld von Literatur und Politik* (with Rolf Selbmann and Thorsten Unger; 1999) and articles on Erich Kästner and Heinrich Heine.

Stuart Parkes is Professor of Contemporary German Studies at the University of Sunderland. His numerous publications include *Literature and Politics in West Germany* and *Under-*

standing Contemporary Germany (1997). *The Gruppe 47 Fifty Years On. A reappraisal of its literary and political significance* appeared in 1999 (with John J White).

Helmut Peitsch is Professor of European Studies at the University of Wales College of Cardiff. His extensive programme of research and publications locates Contemporary German Literature in a broad societal, political, and aesthetic context.

Beatrice Petz is a doctoral candidate in the School of English and European Languages and Literatures at the University of Tasmania, Australia. Her dissertation is on the narrator figures in the post-unification works of Günter Grass. Her publications in the area include the recent article: 'The Toad and the Toady — Günter Grass's *The Call of the Toad*' (1999).

Julian Preece lectures in German at the University of Kent. His varied research interests encompass both German Literatures and Austrian Literature. *Nine Lives. Ethnic Conflict in the Polish-Ukrainian Borderlands* appeared in 1999 (with Waldemar Lotnik). His book on Günter Grass is scheduled to appear in September 2000.

Colin Riordan is Professor of German at the University of Newcastle upon Tyne. He has published extensively on post-war German literature, including books and articles on Uwe Johnson, Peter Schneider, Martin Walser, Patrick Süskind, Jurek Becker, and Uwe Timm.

Carsten Rohde studied German, History and North American Studies in Berlin at both the Technische Universität and the Freie Universität. He is currently writing his doctoral thesis on the autobiographical writings of Goethe.

Wiebke Sievers was DAAD-Lektorin at the University of Nottingham until September 2000. She has returned to the University of Düsseldorf on a DAAD scholarship while finishing her PhD in Translation Studies for the University of Warwick.

Dieter Stolz holds a doctorate of the TU Berlin where he has also taught. He has been Deputy Director of the Literarisches Colloquium Berlin since the beginning of 2000. He is a member of the editorial board of *Sprache im technischen Zeitalter* and has published widely, particularly on Günter Grass (*Vom privaten Motivkomplex zum poetischen Weltentwurf*, 1994). He has edited Robert Menasse's *Trilogie der Entgeisterung* (1997) and Volume 2: *Theaterspiele* of the Grass *Werkausgabe* (Neuhaus/Hermes; 1999); his companion volume of commentaries will appear in autumn 2000.

Susan Tebbutt is Senior Lecturer in German Studies and Head of German at the University of Bradford. She is particularly noted for her work on *Jugendliteratur* and on Sinti and Roma. She is currently translating her edited volume: *Sinti and Roma: Gypsies in German-speaking society and literature* (1998) into German. Reflecting her other interests are co-edited volumes on *Wirtschaftsdeutsch* (1998) and *Ab Initio German* (1999).

Arthur Williams is Professor of Contemporary German Studies at the University of Bradford. He has published on the West German media and, since 1987–1988, has made the Bradford Colloquia and the associated publications a focus of his work. Most recently he has worked on Botho Strauß and W.G. Sebald.

Isabelle Esser (translator of the essay by Stefan Neuhaus) is a Bradford graduate and is currently working as a professional translator and revisor in the commercial sector. **Robert Gillett** (translator of the essay by Astrid Köhler) lectures at Queen Mary and Westfield College in the University of London. **Chloe EM Paver** (translator of the essay by Silke Hassler) lectures in the Department of German at the University of Exeter. Dr Gillett and Dr Paver have both contributed scholarly essays to earlier volumes in this series.